BUILDING THAT BRIGHT FUTURE
Soviet Karelia in the Life Writing of Finnish North Americans

In the early 1930s, approximately 6,500 Finns from Canada and the United States moved to Soviet Karelia, on the border of Finland, to build a Finnish workers' society. They were recruited by the Soviet leadership for their North American mechanical and lumber expertise, their familiarity with the socialist cause, and their Finnish language and ethnicity. By 1936, however, Finnish culture and language came under attack and ethnic Finns became the region's primary targets in the Stalinist Great Terror.

Building That Bright Future relies on the personal letters and memoirs of these Finnish migrants to build a history of everyday life during a transitional period for both North American socialism and Soviet policy. Highlighting the voices of men, women, and children, the book follows the migrants from North America to the Soviet Union, providing vivid descriptions of daily life. Samira Saramo brings readers into personal contact with Finnish North Americans and their complex and intimate negotiations of self and belonging.

Through letters and memoirs, *Building That Bright Future* explores the multiple strategies these migrants used to make sense of their rapidly shifting positions in the Soviet hierarchy and the relationships that rooted them to multiple places and times.

SAMIRA SARAMO is a Kone Foundation Senior Researcher at the Migration Institute of Finland.

Building That Bright Future

*Soviet Karelia in the Life Writing
of Finnish North Americans*

SAMIRA SARAMO

UNIVERSITY OF TORONTO PRESS
Toronto Buffalo London

© University of Toronto Press 2022
Toronto Buffalo London
utorontopress.com

ISBN 978-1-4875-0480-9 (cloth)   ISBN 978-1-4875-3093-8 (EPUB)
ISBN 978-1-4875-2349-7 (paper)   ISBN 978-1-4875-3092-1 (PDF)

Library and Archives Canada Cataloguing in Publication

Title: Building that bright future : Soviet Karelia in the life writing of Finnish North Americans / Samira Saramo.
Names: Saramo, Samira, author.
Description: Includes bibliographical references and index.
Identifiers: Canadiana (print) 20220132518 | Canadiana (ebook) 2022013264X | ISBN 9781487504809 (hardcover) | ISBN 9781487523497 (softcover) | ISBN 9781487530938 (EPUB) | ISBN 9781487530921 (PDF)
Subjects: LCSH: Finnish Americans – Russia (Federation) – Karelia – Biography. | CSH: Finnish Canadians – Russia (Federation) – Karelia – Biography. | LCSH: Finnish Americans – Russia (Federation) – Karelia – Correspondence. | CSH: Finnish Canadians – Russia (Federation) – Karelia – Correspondence. | LCSH: Finnish Americans – Russia (Federation) – Karelia – History – 20th century. | CSH: Finnish Canadians – Russia (Federation) – Karelia – History – 20th century. | LCSH: Finnish Americans – Russia (Federation) – Karelia – Social life and customs – 20th century. | CSH: Finnish Canadians – Russia (Federation) – Karelia – Social life and customs – 20th century. | LCSH: Karelia (Russia) – History – 20th century. | LCSH: Soviet Union – History – 1925–1953.
Classification: LCC DK511.K18 S27 2022 | DDC 305.894/54104715–dc23

We wish to acknowledge the land on which the University of Toronto Press operates. This land is the traditional territory of the Wendat, the Anishnaabeg, the Haudenosaunee, the Métis, and the Mississaugas of the Credit First Nation.

University of Toronto Press acknowledges the financial support of the Government of Canada, the Canada Council for the Arts, and the Ontario Arts Council, an agency of the Government of Ontario, for its publishing activities.

 Canada Council for the Arts   Conseil des Arts du Canada

 ONTARIO ARTS COUNCIL
CONSEIL DES ARTS DE L'ONTARIO
an Ontario government agency
un organisme du gouvernement de l'Ontario

Funded by the Government of Canada   Financé par le gouvernement du Canada

Contents

List of Illustrations   vi

Acknowledgments   vii

Map of Karelia   x

Introduction   3

The Life Writers   11

1 The Call of *Karjala*: Contextualizing the Karelian "Fever"   20
2 "Our Comrades Are Leaving Again": Moving to Soviet Karelia   41
3 "Of Course Not Like There": Karelian Living Conditions as Experienced by Finnish North Americans   59
4 "The Golden Fund of Karelia": Childhood in Finnish North American Karelia   84
5 "Isn't It a Different Land, This Sickle and Hammer Land?": Working in Soviet Karelia   102
6 "All Kinds of Hustle and Bustle": Community Life and Leisure   123
7 "Karelia Is Soaked in the Blood of Innocent People": Writing about the Great Terror   149

Conclusion   178

Notes   187

Bibliography   231

Index   247

Illustrations

1. Finnish Labour Temple, Port Arthur, Ontario, in the 1920s 23
2. Edvard Gylling 31
3. The MS *Gripsholm* leaving New York in 1932 54
4. A view of Petrozavodsk 57
5. Cars in Petrozavodsk 63
6. Foreign worker barracks in Kondopoga 65
7. The Hiilisuo daycare 79
8. Young Pioneers marching in Ishpeming, Michigan, in 1932 86
9. *Fairy Tales for Workers Children*, 1925 89
10. Women working at the Karelian Ski Factory in Petrozavodsk in the early 1930s 109
11. Soviet technology at work building roads in Karelia 112
12. Women measuring logs in Matrosy 119
13. The National Culture Centre in Petrozavodsk in 1935 127
14. Film screening for lumber workers in 1938 135
15. Katri Lammi and Jukka Ahti in New York 173

Acknowledgments

I am grateful for all the ways I have been supported through the long process of seeing this book to publication. It seems fitting to begin these acknowledgments with Varpu Lindström, since this project began with her. Varpu was an inspiring scholar, mentor, and friend, who taught me so much about Finns and social history, but also about generosity, cooperation, and kindness. Though Varpu is not here to see this book, or the York University History doctoral dissertation on which it is based, I have been very fortunate to have had the guidance and friendship of Roberto Perin throughout it all. I am also greatly indebted to Jane Couchman, Marcel Martel, Sheila Embleton, Katherine Bischoping, and Marlene Epp for helping me to think through the project in new ways. I am immensely thankful for the feedback and friendship of many brilliant colleagues at the Migration Institute of Finland, the John Morton Center for North American Studies, the University of Turku, Lakehead University's Department of History and Northern Studies Resource Center, York University Department of History, the Comparative Immigrant Book Cultures Research Group, the History of Finnish Migrations Network, the Finnish Oral History Network, and the Place & Colonialism Reading Group, among other scholarly communitites I have the privilege to be part of. I want to give special thanks to Katie Bausch, Andrew Watson, Malla Lehtonen, Reetta Humalajoki, Anne Heimo, Marta-Laura Cenedese, Pekka Kolehmainen, Niko Heikkilä, Saku Pinta, Ulla Savolainen, and Hanna Snellman for their unwavering camaraderie.

My engagement with this history began with the opportunity to be part of Varpu Lindström's Missing in Karelia research project from 2006 to 2010. Through the project, I learned so much from the expertise of colleagues including Markku Kangaspuro, Alexey Golubev, Peter Kivisto, Irina Takala, Evgeny Efremkin, and Börje Vähämäki. I am grateful to

Raija Warkentin, who generously shared her research materials with me. I have also had help and support from some of the descendants of the Finnish North American life writers. Thank you, Nancy Mattson, Kathy Toivonen, Leonore Heino, Arthur Koski, and the late Eini Tuomi, for sharing your families with me. Thanks also to Laurie Hertzel, who years ago kindly answered my questions about her time working with Mayme Sevander.

I gratefully acknowledge the financial support of the Ontario Graduate Scholarship program, the Academy of Finland, Kone Foundation, and the Migration Institute of Finland, which have enabled this work at different stages. Thank you to Lennart Husband, Robin Studniberg, Barbara Porter, and the University of Toronto Press team for making this book a reality. Thank you also to copy editor James Leahy and indexer Ellen Hawman.

In the process of learning about the Finns in Karelia, I discovered that my family has played a role in this history, too. My maternal grandfather's uncle was among these Finnish North American migrants, my maternal great-grandfather brought Finnish "border hoppers" to the Soviet border, and the Närvänen family has deep Finnish-Karelian roots. My family has, of course, influenced this work in many other more immediate, intimate, and nourishing ways. My warm thanks to my mother and father, Tiina and Jari Närvänen, my in-laws, Lita Boudreau and Lyle and Vicki Nicol, my amazing assorted siblings, Ninja, Jaan, Milko, Jonna, Erna, Bret, Kate, Michael, and Justin, and my nephews and nieces. I am blessed with a wonderful community of family and friends in Finland and Canada (and elsewhere), and you have each made a mark on this work. Finally, my greatest love, thanks, and appreciation go to my partner Luke Nicol and our "raised in the revolutionary spirit" children, Azelia and Maeve.

I dedicate this book to the Finnish North Americans who went to Karelia. May the memory of their commitment to building a better world inspire us to work now for an equitable, sustainable, and brighter future for all.

Map of Karelia in the 1930s. (Inset map by Danloud, reproduced under the Creative Commons Attribution-ShareAlike 4.0 International [CC BY-SA 4.0] licence, https://creativecommons.org/licenses/by-sa/4.0/deed.en.)

BUILDING THAT BRIGHT FUTURE

Introduction

Finnish North American socialist halls buzzed with stories, debates, and rumours about Soviet Karelia in the first years of the 1930s. The Karelian Autonomous Soviet Socialist Republic (ASSR), bordering Finland, represented a radical opportunity to actively participate in building the bright future so many Finnish migrant socialists had long been dreaming of. The awe-inspiring development of the Soviet economy and society sharply contrasted with the anxiety and gloom of North American economic depression and political hostility. In Karelia, there was work for all, free education, free health care, and equality. In Karelia, the Finnish language and migrant work experience were desired assets. From 1931 to 1934 Finns in Canada and the United States were actively recruited to move to Soviet Karelia with the support of the Communist Party of the Soviet Union (CPSU) and the Communist International. With the establishment of the North American Karelian Technical Aid and the support of the Finnish migrant communist press, the Karelian project quickly reached feverish proportions.

Some 6,500 Canadian and US Finns moved to Karelia. In the recruitment rhetoric, Finnish North Americans were to become Karelia's civilizers, bringing modernity and progress to the "backwoods." The First Five Year Plan focused on moving the Soviet Union into industrial maturity at a pace intended to dazzle the world, and the development of Karelia's lumber industry was of national significance. Finnish North Americans in Karelia threw themselves into the building of socialism, through formal employment, voluntary labour, and by participating in a growing, vibrant cultural life. In the process, they encountered difficult living and working conditions previously unknown to them, as well as peoples and cultures that often disapproved of the North Americans' superior rations, privileges, and attitudes. While Finnish North Americans worked on realizing their utopia and overcoming the hardships of their new Karelian life, the Soviet centre moved on.

In the early 1930s, Soviet culture transitioned from the revolutionary ideals that were still advocated in Finnish halls in North America to the Stalinist culture of hierarchy, privilege, traditional gender roles, and surveillance. In the Karelian hinterland, the newcomers were left with uncertain and improvised approaches to leading proper socialist lives. Although the Finnish settlement of Karelia initially served to appease relations with Finland and the Finnish North Americans' lumber and mechanical expertise assured the region's economic development, the Stalinist centre's views on the role of Finns in the Karelian borderland quickly soured. In 1937, as the Great Terror intensified throughout the Soviet Union, Finns became the primary targets for the region's arrests and executions. As the Terror subsided, Karelia was thrown into war preparations and then into battle against Finland, with much of the remaining migrant population evacuated from the region. Postwar Karelia little resembled the place of Finnish North American utopian dreams.

This study turns to personal letters and memoirs written by Finnish North Americans in Karelia to build a History of Everyday Life, analytically grounded in Life Writing Studies. The sources are brought together under the umbrella of *life writing*, defined succinctly by Marlene Kadar as "texts that are written by an author who does not continuously write about someone else, and who also does not pretend to be absent from the text."[1] Finnish North Americans' Karelian narratives allow individual voices to inform us of the world they lived in, offering a more dynamic view of society and community, while also teaching us about self-representation, memory, and relationships with audiences. Through an analysis of personal experiences as made evident through letters written in the 1930s and retrospective memoirs and letters written after the death of Joseph Stalin, this work carefully attends to the everyday, gender, and age, as well as fluid negotiations of self and belonging, contributing important new Finnish–North American–Soviet social historical perspectives.[2] This study is a microhistory of a long moment of change. The migrants' narratives are analyzed in the contexts of the writers' Finnish and North American backgrounds, Finnish-Karelian history and relations, and 1930s Soviet culture, including its ideals, realities, and contestations. Through these lenses, this study emerges as a transnational North American history, largely set in the hinterland of the Soviet Union.

Complicated identity claims based on ethnicity became an increasingly significant and conscious part of the migrants' understanding of their self, place, and role in the socialist project.[3] In Canada and the United States, the migrants very much identified with their Finnish backgrounds and stayed in close contact with the Finnish migrant community, through worksites, ethnic stores, and cultural halls.[4] In the Soviet Union, however, they came to identify – and be identified – with their North Americanness. Unlike other Finns in the region, the Finns from Canada and the United States received preferential treatment and access to food and housing specifically because of their North American background and work expertise. Bringing North American tools, automobiles, household goods, clothing, and experiences, US and Canadian Finns held on to the recruitment messages, which proclaimed them to be the bringers of Karelian modernity. Met with a large population of migrants from Finland,[5] the Finnish Canadians' and Americans' sense of their own Finnishness was challenged. Their unique hybridized language (Finglish) and distinct Finnish North American culture, along with North American social outlooks and lived experiences, clearly set them apart from Finland Finns. During the Great Terror, the migrants' Finnishness and foreignness as North Americans were equally held against them.

The socialism(s) of the migrants further complicated their identities. Though some were Communist Party members, well versed in party rhetoric and policy, I argue most Finnish North Americans on the left engaged with socialism on the everyday level, through community sites and events, the Finnish-language socialist press, children's upbringing, and at workplaces. All of these together resulted in a range of lived "Redness," and personal efforts to live the principles of cooperation, equality, and world betterment in one's own ways.[6] The North American socialist movements – and particularly, in the case of the Karelian migrants, the Communist Parties in the age of the Comintern[7] – connected their members with the global workers' struggle.[8] Finnish migrant socialists saw themselves as members of the international proletariat on a symbolic level, but, on the everyday level, the movements also served to strengthen localized community belonging. In Karelia, many of the migrants came to increasingly identify with Soviet belonging, symbolically through the building of socialism, practically through a solidifying sense and experience of home in Karelia, and legally through the formal adoption of Soviet citizenship (and the relinquishment of Canadian and US passports). These overlapping cultural, linguistic, political, and experienced identities were fluid, changing significance and meaning at different times and in individual ways.[9] To signal these complex physical and psychological mobilities, I primarily use the term "Finnish migrant," as opposed to "immigrant" (except where needed for clarity).

Though the studied letters and memoirs reveal much about the "I" – or individual – who narrates their experiences, the writers simultaneously inform us about their perceptions and relations with others and about the communities to which they saw themselves belonging. Aleida Assmann argues that "human beings do not only live in the first person singular, but also in various formats of the first person plural. They become part of different groups whose 'we' they adopt together with the respective 'social frames' that imply an implicit structure of shared concerns, values, experiences, and narratives."[10] The Karelian life writers most often related with their immediate family, the community they left behind in North America, and the one they formed in Karelia. In telling their own stories, then, the life writers also offer the stories of their collectives.

Considering the letters and memoirs as a whole reveals the entrenchment of core narratives that have come to represent the collective experience of Finnish North Americans in Karelia. Contrasting shared symbols marking shortage and plenty and optimism and despair are common narrative constructions found across Finnish North American life writing on Karelia. Likewise, the Karelian life writing serves to reinforce the migrants' group identity by allowing the individual to speak for the larger community through narrations of collective events and assertions of the communal "truth," which tells the story of a devoted, hardworking people, attacked by the Soviet state.

An important, long-standing formulation of this communal story has been the portrayal of Finnish North Americans as Karelian civilizers and modernizers. This trope can be traced from early Finnish nationalist rhetoric, to Finnish North American recruitment messaging, to 1930s letter narratives that serve to affirm the success of the migrants in the socialist project, through to memoir narratives that claim redemption and purpose in attributing modernity and civilization to their settlement in Karelia. North American migrants did bring new tools and work methods that increased Karelian productivity. Likewise, their imported experience enlivened the Karelian arts and culture scene. However, in another light, settlement in Karelia and the subsequent assertion of belonging and significance can be seen as a further expression of Finnish engagement in broader (settler) colonial projects.[11] As one example of how Finnish settlers claimed Karelia, Finnish place names (some old, some new inventions) were used for Karelian sites in both personal and formal contexts. Here, the English transliterated Russian place name is primarily used, with the Finnish/colloquial name in parentheses – e.g., Petrozavodsk (Petroskoi). The exception is in direct quotes from the life-writing sources. The privilege of voice – whose stories are told and who is given the platform for voicing – likewise ought to be remembered as we encounter repeated claims of the "civilizing" work of Finnish North Americans in the studied life writing (and the migration's historiography). The civilizer-modernizer life-writing trope further suggests the internalization of the local and Soviet social hierarchy and the "psychological barrier" that existed between North Americans and the local population.[12]

Memories conveyed through life writing play a significant role in this work. We encounter memories operating on three levels: memories of the home community and life in Canada or the United States, memories (though often fresh recollections) of daily events in Karelia deemed appropriate to write about in letters, and, in the retrospective letters and memoirs, memories of the Karelian past, including the Great Terror and the Second World War. Through life writing and the negotiation of memory, individuals could formulate the "truth" of their experiences and sense of self. It is pertinent to pay attention to the ways in which memories and time can become conflated and confused, and serve to structure life narratives in different ways. While carefully historically contextualizing narratives to build a community history, this study takes Smith and Watson's observation to heart: despite possible slips in time, order, or factual "truth," life writers are always telling a truth about themselves.[13]

Life writing highlights the migrants' transnational identities, networks, and relationships. Letters link physically separated family and friends through the shared touch of the paper, through the visible offerings of each other's handwriting, and mentally and emotionally through salutations, shared news, and reminiscences, making their impact multisensory and multitemporal. Letters serve as a bridge in the process of migration, addressing the points of origin, destination, and space in between. However, memoirs, too, demonstrate how individuals define and portray home, belonging, and relation. Memoirs often allow us to witness the life writers' fluid movement between times and places through narrative. Though letters and memoirs differ in their temporal vantage points, both provide historians with first-hand accounts of the ways in which migrants' thoughts and identity flowed between the community left behind and their solidifying place in their adopted home. Letters written by North Americans in Karelia demonstrate the transnational flow of goods, money, and ideas and reveal how many migrants continued to maintain a material presence in the home place, for example through the ownership of property. These intellectual and material transfers are also described and remembered in memoir narratives. Staying attuned to the ways both memoirs and letters reveal migrants negotiating identities that coexisted in the home community, in the adopted community, the middle ground of migration, and the ideals of international socialism further contextualizes the wider world within which the Finnish North Americans' Karelian settlement occurred.

Many of the letters and memoirs studied here were written in the Finnish language. The provided excerpts have been carefully translated to maintain the structure and form used by the writer. They have not been polished, and only minor, clearly indicated edits have been made where necessary for comprehension. Uses of metaphor have been translated to best express the meaning and imagery of the Finnish, rather than the sometimes differing English equivalents. I have likewise kept the writers' uses of Finglish hybridized words. The way life writers' narratives have been translated and presented takes seriously David Gerber's contention that "the more we consider the language, form, and content ... as problems we must correct, rather than an opportunity to extend and deepen our understanding, the further we may drift from being able to have the letter instruct us on the mental worlds, experiences, and purposes of the letter-writers."[14]

The voices of the life writers serve as our guide into the daily lives of Finnish North Americans in Karelia. Before delving into the history of the migration and community, I provide brief biographical sketches of the primary life writers studied here. After this, we turn to the broader mechanisms and trajectories that ultimately led over 6,000 US and Canadian Finns to Karelia. Their settlement on the edge of the Soviet Union was no coincidence. An overview of Finnish migrant socialist organizational life in Canada and the United States from the beginnings of mass migration in the 1880s demonstrates a long-standing, though tumultuous, commitment to international socialism and a belief in the possibility of a cooperative Finnish utopian society. The North American Finns who answered the call of Soviet Karelia in the 1930s were no strangers to the "Karelian Question." Karelia had, in fact, played a crucial role in the vision of Finnish culture and Finland as an independent nation since the early nineteenth century. However, claims on Karelia have been highly contested. The region saw disputes, both armed and rhetorical, over who had the right to govern, and the people of Karelia were caught in a struggle over who would be their "civilizer." Due to a unique opportune moment, the assisted migration of North American Finns to Karelia became seen as the solution to quelling turmoil in the Soviet economy, in international geopolitics, and in Finnish migrant enclaves.

From the broad trends that made mass migration possible, the book moves on to personal motivations and experiences. Chapter 2 analyzes how life writers have narrated their decisions to move, travel preparations, journey experiences, and first impressions of the Soviet Union and Karelia. These narrations highlight the impact of age and gender, and the influence of family power dynamics and emotions on mobility. Chapter 3 examines the re-establishment of daily life for the life writers after settling in Karelia. Situating the letter and memoir content within the context of the writers' Finnish North American backgrounds and the ideals and daily realities of Soviet life illustrates some of the challenges and strategies migrants employed to make do in Karelia. An examination of housing, food, clothing, consumer goods, and hygiene highlights the shift in Soviet culture and social politics in the first years of the 1930s. Access to housing, food, and goods, and the overall health of Finnish Canadians and Americans in Karelia clearly demonstrate the disparity in standards of living between these invited foreign workers and other local residents. In addition to developing a vivid new view of everyday life in Karelia and the Soviet Union more broadly, this chapter analyzes how life writers have shaped their narratives on living conditions to convey specific formulations of self and experience.

Chapter 4 turns to Finnish North American children and youth in Karelia. Contrasting their North American socialist upbringing – or being raised in the revolutionary spirit – with transitioning Soviet ideals of childhood and education show how these migrant children became entangled in adult contestations of what the building of socialism entailed. Looking at children's feelings around the decision to emigrate and initial confrontations with language barriers and, then, daily experiences with school, the Communist Young Pioneers, at work, and at play reveals aspects of North American Karelian life previously unaddressed.

Chapter 5 examines employment and labour relations, with attention to gender. The migrants employed agency and adaptation to make the best of difficult working conditions. Finnish North Americans were often rewarded as highly productive Soviet "Shock Workers" and "Stakhanovites," which increased their privileges and heightened their own sense of superiority and obligation over other Karelian workers. These "others," however, often resented and distrusted the North Americans. Examining these tensions and the significant presence of prisoner labourers in the region, the life writing sources reveal a deeply stratified region. The chapter aims to complicate the "hero" narrative often espoused in Finnish North American collective memory and historiography.

Chapter 6 turns to both formal and grassroots cultural and leisure pursuits, including political volunteerism, music, theatre, movies, and athletics. Leisure and sociability provide an entry point for exploring youth culture, dating, drinking, and gender roles in the community. The study of daily life prior to the years of repression and terror makes an important contribution to understanding the migrants' enthusiasm, commitment, and idealism. Furthermore, the chapter argues that retrospective narrations of sociability, cultural life, and leisure have served the life writers on their personal journeys to make sense of the violence and hardships they endured.

The final chapter delves into the Great Terror in Karelia and examines how life writers confronted the difficult task of narrating their experiences. An overview of the Great Terror in the Soviet Union and, specifically, in Karelia contextualizes how these experiences have been written about. Finnish North American letters from the mid-1930s to the first years of the 1940s offer voices never before heard and provide an opportunity to read for glimpses of the Terror in action. What is written and, just as importantly, what is not, may show the tenuous circumvention of censors and self-imposed silences that served writers' "identity maintenance" in the face of crisis. The letters reveal emotions and negotiations of self and place wrapped up in the fear and uncertainty of turbulent times, and the settling in of silences that would enshroud the history of Finnish North Americans for decades. Memoirs and retrospective letter collections written after Stalin's death make it possible to assess the multiple layers of silence in Finnish North American narratives, the scars of trauma, the writers' search for "truth," and the way in which the sources, taken together, promote a collective memory of Finnish North American life in Karelia and their community's loss.

This study takes on the challenge posed by Sara Jayne Steen, who asks us to "dare to cross disciplinary boundaries and treat the biographical, historical, social, political, psychological, economic, and rhetorical contexts in which [life writing is] produced."[15] Turning to life writers' narrations, this book aims to show the spaces, experiences, interactions, and feelings that made up daily life in the 1930s. Reading for both what is told and how it is told, we can better understand the evolving meanings of the Finnish North American migration to Soviet Karelia. Through letters and memoir, life writers marked the sites – geographic, cultural, and emotional – that framed their individual lives. Together, they form a map of Finnish North American Karelia that guides us now to their quest for that brighter future.

The Life Writers

Claudia Mills observes: "The beauty of sharing stories ... is that we get a chance to know, or at least try to know, at least catch a glimpse of, the 'whole person' whose story it is."[1] Setting their Karelian stories to paper, the Finnish North American life writers presented pieces of themselves, of their daily lives, and shared something of the Finnish North American community in Karelia. While the coming chapters build our knowledge of these individuals, a brief introduction to the main studied writers contextualizes their narratives.

Elizabeth (Lisi) Mäntysaari Hilberg Hirvonen moved to Karelia from Duluth, Minnesota, with her second husband, Eino Hirvonen, in March 1932.[2] Lisi Mäntysaari moved from Finland to Canada with her family as an eight-year-old in 1907. It is not known when she moved to the United States. Hirvonen had no known children and moved to Karelia at the age of thirty-three. Fourteen of Hirvonen's letters survive, spanning from 13 October 1932 to 19 July 1939, each written to her sister Anna Mattson, in Grove Park, Saskatchewan. The letters, all written in Finnish, show Hirvonen's early settlement in Vonganperä lumber camp in northern Karelia and glimpses of her daily life in Petrozavodsk, the Karelian capital, where she moved in early 1933. The largely upbeat portrayals of Karelian life become tempered by the dissolution of her marriage, and the silences and anxieties of the Great Terror that ultimately led to the end of both the correspondence and what is known of Lisi Hirvonen.[3]

Aate Veli Pitkänen, born 30 January 1913, moved to Karelia in November 1931 from the Finnish Canadian community of Kivikoski, in the rural Thunder Bay, Ontario, area. Pitkänen, as we will see, came from a remarkably devoted communist family. Arriving in Karelia right around his nineteenth birthday, Pitkänen quickly embraced Karelian community and political life. Pitkänen's available letters begin in November 1933 and end in June 1942.[4] Of the thirteen available letters, eight are addressed to his parents and written in Finnish, four English letters are to his sister and, later, brother-in-law, and one Finnish letter was addressed to his friends and neighbours as a group. These letters contribute to understandings of Karelian youth culture, the impact of return migration, Soviet athletics, and the role of Finnish North Americans in the Continuation War.[5] Aate's remarkable life came to an end in a Finnish prisoner-of-war camp, where he was executed in 1942.

Aate Pitkänen's letters are complemented by a rich collection of biographical materials written and saved by his sister Taimi Davis (née Pitkänen), as well as her letter correspondence with her parents, Kirsti and Antti Pitkänen, which refer to news from Aate in Karelia.[6] **Antti Pitkänen** followed his son to Karelia in the fall of 1934, but quickly returned to Canada in 1935. A letter from Antti Pitkänen to Davis, written 25 December 1933, provides a rare opportunity to analyze the process and decision making involved in migrating to Karelia. Finally, the Pitkänen collection is completed by an astoundingly vivid and forthright letter by Aate Pitkänen's aunt, **Aino Pitkänen**, which details the Great Terror in Karelia, after she and her husband fled to Finland in 1938.

The most challenging collection of letters to work through is that of the Heino family, who moved to Kondopoga (Kontupohja), Karelia, from Menahga, Minnesota, in October 1931. Frank and Justiina Heino, born in 1887 and 1882, respectively, had a mixed family of ten children at the time of their migration. Six of their children went to Karelia: Martta (Martha), born 1911; Kaarlo (Karl/Carl), born 1912; Walter (Valte/Walt), born 1916; Urho, born 1917; Arthur (Arte), born 1920; and Alisi (Alice), born in 1922. Martha moved with her parents and siblings, but also with her husband Arvo Nestor Tieva (1897–1956) and their daughters Florence (1928–1990) and Violet (1930–2019).[7] Kaarlo's wife, Helen (née Niemi), was also in Karelia, but it is unclear whether the couple, who both came from Menahga at the same time, were married before migrating or once they arrived in Karelia, since Helen is found with her family in immigration records.[8] Both Martha and Kaarlo returned with their families to the United States, presumably in 1935.[9] The family experienced immense tragedy in Karelia: Urho and Arte died within three months of each other at the ages of fourteen and twelve; Frank Heino was arrested and executed in the Great Terror; and Walter was killed in action in the Siege of Leningrad.

The available letters were written by Justiina and Alice to the siblings in the United States, including Martha and Kaarlo after their return. The collection poses significant challenges because many of the letters are torn and missing pages, and very few are dated. What can be clearly discerned from the letters, however, make crucial contributions to an understanding of Finnish North American life in Karelia and have, therefore, been included in the study and analyzed with great care. The letters have often been successfully dated to a year range using references to key events, such as birthdays, deaths, the return of Martha and Kaarlo, the arrest of Frank, and even films as markers. Together, the six letters by Justiina and five letters by Alice range from 1932 to 1941. **Justiina Heino**'s letters discuss the work of caring for a large family separated by migration, her daily thoughts of work, Karelian life, and the children, and provide emotionally stirring glimpses of a woman whose heart is broken by the loss of her children, husband, and sense of safety and connection. **Alice Heino**'s letters to her siblings are rare first-hand accounts written by a child coming of age in Karelia. Justiina and Alice's fates are not known beyond the final 1941 letter.

The Heino collection also includes one letter written by **Tauno Salo** to Kaarlo Heino in November 1935.[10] Based on immigration lists, I believe Tauno Salo moved to Karelia with his family from Balsam, Minnesota,[11] and they, like the Heinos, lived in Kondopoga in Karelia. It seems Tauno Salo's father was also arrested and executed in the Kondopoga Paper Factory purge of 1938.[12]

Nine letters written by **Kalle Heikki Korhonen** (who often signed letters as "Korholen") to his daughter Aune Batson have also been analyzed in this study.[13] Korhonen, according to family history, was born in Finland in 1887 and moved to the United States in 1910.[14] He moved throughout the United States and Canada looking for work, and moved to Soviet Karelia in 1930, leaving behind his second wife and sixteen-year-old daughter, whose mother had recently passed away. Korhonen's available letters begin in August 1935 and conclude in October 1939. Additionally, the collection contains one formal letter written by George Halonen on Korhonen's behalf to Aune Batson in April 1939, after correspondence between the father and daughter had broken off.

Compared with the incomplete biographical information of many of the studied letter writers, much is known about **Enoch Nelson**. Nelson's Karelian letters are a part of his brother's significant collection, the Arvid Nelson Papers, housed at the Immigration History Research Center Archives.[15] What makes the Nelson letters especially unique is the fact that Arvid Nelson saved copies of the letters he wrote, providing both sides of the correspondence for analysis. Enoch Nelson's life has also been examined by his nephew, Allan Nelson, in *The Nelson Brothers: Finnish-American Radicals from the Mendocino Coast*, which includes translations of his Communist Party of the Soviet Union "Autobiographical Statement" and rehabilitation notices.[16] Nelson was a second-generation Finn, born in northern California in 1897. He had moved to Karelia already in 1921 but his letters from the early 1930s have been the primary focus for this study. These seven English-language letters, written to his brother and sister Ida, offer a rare view of the newly arriving mass of Finnish North Americans from the perspective of someone already accustomed to Soviet life and speak to industry and employment at this time. Enoch Nelson became increasingly devoted to the Communist Party of the Soviet Union, but fell victim to its repression in 1938. In January of that year he was expelled from the Party and on 5 March 1938 he was executed for alleged counter-revolutionary activities.[17]

Seven letters written by **Karl Berg** to his daughter are available for analysis. Finnish-born Berg left for Karelia from Mather, Pennsylvania.[18] The first three letters, written between May 1932 and April 1935, describe Berg's daily life in Petrozavodsk and his longing to be near his daughter and new grandchild. A letter dated 29 October 1938 places Berg in Finland and refers to other letters that seem to have not made it to the United States. It appears he had asked his daughter to help him get out of the Soviet Union. Three final letters were written in Helsinki, with only one, written on 8 July 1940, dated. Because he migrated as a single, mature man, and escaped during the Great Terror, beyond his letters and the listing of a "Kaarlo Berg" emigrant, no further information about Karl Berg has been confirmed to date.

The Arthur Koski Letter Collection contains six letters written by **Terttu Kangas**, née Järvinen, and one written by her husband, **Antti Kangas**.[19] The Kangas family, including Terttu, Antti, and their three children, Martha, Olavi, and Urho, left behind the Finnish community of Drummond Island, Michigan, in the fall of 1933. They moved to the village of Lohijärvi, some 20 kilometres from Petrozavodsk, and most of what is known about their lives came from the letters written by Terttu to her sister Toini. From these letters, which were written between November 1933 and January 1939, we know that Antti and the eldest son, Urho, worked in the lumber industry, Olavi struggled with schooling, Martha pursued teacher training, and Terttu took on various odd jobs throughout the years. While Terttu's letters provide detailed descriptions of daily life, Antti Kangas's single letter, dated October 1934, is addressed to the "Comrades" of Drummond Island. This letter has a much more formal tone than Terttu's letters, and aimed to address questions and concerns about the Karelian project. It is optimistic in its portrayal of socialism at work and hoped to deflate rumours about Karelian life. Antti Kangas's letter demonstrates the rhetoric and ideology that accompanied the migration of Finnish North Americans, and the role of the personal letter in transferring information between the Soviet Union and North American socialist circles. Terttu Kangas's letters reveal that her family made it through the peak of the Great Terror, with each member mentioned in her final letter, dated 30 January 1939. Beyond that, the only additional information about the family that has been found to date is that Urho Kangas died in a gulag in 1943.[20]

Two letters written by **Elis Ranta** have been analyzed in this study.[21] Ranta was born in Finland in 1891,[22] moved to the Great Lakes region of the United States as a young man, and met and married a nineteen-year-old Finnish migrant, Alli, in 1916.[23] The couple moved from Waukegan, Illinois, to Monessen, Pennsylvania, where their daughter Viola was born in 1918. The family set sail for Karelia on board the *Gripsholm* on 30 July 1932. They were first sent to Uhtua, where Elis worked as a baker and Alli worked as a school manager. Viola left school and began work at the age of fourteen as a typist. The family moved to Petrozavodsk in the spring of 1933, when Ranta was employed as a professional musician, working with the radio orchestra and as the Ski Factory Orchestra's director. Ranta's letters are the only ones in the studied group that were sent to Finland, rather than to Canada or the United States. Elis Ranta's letters to his brother in 1933 and 1934 demonstrate the struggle between his delight in being able to work as a full-time musician and his lingering homesickness, as well as the contestations between a father and the will of his teenaged daughter. Elis Ranta was arrested during the Great Terror and died in a gulag in 1940.[24] Alli, Viola, and Viola's sick daughter, Lorein, whose father had also been taken in the purges, were sent to the Urals for the war years. They returned in late 1944. Alli died in Karelia in 1979 and Viola moved to Finland in the early 1990s after retiring. The family's biography is enriched by **Viola Ranta**'s six-page, unpublished memoir, written in 1992. This brief yet powerful narrative depicts Viola's abhorrence for Soviet life from the first days of arrival through the ongoing struggles that confronted her life.

Reino Mäkelä's life writing makes a unique contribution to the study, since we have access not only to four letters that he wrote shortly after moving to Karelia in 1931, but also fifty-six letters he wrote to his childhood friend between August 1958 and October 1979.[25] He was born in Ishpeming, Michigan, on 19 April 1915, and moved with his parents and two brothers to Karelia in 1931. Mäkelä's letters from October 1931 to March 1932 provide insights into Finnish North American youth culture in Soviet Karelia. The large collection of letters written after Stalin's death focus primarily on day-to-day descriptions of life, and prove quite useful in considerations of what is *not* said when one narrates one's life experiences. Mäkelä's collection at the Immigration History Research Center Archives also contains two letters, dated 20 February 1932 and 5 April 1932, which are addressed to the same recipient, "Benny," but are written by a different Reino. **Reino Hämäläinen** was born in 1915 or 1916, and moved to Karelia from Waukegan, Illinois, in 1932 with his parents and brother.[26] Like the 1930s letters from Reino Mäkelä, Hämäläinen's letters offer a unique view of youth culture and leisure in Soviet Karelia.

The twenty-seven letters and two Christmas cards written by **Jack Forsell** to his niece, Janet, in Thunder Bay, Ontario, represent a nearly twenty-five-year-long correspondence from February 1972 to December 1996.[27] Over the course of the years, Forsell shared much of his life story with Janet. Forsell was born in 1906 in the Dog River Valley (rural Thunder Bay, Ontario, area), where many Finns tried their hand at farming and forestry. He moved to Karelia in the fall of 1931. There, he married a Finnish North American, Elvie, in 1932, and they had two children, though he and Elvie outlived them both. Jack and Elvie spent the rest of their lives in Karelia. The remarkably rich letters slip between talk of daily life in a transforming USSR to memories of 1930s Karelia, war, and boyhood memories from the 1910s and 1920s, and leave the reader wanting to hear more. As Forsell aged, he lost his eyesight, and wrote blind in handwriting that became large, thick, and wayward by the final letters. On 23 June 1997, **Elvie** wrote to Janet that Jack Forsell had died.

Also providing an opportunity to analyze retrospective narratives are four letters written by **Harold Hietala**.[28] Hietala was born in Port Arthur, Ontario, on 29 April 1918. He moved to Karelia with his family in 1931, where he married US Finn Leini Leipälä. Harold Hietala was captured by the Finns during the war, and when he was returned to the Soviets, he was imprisoned for three years.[29] Harold and Leini Hietala participated in Varpu Lindström's Karelian research in August 1988. The four letters were written to Lindström after participating in the research project, Harold reflecting on his role as interview subject. **Leini Hietala**'s life-history interview has also been used in this study.[30] The couple returned to North America (Thunder Bay) in 1993. Harold Hietala died in December 2009 and Leini Hietala in December 2015.

Klaus Maunu was born in New York in 1924. He moved to Karelia as an eight-year-old from Pike Lake, Ontario (rural Thunder Bay). Maunu wrote his life story in three instalments after moving to Finland in the 1990s.[31] The first, "Muistoja lapsuus ja poikavuosilta" ("Memories of childhood and bachelor years"), which is of most interest to the present study, details his life in North America and Karelia up to the 1941 war evacuation of Karelia. This memoir provides insights into daily life and the perceptions of a child migrant, remembered decades later. The second instalment focuses on his experience in evacuation in Arkhangelsk. The final and longest instalment, "Piikilangan takana" ("Behind Barbed Wire"), narrates his life in the "work army" (gulag) from 1942 to 1946.[32]

Paavo Alatalo moved to Karelia from Ohio in the spring of 1931 as an eleven-year-old boy. His unpublished life writing serves as auto/biography, narrating his own life, as well as his wife's story. Written between 1998 and 2002, "Sylvin ja Paavon Tarina" ("Sylvi and Paavo's Story") aimed to record family history for younger relatives.[33] The narrative further strikes readers as an outlet for dealing with the grief of his wife's death, which occurred just before he began writing. Like Klaus Maunu's narrative, the majority of the life writing is dedicated to the war years. However, the description of his early life adds to our understanding of the Finnish North American migration, the school experiences of children in Karelia, and the impact of the Great Terror as felt through the loss of his first love.

Allan Sihvola began to write his autobiography at the age of seventy-four.[34] Sihvola's family moved to Karelia from Warren, Ohio, in 1933, when Allan was thirteen years old. Sihvola comes across as a very detail-oriented person, as his life writing provides vivid descriptions of his everyday life beginning with his early years in the United States. This memoir contributes rich imagery of Finnish North American culture and leisure in Karelia, as Sihvola was himself an active musician. Sihvola's narrative addresses quite openly the Great Terror and the fears in the community, in contrast with other writers. In addition to the losses he endured in Karelia in the late 1930s, Sihvola, too, was sent to the gulag after being released from the army in 1943. Though captive in the Ukraine, Sihvola was assigned to the orchestra and travelled to various camps and military operations for the next three years. He returned to Petrozavodsk in late 1946. Like Ranta, Maunu, and Alatalo, Allan Sihvola moved to Finland in the 1990s. He died in 2009. An edited version of Sihvola's autobiography was published posthumously in 2021, but the original is analyzed here.[35]

Kaarlo Tuomi moved to Karelia in 1933 at the age of sixteen with his parents and sister, leaving behind Rock, Michigan. Tuomi's short memoir appeared in *Finnish Americana* in 1980, and blends the community history with his own experience.[36] This personal account of the migration and the Great Terror was among the first published, and Tuomi acknowledged that the topic had been understudied because it was "too hot to handle."[37] Tuomi's "The Karelian 'Fever' of the Early 1930s," focuses on the period leading up to the Second World War. However, in 1984 Tuomi also published a memoir that described his work as a KGB spy in the 1950s, and later as an FBI double agent.[38] The focus in this study, however, has been on Tuomi's narration of the 1930s.

Karelia: A Finnish-American Couple in Stalin's Russia, 1934–1941 tells the story of **Lauri and Sylvi (anglicized Sylvia, née Kuusisto) Hokkanen's** time in Soviet Karelia.³⁹ This memoir, published in 1991 in the United States, brought the personal narratives of Karelian return migrants to North American audiences. The newlyweds, Lauri aged twenty-five and Sylvi twenty-one, left Sugar Island, Michigan, and were among the last Finnish North Americans to migrate to Karelia. Once the Hokkanens returned to the United States, they shared very little about their experiences in the Soviet Union, until their daughter, Anita Middleton, encouraged them to write a memoir. The memoir, written with the help of Middleton, moves back and forth between Lauri and Sylvi's narration. While little is known about how the couple's memories were divided into the resultant shared narrative, *Karelia* presents two very distinct voices and perspectives of their time building socialism in Soviet Karelia. Lauri Hokkanen died at the age of ninety-three, in 2002, and Sylvi passed away a few months later in January 2003.

Vieno Zlobina was born 18 September 1919, in Cobalt, Ontario. Her parents, Elis and Emma Ahokas, were founding members of the Säde (Ray) Commune, and moved to the Olonets region of Karelia in the spring of 1926. Zlobina lived in Karelia until 1965, experiencing the early Finnish North American commune movement, the impact of the arrival of the recruited US and Canadian Finns in the 1930s, the Great Terror, the War, and the shift to post-Stalinist life in the USSR. In 2017, the Migration Institute of Finland published Zlobina's memoir in both English and Finnish, and a Russian-language version was made available in 2019.⁴⁰

Mayme Sevander's name is closely linked to the story of Finnish North Americans in Karelia. Sevander, née Corgan, moved to Karelia in 1934 from Superior, Wisconsin (via New York City), at the age of ten. Her father, Oscar Corgan, was an influential Finnish migrant organizer and leader on the left, and the long-time editor of *Työmies* newspaper. He served as the final director of the Karelian Technical Aid, which oversaw the fundraising, recruitment, and transfer of Finnish North Americans to Karelia between 1931 and 1934. Believing in the Karelian project, and having sent thousands of people ahead, Corgan, his wife, Katri, and their three children moved there, too. The family embraced the building of socialism, but Oscar Corgan was arrested in 1937. The Corgan family, like others in Karelia and across the Soviet Union, faced significant hardships through the Great Terror and the Second World War. Mayme, however, came out well educated, employed at the national news bureau, married, and a mother. She even joined the Communist Party in 1960 because, in her words, she "believed in Krushchev's integrity, and I decided that to turn my back on the Soviet Union and the great experiment of communism would be a betrayal of my father's memory."⁴¹ The

Corgan family did not know Oscar's fate until 1991: he had been shot two months after his arrest.

Mayme Sevander fervently believed in the idealism and socialist principles that Finnish North Americans – or "My People" as she referred to them – brought to Karelia, and so many died for. In 1992, Sevander published *They Took My Father: Finnish Americans in Stalin's Russia*. This memoir, written with American journalist Laurie Hertzel, tells the story of the Corgan family and Mayme's life in the Soviet Union. However, Sevander was not satisfied to end there; she committed to telling the story of Finnish North Americans in Karelia as a whole. She researched, wrote, and published two more English-language works, *Red Exodus* and *Of Soviet Bondage*, and the Finnish *Vaeltajat*, which synthesizes her other publications.[42] While *Red Exodus*, *Of Soviet Bondage*, and *Vaeltajat* approach the topic of Finnish North Americans in Karelia as research subject, Sevander's personal involvement in this history results in chaotic, dynamic, emotional, and ground-breaking narratives that blur the autobiographical and the researcher's distance. Sevander's contribution to what is known about US and Canadian Finns in Karelia has been invaluable. She died in 2003, still devoted to unearthing the history of "Her" People.

These voices have never before been academically analyzed and, with very few exceptions, have remained publicly unknown.[43] Together,[44] they provide intimate insights on life in Soviet Karelia from excitement to heartbreak. The letter and memoir writers guide us through our exploration of daily life, and their writing allows us to consider the ways they shaped their stories to represent themselves. We turn now to the multiple paths that ultimately led these life writers to Soviet Karelia.

Chapter One

The Call of *Karjala*: Contextualizing the Karelian "Fever"

The migration of over 6,000 US and Canadian Finns to Soviet Karelia in the early 1930s was not a spontaneous "fever." Though individual migrants may have made quick decisions that altered their life course, Finnish North Americans' collective fate in Karelia had begun to form over a hundred years before the life writers set foot on Soviet ground. The collective movement can be best understood as part of the Finnish North American traditions of international socialism and utopianism, and the long-standing geopolitical and geocultural project of Finnish Karelianization. Karelia, or *Karjala* in Finnish, has for many generations occupied a central part of the Finnish people's sense of self, past and future. By joining in the recruited immigration of the 1930s, Finnish North Americans became participants in the contentious negotiation of Finnish–Russian relations, and the developing mechanisms of Stalinism.

Finnish North American Trajectories

The Karelia migration of the 1930s was a manifestation of Finnish North American international socialism, developing through twists and turns since Finns' early settlement in Canada and the United States. The call of *Karjala*, furthermore, coincided with a period of political and economic instability in Finnish enclaves. By examining the course of Finnish socialist organizational life in North America, we better understand the socio-political experiences and world views that migrants brought with them to the Soviet Union in the 1930s.

While a small group of early Finnish emigrants had already headed to Delaware in 1637 as a part of a Swedish colonization effort, and others sought riches in Alaska and California before the 1860s, the mass movement of Finns to North America took off in the 1880s. Mass migration was fuelled by poverty, unavailability of land in the countryside, unemployment in the cities, and the political and social clashes between Finnish nationalist determinism and the Russian centre. By 1930, Finnish-born residents numbered over 100,000 in the United States, along with thousands of US-born Finnish descendants. The 1931 Statistics Canada census reported that 43,885 people of Finnish origin lived in Canada, including 30,354 who were Finnish born.[1] Peter Kivisto contextualizes the place of Finns by stating that, while Finns "represent a relatively small immigrant group in the United States, their settlement patterns were such that, as an ethnic group, they had a rather profound impact on certain locales."[2]

Ontario, especially in the northwest, the Prairies, and British Columbia were the primary destinations of the majority of Finns to Canada. In the United States, the Great Lakes region proved most attractive, but sizeable Finnish communities could likewise be found on the west coast from Washington to northern California, in the Dakotas, and the east coast. While the government of Canada officially welcomed Finns to work in agriculture, many instead found employment in lumbering, mining, railroad construction, and fishing. Finns in the United States pursued similar occupations. Wage work, rather than farming, proved the norm among Finns in North America. In both Canada and the United States, Finns typically settled in rural areas and towns rather than in large urban centres. Finnish women arriving at the turn of the century, however, were an exception, most commonly pursuing employment as domestics and in the service industry in cities. Finnish migrants' "America" letters depict the active evaluation of earning potential, whether that meant frequently or seasonally changing jobs, or moving to where wages were best.[3] Experience with different occupations, job sites, and locales resulted in a wide array of skills and knowledge that ultimately made US and Canadian Finns appealing for recruitment into the Karelian project.

Finnish Migrant Socialisms

In the words of Varpu Lindström, socialism for Finns "was not a philosophy abstracted from the experience of the ordinary people, but was an integral part of the day-to-day life."[4] The era of mass migration from Finland to North America coincided with the quickly growing popularity of social democracy in Finland and the decline in the Finnish State Lutheran Church's power, but living and working conditions in Canada and the United States were a strong push to the left for many migrants. In the United States it is estimated that no more than 25 per cent of Finns had joined a church by 1900.[5] Even more strikingly, the 1931 Canadian census revealed that only 3 per cent of Finns were affiliated with a church.[6] Instead, socialist organizations largely came to meet the multiple social, culture, and political needs left unfulfilled by early Finnish migrant churches, plagued by lack of funds and clergy, and an inability to resonate with the concerns of immigrant daily life.[7]

The temperance pledge was welcomed by many who desired moral guidance. The temperance movement concretely worked to combat the alcoholism prevalent among new migrants, but also gave spiritual direction to those feeling lost and lonely. Carl Ross estimated that in the United States, some 200 Finnish temperance societies had been formed by 1900 and that they "outstripped the church, [and] became the incubator for Finnish immigrant culture, and the umbrella under which its institutions arose."[8] Along with the formation of Finnish temperance societies came the ubiquitous Finnish *haali*, or cultural hall. For example, the Finns of Savo, South Dakota, built their hall in 1899, the communities of Copper Cliff, Ontario, and Virginia, Minnesota, both built halls in 1906, the Port Arthur, Ontario, Finns in 1910, and, in Minneapolis, Minnesota, a hall was built in 1913. In the safety of the Finnish hall, migrants could come together to speak their language, celebrate their traditions and customs, and partake in the busy social calendar.

Hall members frequently staged *iltamat*, or evenings of entertainment, that featured a variety of activities ranging from dances, musical acts, and guest speakers, to dramatic performances. Finnish women were instrumental in organizing these popular community events. Additionally, halls were home to a wide array of clubs, groups, and organizations. From childhood to old age, Finnish migrants could partake in athletics, sewing circles, theatre troupes, or politics, to name just a few options. The vital place of the *haali* in Finnish Canadian and Finnish American lives would be replicated in Karelia in the Cultural Houses and Houses of Enlightenment, which stood as hubs of cultural life. In the words of Edward Laine, halls "provided a refuge or sanctuary for the immigrant community where its members could immerse themselves in the comfort of their commonly-held Finnish cultural heritage and, increasingly, to dream of the coming era of social democracy."[9]

From their arrival in North America to the move to Karelia and beyond, Finnish leftists worked their way through a number of political movements and parties, making a lasting mark on broader North American political and social spheres.[10] Tracing Finnish North American involvement in these movements clearly demonstrates a collective desire to carve out a place of their own within international socialism. With socialist movements focused on both domestic and international betterment, Finnish migrants could feel they were working toward a better life for those in North America, for family and friends remaining in Finland,

Figure 1 Finnish Labour Temple, Port Arthur, Ontario, in the 1920s. Archives & Digital Collections at Lakehead University Library, accessed 18 July 2021, https://digitalcollections.lakeheadu.ca/items/show/11.

and the greater good of the world's workers. For many Finnish migrant leftists, Karelian émigrés included, involvement in socialist movements in practice meant not just reciting party doctrine, but fostering a community that collectively worked to enact meaningful, tangible change to their day-to-day lives. For the thousands ultimately disheartened by North American life and the slow progress of revolution, the opportunity to move to Karelia offered another chance to work directly to meet workers' needs and to establish a Finnish socialist utopia.

An early example of Finnish political organization is the *Työväenliitto Imatra*, or Imatra Workers' League, formed in 1890. This organization operated as an inclusive mutual aid organization that advocated a broad type of socialism to better the lives of workers. Imatra grew to claim thirty-two locals in the United States and Canada, many of which evolved from temperance societies that had adopted a socialist point of view. Imatra waned with the founding of the Socialist Party of America (SPA) in 1901 and the Socialist Party of Canada (SPC) in 1903. Forming their own locals, the Finnish membership constituted approximately two-thirds of the total party membership.[11] However, the Finns' relationship with the socialist parties at large was strained. Finns in the US party faced anti-immigrant attitudes from the leadership,[12] while the Canadian leadership's sole focus on the long-range goal of Marxist world revolution did not suit Finnish interest in addressing the immediate needs and demands of workers.[13] In response, many turned to unionism. In particular, the direct action approach of Industrial Workers of the World (IWW or Wobblies) resonated with many Finns in Canada and the United States and would last decades.[14]

As they struggled to claim their space in broader North American socialist movements, both US and Canadian Finns began to form their own national organizational body. After an early attempt to organize across political and religious lines through the Finnish National League, leftists established the Finnish American Socialist Federation (FASF) at a convention in Hibbing, Minnesota, in the summer of 1906. The Federation proved to be a popular outlet for Finnish migrant political action and cultural pursuits. Although at its founding the Federation was officially affiliated with the Socialist Party of America and remained a language branch of the party until 1920, the relationship was far from unanimously accepted and many members were committed to the IWW. By 1920, with the dawn of international communism, the Federation was strained by internal divisions between the socialists, communists, and industrial unionists, with the communists eventually winning control. In Canada in 1911, the founding of the Finnish Socialist Organization of Canada (FSOC/FOC)[15] coincided with the emergence of the new Social Democratic Party of Canada (SDPC), in which Finns played a significant role. However, the FSOC ultimately moved through affiliations from the SDPC, to the One Big Union, finally aligning with the Communist Party of Canada (CPC).[16]

While much of Finnish socialist involvement focused on revolutionizing existing society, a deep vein of utopianism ran through the Finnish migrant left. The best-known utopian attempt is that of the Kalevan Kansa Colonization Company, which from 1901 to 1905 sought to build a new society on Malcolm Island, British Columbia, on traditional Kwakwaka'wakw territory.[17] Led by Matti Kurikka and his unique brand of socialist theosophical ethnonationalism and the Marxist A.B. Mäkelä, the Kalevan Kansa aimed to be freed from "wage slavery" and the capitalist cash system by producing commodities that could be traded both internally and externally. However, despite reaching a peak of some 300 members, rapidly growing debt, poverty, personality clashes, and a community tragedy, mixed with the difficult demands of building a self-sustaining community out of rugged, remote bush, proved too much. The (first) dream of Sointula, or the Place of Harmony, ended on 27 May 1905 when the Kalevan Kansa dissolved. Another example of Finnish North American communal utopianism, though lesser known than the Sointula experiment, is the history of Drummond Island, Michigan. Finnish migrant Maggie Walz – at first a follower of Kurikka – became a government land claim agent in 1905 in order to recruit desirable Finnish residents to the island who would participate in cooperative, temperate, Christian life.[18] The several hundred residents proved more aligned with socialist principles than with Walz's ideals, and the socialists took over the colony in 1914.[19] Finnish socialist activity continued on the island until the late 1930s,[20] but the utopian aim of cooperative living never came to fruition. The dream of Karelia as a workers' paradise, as envisioned by the Finnish migrant communities that fuelled the migration, can be seen as a continuation of their North American utopianist tradition. Some migrants even had direct first-hand experience with these earlier projects, like Martti Hendrickson in Sointula, and the Kangas family, whose letters we will become well acquainted with, who moved to Karelia from the Finnish community of Drummond Island.

Cooperativism was a primary feature of Finnish migrant socialist and utopian philosophy and practice. For example, Finns had already established sixty to seventy cooperative stores in the United States by 1919 and the movement remained strong into the 1950s.[21] Perhaps even more important than their role in providing material goods, co-ops organized social, cultural, and athletic activities for Finnish migrants.[22] By the late 1920s, the cooperative movement was embroiled in controversy as active members fought over whether communism or political neutrality would govern the co-ops. The fight was especially pronounced in the United States. Ultimately, in the spring of 1930 the communists were ousted and links to the party were severed, though the communists would mount take-over efforts in the following years. Many communist co-opers, including Mayme Sevander's father Oscar Corgan, turned to the Karelian project.

Coming to Communism

With a keen eye on movements in Russia, Finns in both North America and Finland were profoundly affected by the Russian Revolution. Reflecting on the early days of the North American communist movement, Elis Sulkanen, a well-known Finnish migrant organizer, remarked: "With ludicrous devotion did we sit in meetings of the underground branches, where the mentioning of the name of Lenin made the heart throb ... In mystic silence almost in religious ecstasy, did we admire everything that came from Russia."[23] In both Canada and the United States, Workers' Parties were created as public fronts for the underground communist parties. Their creation coincided with the adoption of a new United Front policy by the Third World Congress of the Communist International, which could not have come at a better time for Canadian and US communists. For the infant communist parties, an opportunity to call to action anyone who had marvelled at the creation of a workers' state in Russia proved very beneficial. With an emphasis on unity, fractures in existing socialist parties and organizations could be used to gently coax new members toward communism.

While many Finns had individually been moving toward United Front Communism, the Finnish American Socialist Federation became affiliated with the Workers' Party of the United States in late 1921 and the Finnish (Socialist) Organization of Canada joined the Workers' Party of Canada at their conference on 16 February 1922.[24] This meant that all FOC and FASF members also became members of their respective communist parties. The automatic membership proved very significant. Consider, for example, that by 1930, the FOC boasted over 6,000 members and half of the members of the Communist Party of Canada in the 1920s came from the membership of the FOC. When other segments of the CPC witnessed stagnation or even a drop in party membership, Finnish membership continued to grow.[25] In the United States, Finns, through the FASF, accounted for some 40 per cent of the Communist Party of the United States of America (CPUSA) membership.[26]

In the workers' parties, in addition to a national body, federations based on language accommodated the majority of their supporters, who were affiliated first with their cultural socialist organizations. Because of their strength in numbers and the experience contributed by radical immigrants, such as Finns, Jews, and Ukrainians, language groups were viewed as key pillars to the organization's structure, right from the foundation of the parties.[27] These ethnic branches were to have their own constitutions and by-laws, and hold their own conferences, with an emphasis on maintaining the official party line at all times.[28] This model suited Finns who had worked with other political parties in the past.

The Finns became the financial backbone of the Canadian and US communist parties. For example, in Canada, with 2,028 members out of the reported 4,808 in 1923, the Finnish elements contributed a disproportionate two-thirds of the party's total revenue, through fundraising and dues payments.[29] At times Finns supplemented the parties even further. In 1922, Finnish Canadian communists donated $2,000 to help launch the English-language party organ, *The Worker*.[30] US Finns provided $25,000 for the establishment of *The Daily Worker*.[31] This was in addition to funding their own Finnish-language papers, *Vapaus* and *Työmies*.

The Finns' relationship with the communist parties turned sour, just as the Workers' Party fronts were being dismantled. In 1924, the

Communist International adopted a "bolshevization" policy which, in part, meant the abolition of all language federations. In the words of Auvo Kostiainen, bolshevization was intended to "destroy the last remnants of socialist and social democratic thought among the world's communists."[32] The Comintern viewed the North American communist movement as splintered and failing to follow the official international party line. An emphasis on a "working-class language" was the solution supported by the Communist International. Unfortunately for the more than 80 per cent of non-English-speaking members, this unifying language was to be English.[33] While communist parties in other countries were largely structured unilingually, both the Canadian and US parties were created through the amalgamation of numerous linguistically and culturally differing organizations, and, thus, breaking the original branches into smaller cells proved almost impossible. In the North American context, bolshevization essentially meant the assimilation or "Americanization' of migrant communists. In an attempt to counter the very profound concern expressed by the non-English branches, the Comintern and, in turn, the North American leadership argued that an inability to effectively communicate in English could be manipulated by the bourgeoisie.[34]

The bolshevization crisis not only alienated Finns and other language groups from the wider communist movement but also resulted in extreme divisions within the Finnish branches. Hostile in-fighting, neglect of the rank and file, and, ultimately, a rash of expulsions marked the end of moderation in the communist parties of Canada and the United States. By 1930, after years of struggling to maintain their original position within the North American communist movement, less than 10 per cent of the Finns who had aligned themselves with communism at the beginning of the decade remained members.[35]

By the 1931 establishment of the Karelian Technical Aid to recruit Finnish Canadians and Americans to Soviet Karelia, the Finns' relationship with the communist parties of North America was complicated, to say the least. Although the Karelian project was officially sanctioned by the Communist Party of the Soviet Union and Communist International, the Canadian and US parties, as we will see, were very reluctant to grant remaining Finnish members permission to participate in the immigration scheme. Therefore, the vast majority of the Karelian migrants were not card-carrying communists, but rather those who had lost their long-standing social, cultural, and political place in the North American left movement and, in even greater numbers, their children, who had been raised in the revolutionary spirit.

Finns Divided

The Finns' bitter experience with formal North American communism in the 1920s was not an isolated event of dissatisfaction and dissension, neither between Finnish migrants and the leftist political movement in North America, nor among Finnish socialists themselves. As evidenced by the continual shifts in allegiance, members of the Finnish socialist movement could not find a political party or philosophy to unite them as leftist Finnish migrants. Though committed to the establishment of a new world order through varying forms of socialism, they were also caught up in trying to find their place in Canadian and US society while holding on to their native Finnish culture. Different geographic and employment realities also separated the needs of Finns spread throughout Canada and the United States. The contesting pulls could find no simple compromise, and hostilities between socialists of varying shades of red were an ongoing feature in the history of Finnish North Americans up to the Karelian exodus and beyond.

The wave of migration that followed the Finnish Civil War of 1918 brought with it bitterness that succeeded in dividing Finns so thoroughly that the remnants are still palpable today. Economic competition heightened political tensions among Finnish "Reds" and "Whites" in North America. The persecution of socialist sympathizers in North America, often referred to as the "Red Scare," affected many Finns. Not only were Finnish migrant socialists attacked by the Canadian and US governments and nativist groups, but the Depression led to a no-holds-barred attack by organized conservative Finns. The involvement of so many Finns in the frequent labour disputes and disruptions of the early 1900s caused employers to be wary of hiring Finns, believing them all to be radicalized. This meant that even those "Church Finns," vehemently opposed to the activities of the socialists, were often unwelcome at worksites.[36] In response, conservative Finns rallied together in Canada and the United States to publicly distance themselves from Finnish leftists.[37] In the United States, non-socialist Finns organized the Lincoln Loyalty League in 1918. Canadian Finns attempted to come together under the Kansallis-Liitto (Finnish National Federation) in 1917 and other similar groups over the years, but had lasting success with the Central Organization of Loyal Finns in Canada in 1931. With these organizations, Finnish conservatives promoted their own well-being, asserted their North Americanness, and also informed prospective employers about those with known, or even suspected, ties to socialism or unionism. Varpu Lindström has demonstrated how the rise of conservatism and right-wing movements among North American Finns influenced decisions to move to Karelia.[38]

Karelia and Independent Finland

For Finnish migrants, on both the political left and right, ideas about Karelia were interwoven with ideas about the homeland. In the decades following the transfer of control from Sweden to the Russian Empire in 1809, which gave Finland autonomy, a new Finnish nationalist spirit, *Fennophilia*, emerged. The cultural and linguistic renaissance, led by writers and scholars, such as J.V. Snellman, Johan Ludvig Runeberg, and Aleksis Kivi, also resulted in the *Kalevala*, the epic of the Finnish people. Elias Lönnrot published the first version of the *Kalevala* in 1835 and the second, elaborated and now standard version, in 1849. Lönnrot and others travelled through the borderlands of Finland and Russia gathering oral folk poetry that told the mythological origins of Finns. However, to complicate the claim on these ancient Finnish roots, the *runos* were primarily preserved among the Finnish and Karelian speakers of Karelia, securely in the clutches of the Russian Empire. Regardless, Karelia came to be seen as "the cultural cradle of Finnishness."[39] Yet, the *Kalevala* stood for even more than just a glorified Finnish past. The poems, as Eino Friberg writes, were "proof of an ethnic entity previously underestimated, and an argument for its coming to full expression."[40] From the newfound roots and national identity, Finnish nationalists believed they had an obligation to modernize the local Finnish, Karelian, Ingrian, and Veps populations of Karelia, uplifting them with Lutheranism and Finnish culture.

As Finland asserted its independence from Russia and its place in the international order at the turn of the twentieth century, Karelia continued to function as a significant site culturally and politically. Almost immediately following the passage of the Declaration of Independence by the White-led Finnish Senate on 6 December 1917, the government was committed to securing Karelia and the Petsamo region in the far north. By the New Year, Finland's independence had been recognized by the Bolsheviks and other foreign powers. Lenin initially agreed to cede Petsamo to the "Socialist Workers' Republic of Finland," but the question of Karelia was left unresolved. Hostilities and divisions arising from contesting views on the political structure of Finland erupted into a bloody civil war in early 1918. In April, the Finnish White Guard called in German supports and defeated the Red Guard in a series of raids. Though the war was officially over on 15 May, Reds were severely persecuted, abused, and even outright killed in the aftermath, and the wounds of civil war have stayed in the forefront of public memory for generations and even followed Finns across the ocean.[41] In the tumultuous transition from Russian Grand Duchy to post–Civil War independent Finland, Finnish migration to North America peaked.

Having forcefully secured their power in Finland, White Finns turned again to Karelia to continue their work. Still set on bringing Karelia into the Finnish nation and holding on to the *Fennomania* of decades past, the White Finnish government began extensive agitation campaigns among the Finnish and Finno-Ugric speakers of the region in an attempt to turn the people against the Bolsheviks. In August 1918, Finnish border guards pushed into Repola and convinced the people to join Finland. Similar expeditions and missionary work continued over the course of the next years, with the aim of converting the poor population of the borderlands into Finnish nationalists.[42] Meanwhile, the Finnish Red Guard, exiled in North America, Sweden, and Soviet Russia, regrouped and continued the work of building Finnish socialism. In August 1918, the Finnish Communist Party was established in Moscow. The Red leadership also began to look toward Karelia.

Edvard Gylling and the Red Finn Homeland

In Sweden, a Finnish exile, newly converted to communism, began to formulate plans that would result in the creation of the Karelian Workers' Commune. Edvard Gylling, born to a wealthy middle-class family in Kuopio in 1881, was a self-described "right-wing socialist,"[43] who opposed revolution and emigration, instead supporting parliamentary reform.[44] When the Civil War began, he was nonetheless selected to serve as the Red Guard's Chief of Staff in 1918, following a brief stint as Minister of Finance in the revolutionary government. After being charged with treason by the White Finnish Senate at the close of the Civil War, he found refuge in Stockholm. There, he devised a plan for a Red Finn homeland that included Karelia and the Kola Peninsula, with Red Finns as leaders, the Finnish language and culture as its cornerstones, and the right to self-govern matters of local policy, education, and finance.[45] With the population envisioned to be at least half Finnish and Karelian, the Soviet Karelian commune would serve as the perfect centre for the future "Soviet Republic of Scandinavia."[46]

Soviet Russia had not signed a peace treaty with Finland since the conclusion of the First World War. Already consumed with controlling Polish ambitions in the Ukraine, the Finnish pursuit of Karelia and their close relationship with Germany added unwelcome stress to Russian foreign affairs. Karelia had gained greater importance for the Russians after the completion of the Murmansk Railway in 1916, providing an important route to the open sea. Peace with Finland was seen as a key to ensuring ongoing access. However, in addition to

Figure 2 Edvard Gylling. Photo courtesy of the Karelian Research Centre Russian Academy of Sciences.

making dramatic territorial demands,[47] the new state of Finland also insisted on self-governance for Karelia. Gylling was called to meet with Lenin in May 1920. His plan to bring Finnish autonomy to Karelia under the Soviet realm was seen as the compromise to winning Finland's favour.

On 7 June 1920, the All-Russian Central Executive Committee issued a decree that established the Karelian Workers' Commune, just days in advance of the opening of a new round of peace negotiations with Finland.[48] The commune was created as a buffer between Finland and the Soviet Union, to prevent Finnish annexation, to counter White Finn agitation and sway loyalties to the Soviets via the Red Finns, and to pacify unrest by improving living conditions through regional development.[49]

However, the founding of the Karelian Commune did not make Finland automatically agreeable to signing a peace treaty with Russia. Finland wanted more say in the terms and extent of Karelian autonomy. Therefore, the Soviets, desperate for peace, continued to broaden the scope of Karelia's self-governance, conceding to practically all of Gylling's requests, including control over local revenues. As Markku Kangaspuro succinctly concludes: "Without the threat that Finland posed to the Murmansk railroad, no autonomy of this scale would have been possible. Had not Karelian autonomy had this dimension of international politics, Red Finns would never have gained the central role in Karelia they now were to enjoy."[50] Under the pressure of signing the peace, Gylling's Karelia became the area with the most wide-ranging autonomy in all of the Soviet Union.

Korenizatsiia and "Karelianization"

With the green light given to begin building a Red Finn commune in Karelia and the threat of Finnish annexation eased (at least temporarily), the fall of 1920 also marked the beginning of a Soviet era of minority accommodation, or the strategy of *korenizatsiia*. At the end of the tsarist regime, about 50 per cent of Russia's population was non-Russian, and the revolution and Russian civil war had done much to awaken minority nationalisms.[51] On 10 October *Pravda* published an article written by Stalin, in his role as People's Commissar of Nationalities, that called for an "indigenization" of the borderlands to foster cultural and linguistic development, along with economic and resource development.[52] By the Tenth Party Congress in March 1921, *korenizatsiia* had become official policy. Though vaguely defined, Lenin's Russia was to be a federalist union supported by the restricted autonomy of the vast state's minority nationalities. The Bolsheviks were aware of the "backwardness" of rural Russia and saw roads, electricity, postal service, and improved hygiene, among other factors, as crucial to achieving modernity.[53] Autonomy, then, was the key to realizing these beacons of modernization. By installing locals to administrative posts and allowing some level of self-governance on local issues, the Soviets envisioned a cultural uplift among the minority groups, which in turn would ensure loyalty.[54] Soviet *korenizatsiaa* perfectly suited the Red Finns' aspirations.

The Karelian leadership team consisted of Red Finns in all top posts. Edvard Gylling was positioned as Permanent Chairman of the Karelian Council of the People's Commissars, while his long-time colleague, former Finnish Social Democrat Kustaa Rovio, served as First Secretary of the Karelian Communist Party. The Red Finns were focused on building a new homeland for Finns and saw themselves as the natural leaders of the people. Yet, claims of the region's Finnishness were tenuous. Finns actually accounted for less than 1 per cent of the population.[55] In addition to ethnic Finns who had roots in Karelia, the region's Finnish population comprised no more than 10,000 Red Finn refugees (including Social Democrats, communists, and other leftists) who had fled Finland during and after the Civil War, and a steady flow of illegal border-hoppers (*loikkarit*), of whom an estimated 3,000 to 3,500 settled in Karelia.[56] Ethnic Karelians represented some 40 per cent of the population in the 1920s but Russians were the most numerous in the region.[57] In population counts taken during the transition from the Commune structure to the Karelian Autonomous Soviet Socialist Republic (KASSR) in 1923, Russians represented 55.7 per cent of the total population.[58] In Petrozavodsk, the Commune's capital, Russians accounted for some 90 per cent of its residents in 1926.[59] Furthermore, between the establishment of the Karelian Workers' Commune and the end of 1924, the region's borders had been redrawn at least six times, further diluting the Finnish and Karelian character of the region, due to the inclusion of additional ethnically Russian areas.[60]

Given the region's ethnic reality, the question of what would be the Commune's primary language of administration and education was an important and difficult one. In Karelia, Russian, Finnish, Veps, and three main dialects of Karelian were all represented. Northern Karelian was very similar to Standard Finnish, while the southern dialects were quite distinct.[61] Karelian speakers far outnumbered Finnish speakers in the region, but the Karelian language had yet to be standardized and had no literary form, so choosing Karelian as an official language would have been a complicated matter.[62] Furthermore, in the minds of Finnish ethnonationalists, like Gylling, the Karelian language was little more than just another dialect of Finnish.[63] Russian language, though well represented in the region, would have made the establishment of the autonomous region largely redundant in the view of *korenizatsiia* and, in Kustaa Rovio's words, "nonsensical."[64] Both Russian and Finnish were given official-language status, but between 1921 and 1935, Karelia became increasingly Finnicized.[65]

Finnish-language newspapers and libraries were established as a passive form of expanding Finnishness in Karelia. From 1922 onward the formal policy of "Karelianization" was actively pursued.[66] As an indication of what the Karelian Commune's true objectives were, the policy, in actuality, meant elevating the status of the Finnish language – or "Finnish-Karelian," as it was tokenized - and the assimilation of Karelians and other Finno-Ugrians into Finnish speakers. As an example of the policy's scope, consider that out of 420 schools in the region in 1920, not a single one used Finnish as the language of instruction.[67] By the time Finnish North Americans were arriving in the 1930s, all of Karelia's schools were Finnish.[68] Likewise, regional records and most interactions with the administration had become Finnish.[69] The demographic reality in Karelia suggests that the Soviets were using Red Finns in Karelia to appease Finland and the discontented borderland residents, rather than promoting the region's indigenous cultures.

Labour Recruitment

The Red Finn leadership envisioned a prosperous and dynamic republic. Under the Soviet Union's liberal New Economic Policy (NEP) of the early 1920s, Karelia was poised to become a leader in the lumber industry, thanks to its significant and accessible forest reserves. Red Finn Karelia had been granted the right to keep 25 per cent of lumber export profits,[70] which could, in turn, be used to further diversify the economy, and especially to develop a lumber processing industry. However, revenue from exports at this time proved insufficient to fund processing facilities and, though, overall, Soviet Russia was experiencing unemployment, the local labour force was too small and inexperienced to meet the region's demand. In 1920, the Karelian population was approximately 210,000, with the majority employed in small-scale agriculture and only 2 per cent in industrial work.[71]

Edvard Gylling's solution was to relocate 80,000 Finnish workers from Finland and North America by 1923. The plan, however, was a complete failure. In fact, by 1923, Karelia had experienced a net loss in population, due to war and starvation in the Finnish borderlands.[72] Furthermore, Karelian recruitment efforts made the Soviet centre uneasy and drew closer attention to activities in the region. Very few Finnish foreigners accepted Gylling's invitation. Instead, newcomers primarily came from other parts of the Soviet Union, recruited to work along the Murmansk Railway by the central government.[73] Another sore point for the Red Finn leadership was the ever-growing presence of over 10,000 prisoner labourers in Karelia by 1926.[74] Gylling's silver lining was the arrival of a few hundred Finnish North Americans in the early 1920s.

Early Finnish North Americans in Karelia

Finnish North Americans were never far behind the news from Soviet Russia and always proved quick to help. By 1921, Finnish North Americans had already reorganized their "Society for the Technical Aid of Soviet Russia," active since 1919, into the "Society for the Technical Aid of Soviet Karelia," also known as the "Soviet Karelian Aid Committee."[75] Vieno Zlobina remembered Cobalt, Ontario, Finnish socialists' participation in these fundraising efforts as "an impressive demonstration of the internationalism of the community."[76] In conjunction with this fundraising limb, US and Canadian Finns formed the Karelian Workers' Cooperative that sold bonds to migrant communists and used the profits to further aid the Karelian project. The Karelian Workers' Cooperative managed the monies raised and handled the transfer of goods to the Soviet Union. By the beginning of 1922, the Finnish Socialist Federation reported that the Karelian Aid program had raised $4,696.27 in cash and countless – and, in fact, uncounted – more in material goods.[77]

Finnish North Americans also established Karelian labour cooperatives. After 1921, as part of the NEP, the Comintern encouraged international communists to form cooperatives and to apply for licences to work in Russia. Many Finnish North Americans founded such companies but they did not meet the requirement of having five members, so the Karelian Aid office reformed the cooperatives into larger units.[78] Ultimately, about six Finnish North American cooperatives, or communes, became active in the Soviet Union in the 1920s from the far north to the Black Sea to the Kuzbas.[79] While Gylling certainly hoped for Finnish migrants to come to Karelia and the Comintern encouraged the formation of cooperatives, no formally organized Soviet recruitment efforts were made among Finnish North Americans.[80] This lack of official direction, then, may explain why, despite the Karelian leadership's focus on the lumber industry, the 1920s arrivals from Canada and the United States did not work in the forests. Instead, most participated in agricultural work and the fishery.

In a letter dated 22 January 1921 from Arvid Nelson to his brother Enoch, Arvid reported that the *Työmies* newspaper's building in Superior, Wisconsin, was being used as the Karelian Committee headquarters.[81] Arvid's letter reveals that in addition to raising funds, the Superior office was also looking for US Finns to go to Karelia. He sent his brother an application for the "bona fide red Finnish republic," adding that he would gladly send additional applications for any of Enoch's interested friends.[82] Enoch Nelson did fill out the application Arvid sent and, in May 1921, he became one of the early US Finns to head off to build socialism in Soviet Karelia. Enoch's letters to Arvid, offering much insight on the daily life of a foreigner in 1920s Soviet Russia, show him moving between jobs and travelling remarkable distances. At first working in the Lake Onega area of Karelia, Enoch moved far north to Knäsö on the Kola Peninsula in April 1923. There, Enoch joined with the Karelian Fish Trust, established by a small group of fishermen from Astoria, Oregon. Differing from the farming collectives, the Trust aimed to become a major fish cannery station, but their limited catch did not allow them to recoup the expense of the canning machinery. Further, as Enoch Nelson alleged, the machinery was ill-suited to the processing of herring, the main species present in their region of the White Sea.[83] Unfortunately, not much is known about the Karelian Fish Trust at this point, but less than a year after Enoch's arrival in Knäsö, the Trust had gone bankrupt and most members had returned to the United States.[84]

In May 1924, Enoch settled 3,000 kilometres south of Knäsö, at the Finnish North American collective farm "Kylväjä," in the District of Rostov, between the Azov and Caspian seas. Fortunately, more is known about the Finns of Kylväjä. The Seattle commune, as it was often called, was founded by six Finnish farmers in Washington in 1921 but within a few months, dozens more had joined the cooperative. In addition to giving their labour to the Soviet Union, members each paid $500 toward the machinery fund, $100 for necessities for the first year, and each had to pay their own travel expenses.[85] Agreeing to take a loss on their investment if they decided to leave the commune, the members made a significant commitment to Kylväjä. The amounts required to participate in the cooperative project suggest that the members were quite well-off, and propelled to move to the Soviet Union by idealism, rather than economic necessity. The first group of seventy-two communards left for Russia in August 1922 and by the end of 1924, the commune had approximately 150 members, many having already come and gone.[86] Enoch Nelson stayed only until early 1926.[87] Overcoming initial problems with the land, housing, health, neighbours, and machinery, the Commune managed to become a model in collective farming. However, as Kylväjä began to flourish, the Finnish and Finnish North American character of the farm came under attack. Many Finns chose to move north to Karelia, perceived as a Finnish region, to try their hand at further collective farming.

Among the Finnish North American cooperatives from the 1920s, the name of Säde Commune is most often mentioned, and Enoch Nelson likely knew much about the Finns' work there. Säde was established in 1922 by Finnish Canadian socialists in Cobalt, Ontario, and the first nine families arrived in Karelia in 1925.[88] Vieno Zlobina moved with her parents to Säde in the spring of 1926. Säde earned a reputation as an exemplary collective, and the Finnish Canadians were featured in agricultural manuals, newspapers, and even a dedicated book written by a leading Soviet agronomist. Unlike other communes of the 1920s, Säde remained an active farm and model for collectivization into the 1930s.

Through the success of Säde and Kylväjä in the 1920s, Finnish North Americans made a mark on Karelian and Soviet development and proved their capabilities as builders of socialism. By actively raising money for Soviet Karelia through the early Karelian Aid campaign and the Worker's Cooperative Bonds, Finnish Canadians and Americans took a stake in the Karelian project. Involvement in these early Karelian undertakings are examples of the Finnish North American commitment to international socialism and the ongoing belief in the possibility of utopia. With a flourishing Finnish-language North American leftist press and with the reports and letters of those who went to Karelia, Finns in Canada and the United States were well aware of the Red Finns' work in *Karjala* and eagerly looked for news from the Soviet Union. Though the Säde Commune continued into the 1930s, the trickle of Finnish North American migration in the 1920s came to a halt by mid-decade. Finns in Canada and the United States were by then embroiled in conflicts over the Bolshevization of the communist parties and the crisis of the cooperative movement's political direction. In Soviet Russia, the state began to reformulate its approach to building their socialist union and interest in foreign workers was put on the back burner.

Reformulating the Soviet Economy

By the late 1920s, the New Economic Policy had enabled the reconstruction of the postwar Soviet economy. While it had served its purpose, the NEP had also compromised the ideological position of the Bolsheviks. With Stalin now in charge and the Party and central government having become largely synonymous, the Bolsheviks began to tighten control over their vast territory and worked at centralizing all elements of Soviet life and economy. In addition to the expulsion of "kulaks" and forced agricultural collectivization in the name of unity, the Soviet government refocused its limited resources and efforts into priority industrial development. "Class A" production of raw goods, like coal, iron, and timber, were increased at the expense of consumer goods.[89] The economic strategy of the coming First Five Year Plan had significant repercussions on Karelian development and autonomy.

Karelia's privileges were not secured by constitution. As long as the Bolsheviks were focused on the spread of socialism, Karelia would be safe, but as soon as the state's focus began to shift, Karelia's future was insecure. Nick Baron convincingly argues that Stalin's growing interest in centrality was fundamentally at odds with Karelia's ambitions, due to its irreversible position as a hinterland.[90] Karelia's vision of its own development, as highlighted in its 1926 General Plan, included the construction of municipal amenities, housing, transportation, hydro power, food production and processing, and diversified industry.[91] However, the Soviet centre began to peel back Karelia's ability to control its budget and industry. The Soviet Union's main objective by 1929 was the accumulation of hard currency from export. Instead of building up wood processing, or much of anything else for that matter, the centre focused on selling raw timber at the lowest prices on the market.[92] To ensure expediency in meeting the goals of the "optimum variant" of the First Five Year Plan, the Soviet government nationalized forest administration, taking away Karelia's main sources of revenue through the Karelles Timber Trust and the Kondopoga Paper Mill.[93] Finally, the centre repealed Karelia's economic autonomy over its budget in early 1931. The envisioned role of Karelia had transformed from a future showcase of socialist development to little more than virgin forests ready for reaping. However, the overarching goal of rapid industrialization gave the Red Finns their final chance.

A Final Push for Red Finn Karelia

The Soviet Union began to suffer from a labour shortage by 1930. Backwoods Karelia had always had a difficult time attracting and keeping workers, and with the Five Year Plan in action, the shortage was felt even more acutely. The Karelian timber industry was largely dependent on expensive seasonal labourers and forced labourers, who by 1930 numbered 65,000 in the region.[94] Though even less worried about the region's ethnic composition than before, the central government had to concede that Karelia's labour needs were not being met adequately or efficiently. Karelia lacked both modern timbering specialists and equipment.[95] After continually rejecting Gylling's requests to recruit Finnish workers, the 1930 Party Congress agreed to invite foreign experts to fill labour needs. Furthermore, Gylling had the opportunity to present his proposal of bringing Finnish North American expertise directly to Stalin and Molotov, which led to the passing of resolutions on immigration. Likewise in 1930, the Communist International summoned US Finnish Communists John Wiita and Matti Tenhunen to Moscow to provide information about the rampant in-fighting among the Finnish North American left. During this time, the two were also sent to meet the Karelian leadership, where it was agreed that the transfer of migrant Finnish communists could be beneficial to both Soviet Karelia and North America.[96]

It was clear that the North American workers had to be experienced and bring all the tools of the trade, and it was imperative that they be Finnish. The timing was right also from the Finnish North American perspective. Many had become estranged from the communist parties of Canada and the United States and unable to collectively unify under any other socialist banner. The increasing strain of the Depression was made worse by the organizing efforts of White Finns, who sought to block leftist Finns from worksites. It seemed the society Finnish migrants had been working toward since the early political and cultural organizations of the turn of the century were becoming further out of reach than ever. The call of Karelia spoke to those who had not given up on the utopian dream, among them the Finnish North American youth, raised in the revolutionary spirit.

The Culture of Stalinism

Finnish North Americans arrived with the cultural baggage of their North American migrant political and cultural experiences and found themselves negotiating their way through differing notions of what building socialism entailed and the role of Karelia in that project. Though the Red Finns maintained their commitment to make Karelia Finnish, the Soviet centre saw the recruitment of foreign workers in purely economic terms and demonstrated increasing hostility toward the non-Russian population. As the Soviet state restructured centre–periphery relations and its economic priorities, it also re-envisioned what it meant to be Soviet. The arrival of Finnish North Americans in Karelia coincided with the transition from revolutionary values and practices to the emerging culture of Stalinism. Just as Stalin's regime insisted on stringent control of all levels of governance, economy, and industry, the newly espoused Soviet culture had little tolerance for contesting cultural values. The task of Soviet centralization extended to the moulding of a new united Soviet identity, based on Russianness.[97] As subsequent chapters will demonstrate, Stalinism as a culture entailed elaborately constructed social hierarchies, a renewed focus on traditional family and gender roles, and the promotion of luxury and merriment with little regard for the reality of daily life experienced by the majority of Soviet citizens – all of this along with the use of repression and terror against the population. The cultural shift occurred unevenly and haphazardly, especially in hinterland regions like Karelia. Finnish North Americans were left to make sense of this new world of contradictions.

Conclusion

US and Canadian Finns who moved to Soviet Karelia in the 1930s collectively participated in the evolving politics of the "Karelian Question" and continued in the tradition of Finnish North American engagement in utopianism and international socialism. When faced with irreconcilable conflicts within the left, an organizing right, and an unfriendly North American economic and political state, the call for a Finnish workers' utopia in Karelia seemed to come at the perfect time. As news of the creation of a Finnish workers' republic was reaching North America, the effects of the Great Depression and the Red Scare were beginning to take their toll. Yet, the fates of individual migrants were entangled in the broader currents of communism and geopolitics. By 1931, Finnish North Americans had been framed as the region's saviours – saviours of the Finnish ideal for Gylling and saviours of the Soviet centre's floundering economic machinery. The migrants were ready to build a Finnish socialist society, prepped by decades of fresh starts and disappointments. However, the tide had already begun to turn against Karelian autonomy, the Finnish presence, and foreigners in the Soviet Union, more broadly, just as the new Soviet Karelian Technical Aid office opened its doors in New York on 1 May 1931.

Chapter Two

"Our Comrades Are Leaving Again": Moving to Soviet Karelia

"Far away to Asian expanses / Our comrades are leaving again, / Knowing so well they stand no chances / Of winning without taking pains," begins a poem written in honour of the Finnish North Americans who set off for Karelia in the 1930s.[1] While the required "pains" referred to in the poem most directly address the challenges inherent in the building of socialism, the stanza also speaks to the difficulty of migrant life in North America during the Depression and the effort and feelings involved in the decision to migrate. An overview of the collective motivations for emigration and the mechanisms of recruitment highlights the many factors that propelled the Finnish North American migration to Karelia in its scope and intensity. The Karelian life writers offer their insights on what it meant to engage in the Karelian project, reflecting on personal decisions to move, the preparations for departure, the voyage, and their first impressions of life in the workers' state. Since most preparations played out in the North American home community, preceding the establishment of available letter correspondences, memoirists have produced fuller accounts of their motivations and travel than letter writers. When letters do directly address the move and initial arrival, we gain a sense of the emotional and sensory whirlwind that accompanied migration.

Recruitment

US and Canadian Finns were recruited into the Karelian project through a complementary campaign by the Finnish-language communist press and the North American Karelian Technical Aid, in collaboration with the Soviet Karelian leadership. The Finnish-language socialist press played a significant role in shaping the world views of Finnish North American leftists and ultimately, in fuelling the "Karelian Fever." The communist press, *Vapaus* and *Työmies* in particular, juxtaposed reports of a thriving Soviet Union alongside devastating depictions of how the Depression was ruining the lives of workers in Canada and the United States. The newspapers successfully built up a sense of panic. They seem to have exaggerated the impact of the financial collapse, and readers were made to believe that if they had not yet felt the Depression's blow, it was fast approaching, and that workers were specifically targeted by the capitalist crisis.[2] Karelia, on the other hand, was presented as a place where there was work, plenty to eat, a good educational system, the ill and elderly were cared for, and workers and peasants could influence policy and society. Though the press had an ambivalent view of the migration, due to its inherent impact on the strength of the North American revolutionary movement,[3] the promotion of contrasts between "here" and "there" served as a de facto endorsement.

Working with the press and bringing the Karelian project to Finnish communities across Canada and the United States were the recruiters of the Karelian Technical Aid Committee (KTA), who formally carried out the recruitment objectives of the Soviet and Karelian leadership.[4] The KTA was headed by Matti Tenhunen, a long-time leader in Finnish leftist circles in the United States who had recently been ousted from the Co-operative Exchange Board in the mass expulsion of communists. Tenhunen knew Finnish North America well, and had proven his commitment to the Soviet Union during his many travels to Moscow and Karelia. Tenhunen began his work in January 1931 as the coordinator of committee activities and was in charge of the foreign section of the Karelian Resettlement Agency, a Soviet entity.[5] The New York City office, located in Harlem, officially opened its doors on May Day of that year. Kalle Aronen worked as the chair of the KTA in the United States until 1932. Oscar Corgan replaced Aronen and ran the office until 1934, when it was closed. In Canada, John (Jussi) Latva represented the Karelian Technical Aid, and an office in Toronto operated from 1931 into 1935. Tenhunen, Aronen, and Corgan ultimately brought their families to Karelia, while Latva remained in Canada. In addition to these formal paid positions, the Technical Aid found volunteer recruiters in larger Finnish enclaves, to keep community enthusiasm alive.[6]

The KTA's responsibilities included recruiting suitable migrants, working with Soviet authorities and North American Finnish workers' federations to select candidates, organizing the appropriate paperwork, acting as liaison with the shipping companies, and raising funds and equipment for Karelia and the Soviet Union through the Machine Fund. Tenhunen, Aronen, Latva, and Corgan were employees of the Resettlement Agency and, therefore, reported to the Soviet Union. Their wages and the operations of the committee were funded by voluntary donations from Finnish North Americans and by commissions from the shipping companies, mainly the Swedish-American Steamship Company. With wages dependent on arousing interest in the Karelian project, the KTA proved successful at securing its income. During its three years of operation, the New York office reportedly secured $162,146 in donations, in addition to commissions of $11.50 per adult and $5.75 per child on every sea fare sold.[7]

Recruiters criss-crossed Canada and the United States, speaking at Finnish halls and regularly contributing to Finnish newspapers to spread the word about Karelia. In order to meet their quotas and to earn their commissions, recruiters used multiple messages to broaden the appeal of the Karelian project. Some of the main themes included selling Karelia as a place for all workers, regardless of specific political orientation; Karelia as a Finnish homeland; and Karelia as a place of work and free education and health care for all.[8] The recruitment messages also spoke to people's sense of pride: Finnish workers were the ones needed! A significant proportion of US and Canadian Finnish cultural organizations had made the ideological move toward communism, yet the increasing hostility of the Canadian and US party leadership toward ethnic language groups had alienated much of the rank and file. Karelia's focus on the recruitment of specifically Finnish workers supportive of the Communist project provided a new, tangible way for Finnish migrants to work for the cause while maintaining their Finnishness. Varpu Lindström and Börje Vähämäki argued that North American Finns were drawn to Karelia because the Soviet Union and the recruiters promised a "more cooperative and freer intellectual climate" than what was available for socialists in interwar North America.[9] The recruiters knew first-hand the persecution of socialist sympathizers in North America. The "Red Scare" affected many Finns and the rise of conservatism and right-wing movements among North American Finns contributed to the hardships. Depictions of a Finnish workers' state full of like-minded individuals appealed to many frustrated Finnish North American leftists. While right-wing Finns used nationalism to justify their attack on socialists in both North America and Finland, the recruiters and press manipulated the Left's own nationalist sentiments to encourage migration to Karelia, long considered a vital part of the Finnish homeland and the source of the Finnish epic *Kalevala*.

The perceived accuracy of the recruiters' promises divided those who left Karelia disenchanted. On route to Karelia, Mayme Sevander recalled meeting disgruntled American returnees in Sweden, where both parties awaited the next step of their voyage. An angry man yelled at her father, KTA recruiter Oscar Corgan, "Some paradise! Some utopia! Everything you told us was a pack of lies!"[10] Another man came to Corgan's defence: "He didn't lie to us. If we had listened to the words of Oscar Corgan, we would never have gone. He told us it wouldn't be easy. Don't you remember when he said it would be just like being pioneers again? He promised no paradise. We just didn't listen."[11] Given the reality of the harsh living and working conditions in Karelia, did the recruiters adequately forewarn interested emigrants? Was Karelia depicted in accurate terms? Did the lucrative shipping commissions motivate recruiters to downplay the negatives in favour of attracting more emigrants? Unfortunately, no recruitment speeches have been found to detail exactly what attentive crowds in Finnish halls were told about Karelia. However, there is evidence to say that recruiters did make efforts to inform interested people about the nature of the project, who its ideal candidates were, and the reality of the early phases of life in Karelia. In his frequent correspondence with the Finnish left press, Matti Tenhunen aimed to clarify misconceptions and romantic notions of Karelia induced by the "Fever" and to temper the press's tendency to depict the USSR in glowing terms. In May 1931, Tenhunen explained that "the emigration to Karelia should not be an emotional movement."[12] Furthermore, emigration was not to be viewed as a cure-all for economic woes. Tenhunen believed that the ideal candidate had to have something to offer Karelia, and "the idea that a strong desire for emigration should be enough ... is completely incorrect." Looking back, Sevander interpreted Tenhunen's message as: "The wrong notion: I've got to get going because there's no way to get along here any more [*sic*]. The right notion: I've got to get going to help train the local labor force; I can't be a burden to Karelia; the most important professions are: loggers, farmers, steel workers, printers, quarry specialists. I've got to pay my own passage to Leningrad, a little help may be found, but not to turn to the KTA."[13]

Politics or Economics?

Since the late 1970s, when the earliest studies of Finnish North Americans in Karelia appeared, there has been great interest in understanding what compelled thousands of people to move to Karelia in such a short span of time. Much of the debate has focused specifically on whether politics or economics motivated "Karelian Fever." With the rich history of Finnish migrants' involvement in socialist politics in early twentieth-century North America, many have looked to political ideology to explain the feverish pace and scope of the migration. The trajectory of North American Finnish radical communities in the decades leading up to the 1930s set the stage for a mass migration to Soviet

Karelia in many ways. The Finnish North American left expressed widespread admiration for the development of the Soviet Union and looked for ways to participate. Mayme Sevander's work, which combines community study with autobiography, best exemplifies the adamant insistence that the migration was ideologically motivated. For Sevander, the migration exemplified a "commitment to the Cause, the sincere desire to render practical and material assistance to young Soviet Russia. The exodus can be considered a mass manifestation of idealism!"[14] For Sevander's family and others, the migration "took on the aura of a religious crusade."[15] Ideals were also significant for Finnish North American communards who had already set off in the early 1920s. For the Säde Commune formed in Cobalt, Ontario, as Vieno Zlobina remembered, "stipulations were rigorous: high ethical standards and devotion to the cause of socialism were required from the members."[16] The money Finnish North Americans committed to the Karelian project suggests that more than dire economic conditions propelled the movement. Reino Kero argued that those who left were not from the poorest ranks, nor were many totally unemployed at the time of departure.[17] Recruits were expected to pay their own fare, an "entrance fee" of several hundred dollars, to provide tools and household goods, and to make significant monetary contributions to the Machine Fund. In fact, questions on the application for emigration focused on determining how much money an applicant could contribute to the cause.[18]

However, Golubev and Takala have demonstrated that despite formally being required to cover their own travel costs, many migrants, in fact, required the assistance of the KTA to undertake the move.[19] The height of the exodus coincided with the depths of economic depression, and migrant workers, already typically living with negligible means, were among the first to feel the burden of layoffs and work reductions.[20] Michael Gelb recognized that while politics played a role, the Finnish American movement to Karelia also consisted of many "economic refugees."[21] Some have downplayed and even downright denied the political motivations for migration, asserting that economic factors entirely accounted for the scale of the migration. Miriam "Margaret" Rikkinen, who moved to Karelia at the age of nine, insisted in an interview in 2000 that "there was no question of the Left or Reds ... Unemployment caused it, the whole thing."[22] Many of those who returned from Karelia to North America at a time of increasing animosity toward "communists" and misgivings about the Soviet Union strove to distance their families from the "Red" label. The examples of Sevander and Rikkinen illustrate how those who experienced the migration first-hand have typically upheld the staunchest positions.

Communists among the Migrants

Official Communist Party members were only intended to make up a small percentage of the total number of Karelian recruits, and ultimately amounted to less than 15 per cent of all migrants.[23] The communist parties of Canada and the United States knew that their success depended on holding on to their existing membership. The Finns, though continuously embroiled in contestations over the rights of ethnic language branches, still represented a significant portion of the parties' overall support. William Pratt's examination of the CPUSA's reaction to the recruitment of Finnish communists succinctly demonstrates the ambivalence surrounding "Karelian Fever." On one hand, the CPUSA, much like the CPC, opposed the project outright. Just before the official launch of the Karelian Technical Aid, the US Politburo reacted to the announcement that an initial effort to recruit 800 Finns was under way. A December 1930 motion proclaimed: "such a mass immigration of the Finns who are close to the Party will seriously cripple our mass work among the Finnish population in the United States, and in our opinion the comrades in Karelia should recruit a smaller number."[24] As Karelia's desired number of immigrants grew into the thousands by the spring of 1931, the Canadian and US parties' relationship with the KTA grew tense. Pratt concludes that the District was right to worry; though the recruits were intended to include only a maximum of 10 per cent party members, up to 20 per cent of the Great Lakes region's District 9 members joined the migration.[25] By early 1932, the District sounded the alarm: "The Karelian migration from this district threatens to develop to serious proportions, liquidating our mass organizations and withdrawing financial support from the co-operatives: the district and center must act on this quickly."[26]

However, the party's opposition was necessarily tempered by its commitment to international communism and the direction of the Comintern. The District's motion continued by stating "we realize that the decision will have to take into consideration other things besides our own interests, and the question should be taken up with Moscow ... with the understanding that whatever decision is made will be carried out unquestionably."[27] Recruiters for the Karelian Technical Aid could act confidently, knowing their work had the backing of the Soviet Union, to whom the parties had to defer.[28] Correspondence between KTA head Matti Tenhunen and CPC leader Tim Buck reveals Tenhunen's advantage. In May 1931, Tenhunen coolly reminded Buck that "I think it is error from part of [party] comrades if they think that this matter of bringing over about 3,000 workers from US and Canada before the end of the year is for discussion."[29]

Of the letter writers and life writers studied here, two families stand out as having made the decision to emigrate based largely on communist political conviction. The Pitkänen family's history reveals an iron dedication to the revolutionary movement. Radical philosophies, newspapers, organizations, labour actions, leftist symbols, and a profound stake in the development of a workers' state in Russia permeated the Pitkänen family's rural Ontario life. Taimi Pitkänen (later Davis), daughter of Antti and older sister of Aate, was the first of the family to go to the Soviet Union. Recognized as an up-and-coming labour leader and political student, Taimi, at the age of nineteen, was sent to the USSR in a group of Young Communist League (YCL) delegates in 1930. With the alias Liz Alton, Taimi set off in the fall on the secret mission with four other Finnish migrant teenagers.[30] She spent about a year in the Soviet Union, studying at the Young Communist League School in Moscow and travelling throughout the country, as far north as Arkhangelsk, doing practical work, and seeing the Soviet model in action.

Aate Pitkänen was not far behind. Following in his parents' footsteps, Aate had further strengthened his commitment to the work he had begun in the Pioneers and YCL by becoming a card-carrying member of the Communist Party of Canada at the age of seventeen.[31] In 1931, when the first group of young Finns from Kivikoski left for Karelia, Aate Pitkänen was among them. With one bringing back to Canada knowledge of the Soviet system and the other contributing Canadian work experience to the Karelian hinterland, the Pitkänen siblings met one final time at the Moscow train station.[32] Aate was joined in Karelia by his father Antti Pitkänen in the fall of 1934. However, Antti quickly left in 1935, seemingly frustrated by being denied a transfer of his Communist Party of Canada membership to the CPSU, and by the distance separating him from his wife and daughter in Ontario.

Like the Pitkänens, the Corgan family also exemplified a life dedicated to the workers' struggle. In addition to serving as the last director of the Karelian Technical Aid in the United States, Oscar Corgan had devoted his career and personal life to the Finnish leftist press (as long-term editor of *Työmies*), the Finnish socialist cooperative movement, and, later, the Communist Party. Much like Aate and Taimi Pitkänen, the Corgan children, Mayme, Paul, and Aino, were raised to be "Little Reds." According to Mayme Sevander's memory, when the family began their journey to Karelia in April 1934, Oscar Corgan explained that the move was "in keeping with his principles."[33] Confirming the political conviction motivating the Corgan family's emigration, Sevander further explained that US communist leaders, like her father, were "under the influence of standards of the communist doctrine which had the force of a fundamental religion. Such an inflated and glorified image of Communism and Soviet Russia ... left no room for doubt or analysis."[34] Sevander, likewise, recalled her own childhood excitement about going to "live these ideals ourselves" in Karelia.[35]

Raised in the Revolutionary Spirit

While the examples of the Pitkänen and Corgan families demonstrate that certainly some of the Karelian migrants were primarily motivated by a profound commitment to communism and the building of the Soviet Union, most left with a more subtle connection to the radical movement. In the debates about political or economic motivations, an important sociocultural element of the migrants' background has remained inadequately expressed. Though many of the migrants would not have characterized themselves as fundamental communists, their family and personal histories reveal a life and upbringing deeply rooted in the support of the workers' cause. Even if labelled as "hall socialists," or those who turned to the socialist halls and organizations to fill social and cultural needs more than political ones, these Finnish North Americans nonetheless spent their time attending the events of socialist organizations, reading the Left press, and donating their money and time to socialist causes. Regardless of whether the migrants were card-carrying members of the Communist Party or were active in agitation work, the vast majority of the Finnish North American emigrants were raised and cultured in the revolutionary spirit. They embraced the Karelian migration with an understanding of the workers' struggle and sympathy for the Russian revolutionary state. By recognizing the prevalence and importance of left-ally culturing, it becomes clear that discussions about migration motivations need not be fixated on questions of absolute commitment to communist ideology nor on arguing away the importance of politics.

The Hokkanens' memoir depicts the multifaceted factors leading to their decision to move to Karelia, but also helps us to better understand the overall nature of the Finnish North American emigrants. Sylvi and Lauri, like many others in the Karelian migration, were young, newlywed, and had not yet settled into their adult married lives. Sylvi explains that they were "getting along all right," since "those living in the country had not been hit as hard by the Depression as city dwellers."[36] However, she explains that "the future did not look promising in the United States at that time."[37] They believed that, in Karelia, "there would be an opportunity to work for a better life with a good chance of success."[38] Sylvi Hokkanen's explanation of their financial position at the time of emigrating confirms that while the couple had not faced abject poverty, nor had they felt the most severe repercussions of the economic depression, they, like many other youths in Canada and the United States, lived with the reality of curtailed opportunities.[39] Sylvi Hokkanen characterized herself and Lauri as "more or less apolitical" and believed this factor, along with their lumber and teaching backgrounds, qualified them for Karelian immigration.[40] However, both Sylvi's and Lauri's parents had joined the US Finnish socialist movement at a young age, turning to communism after the Russian Revolution.[41] Both had grown up with the workers' slogans and anthems, but, in Sylvi's words, "we hadn't, as yet, fully understood what they were striving for, or what the true meaning of communism was."[42] While Sylvi and Lauri never characterized themselves as active or ideologically convinced communists, their family and social backgrounds substantiate that they, like the significant majority of emigrants, lived their day to day in the revolutionary spirit. Like so many others, this leftist culturing combined with the economic uncertainty of the future and their youthful adventurousness propelled the Hokkanens to join in the Karelian project.

Who Went?

Between 1930 and 1934, some 6,500 Finnish North Americans moved to Soviet Karelia, joining the smaller and less organized migration of hundreds in the 1920s. Finns from the United States formed almost 60 per cent of this migration,[43] but given Canada's smaller Finnish population, Canadian Finnish communities made a significant contribution to the movement. The Soviet government directed the Karelian Resettlement Agency and the Karelian Technical Aid to find young, single, "politically reliable" tradesmen who could also financially contribute to Karelian development. Though it must be remembered that lists of migrants are many, varied, and can be unreliable, they demonstrate that the composition of migrants was much more diverse than the ideal candidates sought out by recruiters. Golubev and Takala's and Evgeny Efremkin's demographic analyses have concluded that migrants from the United States were on average older and more likely to move as a family unit than migrants from Canada.[44] While 72 per cent of Finns from the US were over the age of thirty, only 44 per cent of Canadians were.[45] Seventy-nine per cent of US Finns migrated as a family unit and 64 per cent of Canadians.[46] Efremkin notes, however, that even those registered as single often migrated as a part of a kinship chain. That is, they followed or travelled with aunts, uncles, siblings, and extended family.[47] Much less is known about the demographic profile of women. Only the rare single woman appears in the available documentation, and little detail is given about women generally, since often only the husband's or father's information was recorded. Terttu Kangas reported to her family that single women were not granted permission to go to Karelia, unless they went with their father.[48] The recruiters successfully found men eager to work in the lumber industry, but, as we will see, they did not necessarily bring the expected expertise or commit themselves to employment in one sector. Overall, as life writer Kaarlo Tuomi summarized, the migrants typically met the basic requirements of having "reasonably good health, two strong hands, the skills and enthusiasm for building a new society, willingness to endure some hardships until the paradise was built, the reference of an [North] American Communist affiliated organization, a supply of tools and winter clothing and enough money to make it to the border."[49]

Deciding to Go

Going to Karelia was not always as simple as just deciding to move. In a top-down chain of command from the Kremlin to the Karelian leadership to the KTA, and then the Finnish branches of the North American communist parties, interested Finns often faced long delays or even outright rejection. Through the Karelian Technical Aid, interested persons had to apply for permission to move. Mayme Sevander has outlined the application process:

> First the applicants filled in forms, attached three passport photos and a doctor's certificate to it.
>
> Second, these papers went to a general meeting of a local Finnish Federation. Here a decision was passed on the applicant's political and trade abilities. If satisfactory, they were signed and sealed by the presiding officers and sent on to the KTA offices.
>
> Third, a committee of three, two from the Finnish bureau and one from the KTA, after a final examination and approval of the papers, forwarded them to Narkomtrud (Labor Commissariat) in Petrozavodsk. This was the final stage of the visa application.[50]

Golubev and Takala have identified a similar application process, adding still a final step in Moscow, where the visa was ultimately conferred (or not).[51] Candidates had to strike a perfect balance between a commitment to the class struggle without threatening the work and strength of the North American communist movement, and offering sufficient funds and skills to contribute to developing socialism in Karelia without bordering on being "bourgeois." William Pratt has argued that non-party members "had fewer hurdles" to overcome, while Communist Party members had to prove that they had already secured employment in Karelia, and party and cooperative leaders were typically rejected.[52]

Upon acceptance into the "Karelian Project," the applicant then confronted the challenge of sorting out their lives and relationships and preparing for the significant move. While the available sources do not typically offer any sense of how the decisions and permissions to move were reached, a letter written on Christmas Day 1933 by Antti Pitkänen provides a rare opportunity to learn about the process of application and acceptance, and the personal side of making the decision to move. Writing to Taimi in Sudbury, Antti informed her of the news:

> I have received word from Comrade Latva that I could not even in my dreams await anymore and now there is negotiation or rather, yesterday I informed your mother of what I did almost three years ago without her permission. She has not yet been too judgemental, only asked that it not happen before summer. Permission is not yet final only it said that a month before spring work begins we must have arrived if any other comrades can be found to come along and he expects that in the west there are two families that can go, and if so then we are to be ready to go in February. The place where we are supposed to go is a new settlement 20 kilometres from Petroskoi. I do not know why that application has been buried there for so long and now if there is an opportunity and it is put off, well it may be put off for the last time. And even if not, if I am to go at some point, putting it off won't fix it … That brings me to ask what you say to these news.[53]

Antti's letter clearly demonstrates the long wait – three years in this case – after filling an application, and how official word from Latva in Canada or one of the KTA directors in the United States meant a sudden jump to departure.[54] In Antti's statements about whether he should delay departure, he demonstrates the decision-making processes that likely also played out in the minds and homes of other Finnish North American could-be migrants. Likewise, reading into how Antti had applied to move without his wife's permission or perhaps even knowledge, and how he sought Taimi's opinion and seemingly approval, offers a subtle glimpse of the family operations and negotiations that surrounded "Karelian Fever." Ultimately, Antti Pitkänen left Kivikoski in August 1934, but the available letters do not show how it was that he came to leave much later than the originally planned February departure date or whether he received the blessing of his daughter or wife, who herself had refused to go.

52 Building That Bright Future

The decision to move to Karelia could reveal the power structure of a family. When resistance to migration arose, many families were not comfortable with the idea of separating, even temporarily, in order to take advantage of the Karelian opportunity. However, the move was often made without full family consensus. When Vieno Zlobina's family was preparing to move in 1926, her mother was very hesitant, but "father was determined to go and mother had to remain of the same opinion."[55] Klaus Maunu's family had already lived in the Soviet Union on the "Työ" Commune in the 1920s, but his mother had not been happy there.[56] In order to return to North America, Maunu's parents reportedly agreed to return to the Soviet Union a few years later, when further development had taken place. Three and a half years later, in 1932, Maunu's father began to make arrangements for their move to Karelia without his wife's endorsement and without discussing the plans with their child.[57] With men as the primary breadwinners in most Finnish migrant homes and the movement primarily targeting men, the opinion of the male head of the household often overruled women's thoughts and feelings about moving. Likewise, when the Depression challenged men's positions as breadwinner and women provided the family's steady income,[58] some, like Kaarlo Tuomi's stepfather, battled their egos and looked to Karelia as a chance to restore their masculinity.[59] Tuomi recalled that "my mother was not eager to leave the United States, but, as a faithful wife, she went along with his travel plans."[60] Family power dynamics held much sway in the decision to move to Karelia. Tuomi sums up the point, with regard to his own feelings about the move: "my stepfather wore the pants and his mind had to be the family mind."[61]

Preparing to Move

Once the decision had been made to move to Karelia, the emigrants had to prepare. One of the first considerations was what to do with property and belongings. Many did not have the hard dollars needed to pay for the sea voyage and other moving expenses, which could easily amount to over $400, so liquidating possessions was necessary.[62] Allan Sihvola's family sold most of their belongings in an auction, but given the economic conditions of the time, many struggled to sell their goods and especially to secure a fair price.[63] The Finnish press and Communist movement negatively portrayed those who wanted to hold on to their North American assets, either to wait until the market had improved or in case they wanted to return, as uncommitted to the cause.[64] Personal letters from Karelia, however, reveal that many migrants did leave behind unsorted matters regarding property and other assets.[65]

One could not expect to arrive in Karelia empty-handed. The migrants seem to have been generally aware that they were to pack enough provisions to see them through the first years of Karelian life. Some brought whatever they could, like Paavo Alatalo's family, who took along "many trunks and large boxes" and everything from furniture to a gold coffee service set "because we were instructed to provide everything for 3–5 years."[66] Vieno Zlobina's mother struggled to decide what to bring to the Säde Commune and "a lot of pain was caused by the new carpet that we had to leave behind."[67] Others, especially unsettled youth and newlyweds, had little to bring. Sylvi and Lauri Hokkanen had no savings to spend on buying new goods for Karelia and packed what they had: some clothing, tools, and a hideaway bed.[68]

When belongings had been sorted into what was to be sold, given away, and taken along, the Finnish North American migrants had to say goodbye to their communities. Remembrances of farewell parties appear in most of the memoirs. Some describe casual and very personal events, where friends and family sent off emigrants with their warmest wishes. For example, Sylvi and Lauri Hokkanen were given a "going-away party. It was held at the Hall. We danced and enjoyed the usual cakes and coffee. A collection had been taken earlier, and at the party we were presented with a 'going-away' gift: a genuine Hudson's Bay blanket."[69] Other farewells were much more political, with party speeches and inspirational workers' songs. Allan Sihvola remembers that he and the other youth left the New York Labor Temple "farewell meeting" early, suggesting the event may have been more political meeting than party.[70] Owing to the stature of Oscar Corgan in the Finnish left movement, Mayme Sevander remembers their farewell event as "the biggest party I had ever seen. The Finn Hall was all lit up, and the tables in the auditorium were spread with white cloths and covered with pots of coffee, platters of cookies, and little bowls of candy ... More than four hundred people packed the hall to say goodbye to my father, and we listened to speech after speech until we [the family children] were yawning so hard we thought our faces would split."[71] Public farewells helped migrants reaffirm their decision to move to Karelia and made them feel as if they were in fact contributing to the greater good. Saying goodbye to family and close friends, though, undoubtedly stirred many complex thoughts and feelings.

Making the Move

Memoir descriptions and the rare letters sent during travel or upon first landing in Karelia allow readers today to gain an appreciation of the journey to Karelia. For many, the trip began with a train ride to either New

Figure 3 The MS *Gripsholm* leaving New York in 1932. Public domain, courtesy of Swedish Maritime History Museum.

York City or Halifax,[72] where the overseas voyage began. For some, hard hit by economic conditions, the cost of the train ticket was prohibitive. To make do, while his wife Aino and other women in their group enjoyed the comforts of the coach interior, Eino Streng and the men rode the rails in cargo cars, hoping not to get caught.[73] Reino Hämäläinen's letter to his friend Benny in his hometown of Waukegan, Illinois, depicts his journey to New York City, his awe of the Appalachian Mountains – "my neck was sore for I was looking at the scenery all through the mountains" – and his boyish cavorting around the big city.[74] Some drove their cars to the port cities, planning to sell them to help cover the expenses of the trip, donate them to the KTA, or to bring them to Karelia.[75] Others, like the Hokkanens, rode the bus.[76] For US Finns, especially, it was not uncommon to wait in New York City for several weeks or even several months for the finalization of travel documents and arrangements. Allan Sihvola's family left Warren, Ohio, in the fall of 1931, believing that their travel arrangements would be sorted by the time they got to New York.[77] However, upon arrival, they were told that they would not set sail until the spring, and were left to figure out how to get by until then.

Reino Mäkelä's family left New York City on 16 September 1931 at four o'clock, with a three-hour docking in Halifax, where an additional ninety-four Karelia-bound passengers embarked.[78] The nine-day voyage to Gothenburg, Sweden, was activity packed, as described by Mäkelä:

"We had dance and music by a Canadian. We saw three shows. We had a pioneer and YCL meeting every other day in the public room. The older folks held a meeting and a program every day."[79] Reino Mäkelä's experience had much in common with descriptions offered by others who travelled the same route, like Paavo Alatalo in May 1931, Viola Ranta in 1932, and Mayme Sevander, whose family departed in April 1934. Sevander explained how the Karelian emigrants, once on board, elected committees to oversee social, political, and cultural needs over the course of the voyage.[80] The posts were split equally between US and Canadian Finns, and the executive consisted of a chair, secretary, and a ten-person board. Additional committees included correspondence to communicate with the Finnish-language press in North America and Karelia, a cultural committee, an organizational committee that included programming, and a children's committee. Sylvi Hokkanen also explained the organization of life on ship at the peak of "Karelian Fever": "These earlier groups were well organized with elected officials, entertainment committees, and rules of conduct. They held meetings and social events, and in this way kept up their spirits and their sense of camaraderie."[81] By Sylvi and Lauri Hokkanen's departure in late May 1934, the voyage had a different atmosphere. Sylvi noted that "there were only about ten people in our group, and we held no political meetings, no programs, no flag waving or hurrahs as the earlier, larger groups had been in the habit of doing."[82] Regardless, Sylvi believed that "although we did none of these things, we were also a dedicated group and on the way to help as best we could in building a workers' land."[83]

In Sweden, where most Karelian migrants first landed, Finnish North Americans were greeted by the celebratory spirit of international communism. Local communist groups, especially children's and youth's branches, put on programming for the visitors.[84] From the port of Gothenburg, the Karelian migrants would head to Stockholm by train to await the next leg of the trip: a two-day sailing to Leningrad. Another train trip brought Finnish North Americans 400 kilometres north to Petrozavodsk (Petroskoi), where the regional Resettlement Agency would send newcomers to their new homes and worksites across Karelia, sometimes several hundred kilometres farther.

Landing: First Impressions

Having himself already been in the Soviet Union since 1921, Enoch Nelson commented on the North American migrants arriving in late 1930: "The people coming over here now have it much easier than what it was when I came over but even then it takes them a few days to get used to things because we have so many things different from what it is there."⁸⁵ For many newcomers, though, it likely felt like more than a few days were needed to adjust. How the migrant life writers expressed their feelings about initial impressions varied widely.

The study of life writing provides an opportunity to analyze both the literal, experiential level of what is told and, also, the ways that the form of writing can be employed to further what the writer hoped to accomplish by setting pen to paper. Early letters from Karelia often served to reassure family and friends that the migrant had arrived safely and was content with their new situation. Reino Mäkelä normalized his impressions of Karelia by relaying encounters with old friends who had migrated before him and emphasizing the Americanness of the movies and youth culture.⁸⁶ In Terttu Kangas's first letter to her family, she twice mentions that people at home ought not to await their return any time soon, confirming that the move had been a good idea and that she and her husband were satisfied with their decision.⁸⁷ These positive exclamations may have hidden feelings of uncertainty and discomfort experienced by many migrants. Some, for example, had their belongings taken by officials upon arrival without explanation or recourse, and some were separated from their family members and sent to different villages.⁸⁸

Unlike the reported first impressions found in letters, those in memoirs serve a different purpose. Without denying the validity of the migrants' early impressions, many of the memoir sources seem to utilize common literary conventions to structure the overall arc of their narrative, expressing their feelings about the move in general and linking the beginning of life in the USSR with the ultimate outcome of their experiences in the late 1930s and 1940s. In Paavo Alatalo's life writing, the travellers' spirits were high during the entire voyage. However, the narrative switches in tone with their "cool" reception in Leningrad.⁸⁹ After arriving in Karelia, "the mood was depressing," with lice and cockroaches depicted as the newcomers' welcoming committee.⁹⁰ Viola Ranta's life writing oozes with disdain for having been forced to move by her parents and her abhorrence for life in Karelia. Fittingly, Ranta's description of arrival in Uhtua in August 1932 uses pathetic fallacy to emphasize her misery. After a short two days of good weather, Ranta claims "then it started to rain and that water came every day until it turned into snow."⁹¹ Allan Sihvola remembered the surprise of seeing several funeral processions in Leningrad during the day or two they spent there on route to Karelia; he was left wondering why so many people had died.⁹² For sixteen-year-old Kaarlo Tuomi, the early images of the Soviet Union were burned into his memory. For 800 kilometres, from Leningrad to Kem in northern Karelia, desperate exiled peasants, accused of being *kulaks*, filled the train.

Figure 4 A view of Petrozavodsk. "Petroskoi hyppyrimäeltä nähtynä, taustalla Ääninen" by Jalmari Aarnio, 1942–3. Courtesy of the Finnish Heritage Agency.

These "broken people," as Tuomi remembers, "were literally dying of starvation before our eyes."[93] These displaced peasants, while undoubtedly making a significant impression on him, also seem to serve Tuomi's life writing by foreshadowing the coming fate of Finnish communities. Lauri Hokkanen's first impressions also foreshadow the Soviet corruption, labour inefficiencies, and food shortages that would soon become familiar.[94] Allan Sihvola noted that already at the Petrozavodsk train station some decided to return to North America, "but for the majority, enthusiasm closed their eyes to the first shortcomings."[95]

The memoir sources offer vivid first-impression descriptions of where they settled. These early depictions, not found in the available personal letters, allow readers to build mental maps of what Karelian towns and villages looked like in the early 1930s. Sevander described Petrozavodsk, Karelia's capital and largest centre: "It looked somehow medieval. The main streets were cobblestone, but the rest of the roads were dirt, with car tracks and the clear prints of horses' hooves in the dust. There were no sidewalks. Most of the buildings were small, unpainted log homes with shingled roofs and dirty windows. Smoke from a thousand chimneys rose straight up."[96] Sihvola's family was brought to the lumber camp

Rutanen, some 20 kilometres west of Petrozavodsk, in a forest network of small camps. Much like the other lumber camps, Rutanen, as described by Sihvola, consisted of "two living quarters, of which one was made of boards and the other logs. Additionally, there was a dining hall with kitchen, a laundry hut, a clothes drying room for the bush workers, a horse stall, sauna, a pig stall and blacksmith's shop – all log buildings."[97] Uhtua, the commercial centre for northern interior Karelia, approximately 100 kilometres south of the Arctic Circle, was on the northern shore of Lake Kuyto. Many North Americans were sent to the Uhtua area's lumber camps. Lauri Hokkanen described arriving in the town, after travelling almost 200 kilometres west from Kem, on the White Sea, in the open box of a truck: "There was no railroad, only a poor gravel road from the Kem station. The town did have a clinic and a hospital, grocery store, schools and the usual government offices. A liquor store was a recent addition ... There were also docks along the shore for ... small ships and tugs."[98] These portrayals of select Karelian towns and lumber camps help to build a sense of North American Finnish everyday life, contextualizing the detailed descriptions of living conditions, working conditions, and leisure found in personal letters.

Conclusion

Stories, debates, and rumours of Karelia captured the imaginations of Finnish North Americans in the first years of the 1930s. The development of the Soviet economy and society contrasted with the anxiety and gloom of North American economic depression and political hostility. With the establishment of the Karelian Technical Aid and the support of the Finnish-language communist press, recruitment for the Karelian project reached feverish proportions. A study of Karelian memoirs and personal letters provides new insights into the decisions, preparations, and travel that led so many to move to Karelia. The migrants' first impressions allow for an analysis of the narrative structure of life writing and also refocus attention on the experiences of the individuals that collectively make up the Finnish North American movement. Arrival on Soviet soil intensified the diverse and complex decisions and emotions that led to Karelia. As the poem for emigrants recognized: "Our comrades are leaving again, / Knowing so well they stand no chances / Of winning without taking pains." A spirit of optimism drove many of the migrants to look beyond the hardships they saw, believing, as the final stanza of the poem reminded, "Many an obstacle you may not know / This faraway journey will bring. / But once overcome, the day will glow / With created light and workers will sing!"[99]

Chapter Three

"Of Course Not Like There": Karelian Living Conditions as Experienced by Finnish North Americans

"Still last fall when we came the stores were pretty much empty," wrote Antti Kangas. "But now," he continued, "the situation is entirely another[.] goods there are starting to be all kinds, of course not like there."[1] This letter, the only available one written by Antti Kangas, was composed in October 1934 and addressed to the "Comrades" of Drummond Island, Michigan, from where he and his family had left a year earlier. Kangas's statement demonstrates how Finnish North Americans walked a fine line in their correspondence. Most writers made an effort to emphasize the positive in their new Karelian lives, like the apparent increase in available consumer goods. Some aimed to assure their friends and family that they were healthy, happy, and had made a good choice in migrating. Many, like Kangas, hoped to further the Karelian project by convincing others that they, too, should be good comrades and move or, at least, send money and needed goods. A close reading of letters and memoirs, though, also reveals the migrants coping with how things were "of course not like there," in the North American communities left behind. Nowhere are Finnish North Americans' efforts to assess the positives and negatives of Karelia more visible than in their discussions of housing, food, clothing, everyday items, and health and hygiene.

Moving to Soviet Karelia involved the re-establishment of daily life, and this chapter considers how Finnish North American narratives addressed new living conditions. Situating the letter and memoir content within the context of the writers' North American migrant backgrounds and the ideals and daily realities of Soviet life illustrates some of the challenges and strategies of making do in Karelia. The arrival of Finnish North Americans coincided with the Soviet Union's dive into rapid, at-all-costs industrialization. During this time, people in the Soviet Union experienced shortages and a drop in their overall standard of living, alleviated only by minor improvements in the availability of certain consumer goods. An examination of housing, food, clothing, and consumer goods also highlights the shift in Soviet culture and social politics in the first years of the 1930s. Focusing on these early years of Finnish North American life in Karelia, an analysis of both the 1930s letters and retrospective memoirs illustrates the symbolic and collective significance of home life and, especially, food. While men and women alike were concerned with securing an adequate place to call home and required nourishment, the attention given to the topics of housing and food, and the ways they are discussed, reveal a gendered social order and narrative structure. Access to housing, food, and goods, and the overall health of US and Canadian Finns in Karelia clearly demonstrate the disparity in standards of living between these invited foreign workers and the local residents and Finnish border hoppers.

Soviet Housing Overview

In revolutionary Russia, all aspects of life were to be rid of bourgeois values and ways in favour of new selfless and ascetic styles and methods. Home life was a primary target for this Bolshevik reformation, and living spaces and the functions of the family were accordingly reimagined. Women's break with the domestic life, a focus on communality over the traditional family unit, and self-disciplined functionality of spaces and objects were cornerstones of the revolutionary vision.[2] Throughout the Soviet Union, people were to be revolutionized by detaching daily activities from the home, with each task given its own appropriate communal space. Paid work was to occur outside of one's living space. Cooking and eating were to take place at workplace cafeterias and canteens, or in the shared cooking facilities found in communal apartment buildings and barracks. Special club rooms and Red Corners served as formal political study and participation sites. Children were to be sent to day nurseries and schools. Family members were often assigned different shift schedules, further entrenching this separation. With the day's routine divided into specialized sites, the Bolshevik project specifically targeted family cohesion. The move away from single-family homes to communal housing throughout the Soviet era was ideally a "revolutionary experiment in living" and, in reality, a response to a severe housing shortage.[3] By 1930, it was not uncommon for people to have less than five square metres of personal living space.[4]

Despite attempts to alter the form and spaces of daily life, the Communist Party began to turn its back on efforts to revolutionize the home and family life during the First Five Year Plan. A plummeting birth rate and the exorbitant costs of establishing communal life pushed the Soviet official line to reinstate the family unit's central role, the woman's primary role in domestic and family labour (while maintaining full-time paid work), and the value of single-family apartments. In the 1930s, people's living spaces were still to represent how Soviets ought to live and behave, but now focused on exemplifying the purported abundance and quality of communist life. Soviet images and writing began to place emphasis on making homes comfortable. A focus on the new Soviet "cultured life" brought domestic niceties back into fashion.[5] By the mid-1930s, homes were to be not just clean, but also decorated to become "advanced and cultured."[6] North American department store wares provided the Soviet government with images of appropriate domesticity.[7] According to David Hoffman, acquiring "expensive furniture of Karelian birch" had become an aspiration of many Soviet Stakhanovites and urban elites by the late 1930s.[8] These Karelia Ski Factory luxury goods,[9] though, were not common in the living spaces of those in the region.

The reality of housing shortages challenged the Soviet regime's ability to successfully implement their ideals. With a stark contrast between the revolutionary vision of communist life and the evolving official view of what it meant to live in Stalin's Russia, the typical home was caught somewhere in between. The uneven distribution of material goods and housing funds meant that each region, especially those farther from the centre, like Karelia, created its own version of Soviet housing policy. Ordinary people made do with whatever was available to fit their needs, employing great creativity. The burden overwhelmingly fell on women. In Attwood's words, "while the home was now presented as a place of comfort and support, women were its providers rather than recipients."[10] Women's domestic labour in Karelia linked life in the hinterland with formal Soviet expectations of family life in the 1930s.

Karelian Housing

Overall, housing and living conditions in Karelia were markedly different than in Canada and the United States, even considering the Depression-era standard of living. Though working-class and with few extras in the North American sense, many Finnish migrants had enjoyed indoor plumbing and electricity,[11] relatively spacious homes (rented or owned), and a wide array of consumer goods. In Karelia, Canadian and US Finns, according to Irina Takala,

> were not used to living in barracks in groups of 5 to 6 people per room without any conveniences (one washstand for 3 barracks). Some organizations had 2–3 families accommodated in one room. In the

rooms unsuited for the Karelian winter, there were no lights, there was no furniture, and they were swarming with insects. The accommodation situation was best in Petrozavodsk and in the villages where foreigners built housing themselves but here was a permanent shortage of materials, transport, money and so on.[12]

Though such a description may seem exaggerated, Golubev and Takala have identified countless examples of inadequate housing across the region,[13] and the themes of unfamiliarity and shortage are echoed in migrant life writers' depictions.

While actually recruiting only a fraction of the desired number of newcomers, Karelia's towns and villages, especially Kem and Petrozavodsk, could not meet housing needs.[14] By the early 1930s, as Nick Baron summarizes, "Karelia's resettlement and recruitment initiatives suffered not only because of the better opportunities that industrialization offered workers elsewhere, and the resistance of local authorities in recruitment areas, but because living conditions and food supplies in the autonomous republic were miserable."[15] Therefore, officials in Karelia took special measures to assure that Finnish North Americans, especially, would be met with better-than-average living conditions.[16] They made their homes in apartment buildings and logging barracks, many of which were built with scarce materials and tools by the migrants themselves. Families often shared single rooms in Karelia's towns and villages, and at worksites, lived in open sections of large, primitive camp dwellings, familiar to Finnish migrant men who had worked in North America's lumber and mining industries. Once the purges began, outcast families of arrested "enemies of the people" found shelter outside of the towns and villages in abandoned barns, saunas, or huts. The migrants did their best to make do with the situation at hand. Living in such close quarters, however, could place people in unpleasant positions. As an example, for the non-smoking Ranta family, sharing a single room with heavy smokers proved very difficult and awkward.[17] Karelian living conditions, however, posed many additional challenges.

The Second Five Year Plan for Karelia aimed at the wide-scale electrification of the region, with a focus on industry.[18] While electrified homes were not the norm in the early 1930s, Finnish North American narratives show that some places did have power. For example, the ski factory barracks had electric lighting, but residents, as Sylvi Hokkanen explained, were prohibited from using electricity for other purposes, such as heating electric hot plates.[19] In Komulainen's autobiographical novel *A Grave in Karelia*, "bright electric lights illuminated" Nikolai's logging camp barrack.[20]

Figure 5 Cars in Petrozavodsk (*Neuvosto-Karjalan 15-vuotiaan taipaleelta*, 16).

Even if fortunate enough to have electric lighting, Finnish North Americans who had lived in Canadian and US towns and cities had much to learn in Karelia. Many Finns in North America had become accustomed to indoor plumbing and now had to haul in water and share outdoor privies. In Petrozavodsk, some had their water delivered to the barracks daily, while others drew water from shared wells in the yard, which froze in the cold months.[21] A bucketful of clean water had to be carried indoors, and a slop bucket of dirty water out to the yard. Heating one's space proved difficult too, with no central heating and little available to freely burn. Though working to keep the fire going throughout the day and night, Mayme Sevander remembered that they "could sometimes feel the wind howling through the thin walls."[22] Great care had to be taken to prevent fires. Reino Mäkelä wrote about the fire that started in their room: the log walls began to burn from the constant heat of the room's stove, which was set right against the wall.[23] Remembering her family's time in exile in a large sixty-family barrack in Latushka,[24] Sevander shows how battling against the cold Karelian winter inspired communality: "The wooden building was uninsulated and had only drafty, single-pane windows ... We banded together and did what we could to weatherproof the barracks. We stockpiled logs for fuel and assigned families with the smallest children to the warmest part of the room."[25]

Women's Cozy Homes

The task of creating a semblance of domestic comfort fell on women. This is also reflected in life-writing conventions. Women's letters and memoirs provide insights on domestic interiors, conspicuously missing from men's writing. For example, in the Hokkanens' shared memoir, Sylvi's voice depicts the home much more clearly than Lauri's. Mayme Sevander offers descriptions of her home and mother's work, whereas the unpublished memoirs of Allan Sihvola and Paavo Alatalo do not provide the reader with any sense of what their home was like. Elis Ranta did tell his brother in Finland that in the United States his family of three had been accustomed to three or four rooms, plus a separate washroom, but in Petrozavodsk they shared a single room with another family.[26] Otherwise, Ranta does not elaborate on how they organized their space in order to manage two families in such close quarters. When men do discuss living areas, their narratives focus on the structure of the building and what it was made of, much more than what was inside of it. The memoir of Klaus Maunu serves as a prime example, offering details about the construction of his family's detached home, but saying nothing about the home interior, or even how many rooms it had. The mentions that can be found focus on the lumber camp barracks, which were often predominantly male spaces. This gendered division in the narratives reflects the more obvious gendered division in home responsibilities.

Women used their Finnish and North American backgrounds and know-how to create a homey atmosphere out of next to nothing. Eventually granted a private room, Sylvi Hokkanen remembered that, there, she "even enjoyed keeping house."[27] Terttu Kangas told her sister about their acquaintance, Tilda Korpi, who had made her family's small room "really pretty" by painting it herself.[28] Sylvi decorated their room in the ski factory barracks in Petrozavodsk with her favourite colour green, and with pictures and photographs, and hung cheesecloth curtains that she had sewn.[29] Space could be created in crammed shared rooms by building racks to stack beds on top of each other.[30] Mayme Sevander remembered her family's arrival in Petrozavodsk:

> My mother did her best to make the place homey. She strung up a curtain to divide the room in two. In one half was the day bed, where Aino and I slept, and a big steamer trunk that Paul curled up on at night. My mother

Figure 6 Foreign worker barracks in Kondopoga (*Neuvosto-Karjalan 15-vuotiaan taipaleelta*, 32).

hung their wedding picture and a photo of my [deceased] brother Leo on the bare wall, unpacked the dishes and kitchen utensils, and that was our home."[31]

Like Mayme's mother, women in Karelia and across the Soviet Union used partitions, curtains, and screens to create the illusion of space and privacy in their small rooms.[32] The value of curtains, lampshades, tablecloths, flowers, and carpets exceeded their practical utility by also functioning as key symbols of 1930s Soviet "cultured life."[33]

While Moscow urbanites may have seen depictions of cultured domestic comforts in model store window displays or culture exhibits, and workers may have aspired to the material comforts that accompanied Stakhanovite status, it is unclear how and whether such messages and standards translated into the Karelian context. According to Irina Takala, "the fact, that even in the unbearable conditions of life in the barracks Finns wanted to create something like cosiness and cleanliness, was seen by their neighbours as bourgeois and lower-middle class characteristics."[34] Home interiors came to mark very different social and cultural realities between Karelia's ethnic populations. Furthermore, though official Soviet rhetoric espoused the merits of cultured life and communist consumerism, Takala's findings suggest that such practices had not been broadly adopted by Karelian people. Instead, the realities of poverty, shortages, and never-ending hard work precluded widespread participation in Soviet-proscribed culturing.

Food

In Finnish North American life writing food occupied a central role and came to represent the positives and negatives of life in Karelia. At least at some point in the 1930s, securing adequate nourishment became a preoccupation of most Finnish North Americans in Karelia, as with most people in the Soviet Union. However, the letters and memoirs also demonstrate how "food carries fundamental symbolic and ritual meanings that go well beyond its importance for survival."[35]

The Soviet Union has the dubious reputation of having been, in Jukka Gronow's words, "the only modern state, which has adopted bread cards during peace time," in addition to wartime.[36] The Soviet Union enforced rationing in the periods of 1917–24, 1928–35, and 1939–47. While rationing assured that most Soviet citizens would have access to at least some food, the program's structuring entrenched what Julie Hessler has referred to as a "geographic hierarchy of supplies and the social hierarchy of access."[37] Food and other material goods were not evenly available throughout the Soviet Union, with the cities typically having greater access. As an example, according to Gronow, Moscow, with 3 to 4 per cent of the Soviet Union's population, received half of the country's available meat and margarine in 1935.[38] Moscow was the centre of the Soviet administration, with a significant number of party elites living and working there. Their status granted them access to foodstuffs and quantities largely unheard of beyond the capital and the privileged inner circle. Beyond geographic disparity, the Soviet social hierarchy and system of rations meant that occupational group, political history, and, often, ethnic background determined what and how much one was entitled to.

Antti Kangas reported to his comrades in Drummond Island about the conditions he saw in Karelia. He noted: "here there's one good thing that if something is lacking then it is lacking for everyone because here there are none of those better and worse People."[39] Perhaps the equality that Kangas admired could be seen among Finnish North Americans, but the statement downplayed major social inequities. While not the life of caviar and champagne[40] enjoyed by Moscow party officials, Finnish North Americans had privileged access to food and goods in Karelia in the first years of the 1930s. Motivated to attract and retain North American lumber and mechanical expertise, the Karelian leadership and Soviet centre redirected limited food resources toward Canadian and US Finns. These "foreigner's rations" were much better than those given to the local population and immigrants from Finland.[41] According to Aino and Eino Streng, a full-time working North American was allotted 800 grams of bread per day, and monthly rations that amounted to: a kilo of butter, two kilos of sugar, 3 kilos of oats or macaroni, three kilos of meat, two kilos of *silli* (pickled herring), and one to two kilos of caramels.[42] However, a real discrepancy exists between what was technically allotted, what was actually available, and how migrants remembered available foods. Viola Ranta's recollections suggest a less-than-adequate diet and emphasize the difference between Finnish North Americans' and Karelians' diets:

> We had the foreigner's rations, which included salted meat, rancid butter, sugar, tea, caramels, hulled grain, flour. Other folk got just black bread, salt and tea for rations. Was it a wonder then, that we were insulted by all kinds of names when they saw hunger and we had these kinds of rations. If only they had even been decent foods.[43]

Ranta's "Life Story" is characterized by a deep bitterness about her life in Karelia and she is especially negative about her experiences with food. Though recognizing the unfair rationing system, Ranta still dismissed the extras her family and Finnish North Americans were afforded as not sufficiently "decent."

From the perspective of Karelians and Russians, the Finnish North Americans had more-than-adequate rations.[44] As Gronow confirms, "almost anything – other than very basic goods, such as plain bread, cabbage, potatoes, or vodka – was a luxury in the eyes of Soviet citizens and the authorities."[45] According to Irina Takala, unhappy locals rallied around the phrase "Americans came here to eat our bread!"[46] Yet, from the perspective of the high North American standard of living, even the above-average provisions were shocking and disappointing.[47] It is also worth remembering that while the North Americans were technically allotted superior rations, frequently the promised goods proved to be just a "set of aspirations."[48]

In the United States by 1930, people – albeit not universally – had become overall accustomed to "much more fruit, particularly citrus, many more vegetables, especially green ones, significantly more milk and cheese, less flour and cornmeal, fewer potatoes, and less red meat."[49] The Karelian diet was a significant change. Like many regions of the Soviet Union, Karelia was very dependent on food import and could not meet its own needs.[50] Karelia faced shortages of meat, butter, vegetables, and even canteens to feed its population.[51] Many North American families had only rarely had fruit and fresh vegetables in the midst of depression conditions,[52] but their near total absence from the Soviet diet was noteworthy and especially had an impact on the memories of child migrants. Mayme Sevander's childhood recollections revealed that "in

Karelia, there were no oranges or bananas. In Karelia, there was no fresh fruit at all."[53] Vieno Zlobina's memoir echoes Sevander's.[54] Mary Leder remembered the role of food in social conversations with other foreign émigrés in Moscow:

> Food was, indeed, a constant topic of conversation ... we fantasized about eating, especially about the foods of our childhoods and younger years, which many of us had spent in distant countries. We did this in fun, not in self-pity. After all, we were not starving. Our stomachs were seldom full, but we had enough nourishment to keep our bodies and souls together.[55]

As foreign workers, Leder and her Moscow friends, like Finnish North Americans in Karelia, enjoyed privileged access to foods, but familiar foods and diets still retained a special place in their thoughts.

Karl Berg diplomatically summed up food in a 1932 letter: "Food you do get here even though it is not so varied but, yes, with it you get by."[56] Descriptions of food found in letters written in the 1930s successfully show, from the Finnish North American perspective, what foods could be found in Karelia, the value of particular foods, and how the letter writers shaped their narratives to convey health and success to their correspondents. In her first letter from Lohijärvi, some 18 kilometres from Petrozavodsk, Terttu Kangas assured her father and siblings that "Yes you manage here[.] foods here are almost the same kinds as there on the island except eggs and milk you can't really get lots yet. We have a baker [who] came from America [and is] really good. Even here the bread isn't from bare rye, it has 30 per cent white flour."[57] Terttu used food to assure her family of her health. It seems she employed the baker's American-ness to build on her assurance of well-being and normalcy. Terttu did not hide the shortages. On one hand she claimed food was the same as at home, but without eggs and milk, which had been staples of the rural Finnish diet in North America. Likewise, she had clearly noticed differences in the available bread, even with the skills of an American baker, but tried to emphasize its "purity," mentioning the 30 per cent white flour.

Terttu's comments fit well with broader folk symbolism surrounding bread. Farb and Armelagos point out that "the important metaphorical associations a society has are usually with the staples."[58] Certainly bread served as a primary staple in Karelia and throughout the Soviet Union. By 1933, Soviets were eating only one-fifth of the amount of meat and fish they would have eaten in 1900.[59] Bread and other coarse grains tried to fill the gap. Bread was made from whatever was available, often making it difficult to digest, poor tasting, and, at times, unrecognizable.[60] Soft, white bread communicated a life far different than that of the rough, sour, and dark bread. In her study of food in the life stories of Mennonite women from the Soviet Union, Marlene Epp noted that "white bread, a symbol of prestige and plenty, marked a departure from hardships."[61] When Mayme's brother Paul Corgan got his first paycheque, which was to support the family, he bought a loaf of white bread and a jar of jam. Sevander remembered: "We celebrated that night. It was the first white bread any of us had had in months; we always ate the Russian brown bread because it was cheaper and more filling."[62] Sevander's statement reveals that, while it may have tasted delicious, the white bread had more celebratory symbolic value than nutritional sense. According to Farb and Armelagos, "once a particular food has been elevated to symbolic status its nutritional use may become secondary."[63]

In a letter written to her sister Toini, Terttu Kangas, like Finnish letter writers in North America generations earlier, used the image of sweets and baking to represent an improved standard of living.[64] Instead of directly addressing whether they had steady access to protein or vegetables, or other pillars of sound nutrition, Kangas emphasized the availability of "*pulla* [coffee bread] and *keekiä* [Finglish "cakes"] and all kinds of baking but coffee [we] still can't get except with foreign money."[65] As Epp has shown, sugar acts as a symbol of abundance and metaphor for better times.[66] Terttu Kangas's cakes allowed her to assure her family that she was fine and stood in for her sweet life, so to speak. Sweets were also sent from North America to Karelia. Care packages from relatives and friends often contained treats like cookies, candies, chewing gum, and especially coffee.[67] These specialty foods provided a nostalgic taste of the sweetness of distant homes and communities.

Coffee holds an incomparable place in the narratives of Finnish North Americans in Karelia. Like sweets, the absence or availability of coffee act as symbols of shortage and plenty, of hardship and prosperity. Roland Barthes argued that "coffee is felt to be not so much a substance as a circumstance."[68] Indeed, coffee serves a vital social role in Finnish culture[69] and is the beloved national beverage, enjoyed several times a day. In Karelia, however, coffee was a very rare treat and Russian *chai* (tea) was the standard local beverage. Whether simply indicative of a love of coffee or suggesting that recruiters warned candidates about the lack of coffee, among the few items brought to Karelia by Lauri and Sylvi Hokkanen was a pound of their favourite coffee.[70] It seems Elis Ranta's family also brought coffee from the United States. Ranta casually asked his brother in Finland to send him some: "Apparently you can send duty-free a kilo of coffee, so I was thinking that maybe you brothers there could try to send us a coffee package. We have scrimped American coffee so far, but now it's starting to run out and it might be sad to be without coffee when you are used to it."[71] Ranta specified that wrapping it in cloth, rather than paper, would assure its safe arrival. Sylvi Hokkanen remembered that "we felt the lack of [coffee] deeply but also found it a great pleasure when we did have some."[72] The life writing, indeed, suggests that the absence of coffee was a "sad" state, but, conversely, memories of the availability of coffee have taken on the significant symbolic representation of fortune and prosperity in the mythology of Finnish North American Karelia.

It seems the smell of coffee and a warm cup in hand could, at least temporarily, ease the hardships of Karelian life and inspire camaraderie fit for a workers' paradise. Lauri Hokkanen remembered the woman who cooked for the workers at the Vonganperä lumber camp: "One evening she dipped into her personal supply of coffee and made a pot for all of us. It was a real treat. We had all been sitting there quietly around the fire but when the coffee came, everyone began to talk. What a difference coffee can make, especially to people who haven't had any for a long time."[73] The rare cup of North American coffee could flood the drinker with nostalgic emotion. In 1989, Harold Hietala explained how the first cup from a package from Canada made him and his wife "imagine being again on the other side of the ocean."[74] Barthes identified coffee as symbolizing "neighbourliness" to North Americans, and the same can be said for Finns.[75] Reino Hämäläinen noted that "this place is darn good any place you go the people allways [sic] want to feed you with something. Coffee and coffee is what they usually serve out here."[76] The rare scent of coffee infiltrating the communal apartment corridors or barracks brought eager visitors. Sylvi Hokkanen recalled: "whenever anyone was lucky enough to have coffee to make she would soon find unexpected company at her door."[77] Coffee brewing, as this and other examples demonstrate, was a woman's task.

Though women brewed coffee and served small meals at home, Finnish North Americans' daily meals were to be offered at state-run cafeterias or canteens. Eating communally was part of the Soviet welfare vision and a sign of communist life, and, by 1935, 60 per cent of families in the Soviet Union ate at their workplace canteens.[78] Workers received vouchers for food, which were traded for meals at the dining halls. Finnish North Americans were to be fed in special canteens for foreigners. Aate Pitkänen detailed his cafeteria's offerings for his sister and brother-in-law in 1934:

> I still have an *Insnab* book that is I get my stuff from the foreigners supply store. I give my food coupons to the "Ruokala" [cafeteria]. Boy! And I eat plenty. This restaurant of ours happens to be a good one, well managed.

We have 3 meals a day. Breakfast is tea with sugar, porridge, 3 slices of white bread with a hunk of butter, porridge you can eat all you want. Dinner is soup, velli [thin porridge] or something else and few slices of white bread and all you want of brown, and tea with sugar. Supper is the best meal and you can get second and even 3rd helpings of soup or spuds and gravy, but the best and richest grub ... is desert [sic]. I always eat 2 and 3 helpings unless I'm sick very bad. I tell the women that "pitää kokkien mieliksi syötä" [have to eat to keep the cooks pleased]. Then we make tea at home once in a while and buy some biscuits or cakes. Some of the restaurants serve tea in the evenings.[79]

Based on his depiction, Aate seems to have been very well fed and satisfied in Karelia. Upon close reading, Aate's emphasis on "sugar," "white bread," "deserts," "cakes," and "biscuits" reveals rather little about the nutritional content of his meals, or whether the meals contained any meat or vegetables beyond potatoes. Instead, they again show the use of symbols of prosperity and happiness. More striking, perhaps, is how Aate's description is worlds apart from most other Finnish North Americans' food memories.

In contrast, Viola Ranta remembered: "We ate at the cafeteria, but I wasn't able to eat anything for 2 weeks. The potatoes were frozen, sweet, and bad tasting, porridge ingredients were all mouldy, disgusting porridge. Rye porridge then became the food that I could eat. The black bread was so sour and raw that with it you could glue whatever."[80] The ski factory had two dining areas, separated according to Soviet worker hierarchy; one fed the technical staff and the other the non-specialized workers. Lauri Hokkanen had never eaten in the elite dining room, but "was told by some that they had better food."[81] Hokkanen had grown accustomed to the daily offering of sour bread and cabbage soup. Such plain and repetitive food was the standard. Having done some repair work at a collective farm, he recalled their normal meal: "The first course consisted of water that fish had been boiled in. Next we had the boiled fish with sour bread and tea."[82]

Golubev and Takala examined canteen investigation reports and found a scene very different than the one presented by Pitkänen. In early 1932, a Petrozavodsk canteen, designed to cater to a maximum of 200 people, found itself serving 800 people each day.[83] The canteen could not meet the need, and people waited for hours to get what little they could. Golubev and Takala have also pointed to the North Americans' horror to find that "huge accommodations in which hundreds of people dined had no separate facilities for cooking, dishwashing, or food storage. In addition, the facilities were infested with rats and cockroaches."[84]

Why, then, did Pitkänen paint such a rosy picture of the Karelian food offerings? Perhaps he was truly impressed by the food or perhaps it stood in contrast to what had been available at home in Kivikoski, Ontario, during hard times. However, the local bounties described in letters written by his parents, Antti and Kirsti, suggest he had enjoyed a varied and sufficient diet before leaving.[85] Maybe Aate was trying to emphasize the positive against the common negative attitudes to Karelia displayed by returnees and the anti-Karelian segment of Finnish North America. Or, perhaps Aate was simply trying to reassure his big sister and family that he and his father, who had only recently arrived in Karelia, were healthy and well cared for. While the contrasting narrative raises questions and shows the need to approach personal letters with a sharp analytical eye, it also highlights the basic structure of vouchers, foreigner advantages, and the cafeteria meal structure, even if only in the ideal.

Many people were frustrated by the inefficiencies, high costs, and poor quality of canteen dining. Others, still, lacked access to canteens, either because of their rations category or because they lived in an area where a dining hall had not yet been established. For example, after being sent to work in a remote area on the western shore of Lake Segozero (Seesjärvi, in Finnish), the Maunu family had to make a difficult 50-kilometre voyage by land and waterway to get their monthly food rations from a Finnish Canadian lumber camp (Tumba).[86] Terttu Kangas also told her sister that a "restaurant," meaning cafeteria, had not yet been built in the new village of Lohijärvi. It is unclear where lumber workers in the community ate during their shifts or where the food was prepared, but Terttu's description shows that many women were cooking for their families in their rooms on the stoves intended for heating.

"So you asked where I prepare food," Terttu Kangas wrote to her sister in April 1934 from Lohijärvi, "I have in this same room a stove made of tile and it has an iron lid with holes just like in American stoves[.] yes with it I can cook and it is also a heating oven much better than *paksi stouvi* [Finglish for "box stove"][.] our room has been so warm that the windows weren't frozen all winter."[87] Although the communal cafeteria and communal kitchen were symbols of revolutionary life, they were neither the reality nor preference of many women across the Soviet Union. In fact, none of the available letters or memoirs mention a communal kitchen in an apartment building at all. In an April 1934 letter, Elis Ranta explained to his brother that his wife, Alli, did not work outside of the home in Petrozavodsk, but "just prepares food for us, because the communal cafeterias are not yet in the condition that you can go there to eat."[88] Knowing that there were, in fact, cafeterias operating in Petrozavodsk at this time, it seems the Ranta's felt they could better feed themselves at home. Ranta's letters confirm Lynne Attwood's finding that many women in Soviet Russia were disinterested in communal cooking and preferred to take care of their own families.[89]

Though doing their best to maintain a semblance of familiar comfort, the tendency to take care of one's own family made others in the region suspicious of Finnish North Americans' commitment to socialism. When new migrants with their new rations category joined Säde in the 1930s, the original Finnish Canadian communards who had settled there in the mid-1920s noticed that "instead of giving the [extra] groceries for the common table they kept coffee, sugar, white flour, tobacco, and other delicacies to themselves. They baked cakes and pies, generously using the commune's butter and cream, but didn't share them with others."[90] "Thus," Vieno Zlobina remembered, "the members were split in ones who munched sweets, enjoyed coffee, cakes, pirogi, and others who got to watch on and smell the delicious aroma of pastry."[91]

Sylvi and Lauri Hokkanen did not have children and enjoyed a good standard of living, especially since Lauri was a prized Stakhanovite worker. Lauri recalled:

> I could just imagine how difficult it was for a family with a few kids to get along. I remember a time when the lady who did our wash came over for coffee. We had cookies, and when we put butter on them, she was horrified at our extravagance. She was a good worker and so was her husband, but they had four or five children, and it was tough going.[92]

The woman Lauri referred to was a local, and would not have had the extensive rations that the Hokkanens had grown accustomed to in Karelia. It is no wonder that the woman was surprised by what she witnessed: spreading butter, if there even was any to be had, on special cookies would have been unheard of. The seeming abundance and "extravagance" of North American Finns left a lasting impression on the area's local residents. With a large family and meagre rations, all food had to be scrimped and used with great care. Failure to use foods accordingly could have significant consequences for a family. In the face of shortages or hunger, women encountered a difficult challenge. Marlene Epp has shown how women confronted profound emotional and psychological distress when unable to feed their families. Epp argues that since women are typically in control of providing their family with sustenance, "when that domain is threatened by food shortage ... women are accordingly disempowered by the loss of that domain."[93]

Among the Finnish Canadian and American families, like Karelian, Finnish, and Russian families also, women used their ingenuity and know-how to create filling meals out of what little was available. In many cultures, women have been responsible for providing their family with a "proper meal," typically warm and comprising of many courses. Mayme Sevander proudly recalled her mother's domestic work: "my mother was a creative cook; she could concoct a wonderful, nourishing soup out of a handful of potatoes and very little else."[94] Rural upbringing, experience with poverty, and North American depression conditions prior to migration helped Finnish women make the best out of what foods were available to them in Karelia. Cynthia Comacchio recognized that "previous experiences of unemployment and constrained family budgets prepared many working-class families to meet Depression scarcity with well-honed resourcefulness."[95] Comacchio also notes that "mending, sewing, backyard vegetable gardening, berry-picking, baking and canning returned to many homes."[96] Donna Gabaccia draws attention to how migrant women have been seen as especially adept at economizing and making do.[97] These insights can be extended to the experiences and practices of many Finnish North Americans who moved to Karelia. Finnish women from agricultural or working-class backgrounds, both in Finland and after emigrating to Canada or the United States, had grown up with subsistence garden plots, foraging, and the skills of home preserving. Despite the growing modernization of the food processing industry in North America and the increasing availability of canned foods, the 1930s economic downturn meant a return to old-fashioned approaches to food. As an example, the sale of canned goods fell significantly during the Depression, while the sale of canning jars reached record highs.[98] These changes had helped prepare Finnish North American women for life in Karelia.

Though Karelia's small villages and countryside lacked the amenities available in Petrozavodsk, the possibility of growing one's own vegetables and being able to hunt and fish held significant appeal for many Finnish North Americans eager to supplement their diets.[99] For Finns, annual berry and mushroom harvests have been important traditions and could provide diets with vital vitamins and fibre.[100] From available letters, we know that in Karelia Finnish North Americans joined the ranks of those who scoured the forests and clearings for seasonal berries. In fact, telling of the importance of the summer berry harvest, in August 1934, Lisi Hirvonen told her sister that employers provided workers with transportation to go berry picking on their days off.[101] Terttu Kangas told her sister:

> There has been lots of all kinds of berries. I also bottled a whole lot of blueberries and raspberries and a whole lot of lingonberries are in a tub

and *krämperiä* ["Finglish" for cranberry] [we] have a big package so yes here berries you can get *avian kyliksi* [quite enough] But here you can't get at all that kind of berry jar as there [and we] didn't get to buying any there But yes here they have their own ways that berries are canned[.] here they are put in a vodka bottle with tar on top.[102]

Terttu's description shows a familiarity with berry varieties and canning processes. The reference to American canning jars suggests that Terttu had preserved berries before migrating to Karelia. Her statement, likewise, illustrates the array of items missed by North American Finns in Karelia, the shortage of consumer goods in the region, and the common repurposing of available items (vodka bottles, in this case). Learning the local way of preservation shows the adaptation of Finnish North American women to Karelian life. Lisi Hirvonen's late autumn letter from 1932 reports an abundance of berries but "blueberries we didn't get for the winter because had no containers."[103] Fortunately, as Hirvonen describes, she was able to preserve lingonberries in wooden vats. While Sylvi Hokkanen seemed to otherwise hold responsibility for housekeeping and food preparation, her husband Lauri "took care of" the autumn lingonberry pick.[104] In the winter, Sylvi would make a *marjapuuro* (berry porridge) from the frozen lingonberries, using a homemade whisk made of twigs.[105] Making do was an essential part of life in Karelia, and became increasingly important as the 1930s progressed and all of the "extras" of Finnish North American life there were stripped away.

Clothing

The end of the First Five Year Plan, in its cultural shift, marked the end of military, ascetic fashion in favour of "smart clothes, clean shaving for men and the use of perfumes and makeup for women."[106] However, again, the ideal and the reality were at odds. As demonstrated by Sheila Fitzpatrick, "clothing, shoes, and all kinds of consumer goods were in even shorter supply than basic foodstuffs, often being completely unobtainable."[107] Even amid his usual Soviet boosterism, Enoch Nelson conceded that people in Karelia and the USSR were "not rich in clothing."[108] Newly arrived North American Finns stood in sharp contrast to the local population and even Finnish Canadians and Americans who had been in the region since the 1920s. When Vieno Zlobina began school in Petrozavodsk in 1931 after having already lived at the Säde Commune for five years, she noted the differences and her "envy": "They were taller, wore nice clothes, including colourful sweaters, denim jackets, and blue jeans. Girls wandered the streets in slacks, their shoes were seasonal, and everyone had a watch. Many of them wore fancy glasses."[109] In contrast, Vieno had come from scarcity, as was common in many villages and communes. Even as a prized productive agricultural commune, the Finnish Canadian Säde was without boots and adequate clothing in 1930, having its allocation of goods continually left unfulfilled by local officials. Commune chairman Siikanen appealed to government leaders: "It's hard to work in the fields barefoot, our women are staggering in bare feet, and we can't send our children to school without shoes."[110] Not understanding the poverty of the local population, seventeen-year-old Reino Hämäläinen was first struck by what he saw: "They [sic] sure are a lot of dirty people here[.] they seem not to care how they dress. They all ware [sic] boots and torn coats."[111] The newcomers quickly learned that in the Soviet Union, "'fashion' was dictated by the scarcity of manufactured cloth."[112]

The Soviet Union proved unable to meet the nation's clothing needs, especially the continuous demand for women's clothing and woollen garments.[113] Foreign workers had been encouraged to bring plenty of work clothes, but replacements were continually needed. With harsh winters and heavy labour, adequate clothing was vital but quickly wore out. Even though North Americans typically earned double the monthly wages of locals, a work shirt or pair of shoes could each absorb about 20 per cent of a person's earnings.[114] Even if one had the rubles (or better yet dollars) to buy these poor-quality items, stores rarely had clothing in stock. Vieno Zlobina remembered not being able to find ready-made clothing, fabric, or raincoats in Karelia.[115]

Laundering in Karelia also took its toll on clothes. Mayme Sevander remembered: "In New York we had had a separate laundry room, equipped with a wringer washer and plenty of soap, hot water and galvanized laundry tubs. But here, of course, we didn't have those things, and we had to learn to wash our clothes the Russian way."[116] For Hämäläinen, unfamiliar to the "Russian way," the sight "makes one laugh right in front of the one washing."[117] But for women responsible for this work, the difficult task meant dragging clothes to the river and beating them, even in the bitter cold. One had to be careful with clothes in the river for, as Sevander reminded, "it wouldn't do to lose anything, because clothes and fabric were so hard to come by."[118]

When manufactured clothing or fabric were not available, North American friends and family were relied on to send clothing; both new and used were appreciated. Western clothes were also made of better fabrics and proved warmer and more durable.[119] The letter writers asked for and received clothing like sweaters, underwear, socks, woollen long underwear, and especially shoes.[120] Enoch Nelson explained to his brother that "the hardest we are up for yet is footwear as the demand for it is so great that our factories are not able to supply the demands."[121] Adding some official rhetoric, Nelson continued: "In 1932 we made nine times as many shoes and boots as the Tsars [sic] Government made in its best year but this is not enough for the present day demand."[122] In the same letter, Nelson acknowledged – though notably did not offer thanks for – the arrival of a "dress and kimono as well as the overcoat."[123] Clothes were made and remade to meet changing needs and to make the most out of available cloth. Many women still hoped to keep up with American fashions. Terttu Kangas asked her sister to send recent dress patterns and catalogues.[124] Keeping hair stylish was just as important. Kangas told her sister that, in Karelia, you could now get "*permanenti weivi* [permanent wave] as good as there but it still had a bit expensive price."[125] Bobby pins, however, were not available at all. Terttu asked Toini to send some twice in the available correspondence, and it seems her sister complied. Kangas explained that "here there is already starting to be almost everything, except those little things there still are not everything."[126]

Consumer Goods

Terttu Kangas's explanation was quite accurate. In the Soviet Union's rapid industrial development, few resources were left for the production of consumer goods. To attract foreign currency and to provide the symbols of the Stalinist "good life," Soviet production focused on luxury production in the 1930s. Gronow's study of the luxury industry and mass consumerism highlights the resultant scarcity of ordinary items, like buttons and nail scissors, to name only two examples.[127] Even in 1991, Jack Forsell pinpointed the USSR's continual shortage of household goods: "We do know how to make artillery, planes, bombs, rockets & etc, but we don't know how to make nails, pails, pie rollers & other items which we need in our household."[128] Canadian and US Finns had access to the special stores for foreigners, *Insnab* and *Torgsin*. Reino Kero found evidence of *Insnab* stores operating in Petrozavodsk, Matrosy (Matroosa), and Solomennoye (Soloman), and concluded that they were "noticeably better stocked than Soviet stores generally."[129] These stores were, in Irina Takala's words, "the object of envy for local people."[130] Even with access to *Insnab*, though, it was not necessarily possible to get what was needed, let alone one's allotted rations.

When needed items were not available, Finnish North Americans again turned to the transnational flow of material goods made possible by friends and family in Canada and the United States. Items like darning needles, razors, aspirin, iodine, and alarm clocks were much appreciated by their recipients.[131] Fulfilling both practical and emotional needs, North American calendars had special significance for those in Karelia.[132] Calendars were hard to come by in Karelia, usually did not have pictures, and the layout was confusing for some not accustomed to their format. Soviet calendars combined five-, six-, and seven-day weeks to accommodate different work schedules in different industries. Jack Forsell remembered making calendars with scrounged pencil stubs and cardboard.[133] When calendars were sent from abroad, the scenery on the pages gave a glimpse of home and the North American calendar layout kept the migrants connected to the temporal reality of their faraway friends and family.[134] After receiving a calendar, Aate Pitkänen told his parents: "That one calendar was so fine quality that people line up here so they can come and admire it."[135] While exaggerating to express his gratitude, the calendar was nonetheless a prized gift.

The range of practical household goods requested and received, like clothing and needles, for example, offers a sense of everyday material needs not met in the hinterlands of Karelia. With special rations, access to the *Insnab* store, higher wages, and North American clothes and goods, Finnish Canadians and Americans in Karelia, like "foreign specialists' throughout the Soviet Union, were significantly better off than the region's locals. However, perhaps due to their community's insular nature or perhaps because comparisons may have roused censors' suspicions, available Finnish North American letters do not acknowledge their privileged position. Rather the writers noted a change in their own standard of living; North American products were seen by the life writers as crucial contributions to their Karelian lives.

Health and Hygiene

Terttu Kangas reported to her sister that all of their acquaintances had grown plumper and healthier in Karelia.[136] When considered along with other Finnish North American narratives, however, it seems that Kangas was perhaps exaggerating to assure Toini that she was doing well, just as she had assured her father that she had plenty of food to eat. More typical was Lisi Hirvonen's statement. Just a few months after moving to Karelia, Hirvonen light-heartedly reported to her sister: "we have both lost weight but what do you do with excess flesh anyway."[137] Like Kangas, it appears Hirvonen wanted to present herself as healthy and well, though willing to admit that her body was undergoing changes. Strenuous work and living conditions with limited food quickly affected people's weight and bodies. Mayme Sevander's memories of her mother's hands exemplify the physical transformations that occurred. Sevander stated: "Her

Figure 7 The Hiilisuo daycare (*Neuvosto-Karjalan 15-vuotiaan taipaleelta*, 68).

hands, once slender, beautiful and capable, were now red and cracked, the knuckles painfully swollen from arthritis. It hurt me to even look at them."[138] Marina Malysheva and Daniel Bertaux, likewise, found that the life story of Marina Zolotareva, a Soviet "countrywoman," was narrated as the "life story of her body."[139] The very different living conditions, foods, and environment in Karelia impacted the health of most Finnish North Americans; many noted changes almost immediately. Gastric illnesses were the most typical. Both adults and children experienced the ailments that accompanied new foods, a change in caloric intake, new water sources, and other environmental factors. Allan Sihvola remembered that "for medicine there was only dried blueberries and blueberry soup."[140] Suzanne Rosenberg, likewise, remembered the "skin rashes, boils, and other minor troubles" she experienced shortly after emigrating from Canada to Moscow as a child.[141] Others felt the effects of change more drastically.

The Heino family experienced the devastation of losing two young children to illness in their first years in Karelia. Fourteen-year-old Urho and twelve-year-old Arte died within three months of each other, both seemingly from pneumonia.[142] The boys were both fortunate to receive medical care and hospitalization, but they could not be saved. Likewise, Klaus Maunu's newborn baby brother contracted pneumonia at the Petrozavodsk birthing hospital where he was born, and died there after only a few short weeks.[143] Maunu's mother blamed the hospital's poor heating for the death. Though free health care had been a major lure for Finnish North American migrants, gaining access to doctors could be difficult. Irina Takala explains: "Proper medical aid was not always rendered in time and was not accessible everywhere. The lines to doctors were even longer than the lines to the canteens. In some locations there were no doctors whatsoever but just a nurse with a scanty set of medicines who did not understand the patients' language."[144] Encountering diseases largely eradicated among white settler populations in North America by 1930, such as typhoid and smallpox, and tuberculosis, which had seen a significant decrease,[145] came as a horrific shock to the migrants. In lumber camps and away from the towns, illness could run rampant. In Latushka, a typhoid outbreak made thirty-three people sick and claimed the lives of fifteen. Sevander remembered:

> The smell of illness was everywhere. The typhoid was caused by our inhumane living arrangement. Cleanliness was impossible in a place with no running water, a place where so many people lived and cooked and slept in such close quarters. Many people also suffered from lice, and some of the lice carried disease.[146]

The Soviet authorities were well aware of the disease outbreaks and unhygienic living conditions prevalent across the nation. However, the communist regime treated outbreaks of infectious diseases as classified matters.[147] Hygiene became an important concern for the burgeoning communist state, immediately following the revolution. Stalinist *kul'turnost'* encouraged properly cultured Soviet citizens to practise impeccable personal hygiene. Soviet discourse of the mid-1930s promoted cleanliness, discipline, and efficiency, which could be achieved, at least in part, through the use of individual showers over communal bathhouses, and clean bed linens.[148] As with the ideals of housing and rationing, the daily reality of Soviet life, again, often fell short of the ideals of hygiene. According to David Hoffman, despite major formal hygiene campaigns and the work of the *obshchestvennitsa* ("housewife activists") movement, hygiene standards actually fell because resources were entirely directed at industrialization and overlooked the housing improvements and needs caused by the subsequent urbanization.[149]

Without proper funding and restructuring, barracks living, as characterized by Mayme Sevander, left hygienic aspirations as just that: "My family staked out a place in the barracks for ourselves and strung up blankets for privacy. But there was no way to shut out the sounds of the other people, talking, coughing, snoring, belching. Or the smells – the smells of unwashed clothes and unwashed bodies, the cooking smells of cabbage and potatoes."[150] Sevander's descriptions of the sounds and smells of barracks living resonate with what Svetlana Boym has referred to as the "communal trash" of common spaces.[151] Sharing crowded spaces and responsibility for upkeep could strain relationships and emphasize cultural differences. The hygienic standards of Russians often dismayed the North Americans. Allan Sihvola explained that, at the Rutanen lumber camp, the outhouse was clean "because the people were all Finnish."[152] Lauri Hokkanen took it upon himself to teach a Russian family in their barracks how to use the shared outhouse, without standing on the seat. According to Hokkanen, "the Russian family caught on right away and there was no more crap on the seat and they took their turn washing and cleaning."[153] Furthermore, "a few months later, another Russian family moved in and the same thing happened, but this time the first Russian came to me cussing the 'dirty Russians' who soiled our toilet."[154] Hokkanen's description of these interactions echoes the ideas of Finnish North Americans as Karelian civilizer and of long-standing prejudices and stereotypes about local peoples. Finns have a deep-rooted cultural pride in their cleanliness, which can be seen as linking to long-standing internalized colonial ideas about racial and cultural hierarchy.[155] Ernesti Komulainen's *Grave in Karelia* further demonstrates these themes. When Nikolai arrived at the lumber camp, he searched for the Finns' barrack. One bunk was ruled out because a boy was urinating on the steps, but at the last one "he studied the steps and the area near the walls. The snow there was clean, and he turned in without any hesitation. It was the right place."[156] In the wilds of Karelia, urinating near one's living space delineated "civilized" Finns from "others." Komulainen further qualifies the Finns' space as "bright," "clean," "cheerful," and "cozy," in stark contrast to the gloom of foreign Karelia.[157]

Many Finnish women, like Terttu Kangas,[158] who had worked in North America, became housewives in Karelia and took pride in their cared-for homes. However, women from different backgrounds judged each other by their differing cultural values. As Irina Takala explains, "Soviet women, who toiled as hard as men, didn't understand how Finnish women could stay at home with children and called them 'vagabonds' and 'idlers' who are used to 'living at the expense of others' in their bourgeois countries. Finnish women despised Soviet women for their constantly muddy floors and untended children and household."[159]

North Americans in the Soviet Union were also confronted with cockroaches, bedbugs, lice, and other insects in numbers that few had known before their migration. The 1930s letters do not address the constant struggle to keep the parasites at a distance, but they are discussed in all of the memoirs. Letter writers likely wanted to keep up appearances of well-being in their writing. Given the hygienic values of North Americans overall and Finns in particular, the letter writers may also have struggled with a sense of embarrassment about the infestations. For the memoirists, the infestations act as a symbol of primitive living conditions and, on a deeper level, even signal the way that Soviet life ate away at them, mentally and physically. Some insects, and lice especially, as we have seen, posed a very real health hazard, as disease carriers. Memoir descriptions teach us about how they were dealt with.

Kaarlo Tuomi remembered his early encounters with cockroaches: "millions of them nested in the cracks [of apartments and barracks] and the only way to exterminate them was for the people to vacate the houses for a couple of weeks in the winter and freeze them."[160] Of course, with such limited housing and the intensity of the winter cold, in reality, the suggested extermination method most likely meant simply enduring the presence of the cockroaches. Lauri and Sylvi Hokkanen had been warned about Karelian bedbugs before their departure and found that they were, indeed, "a constant problem all the time we were in Karelia."[161] The Hokkanens brought Borax to try to keep them away, but when it "didn't help at all," they tried different techniques, like setting the legs of their bed in pails of water.[162] Americans and Canadians elsewhere in the Soviet Union also engaged in a battle with bugs. Suzanne Rosenberg fought bedbugs with kerosene and boiled her clothes and cut her hair to combat lice.[163] Mary Leder battled the lice that plagued her and her infant daughter during their wartime evacuation with boiling water, kerosene, and pyrethrum, in an attempt to keep typhus at bay.[164] While the letter writers do not address the insect problem, given the physical discomfort of bug bites and the mental anguish and lost sleep caused by their presence, bedbugs, lice, and cockroaches played an undeniable and unwelcome role in the everyday lives of Finnish North Americans in Karelia.

Conclusion

Life writing provides us with intimate views of daily life in Karelia. Letters and memoirs show us ways the writers worked through the significant changes to their standard of living, by making do at the time and retrospectively in giving meaning and order to their personal life stories. The life writers have given us concrete examples of housing, eating, consumer goods, and health. Situating their narratives in the contexts of their North American backgrounds and Soviet policies and practices, we are able to clearly see the discrepancy between the ideal (and the promised) and the realized. Cultural symbols, particularly foods, then, allowed letter writers and memoirists to communicate particular (and changing) images of their lives in Karelia. Through their narratives, we learn about the gendered order of Finnish North American life in Karelia, and the expectation that women maintain a sense of home and comfort for their families. Housing, food, access to material goods, and hygiene unveil inter-ethnic tensions and misunderstandings occurring in Karelia. According to Irina Takala, "the privileged position [North] American Finns found themselves in evoked a natural reaction among the half-starved inhabitants of the republic – they envied the foreigners, they did not understand and did not like them."[165] But the foreigners, likewise, did not understand the people living around them. Mayme Sevander thought back on the 1930s in Karelia:

> With our American clothes, American luxuries and ration cards, we must have evoked some envy in the Russian people. Life in Karelia was rough and difficult for us, but we still had privileges and possessions that most of the natives could only dream about. I didn't really notice such subtle tensions; I was only a child. I don't even know if my parents were aware of them.[166]

Though they were visibly different and privileged to those who had been in the region before them, the living conditions Finnish Americans and Canadians faced were "rough and difficult" for them, based on their own past experiences. While many struggled to make peace with their advantages, it was difficult to acknowledge living a privileged life when, no matter what, daily life was "not like there," as it had been in North America.

Chapter Four

"The Golden Fund of Karelia": Childhood in Finnish North American Karelia

Yrjö Sirola, a prominent Finnish communist in North America, Finland, and the Soviet Union, was said to have called the children of Finnish North Americans "the golden fund of Karelia."[1] Indeed, the hopes and dreams of a thriving communist society rested on the shoulders of these children. In Canada and the United States, they were raised in the revolutionary spirit by their parents, and in Karelia, the developing Soviet state saw children as both the symbol of and the means to a new social order. However, very little has been known about these smallest builders of socialism specifically within the Karelian project. Evgeny Efremkin's statistical analysis of Canadian and US Finns who migrated to Karelia suggests that about one-quarter of all migrants were under the age of twenty, with about half of those under the age of twelve.[2] However, already in 1993, Mayme Sevander warned that the ways Finnish North American emigrants to Karelia have been enumerated through passenger lists or official party records has resulted in the underrepresentation of children. "Special stress should be laid on the fact that the children and young people, who went over with their families, can in no way be left out," Sevander emphasized.[3] In response, this chapter offers a new child-centred view of the Finnish North American migration to Karelia, finding traces of children's experiences and feelings through letters, memoirs, and life-story interviews.[4] I further situate Finnish North American child migrants in Karelia in the shifting ideals of socialist upbringing and education, and highlight the contrast in their North American and Soviet experiences.

I focus primarily on school-aged children up to approximately the age of sixteen. By sixteen, many youth in the Soviet Union had completed schooling and were legally eligible to work adult hours. Likewise, this age marked the transition from membership in the Communist Pioneers to the *Komsomol* or communist youth organization, which was a mark of political and social maturity. These children and youth arrived in Karelia at a unique historical moment, caught between revolutionary ideals and the developing mechanisms of Stalinism in the region. Looking at children's feelings around the decision to emigrate, initial confrontations with language barriers, and daily experiences with school, the Pioneers, at work, and at play reveals aspects of North American Karelian life previously unaddressed. Analyzing Finnish North American childhood also provides an opportunity to contrast their lives with those of local Karelians and Russians, and, thereby, Soviet childhood in the 1930s more broadly. Finally, situating children's everyday lives in the context of adult-driven ideas about childhood and education reveals the symbolic and contested value placed on children. These vantages show how Finnish North American children's multinational identity contradictorily provided protection but also made them susceptible to repression.

North American Context

By the "Karelian Fever," Finnish socialists and communists in Canada and the United States had a long-established tradition of raising their children in the revolutionary spirit. The children of Finnish North American leftists were no strangers to the ideals of communism or the vision of the workers' society they were to build. Finnish parents, like most immigrant parents, worried about the assimilation of their children and the loss of mother tongue and cultural traditions. By the late 1920s, the communist movement in Canada and the United States actively resisted "foreign language elements" in the party, and left migrant families to negotiate and contest their way through an increasingly English-language-oriented political culture that sought to shape their children into Anglo–North American revolutionaries. As Rhonda Hinther has convincingly demonstrated, using the example of the Ukrainian Canadian communists, "youngsters' activities are an important lens through which to understand the significant role of cultural-political activism and the movement's overall efforts to challenge and resist [Communist] Party efforts to control and dictate."[5] Through children's and youth's programming, migrants could instil their own language and culturally specific values in the younger generation, and, simultaneously, youngsters who spoke English could broaden the reach of the migrant socialist community beyond what was possible for the adults who did not.[6] Examining Finnish North American socialist children's education and upbringing shows a commitment to instilling both identification with the class struggle and a sense of Finnish identity.

Figure 8 Young Pioneers marching in Ishpeming, Michigan, in 1932 (IHRCA Paivio, Carl, Papers [IHRCA2014], im171025. http://purl.umn.edu/66851).

Not only were Finnish adults on the left expected to actively engage in party and committee work, activism, and agitation, children were to be moulded into politically and socially conscious people from a young age. Most children of Finnish socialists and communists began their relationship with the movement as infants and toddlers, brought to the halls for meetings, speeches, and entertainments. Allan Sihvola remembered his early days at the Warren, Ohio, Finnish Workers' Society Hall: "When we went to the Hall I was always brought along, whether there was a play, an evening program, a dance, or a meeting. [When I was] smaller during meetings I would always be found in some corner sleeping."[7] Antti and Kirsti Pitkänen, determined to set an example of activism for their children Aate, Taimi, and Taru, always brought them along to events at the Finnish socialist halls. According to interviews in her later life and in her autobiographical writings,[8] Taimi remembered her parents' stern expectation that she and Aate be active in the workers' movement and train for leadership. Simply attending meetings was not enough, let alone sleeping in the corner; the Pitkänen children had to always be prepared to perform.[9] Children were also made aware of current events and struggles of the working class through early exposure to the Finnish-language leftist press. Taimi Pitkänen remembered her family's subscriptions to *Toveritar*, a Finnish socialist newspaper from Oregon for women, and *Vapaus* based out of Sudbury, Ontario.[10] North American children continued to engage with the Canadian and US Finnish communist press in Karelia, through subscriptions to papers, like *Työmies*.[11]

At times, Finnish families on the left organized ad hoc campaigns to circumvent their children's encounters with capitalist and religious values in public schools and in broader North American society. For example, the 7 May 1930 minutes of the Communist Women's Bureau in the Finnish rural community of Tarmola, Ontario, show the women resolving to fight religious indoctrination in public school.[12] As an example of other types of campaigns organized by Finnish socialist families, in 1927 the Pitkänen children were part of a successful strike by the students of the Kivikoski School to fight for the removal of an unsatisfactory teacher.[13] Ties to the communist movement left lasting impressions on children. Vieno Zlobina remembered reciting poems at the Cobalt, Ontario, Red Finn Hall, singing the *Internationale*, and being worried about attacks by White Finns.[14] Though insistent that she was *not* a communist when she moved to Karelia, Sylvi Hokkanen's childhood upbringing in the socialist tradition had stayed with her. On the workers' anthem, Hokkanen wrote: "I'd heard it many times as a child ... But the feeling of solemnity as well as exaltation associated with the 'Internationale' had stayed with me, and I always had to stand whenever I heard it played. Childhood memories and feelings die hard."[15]

Contrasting Ideals of Children's Upbringing

Home- and community-based socialist teaching was complemented by formalized education methods and programs. At the turn of the twentieth century, North American socialists had begun organizing hundreds of local Socialist Sunday Schools for their children and Finns were "particularly active."[16] In addition to generally introducing revolutionary principles, the schools served a further purpose for migrant newcomers. As Donald Wilson argues, "socialist indoctrination by itself was not sufficient, or else they would have sent their children to the [English-language] schools ... Finnish-language education and knowledge about Finland, both unavailable in the public system, led Finnish socialists (and by the same token other foreign-language socialists) to found their own Sunday schools."[17]

By 1930, the Finnish socialist children's Sunday Schools had largely been replaced by branches of the Communist Young Pioneers. Many child emigrants, like Mayme Sevander, fondly remembered their days in the North American Pioneer movement.[18] Like the Sunday Schools, the Pioneers targeted children from the ages of approximately five to fifteen. Also, like the Sunday Schools and more informal family-based leftist upbringing, Pioneer leaders aimed to "instill a working-class education and consciousness which should combat the training and education received from the bourgeois organizations, from the schools, movies, Sunday school, boy scouts and girl guides, etc. all year round."[19] The programming sought to teach children to question the norms of the capitalist system. Critical thinking was particularly encouraged. The cover of the Communist *Fairy Tales for Workers Children*, published in English translation by the Communist Party of the United States in 1925, illustrates the point well, depicting three children gathered around a book with the floating caption "WHY?" repeated nine times.[20]

Like the "bourgeois" scouting and guide movement, the Pioneers held weekly meetings and summer camps, giving children frequent access to their alternative values. Ester Reiter's take on the nature of Jewish communist children's education at Camp Naivelt resonates with the experiences of Finnish children in the Pioneers: "The politics and the serious intentions of the adults to raise children who would understand class struggle were woven into the play of children just being children. Sometimes the political was the play and the play was political."[21] The 1931 booklet "Games for the Pioneer Leader" provides useful insights into the messages that children were being taught and the means used to convey revolutionary values.[22] Although the booklet is in English, the fact that it was "issued by the Young Pioneers of Canada District No. 6[,] 316 Bay St. Port Arthur Ont." reveals that its games were in fact aimed at Finnish children. This location in Port Arthur, Ontario, was the address of the so-called "Little Finn Hall" or the Communist Hall, next door to the – at the time – IWW-affiliated "Big Finn Hall," or Finnish Labour Temple. District Number 6 was the designation of the Port Arthur Finnish Organization of Canada. The use of the English language is indicative of the lost battle of non-Anglo communists over the right to formal communist correspondence in "ethnic" languages, but also of the changing identities of Finnish youth, who were becoming more fully immersed in English-speaking society.

The booklet begins with a section on the "Significance of Games," which are said to be "the training school for serious militant work."[23] Furthermore, Pioneer leaders were instructed to "allow the comrades to participate wherever possible in formulating necessary rules, And than [*sic*] absolutely see to it that they are enforced by the comrades themselves."[24]

Figure 9 *Fairy Tales for Workers Children*, 1925. (https://archive.org/details/Fairy TalesForWorkersChildren).

The names and directions for the games reveal their work as "training schools." Names like "Sock the Scab" and "Competition or Co-operation" successfully conveyed their political orientation, while "The White Terror" would surely have chilled young Finnish participants, well aware of the cruelty of the Finnish Civil War.[25] In "Catching the Shop Nucleus Organizer" Pioneers were to disguise themselves in order to trick the "boss" from discovering the identity of the factory organizer.[26] The aim of "Employment Agency" was for the "unemployed workers" to remain composed and not "loose their grip" when poked and prodded by the "capitalist."[27] Games like "Win a Tractor for the Soviet Union" resonated for Finnish children living amid the escalating "Karelian Fever" and the campaigning of the Karelian Technical Aid.[28]

Indeed, Karelia and Soviet Russia held a special place in the hearts of children brought up on the class struggle. "Hammer, Sickle, Soviet Star, I love Soviet Russia with all my heart," sang Pioneers.[29] Children's affection for the Soviet Union mirrored adults' interest in the world's first workers' state. North Americans of varying political persuasions kept a close watch on developments in burgeoning Soviet Russia. As Julia Mickenberg has observed about the United States in the 1920s and 1930s, "interest in the Soviets' social engineering of children matched interest in their industrial progress."[30] Naturally, for those sympathetic to the revolutionary movement, the Soviet Union provided inspiration and guidance for children's education and the movement more broadly. Regarding the significance of the Bolshevik state, Paul Mishler states: "US Communists identified strongly with the Soviet Union, and their idea of what the Soviet Union was like influenced their political perspective and the political culture that developed among them."[31]

Finnish North American children's socialist upbringing closely resembled Soviet Russian ideas of "Free Upbringing" from the revolutionary period, which had prioritized child-led exploration and learning.[32] However, while Finns in Canada and the United States continued to focus on instilling creative and critical thinking into the years of the Karelian migration, the Soviet Union adopted a drastically different approach with the consolidation of Stalinism. By the beginning of the 1930s, children had little to say about the form or content of their education. Kirschenbaum has characterized the Stalinist revolution in education, from 1928 to 1932, as having "generally favoured the formulaic over the experiential, the state-directed over the spontaneous."[33] It "valued not rebelliousness, liberation, or self-expression but stability, enlightenment, and state-building."[34] The new Soviet upbringing, or *vospitanie*, prioritized "socialization into customs and habits of the established order."[35] Migrants to Karelia, whether formally identifying themselves as communists or not, brought with them their revolutionary upbringing, a deeply entrenched attachment to the plight of workers, a critical eye for identifying injustice, and an emotional attachment to the Soviet Union. The clash between their upbringing and what they encountered in Karelia quickly made Finnish North American children see themselves – and to be seen – as out of place.

Feelings about Moving

Mayme Sevander described the moment she learned her family would move to Karelia:

> My eyes grew wide with excitement. Karelia! We were actually moving to the Soviet Union! Over the years I had attended so many Pioneer camps, so many Communist rallies, and always, the goals of the Soviet Union and its first leader, V.I. Lenin, had been held out as almost unattainable. And now we were going – we would live those ideals ourselves. I was sure I couldn't wait until April 4.[36]

Sevander's enthusiasm suited her exceptional upbringing as the daughter of a leading Finnish American communist and recruiter for the Karelian Technical Aid. Her carefully crafted retrospective statement highlights the success of communist children's upbringing; she was an example of a child committed to the cause and ready to serve the Soviet Union. Other Finnish Canadian and US children, though, did not share Sevander's fervent enthusiasm for leaving behind their familiar lives to build socialism. For some, the weight of the move was obscured by a sense of adventure. When asked what he had thought about his family's decision to move to Karelia, Erwin Niva answered: "it was interesting to get to leave, and a child, of course, doesn't think where they're going as long as they're going somewhere, that is the main thing."[37] Allan Sihvola remembered, "When we left Warren, I didn't know to yearn for my friends staying behind, and now, leaving the state of Mass, it was again the same. I was still so young, a 12 year old kid, that everything just felt like an adventure."[38] For others, departure was excruciating. In her memoir, Viola Ranta wrote, "I begged and cried that let's not go there, but in vain."[39] "I asked my parents even in Leningrad that we turn back on the same ship," remembered Ranta, "I so missed my own homeland that all I could do was cry all the days. How were there enough tears!"[40] Leaving behind everything familiar was very difficult for fourteen-year-old Viola. Even her father's letters to his brother in Finland mention Viola's desire to leave Karelia.[41] Though all of the above examples are based on adult reminiscences, the varied responses to migration highlight the diverse and complex feelings children had about Karelia and their homeland and further illustrate the need to turn to children to better understand the entirety of Finnish North American life in Karelia.

School

Like for most children, school occupied a central place in the thoughts of Alice Heino. In a March 1938 letter, Alice told her brother "I go to school every day except on the rest day," immediately following the compulsory greetings and weather talk.[42] In their six days a week spent there, the Soviet school was a main force in the acculturation of North American children. However, in many cases, the schools were ill prepared to welcome these new students. The large-scale arrival of Finnish Canadians and Americans in Karelia coincided with a unique period in the Soviet approach to education and childhood. Mandatory primary education was instated in 1930, resulting in an explosion in the number of schools, teachers, and students. These new schools lacked sufficient books, materials, and space – students often attended school in shifts – and suffered from a scarcity of trained teachers. Between 1930 and 1933, the teaching profession grew by almost 60 per cent in the Soviet Union.[43] E. Thomas Ewing's research found that in late 1930, Soviet educational planners knew that, due to the massive increase in the demands for education propelled by mandatory schooling, less than one-third of new teachers would receive any pedagogical training.[44] In 1932, 35 per cent of Soviet teachers had less than secondary education.[45] For students in remote or rural areas, and especially in minority-language school systems, the situation was even bleaker. Ewing argues that the policy of *korenizatsiia* resulted in the hiring and promotion of unqualified teachers and officials who met the requirements of being a local.[46] Though intended to support local culture, Ol'ga Iliukha has shown that school materials sent to the Finnish "minority" schools were simply Moscow works, translated into Finnish and "poorly applicable to the local conditions."[47] Inadequate facilities and instructors and unevenly applied curriculum undoubtedly proved to be to children's detriment.

To continue studies beyond basic primary, children who lived in small rural communities or communes – like Leini Hietala, Mayme Sevander, Allan Sihvola, and Paavo Alatalo – went to a boarding school for foreigners, the Internaat, in Petrozavodsk. When asked if she enjoyed living and studying at the Internaat, Leini Hietala replied: "Well I guess it was pleasant there. After school we could run around there."[48] Allan Sihvola's memoir includes a vivid description of the school's accommodations, food, teaching, and camaraderie.[49] Sihvola described his forty-pupil class that studied subjects like music, English, wood shop, Russian, physics, and physical education, taught by Finnish North Americans, Karelians, and Finns.[50] Vieno Zlobina remembered the role of political upbringing in the classroom, as well as school military training. This included learning to "dismantle a rifle, to throw hand grenades, to shoot, and how to use gasmasks."[51]

In the classroom, North American students often encountered a teaching style much different from what they had been accustomed to. Viola Ranta explained: "I tried to go to school, but nothing came of it. It was such different kind of school-going from what I was used to, that I said to my parents that I will not go there for even a day."[52] Mayme Sevander's personal recollections of childhood in Karelia and her research on the North American migrants, as well as Ol'ga Iliukh's study of Karelian schools in the 1930s, identify rigid textbook learning and the presence of fear as key characteristics of the Karelian Soviet school. Sevander observed:

> In American schools there is a complete absence of inhibition on the part of the child. He feels free to approach the teacher at any time and with any question or request ... This method of learning in the eyes of some Karelian teachers in the Finnish schools of the 1930s turned out to be a detriment. One could hear them complain: "Oh, those American kids! They behave at school as if they were at home." Rigid discipline in the schools mirrored the administrative-command system which permeated every field of Soviet life. Such teacher-pupil relations instilled fear and excluded any initiative on behalf of the student.[53]

Likewise, Iliukha argues: "The pupils' independent judicious reasoning came to be more and more regularly replaced by formal rote-learning of the fundamentals given in textbooks and the main theses of Stalin's works and by citations from them."[54] Furthermore, Iliukha contends, "all literature recommended for reading invoked in children, in one way or another, a sense of danger, anxiety, fragility of the surrounding world, instilled hatred for the hostile encirclement around the country."[55] While curriculum formally became more rigid and focused on indoctrinating a very specific political culture, and often with scare tactics, it must be noted that educational directives from above were applied unevenly and differently by individual teachers in varied parts of the Soviet Union, resulting in a range of classroom experiences.[56]

Barriers

The appeal of an emerging Finnish-language workers' society proved very enticing for many Finns in Canada and the United States who struggled to make their way with limited English-language skills and who had been alienated by the revolutionary movement through increasing

Canadianization/Americanization and the Bolshevization of the communist parties. However, for many of the children of these Finnish speakers, the reality of life in a linguistically Finnish, Karelian, and Russian community proved difficult. "I pretty much learned the Finnish language here," Erwin Niva told interviewer Varpu Lindström.[57] "Of course we spoke some [Finnish]," Niva explained, "but the English language among the children was the main language and here with each other we children always spoke English in the beginning."[58] Mayme Sevander remembered: "We were dismayed to find that our Finglish was worthless here, and we would have to learn Finnish practically all over again."[59]

For school-aged children, the learning was expected to be rapid. With the nationalities policy of the late 1920s and early 1930s, the Soviet government instituted schooling in minority languages, and more than seventy instructional languages were in use in the USSR in the 1930s.[60] By 1931, all of Karelia's 275 schools were operating in the Finnish language.[61] Commenting on her son's progress in school, Terttu Kangas told her sister that Olavi was getting by in everything "but the Finnish reading is very slow for him."[62] Even North Americans training to become teachers in Karelia encountered difficulties with Finnish. Sylvi Hokkanen, who studied at the Karelian Pedagogical Institute recalled, "I knew nothing of Finnish grammar. I had grown up speaking the dialect of Varsinais-Suomi region … Like most dialects it was far from book language. During the course of my studies I was often amazed to learn how the correct way to speak or write Finnish differed from what I had known at home."[63] As Sylvi Hokkanen pointed out, it was one thing to speak Finglish or an old dialect of Finnish in the home setting and another to be expected to complete classes and homework in formal, literary Finnish. Paavo Alatalo, who began school in Petrozavodsk in 1933, echoed Hokkanen's point: "I didn't know anything at all about Finnish language, especially grammar, well, [I knew] the spoken language."[64] However, he continued by saying, "Of course we spoke Finnish at home. We didn't even know anything else."[65] Alatalo's comments point to the precarious linguistic balance that many migrants sustained. Alatalo, for example, had completed five years of English-language schooling in the United States, yet maintained that he "didn't even know anything" other than Finnish. While obviously not speaking literally, Alatalo's choice of words addresses the difficulty of not feeling in full command of either language used in daily life, and the competing pulls of assimilation and tradition that weigh on migrant children.

For children who had already attended English schools in Canada and the United States, being sent to Finnish-language school in the midst of so many other changes to their lives could lead to stress and dissatisfaction.

North American children in Karelia were often placed in grade levels that they had already completed before emigration. Leini Hietala felt her two completed school years in Canada "counted for nothing" in Karelia, as she was put back into the second grade.[66] Mayme Sevander was placed in fourth grade in Karelia, though she had been in grade five at the time of her family's departure from New York.[67] For North American children, being placed in grade levels below their age group and perceived competence was a source of embarrassment. The feelings associated with such academic demotion were further worsened by the resultant physical demarcation of those who did not look to fit into their newly assigned grade. According to Sevander, her brother Paul "was placed in second grade, which he hated; he'd been in fourth grade in New York, and he was head and shoulders taller than the other students."[68] Similarly, Paavo Alatalo found himself thirteen years old in the fourth grade, where most students were between nine and ten years of age. In his memoir, Alatalo wrote: "Bitterly I did my best with [Finnish] grammar. For I had to (!) advance to the fifth grade ... I felt myself to be over-aged."[69] Inserting the parenthesized exclamation point in his life writing sixty-nine years after beginning school in Karelia points to the anxiety that Alatalo likely felt about his position in Karelian school and, indirectly, about his ethnolinguistic identity. Neil Sutherland has found that, in childhood recollections, the "factual core" of what happened tends to be "encapsulated in the feelings that it aroused."[70] Alatalo's long-held exclamation of being held back in school succinctly demonstrates Sutherland's observation. For Allan Sihvola, the shock (also exclamation point worthy) of being placed in the fifth grade for his "imperfect" Finnish, after having completed seven grades in the United States, was eased by placement in a class composed of others his age and primarily foreigners.[71]

In 1937, the Finnish language was banned in schools and local administration. Life in Russian-language school made Finnish North American children's previous struggles with the Finnish language pale in comparison. While some children learned Russian quickly and served as important intermediaries for their parents who had not learned the language, many children struggled with the language policy change.[72] Tight-lipped Leini Hietala summed up her experience of moving to a Russian-language school by saying "it was difficult."[73] When asked if she had known any Russian, Hietala answered: "I did know some, but not as much as [I] should have."[74] Paavo Alatalo began his schooling in the Soviet Union at a Russian school, but felt he lost time in his studies because of his inability to comprehend Russian.[75] Sylvi Hokkanen, who had just begun teaching in a Finnish secondary school, was sent to teach at an all-Russian school in 1937. She did not yet really know Russian, and her students could not understand English or Finnish. "My discipline was terrible," Hokkanen remembered,

> I had several young lads in the class who continually disrupted the whole class. I repeatedly asked the principal to come and oversee my lessons and to help me with discipline, but he never would enter my classroom. I thought it was probably his first job as principal, and he was just as afraid of the kids as I was. On the other hand, perhaps he did not want me teaching there since I was a foreigner.[76]

Hokkanen's description highlights the linguistic difficulties of both students and teachers, the prevalence of improperly trained teachers (imagine how the Russian students would have felt about their English US Finnish teacher) and principals, and growing inter-ethnic tensions.

The difficulties of Karelian life, and particularly repression, impacted many children's educational pathways. Though it is common to think about the twentieth century as a decisive transition from child labour to prolonged schooling in North America, many young people continued to contribute to their family income. Children certainly contributed to family labour in the Soviet Union. Lenin's widow, Nadezhda Krupskaya, wrote about working children on collectivized farms in 1932, reminding the reader that "there are no officials whose job is to protect child labor, and it is exploited inordinately."[77] While *kolkhoz* children were expected to engage in heavy, full-time agricultural work from the age of twelve, Finnish North American children joined the workforce in different occupations and at different ages. Viola Ranta, who struggled with Karelian school, joined the labour force at the age of fourteen as a typist.[78] Erwin Niva, also at the age of fourteen, lost a semester of school due to illness, never returned, and instead became a tractor operator.[79] For families who lost a parent in the political turmoil in the second half of the 1930s, children's labour was essential. At the age of thirteen, after the arrest of his father, Paul Corgan, Mayme's younger brother, supported his family by driving horses at a lumber camp.[80] According to Mayme, "Paul knew he was the man of the family now, and he didn't complain."[81] After the arrest of Frank Heino, Alice, at fifteen, tried to find work to help her family's subsistence, but, as she explained to her brother Viljam, "I'm always told I am too young for heavy work and there isn't any light work."[82] While boys, like Niva and Corgan, found work among Finnish North American men, gendered notions of appropriate work hindered Heino's ability to find work. Some balanced school and work, like Mayme Sevander, who wrote: "Not a day of study occurred after grade school without a full-time job. I worked my way through high school, university and M.A. exams and I'm not an exception."[83]

Children's Leisure

Children's lives in Karelia were quite difficult. North American–raised children struggled with the demands of Finnish education and the unfamiliarity of the Russian language. The critical analysis that had been instilled through their socialist upbringing was unwelcome in the Soviet system, and as time passed, so was their suspicious multi-ethnic identity. Some toiled through school to become the required New Soviet Citizen, while others gave their physical labour to build industrialized socialism in the Karelian woods. Life narratives, however, also offer glimpses of Finnish North American children at play.

The Soviet educational structure closely bound in-school curriculum with extracurricular involvement in children's programming. For children who had participated in the Pioneers in Canada and the United States, continued involvement with the program in Karelia offered the relief of familiarity. For those new to the movement, the Pioneers presented children with an opportunity to become involved in a wide array of educational and fun activities. The Petrozavodsk "Palace of Pioneers" offered children "art, handicraft, visual arts, drama, and chess," as well as checkers.[84] Alice Heino told her brother "I go to lots of places to practice pieces. We have lots of those kinds of groups here that I go to. They teach songs, pieces, and poems. Then when there is some evening program we have to perform. I have already performed many times ... I am in the pioneer organization and I have been given tasks."[85] Alice's tone suggests pride and enjoyment in her involvement in the Pioneers. Commitment to Pioneer work could lead to community recognition. For example, on 23 July 1936, *Punainen Karjala* featured a photo and blurb about young Karelian Pioneer Lilja Sorokina for her "diligence and work ethic."[86] Publicly highlighting children's accomplishments mirrored the adult worker hero culture, as we will see. Such acknowledgments in official newspapers encouraged children to aspire to do their best and perpetuated the manufactured image of happy, thriving youngsters in Soviet Karelia. On a practical level, the Pioneers could offer children security and well-being. For example, acceptance to a Pioneer summer camp could provide a child with a "carefree life" and "three square meals a day," as Mayme Sevander described it[87] – both very appealing to families experiencing increasingly difficult times as the 1930s progressed.

In January 1933, twelve-year-old Arte Heino died from pneumonia. Looking through the tragedy of a lost son, Justiina Heino's 25 January

1933 letter to son Waino (Väinö) in the United States depicts the active life of children in Karelia. Justiina wrote: "The children got a day off school on the first of January and then for two days they had a ski competition. On the final day he came home in the evening with a real chill so he went with father to warm up [presumably in a communal sauna]. He had gotten sweaty and then didn't come home but went to the cafeteria from there and still to a friend's place from there. Only around 9 in the evening did he return home."[88]

Justiina's description of Arte's final day of play succeeds in painting an image of a day in the life of a child and Karelian life more generally. Contrasting with the rigid inculcation of schedule, regiment, and punctuality undertaken in Soviet school and Pioneers,[89] the statement speaks to the relative freedom children enjoyed. Arte seems to have spent the day in the company of friends, engaged in school and, likely, Pioneer-sanctioned athletics, briefly returning home and going to the sauna with his father, before heading out again for leisure activities.

Arte's mobility was common to other Finnish North American children as well. In one short letter, Alice Heino told her brother about her involvement in various community activities, her visits to see the "kino" or movie shows, skating, and skiing.[90] In another, she told of hanging around the house with nightly visiting youth, listening to the phonograph, and about attending programs and dances at the Cultural Hall.[91] Mayme Sevander recalled that at the age of thirteen, "I was old enough to go out alone now" to participate with friends in various social and cultural events.[92] In Mayme's and Alice's cases, it is worth pointing out that they were permitted to go off alone, without explicit gendered limitations on what girls could do. Older children were enabled to move through their towns without adult supervision, gaining a first-hand understanding of the social and cultural engagements and clashes occurring across the region.

Other Children

In the streets, at school, and at community groups, Finnish North American children came into contact with local Karelian and Russian children, and the children of Red Finn émigrés. In *A Grave in Karelia*, Ernesti Komulainen provides a vivid description of children at play in Kondopoga:

> Kids were sledding ... Nikolai observed the colourful group as he sat on his trunk. Some of them were American or Canadian Finns; he could pick them out easily from the others by their good clothes and loud voices and

the English language that they used in their play. He could also tell which children had come from Finland because their clothes were of Finnish make, and their spoken Finnish was clearer than that of the American children. They, like the Russian and Karelian children, looked cold and malnourished. The Russian and Karelian kids were wearing padded jackets. All of them were trying to be cheerful and to enjoy the sledding, each clamouring in his or her language, although some of them were shivering and runny-nosed.[93]

Komulainen's portrayal raises some important considerations. While the children were all playing on the same hill, they were, nonetheless, separate, divided by language and appearance. Komulainen showed North American children playing in English, with their Finnish language less "clear" than that of the Finns. Unlike the Finns, Russians, and Karelians, who looked "cold and malnourished," the North American children had "good clothes" and exhibited health in their "loud voices." Given the broader context of Karelian life, the notion of "all of them trying to be cheerful" is striking.

Perhaps tensions between children of different backgrounds made sharing play space difficult. Red Finn child Kyllikki Joganson remembered that between Finnish-speaking children (Red Finns, North Americans, and Karelians) and Russian children, "dealings with them almost never happened."[94] Irina Takala, whose work has provided important findings on the inter-ethnic relations of adults, has acknowledged that "relationships among children were also not very simple."[95] In the schoolyard, Russian children taunted Finns with "finka-blinka" and Finnish children retaliated with "russkii pusskii."[96] Other encounters had darker undertones. Takala's interviews with Paul Corgan revealed fear and bullying based on ethno-linguistic differences.[97] In some cases, though, children interacted together productively. Paavo Alatalo learned to speak Russian through mixed ski competitions and Pioneer events.[98] Whether children approached each other positively or with disdain, a clear line separated Finnish North American children from the others.

As Komulainen's description of children sledding illustrated, Finnish North American children stood out among others for their higher-quality clothes and, as we have seen in the last chapter, overall well-being, thanks to their privileged access to special foods and supplies. Local children often stood out in sharp contrast. Lauri Hokkanen was moved by the health and lives of Karelian and Russian children. He described a visit to the home of a Karelian single mother and observed the health of her children, stating, "They just got to me. I will never forget them."[99] Though Finnish North American adults recognized the plight of local children, materials from the 1930s, and, perhaps more surprisingly, retrospective sources do not connect what they see with the wider context of Soviet conditions. Lauri Hokkanen, in a brief mention of the apprentices at the ski factory, explained: "At first I thought they were only about twelve or thirteen years old, but I was told that none of them were under sixteen. They were small because they had been born during really hard times and hadn't gotten enough food for growth."[100]

"Really hard times" seems to do little justice to the facts, considering that in the famine year of 1921, when these apprentices would have been about two years old, 90 to 95 per cent of children under the age of three died.[101] Likewise, the mass arrival of the Finnish North Americans also coincided with a surge in the number of street children in the USSR. Following the Civil War, Soviet Russia was left with millions of homeless children,[102] but the period of 1932–34 saw another increase caused by forced collectivization, dekulakization, and the famine of 1932–33.[103] The known horrendous living conditions of these devastated children, as evidenced in official inspections of "Children's Homes" shows a significant disparity in the lives and health of Home inhabitants and Finnish North American children.[104] Hokkanen does not demonstrate an awareness of broader Soviet children's experiences, even though writing almost sixty years later.

Local, non-Finnish children took on symbolic significance for Lauri Hokkanen in writing the experiences of his life in Karelia. His description of an "expeditor from the lumber camp" serves as a poignant example: "we found him sitting at the table chewing away on a chicken with several children watching. I could see the kids were hungry and undernourished, but the fat slob ignored them and continued to crunch away, grease dripping down his chin. It was a depressing sight and we were glad to get out of there."[105] Although it is difficult to ascertain to what extent Hokkanen would have been influenced by Soviet characterizations of the bourgeois enemy and his own North American socialist upbringing in the class struggle, his vivid imagery can be analyzed in the wider context of 1930s Soviet discourse. The "fat slob" is a familiar representation of the class enemy, while the children can be seen as portrayals of the tragedy of Russian backwardness and the inspiration for the construction of a new Soviet social order. The image evoked by Hokkanen highlights the distance between the reality of life for many of "Stalin's children" and the ideal of the proud, committed, and healthy Pioneer. In Lisa Kirschenbaum's words, "the clearest symbol of the Stalinist Revolution's success became the beaming faces of Soviet youngsters. The policy of making childhood (appear) happy had at least as much to do with the state's need for disciplined and devoted communists as with the best interests of children."[106]

Conclusion

When asked if her childhood in Karelia was pleasant, Leini Hietala replied, "Well, I don't know, you had to get used to it whether it was pleasant or not."[107] Hietala's response suggests that life for "Karelia's Golden Fund" was a marked change from earlier days in Canada and the United States, and reveals a mix of ambivalent emotions about migration, schooling, communist training, work, play, and their privileged place in the region's ethnic contestations. US socialist pedagogue Jeanette D. Pearl wrote in 1911: "make no mistake, children of 10 and over know much of the sadness and sorrow of life which this system of capitalist exploitation inflicts upon them. Our children are the workers' children; and they have imbibed the suffering and privation of the working class with their mothers' milk."[108] In North America and in Karelia, these children symbolized the new social order. Yet, in their upbringing and experiences in Karelia they carried the burden of an adult movement's clash between ideals and practice. Beginning the work of uncovering the experiences of Finnish North American children in Karelia contributes to a greater understanding of the joys and struggles, and broader social, cultural, and political workings of Autonomous Finnish Karelia in the Soviet project.

Chapter Five

"Isn't It a Different Land, This Sickle and Hammer Land?": Working in Soviet Karelia

Karl Berg enthusiastically described to his daughter how good life was in Karelia in October 1932, emphasizing the availability of work and the rights of workers. Berg concluded by rhetorically asking, "isn't it a different land, this sickle and hammer land?"[1] With regard to working experiences, most Finnish North Americans in Karelia would likely have agreed that the USSR was indeed a "different land." Since the migrants had come to *build* a workers' state, the hours committed to formal state labour were integral to forming their sense of place, purpose, and perceptions of life in Karelia. Examining the theme of work through letter and memoir narratives provides unique, bottom-up insights on the region's economy, industry, and workforce. Narratives about work inform us of social relations in Karelia and enrich our understanding of what it was like to be engaged with the great socialist project.

Most Finnish migrants in North America came from an agricultural background. Many continued to pursue farming – or at least dreamed of one day owning their own farm – but wage work became the standard occupational category for Finns and Finnish descendants in early twentieth-century Canada and the United States. The paid labour of Finnish migrants, like so many others, can be summarized as insecure, seasonal, piece-rate, and strenuous. Finnish men found employment primarily in lumbering, mining, freight handling, and factory production. The families whose experiences are represented in the Karelian life writing demonstrate the typical challenges that faced Finnish migrant families, including the ongoing search for secure employment. Oscar Corgan's work in a coal mine and on the railroad ignited his passion for workers' rights, which eventually led him to leadership roles in the Finnish migrant press, cooperatives, and Karelian Technical Aid.[2] Klaus Maunu's father worked in logging and cleared land at Pike Lake, Ontario, for a family subsistence farm.[3] Paavo Alatalo's father tried his hand at farming on the outskirts of Warren, Ohio, but ultimately moved the family to town so he could work at an iron mill and take on other short-term wage work in the Cleveland area.[4] Allan Sihvola's father also worked at the Trumbull Steel Factory in Warren, Ohio, which significantly reduced wages in 1929.[5] In 1932, the company was forced to shut down half of its operations. Sihvola remembered that the company's management was so "forward thinking" that, instead of completely eliminating workers, they doubled up positions and split the wage in half.[6] The union protested the drop in wages and staged an unsuccessful strike – teenaged Sihvola among the picketers – which left the strikers unemployed. Before moving to Karelia, Elis Ranta worked at a Pennsylvania iron mill for ten years, where the hard, hot work had begun to take a toll on his health.[7] With the economic depression, his hours were reduced to only two to three days per week, and the family struggled to make ends meet. Without a secure job in sight, young Lauri Hokkanen had worked on lake freighters, at lumber camps, and sawmills in Michigan's Upper Peninsula, developing his mechanical skills.[8] Finnish women typically found secure employment more easily than men – though poorly compensated and little less strenuous – as domestic servants, in the service industry, or as cooks and laundresses at work camps.[9] Paavo Alatalo's mother, for example, worked as a domestic servant for three dollars a day.[10] Many other women stayed at home to care for their families, leaving the few available jobs open for men and single individuals.[11] Finnish migrants in Canada and the United States gained experience in many different industries through their ongoing search for secure employment and fair wages and treatment. Such labour experience, paired with their experience in workers' movements, attracted Karelian planners in the Soviet Union.

North American Skills and Karelian Projects

Finnish North Americans found work at many sites in the vast Karelian territory, which spanned over 800 kilometres from the Finnish agricultural commune Säde near Lake Ladoga in the south to work settlements above the Arctic Circle, near Kandalaksha (Kantalahti) Gulf on the White Sea. The Murmansk Railway and the White Sea Canal, both within Karelian borders, provide two examples of significant labour projects that brought thousands into the area, garnered national and international attention, and also resulted in appalling numbers of fatalities. Finnish North Americans' contribution to Karelia's economic development, however, was made primarily in the lumber industry, construction, agriculture, and general mechanics.

Finnish North Americans were invited to Karelia foremost to harvest the region's "green gold." Timber was viewed as Karelia's way forward from backwoods periphery to a modern, industrial economy.[12] The northwestern region of the Soviet Union, which included Karelia and the Leningrad district, accounted for half of the nation's forests and the reserves had been largely unexploited.[13] A shortage of workers, especially in the north, had been the primary impediment to developing the regional timber industry. Finnish North Americans were recruited to fell forests, transport logs, float them in the spring, and work in sawmill operations. Over 60 per cent of the migrants worked in Karelia's lumber industry.[14] The Petrozavodsk area had many successful lumber camps that employed Finns almost exclusively, including Matrosy (Matroosa), Vilga, and Lososinnoye (Lososiina).[15] The Kangas family was based at the Lohijärvi camp, near the village of Lososinnoye, where Antti and his sons worked in the lumber industry, which included building ice roads for lumber transportation. Fifty-five kilometres farther north, along the shore of Lake Onega, the town of Kondopoga (Kontupohja) served as a hub for surrounding lumber camps, with its paper mill and hydroelectric plant. Small lumber camps were also scattered throughout the Karelian territory, along its many lakes and rivers. Uhtua and Kem were two additional centres supporting Finnish North Americans working in the north. The Hokkanens and Hirvonens first worked at Vonganperä commune, outside of Uhtua.

Finnish North Americans were encouraged to bring tools with them and to donate money to the Machine Fund. In Karelia, the migrants' tools, like "Finnish axes" and "Swedish saws,"[16] were renamed and rebranded in the socialist fashion.[17] For example, the Caterpillar bulldozer used for hauling logs was renamed "Stalinets." Foreign tools offered the possibility of significant production increases.[18] Autio-Sarasmo argues that "one Canadian lumberjack cut down a tree in just half the time required by two local lumberjacks. The Canadian lumberjack used a frame saw and a Canadian axe whereas the local workers used Russian saws and axes."[19] Golubev and Takala have also found impressive results: a Canadian lumberjack could cut an average of 12 cubic feet of harvested wood per day compared with the meagre 3 cubic feet cut by lumberjacks from other regions in the Soviet Union.[20] The migrants also donated trucks and tractors that were used to facilitate the transportation of lumber. These technologies and techniques were disseminated by touring experts who visited lumber camps and through the establishment of model camps, like "Internationale" in Matrosy. Interestingly, while contemporary literature tended to refer to all Finnish North Americans as "Finnish Americans," lumber expertise and technology were typically labelled "Canadian."

In addition to lumber exports, Karelia used some of its timber for manufacturing and processing. In the first half of the 1930s, employees of the Kondopoga Pulp and Paper Factory were primarily Finns. Frank Heino was among the Finnish North Americans working there. In Petrozavodsk, the Ski Factory was another largely Finnish operation, with Finns representing 60 per cent of the 500 employees.[21] The Ski Factory had the reputation of being the most productive ski manufacturer in all of the Soviet Union.[22] In the mid-1930s, the factory began to also manufacture furniture. Among the studied life writers, Lisi Hirvonen, Lauri Hokkanen, and Elis Ranta were employed by the Ski Factory. The capital was also home to the large Onega Metallurgic Factory. Finnish North Americans not only worked at the factories, but they had played a significant role in building the operations, going back to the late 1920s.[23]

Finnish North Americans established agricultural communes, most famously Säde and Hiilisuo, which were to produce feed for the 10,500 horses used in the lumber industry and to help alleviate reliance on food imports to the region.[24] Hiilisuo, just outside of Petrozavodsk, became an experimental and educational farm in 1933. In 1933–4, Finnish North Americans were also recruited to contribute to the Karelian fishery on the White Sea and the region's large lakes.[25] To accompany the front-line extraction and production of the lumber camps, factories, and farms, approximately 30 per cent of Finnish North Americans worked in the construction industry.[26] Many also worked building roads and other infrastructure, and on electricity and telephone lines. The available letters and memoirs collectively highlight work in several of these fields.

Working in a Workers' State

Describing just how different life was in the USSR, Karl Berg wrote: "Work is free[.] There is no *Paasia* [boss][.] Workers choose always from amongst themselves a capable leader only they work just the same as others and if we notice some defects then they are always discussed."[27] Berg exemplifies how letter writers were eager to point to the positive qualities of working in a communist state, and to draw a contrast between labour in the Soviet Union and labour in depression-stricken, capitalist North America. The writers emphasized the availability of work, the equality of workers, and access to paid sick leave and vacation. These issues were well familiar to the Finnish North American labour and leftist movement, and many of the migrants had fought for those very rights in the United States and Canada. Unemployment, paltry wages, and poor working conditions were a significant concern in Finnish socialist circles and media. Enoch Nelson explained to his brother Arvid that "I have learned a new way of living out here that is different from the way we used to live in [A]merica and that is that what I earn I spend because I have no reason to save up for hard times or sickness in the family as they are all free of charge in all cases."[28] He elaborated, stating, "Everybody who has money, and every one that works has money, and everyone has a chance to work, has learned the same form of living as I have that it is useless to save money and they spend it as they get it."[29]

The letter writers often referred to the availability of work. For example, Aate Pitkänen wrote to his parents in late 1933: "Yes work there is enough, don't have to worry at least about unemployment."[30] Likewise, Karl Berg explained to his daughter that you did not have to "fear that the work will end."[31] The letter writers wrote even more often about workers' benefits in the Soviet Union. If a worker fell ill, they had access to free health care and paid sick leave. Lisi Hirvonen explained to her sister that "here are free doctors and hospitals and you get wages during your sick leave."[32] Some workers got sent to health sanatoriums, without expense. Enoch Nelson boasted that the sanatorium where he had stayed "has been equipped with a lot of the latest form of electrical and other medical apparatus [sic] and can take care of a thousand workers at a time. There are a dozen doctors with there [sic] staff of nurses and other personel [sic] on the place to take care of the people that come there and all the care is given free of charge to the workers and peasants of the Soviet Union."[33] Kalle Korhonen summed up the importance of paid sick leave in 1937, stating that with it sickness doesn't "feel so heavy."[34] To provide sufficient rest for workers, paid vacations were also provided. In an earlier letter, from 1935, Korhonen exclaimed, with his typical communist zeal, that "In capitalist countries workers do not get a month vacation with full pay but for us IN THE SOVIET UNION IT IS SECURED FOR EVERY WORKER."[35] Terttu Kangas explained in 1934 that vacation pay was calculated by what one had earned in the three months prior.[36] Therefore, she told her sister that her husband Antti had been on a month-long vacation and "so yes it suited him to be on vacation when every day came over 22 rubles ... of pay."[37]

These references to the availability of work, the equality of labour, and state-covered health care, sick leave, and vacation served two main functions: one personal and one social. To the family and friends on the receiving end of the letter, such mentions acted as assurances that the emigrant was personally secure in employment and well supported in their new home. These descriptions further reflect the critical role of procuring stable work in migrant and working-class life. The emphasis on the positive qualities of work in the USSR also served as social reinforcements of the success of the Karelian project, specifically, and the Communist project, overall. Guarantees of employment, health care, and vacation strengthened networks of chain migration to Karelia. These assurances signalled that the North American recruiters had told the truth, and that Canadian and US Finns were better off in Karelia.

Employment and benefits for all also symbolized the success of the revolution. Enoch Nelson's letters characterize the commitment to collective endeavour and show how he took his role in the completion of the Five Year Plan to heart. Believing that the Five Year Plan would be achieved ahead of schedule, Enoch noted that "everybody talks only about getting the plan fulfilled and after this plan has been made there is a noticeable increase in the amount of work that a person does."[38] The Finnish North American letter writers echoed the official vision of work in the USSR. "Work under Soviet conditions," as summarized by Sheila Fitzpatrick, "was regarded as a transformative experience because it was collective and imbued with a sense of purpose. Under the old regime, work had been an exhausting, soul-destroying chore; under socialism, it was the thing that filled life with meaning."[39] The old regime, as described above, also easily applies to labour as it had been known in North America. The attainment of worker equality and universal health care, and the elimination of unemployment in the Soviet Union, as depicted in the Karelian letters, encouraged their recipients – and, thereby, the Finnish North American Left – to keep up their struggle for workers' rights. Though emphasizing the positives of work in the Soviet Union for the benefit of their correspondents and to further justify their commitment to the building of socialism, the letters and memoirs also reveal that working life was fraught with continuous negotiations and fluctuations.

"Change Refreshes"

When Finnish North Americans landed in the Soviet Union, they were quickly "commanded" to a worksite by the Karelian Resettlement Agency. There was plenty of work to be done to build the necessary infrastructure to develop the region and to meet the centre's productivity requirements. Enoch Nelson, writing from Petrozavodsk, told his brother in July 1930 that "I have been changing jobs so often this year that I have also had several places of residence."[40] While some people stayed at the same job for extended periods of time, one is struck by how often a change of work is noted in the Karelian life writing. The early phase of migration was especially characterized by a succession of jobs, often accompanied by a change in residence. Some of these transfers were ordered by the administration; others were self-propelled in hopes of finding more satisfactory work and living conditions; and others, particularly after 1937, were forced by repression, fear, and, then, war.

Lisi Hirvonen's letters to her sister Anna demonstrate the impact of each of these factors. Upon arrival in 1932, Lisi Hirvonen and her spouse Eino Hirvonen were sent on assignment to the Vonganperä camp. While Eino worked in the forest, Lisi reported, "I have been busy doing many different duties picking berries cleaning fish gathering mosses digging up potatoes and many other little jobs."[41] Four months later, Lisi Hirvonen reported that she was "still" working in the laundry.[42] These jobs in Vonganperä were likely all officially delegated. However, self-interest was culminating in yet another change. In the same February 1933 letter, Lisi told her sister that "Eino and I have been here thinking of putting in an application for a town in the spring this place is a bit too far from the railway and too cold in winter I don't know if it will happen."[43] Lisi's next letter, dated 20 April, came from Petrozavodsk, showing that their move had been accepted and happened quickly.[44] In Petrozavodsk, Lisi had happily secured work at the Ski Factory, remarking "I have always wanted [to work in] a factory."[45] Eino, at first, worked at a construction site but changed work again in September 1933, this time finding employment with the touring Finnish National Theatre.[46] Based on the available letters, Lisi Hirvonen stayed on at the Ski Factory until at least February 1938, when she reported that "I'm still in the same job as before and living in the same place" – albeit on her own, having separated from Eino Hirvonen around 1935.[47] However, by September 1938, with the region in upheaval due to repression, and for reasons unknown, Lisi had left the capital area and was unemployed.[48] In the fall of 1938, she returned to a lumber camp for forestry work for some months.[49] Lisi Hirvonen's final available letter, dated 19 July 1939, revealed that she was again back in Petrozavodsk, working at the Ski Factory.[50] Following Lisi Hirvonen's employment throughout her time in Karelia illustrates frequent changes of work, typical of the Finnish North American experience in Karelia. Whether compelled by personal reasons or state-directed transfers, Lisi twice explained the recurrent moves with humour, simply stating, "change refreshes."[51]

The Hokkanen's work history likewise exemplifies the whirlwind of formal work assignments that migrants could encounter. During their first two months in Karelia, in the summer of 1934, Lauri Hokkanen was moved to six different jobs, which can be traced through his memoir.[52] Lauri and Sylvi were first sent to the Vonganperä lumber camp, where Lauri was charged with trimming tree tops at ten kopeks per top, leaving his "hands full of blisters." Next, he was sent to Kannussuo lumber camp, some 10 kilometres away, to make shingles. A few weeks later,

Figure 10 Women working at the Karelian Ski Factory in Petrozavodsk in the early 1930s (photo courtesy of the Karelian Research Centre Russian Academy of Sciences).

Lauri made hay in a five-man team. From there, he was sent to Sakura Järvi camp to drag and float logs. Soon, back in Kannussuo, he was making bricks. Finally, he ended the summer by dismantling a sawmill in Uhtua, then transporting and rebuilding it in Kannussuo. Sylvi Hokkanen also experienced many different odd jobs in their first months in Karelia. Sylvi realized: "Having never done anything but attend school and then teach, I was ill-prepared for any of the work that needed doing at the lumber camps."[53] In Vonganperä, Sylvi was at first without work and left alone when Lauri was sent for shingle and hay work. Sylvi secured a position at Sakura Järvi with Lauri, where she worked as camp cook.[54] Sylvi again followed Lauri to Kannussuo, where first she picked moss for caulking, and then joined in the brickmaking operation.[55] Her assignment was riding a horse around in circles, hour after hour, to mix the clay. Thinking back on her work, Sylvi remembered: "None of these jobs made me feel very important, but at least I was doing something."[56] In the midst of the quick succession of assigned jobs, the Hokkanens arranged a move to Petrozavodsk.[57] In the fall, Sylvi enrolled in the Karelian Pedagogical Institute and Lauri was reassigned to the Ski Factory shortly after.

It must be noted that the history of Finns in North America in the twentieth century also offers abundant examples of chasing work, better wages, and more hospitable working and living conditions.[58] However, moving in the Soviet Union was not meant to be so free. The Soviet government enacted state-wide passportization in 1932, in effect binding individuals to a particular village or town and workplace, and determining access to goods.[59] The internal passport was intended to control people's movement, taking pressure off housing demand and ensuring labourers for each project. Golubev and Takala have discussed how North Americans in Karelia had the formal right to change jobs, but that it was very difficult to do so.[60] However, the available letters and memoirs paint a different picture. The narratives suggest that changing locales and workplaces did require official permission but that Finnish North Americans had little trouble obtaining desired posts. The main insight into how this process may have worked comes from Lauri Hokkanen's memoir. The Hokkanens wanted to move into the city so that Sylvi could attend teachers' college and Lauri could focus on "mechanical and metal work."[61] Their strategy was to send Sylvi ahead to register for school, which was a formally acceptable move, and to use a friend at the Ski Factory to sell the director on Lauri's auto mechanics and sawmill expertise. Apparently, though, it was Lauri's musical – rather than mechanical – skills that ultimately helped him obtain a transfer.

"I learned later," Lauri recalled, "that Laine, the fellow from the ski factory band, had approached Kustaa Rovio, secretary of the Karelian Communist Party, and asked to have me transferred to the ski factory. Hearing that I had already been sent up north to the lumber camps, Rovio had first said it was too late and why hadn't I been sent to Petrozavodsk in the first place. But later he relented and went along with the plan."[62] If Lauri's explanation of how the transfer came to be can be taken at face value, it implies that, in the close-knit Finnish North American community, personal connections could be used to influence the system. Regardless of whether one had the connections or not, Karelia had a severe labour shortage and Finnish North Americans were viewed as the most desirable workers, classified as "foreign experts," whether their experience actually merited such a title or not. As we have seen, Finnish North Americans were in a privileged social category in the region in the first half of the 1930s, which seems to have also manifested in a freedom of movement not necessarily afforded to others. The Finnish Karelian leadership was desperate to retain its foreign workforce and likely "went along with the plan" on more than one occasion. Finally, throughout the Soviet Union, the passport and registration system was "notoriously inefficient," and knowledge of how to manoeuvre around formalities was a part of Soviet life.[63]

Implementing Know-How

Adaptation to Soviet conditions is evident in descriptions of everyday work experiences. An excellent example comes from the letters of Aate Pitkänen. For much of his time in Karelia, Pitkänen worked as a telephone cable linesman. In late 1934, he detailed the kinds of work he engaged in on a daily basis. Working with one other "kid" in Petrozavodsk, he explained:

> We're supposed to be the cable splicers but when there is no splicing, that is, when there is no breaks or new cables to be put in we do almost anything; clean manholes, install phones, tear others down, pull lines, somethings [sic] we're carpenters and blacksmith. If there is cable work we dig our own canals, set our own poles, ring, splice and wipe the joints, and of course we get hell for everything too. While in other places there is different gangs for all the different jobs. We have no truck to take our tools around. Last year we had a two wheeled wheel barrow we were hauling poles with it one day and it fell apart. It could have been fixed but it didn't happen to be ours and the owner took it away. So now when we start on a job in the morning we have everything on our backs all the way from pliers, torches and magnets to shovels, saws, crow bars and cable rolls.[64]

Pitkänen's description illustrates what his job entailed and reveals a great deal about Karelian conditions. For example, Pitkänen explains how he was responsible for the whole of cable work, whereas "in other places there is different gangs for all the different jobs." This point addresses the serious labour shortage in Karelia overall and the difficulty in finding qualified workers for technological jobs. Pitkänen offered a listing of the tools he used at work, giving a sense of what was available locally. Finally, that Pitkänen and his co-worker had to carry their tools on their backs, without even the use of a borrowed wheelbarrow, points to the makeshift nature of Karelian life and work. Not only was his job all-encompassing and haphazard, Aate Pitkänen, in another letter, complained that he was very cold during the winter when working down in manholes or up on

Figure 11 Soviet technology at work building roads in Karelia (*Neuvosto-Karjalan 15-vuotiaan taipaleelta*, 660).

poles.⁶⁵ Knowing the scarcity of clothing and the extreme Karelian temperatures, one can imagine how outdoor work must have felt.

The letter writers and memoirists show us how work in Karelia was characterized by both entry into previously unknown fields with makeshift tools and practices, and the application of past experience and Western technology. For example, in May 1930, Enoch Nelson was building a highway to connect the towns of Uhtua and Kem, improving the transportation of lumber to the White Sea. He told his sister Ida that "we have been given ... order to fulfill to have this highway open for automobile traffic at the end of the summer. This is the first time in my life that I have been working on roadwork but my duties here are to keep the machinery going."⁶⁶ Enoch Nelson, in this case, applied his previous mechanical skills to a new field of work. Aate Pitkänen, as described above, made the best of what was available to him to perform his job. North American know-how was a vital element of Karelian development. In the late 1920s and early 1930s, the Soviet Union was very interested in adopting Western technology and labour practices. Foreign workers were essential to the transfer of this knowledge.⁶⁷ In Karelia, many jobs involved using innovation and knowledge gained from North American work experience. Reino Kero's foundational work, fittingly subtitled *North American Finns as Bringers of Technology in 1930s Soviet Karelia*, details how North American saws, axes, and trucks, especially, were viewed as the key to modernizing and rationalizing the Karelian lumber industry.[68] The Finnish North American lumber camp Internationale, arranged in the "Canadian way," became a Soviet model worksite of national importance.[69] In other fields, North Americans also provided new technologies and methods. For example, Aate Pitkänen described visiting his father's Karelian work camp, where the men had made their own shingle mill using a "new technique."[70] Finnish North Americans could ask friends and relatives to send manuals and information from Canada or the United States, like Pitkänen did at the end of 1934, requesting books on telephone cable work.[71] This transnational flow of information furthered technological development in Karelia. For their part in developing Karelian industry and infrastructure, Finnish North Americans were often rewarded.

Worker Heroes

In the Soviet Union's all-out drive for industrialization and modernization, production quotas were continually raised. Workers were expected to take responsibility for their share in the building of socialism. Those who proved able to consistently meet and exceed labour requirements and embodied the Soviet work ethos were praised and rewarded as heroes. Conversely, those who did not meet goals were shamed and their rations downgraded.[72] To meet the ambitious objectives of the First Five Year Plan, which included astronomical increases in iron, steel, coal, and power production, along with the collectivization of agriculture and the construction of both industrial and residential infrastructure, "Shock Work" became the preferred method. High labour output goals were set for work brigades to fulfil at a rapid pace.[73] The most successful and accomplished workers were endowed with the title of "Shock Worker" (*Udarnik* in Russian, *Iskuri* in Finnish) and represented the idealized labourer. Central administration and localized managers used the honour to fuel "socialist competition" or challenges between work brigades to see who could achieve the highest productivity. In the summer of 1935, miner Alexei Stakhanov's record-breaking labour output propelled him to celebrity status and changed the nature – and name – of hero workers in the Soviet Union. The resulting Stakhanovite Movement publicized exemplary workers and used them to further propagate the image of Soviet culture and advancement.[74] Shock workers and Stakhanovites came to represent a privileged class in the Soviet social system.

North American Finns, as a result of their "foreign expert" status, were already at the top of the Karelian social hierarchy. Their special social position paired with past work experience and culturally scripted devotion to hard work further elevated many of the migrants to the top ranks of the labour force. In the early 1930s, Finnish North Americans, to the disapproval of many in the local population, served as foremen and managers on several of the job sites in the region. Additionally, Canadians and Americans were frequently honoured with Shock Worker or Stakhanovite status. At least four of the studied life writers were granted these work titles and awards. Aate Pitkänen mentions the "Iskuri" prize of fifty rubles he was awarded at the Revolution celebration in November 1933.[75] Antti Kangas's work brigade in the Lohijärvi lumber camp won a Shock Worker prize in 1934.[76] Lisi Hirvonen's work at the Petrozavodsk Ski Factory earned her an all-expenses paid (plus wages) women Shock Worker's trip to Leningrad in March 1935.[77] Hirvonen was a part of a forty-person regional delegation of prized workers who enjoyed their time away from work by visiting palaces, factories, churches, the circus, and an art museum. The perks of her status continued in Karelia. During the revolutionary celebrations of 1935, in the midst of Stakhanovite excitement in the Soviet Union, Hirvonen refers to a "great party for us shock workers at the ski factory" and another occasion when the "shock workers" were treated to an all-night cultural event, which included a play, concert, and dance.[78] In the same year, 1935, Lauri Hokkanen was also honoured as a Stakhanovist for his work at the Ski Factory, for which he received monetary bonuses, praise, and his photo in the newspaper.[79] Although their social status was elevated with the title of shock worker or Stakhanovite, none of these Finnish North Americans emphasized their difference in their life writing. This is fitting with the broader Soviet trend, as identified by Sheila Fitzpatrick: "Nobody who had privilege in the Soviet Union in the 1930s seems to have thought of himself as a member of a privileged upper class."[80] The position of Finnish North Americans in Karelia, however, did not go unnoticed by others in the region.

Working with "Others"

Irina Takala's research demonstrates the "big difference in cultural priorities and value orientation between urbanized North Americans and the people of poor rustic Karelia."[81] This gulf can be clearly seen with regard to workplace interactions and perceived differences in work ethics. In the early 1930s, the Soviet Union pronounced its "civilizing mission" to bring the vast nation "Out of Backwardness."[82] The Red Finn leadership and many in the Finnish North American migration also believed their task to be the culturing and modernizing of Karelia. Bringing new tools and methods, the Finnish Canadians and Americans saw their part in Karelia as crucially important, as exemplified by Mayme Sevander: "The Finns had brought more than machinery and equipment with them; they had also brought knowledge and culture."[83] Sevander noted that Finns in 1930s Petrozavodsk "didn't mix much with the Russian-speaking natives, other than to help them in their work."[84] In Sevander's portrayal of inter-ethnic relations, then, it is possible to see how Finnish North Americans perceived their role in Karelia as educators of the local population. When working on highway construction inland from Kem, Enoch Nelson noted the problems caused by novice "tractorists": "My job would not be very hard if we had some American tractorists on the job but we have to use men who have never seen a tractor as tractorist. This makes the job important."[85] Though not explicitly belittling the skills of the non-American workers, Nelson's statement emphasizes the commonly held belief of North American migrants that their know-how was superior and essential, and that their work with others in the region was inherently "important." In his scathing criticism of life in Karelia, V. Suomela perpetuated attitudes about the differences between Russian and Finnish work ethics. Complaining about the labour laws, he noted that, while they were unnecessary and demeaning for foreign workers, "maybe those kinds of laws are needed for Russians, who are not willing to do work."[86] Finnish North Americans shared with other foreign workers in the Soviet Union the rewarding feeling of being needed and of being glorified as skilled workers.[87] Lauri Hokkanen, who worked primarily with other Finns, remembered that "anything you did was noticed and appreciated, and we were all proud of what we had been able to accomplish."[88] North American Finns had passionately upheld workers' rights in Finland, Canada, and the United States and took pride in their self-ascribed dedication to hard work. By accepting the perks that accompanied their (often self-) proclaimed status as exemplary workers, however, the foreigners created a division between them and other local workers. Sevander explained that "though the Finns tried to teach the Russians their skills and shared their tools, the two cultures didn't mix well. The Russians weren't always receptive to having immigrants tell them how to improve their country, and most of the Finns didn't make an effort to assimilate."[89]

Aggravating relations was the fact that Finnish North Americans earned much higher wages than Karelians and Russians. For example, Sylvi Hokkanen, as a teacher, earned four times the average local wages, and Lauri, as a Ski Factory foreman, earned double average wages.[90] Though the Hokkanens were both employed in skilled work, even North Americans without qualifications automatically received higher pay.[91] Such inequalities led to the resentment of the foreigners and – at times – indifference to work quality and output.[92] As a further consequence, local workers were often unwilling to take direction from North Americans or to adopt new work methods or technologies.[93] In a vicious cycle, such resentment, in turn, made many North Americans view local Russians and Karelians as poor workers and "backwards."[94] As a result, Karelia was ethnically stratified, with Finnish North Americans forming an insular community. Inter-ethnic interaction was largely limited to the workplace.

One group of labourers in Karelia is noticeably absent in the Finnish North American narratives. At the beginning of 1931, Karelia had over 70,000 forced or prisoner labourers, who accounted for a significant percentage of the region's productivity, especially the building of the Murmansk Railway, the White Sea–Baltic Canal, and in lumbering.[95] In 1934, Suomela wrote about the prisoners in Karelia, noting that they were transported in Petrozavodsk "like animals" but "with the difference that beasts' mouths cannot be shut like these miserables. Quietly, depressed, half-naked, wrapped in sacks and rags, men, women, old grey-haireds, [as well as] young, school-aged."[96] Though Suomela's description suggests the prisoners posed little threat, Nick Baron found evidence that other inhabitants in the region feared their presence. An August 1930 report from the Medvezhyegorsk District, 200 kilometres north of Petrozavodsk, "stated that camp inmates were roaming freely throughout the district, wreaking havoc and terrifying the local population to such an extent that citizens were too frightened even to collect berries and mushrooms in the forest."[97] The only mention of these labourers in the studied letters and memoirs comes from Karl Berg. In his glowing endorsement of life in Karelia, Karl states, "No here there is no *vanki* [prisoner] labour except in the case that you do something bad and end up in jail but that is your own fault."[98] Concluding that doing "something bad" was "your own fault," Berg echoed formal Soviet attitudes towards the numerous *kulaks*, and even "saboteur" engineers and specialists,[99] who were sentenced to work in the region's prison camps, including Medvezhyegorsk and Belomorsk. Only a few years after Karl Berg wrote about the prisoners, many Finnish North Americans became personally acquainted with work in the prison camps.

Gender at Work

Inter-ethnic interactions and attitudes in the workplace reflected the Soviet social hierarchy. An analysis of gender and work in the Karelian life writing further exemplifies cultural categorizations. The gendered division of labour took on ambivalent forms and meanings in the socialist world. The equality of men and women in work, wages, and political rights was espoused in Soviet rhetoric, but, as we have seen, women still retained primary responsibility for the home sphere. Finnish North American letters and memoirs reveal further social constructions of what work was appropriate for men and women. Enoch Nelson wrote to his brother in 1933 that "I and the family are getting along as well as can be expected but as the plans of the Soviet Union are short of laborers the wife is also working and of course earning money."[100] Nelson's phrasing suggests that despite the Soviet push to move women into the workforce, his wife's employment was either not the norm or not the ideal. Others, too, preferred their wives to stay at home, despite what a woman herself may have desired. Justiina Heino, concerned about the family economy, wrote to her daughter: "I've been thinking that I've got to go find some type of work. We really should get clothes but father is against it saying to try to patch them one more time and make cheap food."[101] In an interview in 2002, Paavo Alatalo explained that his mother did not work in Karelia during their first several years there: "Mother was just at home. She did want to work ... Father wanted her to be at home and taking care of the home and mother just wanted to work somewhere, so she, too, could get those work years."[102]

When women did work, there was the question of what work was appropriate for them. In her first letter from Karelia to her sister, Terttu Kangas wrote, "I haven't been at work here yet except two days sawing firewood [.] here there doesn't seem to be any women's work but here women do not have to work like some there seem to think."[103] Kangas took for granted that her sister would understand what she meant by "women's work." Her statement also addressed the North American communities' prevalent perceptions about Karelia. A few months later, Kangas further explained her experiences with work and offered more insights on women's work:

> I haven't been really in a permanent [full-time] job this winter I have knitted a lot for people and day care children clothing now I am again in the forest with other women sawing firewood[.] yes it's fun being at work when you have a big bunch of *akoja* [hags] it's not so hard the work as there in America people think[.] yes a woman does it just like a man too[.] Yes I could have gotten [work] as a daycare worker if I had wanted but with spring here I don't have the mind for indoor work when you can be outdoors.[104]

Knitting, daycare work, and sawing firewood in a gang of women were all women's work, based on Terttu Kangas's description. Again, she referenced the North American notions of what women were doing in Karelia. In both cases, Kangas assured her sister that Karelia was not so different from the United States; women did not have to work and that the work was not so hard.

If North Americans both there and in Karelia had concerns about appropriate women's work, they were quite taken by the work of local Karelian women. Lisi Hirvonen wrote to her sister about two women who worked directly in lumbering. That Hirvonen knew of only two women in the industry shows that it was largely considered a male occupation. She explained that one of the women, whose ethnicity was not mentioned, worked as an *ylösottaja*, or a log measurer and labeller, and "the other one does everything that the men do she is one of these Karelians she married a Canadian."[105] Hirvonen was not the only one struck by how Karelian women did what was seen by Finnish North Americans as men's work. In Lauri Hokkanen's memoir, local women workers were referred to as "big ... like a prize fighter," "powerful-looking," "Katinka," and "built like a wrestler, a powerful Katrinka," developing an image much different from how North American Finnish women were depicted.[106] Both Lauri and Sylvi Hokkanen recounted their surprise to learn that Karelian women typically rowed boats. When a young Karelian woman was among Finnish North Americans, however, according to Sylvi, "our men told her to sit in the bow while they did the rowing."[107] Sylvi believed that such differences reflected broader cultural distinctions: "She was accustomed to doing men's work as is generally true in societies not as far developed as ours."[108]

Karelian lumber camps, as in North America, were a predominantly male space where rough masculinity was on display.[109] For the women and children who were there, the environment could feel inhospitable. Sylvi Hokkanen, for example, remembered her discomfort of being around the "lumberjack humour" the men enjoyed "as men are apt to do."[110] For men, however, the lumber camps served as a place where masculinity was solidified.

At the age of seventeen, Kaarlo Tuomi and three other "older" Finnish North American "boys" were chosen to go to Matrosy to study the "fundamentals of lumbering," which included "cutting logs and pulpwood, sharpening saws, hauling logs and grading them according to quality."[111] Tuomi's 1980 memoir essay opens up this training or apprenticeship system in Karelia, and also reveals something about the ideals of gender and the coming of age for young workers. Tuomi remembered: "The instructors were old lumberjacks from the States and they sweated us

Figure 12 Women measuring logs in Matrosy (*Neuvosto-Karjalan 15-vuotiaan taipaleelta*, 56).

as we learned the trade. After four months we were able to fulfill the quotas with our own tools and equipment which we had to build from scratch. Now we were considered men."[112] Training to become "foremen or scalers," as portrayed by Tuomi, entailed the hierarchical "sweating" by senior workers, and masculine status was achieved through the fulfilment of quotas and using the products of one's own labour (note the lack of manufactured tools).

In addition to a commitment to hard work, Finnish North American masculinity was also characterized by the solidarity of the work gang. Finnish North Americans wanted to uphold the labour practices and policies they had fought for with unions and socialist organizations before moving to Karelia.[113] During the Second Five Year Plan, the Soviet Union turned away from equal payment but this "went against the grain" with North Americans.[114] The new form of worker "differentiation" served as a valuable tool in upholding and expanding the Soviet hierarchy by clearly distinguishing worker heroes from "slackers."[115] After being told they were to rank the productivity of each member of their lumber gang to determine wages, Lauri Hokkanen explained "we had been taught that even though some people weren't physically able to do as much as the others, they deserved full pay if they were doing their best. I believe all of us – Americans and Canadians – felt this way."[116] Despite official policy, the Finnish North American lumber workers at the Sakura Järvi camp decided on equal pay, confirming the masculinity of each "one hundred per cent productive" member.[117] Ian Radforth has argued that Finns working in northern Ontario bush camps actually preferred to be paid by individual piece rate, because their logging experience ensured that they typically earned higher wages this way.[118] The preference for equalization in Karelia, then, suggests that the Finnish North Americans' adherence to a masculinity based on group identity and collective hard work was also specifically socialist.

Changes

Reading the letters and memoirs for the gendered organization of work and the perceived role and status of the immigrants vis-à-vis the local worker population shows a group negotiating its place in Karelia. The process, however, was interrupted by external forces imposing their will. While Finnish North Americans were at the top of the social hierarchy in the early 1930s, after the autumn of 1935, being Finnish in Karelia took on new meanings. The migrants became faced with forceful Russification and outright hostility to Finnishness, as we will see. The studied life writing offers limited glimpses of how these changes began to impact work experiences. These later experiences draw a sharp contrast to the positive depictions of working life found in so many of the Karelian letters. Sylvi Hokkanen's memoir recounts the devastating impact that the abolishment of Finnish education had on her career. After having been able to teach only one year of Finnish school after her graduation from the Pedagogical Institute, Sylvi was assigned to a Russian school, with limited Russian-language skills.[119] There, she "could not make a go of it."[120] Sylvi remembered: "She [a Finnish North American friend] soon lost her job because she was a 'foreigner' and 'foreigners' were not allowed to teach in Russian schools at this time. In my case, the situation became so difficult that I finally just stayed home, and no one ever came around to ask why I didn't come back."[121]

Due to the restrictive atmosphere in Karelia in the late 1930s, it is unsurprising that little direct mention of the Finnish repression can be found in the available letters from the period. However, the Heino letters serve as a poignant example of the changing position of Finns and North Americans in Karelia and the difficulty of getting by after a family member's arrest. In an undated letter, likely written in Kondopoga in 1937 or early 1938, Justiina Heino explained how "here they are taking Finns out of lots of management tasks and replacing with Russians ...

The whole factory is Russians and wages are heavily dropping."[122] Making do was a "struggle" for the Heino family at this time due to diminishing wages, price increases, and food shortages.[123] However, after Frank Heino's arrest, sometime in 1938, life became even more difficult. A partial letter from Justiina shows increasing Russification and the need for more income:

> should know Russian to get [a job at] a cafeteria, a children's nursery or to bake but everything is in the Russian language – you should know how to speak Russian – but for an old woman it's hard to learn. Bush work was promised but I'm not used to bush work so I'm a little scared but that won't help because I've got to get something [some work]. Walte's wages aren't enough now that father isn't earning. Alice is still too young. She's asked for some but can't get any ... you can only get it when you turn 16 years old.[124]

Alice Heino's letter from the same period confirms that Justiina had, in fact, taken up forest work, despite her concerns.[125]

In 1938 and again in 1940, the Soviet Union introduced new labour laws, which further impacted work experiences. The new laws –"a losing proposition for all workers," in Lauri Hokkanen's words[126] – imposed harsh penalties and fines for tardiness and absenteeism, and made leaving a job more difficult.[127] Sheila Fitzpatrick has argued that the impact of the new labour legislation for the average worker "was probably much stronger than that of the Great Purges."[128] In an area as small as Karelia that faced such an enormous extent of repression, the argument does not stand up, but the new rigid rules undoubtedly made their mark. In fact, Lauri Hokkanen's narrative eases into a more difficult discussion of the Karelian purges through his memories of the 1938 labour laws.[129] Both newly tightened labour discipline and Russification changed the nature of work for US and Canadian Finns in Karelia.

Conclusion

In the "sickle and hammer land," the workplace was a central component of a person's life, being closely linked with one's place of residence and rations and bound to the haphazard whims of the communist centre. By focusing on life writing, we gain intimate insights of practice and policy in action on the everyday level. By writing about work, letter writers helped their correspondents to better understand the new lives they were building and established bridges between the Finnish North American workers' movement and the communist state. The frame of work also allowed the life writers to situate themselves into the Karelian project. Life writing shows North American tools and techniques at work, but also how Finnish North Americans came to see and position themselves as the modernizers and civilizers of the region. The letters and memoirs provide us with access to the Soviet social hierarchy, the gender of work, and the shifting position of Finns in Karelia, while also showing the life writers' work of making sense of the society, places, and everyday life they encountered.

Chapter Six

"All Kinds of Hustle and Bustle": Community Life and Leisure

A November 1933 letter from Aate Pitkänen to his parents describes "all kinds of hustle and bustle" in Petrozavodsk, including athletics, community evening programs, official Soviet celebrations, and youth organizations.[1] The 1930s witnessed a cultural revolution in the Soviet Union. As we have seen with family and domestic values, Stalin's Russia turned away from the ideals of ascetic revolutionary communality in favour of illusionary portrayals and rhetoric espousing a life of happiness and plenty. State-proscribed popular culture, celebrations, and leisure time were to instil principles of productivity, hierarchy, and unswerving commitment to the Communist Party of the Soviet Union. Although the CPSU provided its citizens with carefully planned pastimes, festivals, and venues to promote the "culturing" and political education required of "advanced" socialists, ordinary people shaped popular culture and exercised power by selecting which activities they would participate in, by approaching leisure and entertainment as personal social outlets, and by determining for themselves to what extent they would engage with the party's political messaging.

Commenting on the youth culture he found upon arrival in Karelia, Reino Hämäläinen wrote that "these people wouldn't go back to the states for no money and neighter [*sic*] would I. They seem to like it so darn well and seem to have a lot of fun here. They know the place and got places to go."[2] Alongside the serious business of building communism through large-scale work projects and formal political education, Finnish North American youth in Karelia were coming of age. Though youth and youth culture have not previously been used as frames for analyzing the Finnish North American migration to Karelia, 43 per cent of Canadian migrants and 26 per cent of Americans arrived between the ages of thirteen and thirty.[3] By attending to youth culture, we see that these young Canadian and US Finns represent a fascinating subsection of radicalism; raised in the revolutionary spirit, they brought to Karelia their own socialist idealism and particular understandings of the Soviet project.

The study of community leisure during the early years of settlement in Soviet Karelia allows us to see the enthusiasm, commitment, and idealism applied to the collective work of building socialism, often left buried and forgotten under the weight of repression. US and Canadian Finns replicated familiar North American proletarian entertainments and pastimes, providing them with a sense of community continuity in Karelia.[4] Empowered by the official recognition of Finnish as the region's main non-Russian culture and language, Finns framed their community and artistic contributions as invaluable to the culturing of the region. Their cultural work, though, further demarcated the insular spaces of the Finnish community in Karelia. This chapter situates the social and cultural world of Finnish North Americans in Karelia in the contexts of the broader cultural program of the Soviet Union in the 1930s and the Finnish North American tradition of working-class community life.

Responding to Return Migration

Despite rosy letter portrayals, living conditions in Karelia were simply too much to bear for many Finnish North Americans. The realities of housing, food, and consumer good shortages, difficult working conditions, and, often, feelings of homesickness made past experiences in Canada and the United States seem much better than the building of socialism. Many, then, chose to leave. By the careful calculations of Golubev and Takala, between 1,300 and 1,500 Finnish North Americans left Karelia between 1931 and 1935.[5] Those who left were often very vocal about what they had experienced in Karelia, causing controversy and uncertainty in the Finnish communist communities in the United States and Canada. The Finnish North American left-wing press that opposed the Karelian migration, like the IWW's *Industrialisti* and the Canadian Social Democratic paper *Vapaa Sana*, published negative reports about Karelian life.[6] Such accounts left communist organizations, such as the Finnish Organization of Canada, and papers, like *Työmies* and *Vapaus*, on the defensive. The negative depictions and rumours circulating in Canadian and US Finnish communities compelled some letter writers in Karelia to address the situation first-hand.

"Boy there's a lot of people going back. There's a real migration," Aate Pitkänen wrote to his sister Taimi in March 1933.[7] In fact, 1933 and 1934 saw the most Finnish North Americans leaving Karelia.[8] With return migration clearly on his mind, a few days later, Pitkänen explained to friends how he understood the return of so many:

> There is some truth to the fact that some at times experience difficulties and setbacks. Then when that first *trupelli* [trouble] begins to brew in the mind, it brews and brews, expands and takes root, and every little *trupelli* is put to brew, so in the end nothing seems good, and there is no consolation except one and only saviour, and that is to get back to *kultala* [land of gold].[9]

Later that year, Aate again shared his views on people's decisions to leave Karelia:

> In the first place some people come here for mere adventure, to see the place. They come here, see all kinds of short comings [*sic*] and the good points just seem to fade away in the bad ones. Day in and day out they roll these thoughts in their brains & think of good old American times.[10]

North America had, again, become a *kultala* in the minds of some, despite how bitter disappointment with life in Canada and the United States had been a main catalyst for the "Karelian Fever." "With young people," though, explained Aate, "it's a little different."[11] He continued:

> A lot of them come here alone, their parents staying in America ... They get homesick, and in many cases their folks from back there coax them to come back. They don't think any further and can't resist it. Some of them are here with their folks and when the folks go back they say "I wanna stick by my Pa and my Ma." In general they haven't got a backbone. All they think of is fun.[12]

Those brewing on their misery, as depicted by Aate, were accused of failing to work for improvements. "They don't stop to think of the achievements or the other side of things, or how to better things," wrote Aate, "They don't bother with meetings, educational classes, etc. They run up against some short coming, can't get over it, pack up their trunks and there they go."[13] Writing about family friends who left, to the disapproval of the Pitkänens,[14] Aate said that they did not "fight against the difficulties and I can say that they did not even want to, for Aho, at least, did not make *any* effort to get involved with any organization or education, etc. any more than Martta did, and there they could have brought the negatives to light and worked collectively to improve them."[15] Similarly, Terttu Kangas explained to her sister that one Selma Mäki, who had left Karelia, had not worked hard enough "to build a socialist society."[16] Antti

Kangas, Terttu's husband, wanted to set the record straight about return migration and conditions in Karelia in a group letter to the "Comrades" of Drummond Island. He accused returnees of spreading false rumours about Karelian life and how others there were making out.[17] The "truth," as Kangas saw it, was that "a person who just wants to live off their own work, then, yes, their place is here."[18] Despite what he depicted as small shortcomings, Kangas believed that "we here are with sure steps moving toward improved economic and cultural life."[19] The authorities also recognized the failures in community building. "The Y.C.L. & Party have been taking big steps to avoid this migration," Aate wrote to Taimi, "This Anglo American Youth Club is one of them and a good one."[20] For these letter writers, the antidote to Karelian hardships was getting involved and staying active in community life. Mayme Sevander, writing some sixty years after Aate Pitkänen and Terttu Kangas, understood return migration in similar terms. Sevander explained that many left Karelia,

> but thousands stayed. We stayed ... But when people are honest and hardworking they don't let the circumstances get the better of them. They look forward to a happier future. Many built families, had children, worked for the common good and are rightfully proud of their contribution to that multi-suffering land called Russia.[21]

If one chose to engage, opportunities for building community and improving local life were abundant, as illustrated by the Karelian life writers.

Political Volunteerism

Building socialism involved developing one's own socialist consciousness. Soviet Karelia provided the immigrants with many opportunities to engage in their personal socialist education and to work for the common good. Some, like Kalle Korhonen, immersed themselves in formal political study. Korhonen explained to his estranged daughter in 1935 that he had spent the previous three years completing "Communist University" through correspondence.[22] Korhonen's writing consistently utilized official party language and themes, showing that, if he had not yet become a member of the CPSU, he was at least working toward that goal. Admission into the increasingly withdrawing Communist Party of the Soviet Union was far from certain, even for those who had been members of the Communist Party of Canada or of the United States. Antti Pitkänen, Aate's father, had been an active CPC member since 1925, and applied for Soviet Party membership once in Karelia. His

Figure 13 The National Culture Centre in Petrozavodsk in 1935 (photo courtesy of the Karelian Research Centre Russian Academy of Sciences).

application, however, was declined, and this may have precipitated his hasty return to Ontario.[23] Anatoli Gordijenko has found that Aate Pitkänen remained an active YCL member into the 1940s, nearing the age of thirty, but seemingly never became an official party member.[24] Mayme Sevander joined the Communist Party only in 1960.[25] Based on the Hokkanen's discussions about politics, it seems unlikely that either Lauri or Sylvi would have been members. Sylvi Hokkanen recalled: "We knew only a few party members, and a few more who were candidates, but it was something that was not much discussed. Political matters in general were not discussed as freely over there as in the United States."[26] With no mention found in their writing and with limited biographical information, the party statuses of the other life writers are unknown. Even without formal party responsibilities, Finnish North Americans in Karelia participated in many forms of political activity.

The letter writers described their community political work in terms that likely resonated with their correspondents, who were familiar, if not active, with the Finnish North American Left. Building socialism in Karelia also meant actually building the worksites, villages, and towns where the migrants settled. Much like community *work bees*, Finnish North Americans, like Mayme Sevander's father, Oscar Corgan, joined "*subbotniks* – a volunteer labor force that met on Saturdays to build necessities for the city, such as housing, plumbing and sidewalks."[27] Lisi and Eino Hirvonen quickly joined in community work with other Finns in Vonganperä, with Eino serving as a voluntary inspector of schools and Red Corners, and Lisi participating in women's fundraising efforts.[28] After moving to Petrozavodsk, Lisi Hirvonen wrote to her sister that "we have joined the *Mobriin Oso* [International Red Aid/MOPR] and the labour union's athletic club [.] there sure is bustle. Two nights a week there is the political circle meetings."[29] Viola Ranta remembered that her mother Alli was "enthusiastic about building that bright future and joined the Red Cross and women came to our home to have all kinds of meetings and singing practices."[30] Aate Pitkänen wrote home about the kinds of activities that he had been involved in with other Finnish North American youth. "Even tonight," wrote Pitkänen,

> we went to the Radio studio to perform a group poem. We often go there. We are in our workplace youth league's *agit brigaadissa* [agitation brigade] and we help with the radio program. Here also slowly organized an English Language Youth Club. We present English language programs (this is not workplace, but General City Club), a wall paper, lessons of different kinds, technical, political, dramatic, Russian language, etc. I am the organizer of political education.

Alice Heino proudly described the *tehtävät* (tasks) assigned to her by the Young Pioneer group.[31] She told her brother that she had joined many groups, or *piirit*, where she learned songs and poems that they frequently performed for community evenings of entertainment (*iltamat*).[32] Involvement in Young Pioneers, Youth Leagues, unions, and study groups, among other politically motivated activities, provided Finnish North American migrants with continuity. These activities were well known among the communities that formed around US and Canadian Finnish socialist halls. Throwing themselves into community life may have eased the transition into Karelian life and provided space for social interaction with other newcomers. Writing home about participation in such activities served to illustrate the flourishing culture of the Soviet Union and Karelia, and reassured correspondents that the migrant was doing well.

Others depicted their participation in political organization with little enthusiasm. Teenaged Reino Hämäläinen explained to a friend: "Out here we have to join mostly all kinds of clubs and have to go out and practice our military on free days. You have to join the Y.C.L. and a lot of other clubs in the same line."[33] Hämäläinen's three uses of "have to" suggest how strongly "volunteering" was encouraged and perhaps serve as a reminder of teenagers' dislike of being told what to do. Similarly, Sylvi Hokkanen wrote, thinking back on her years in Karelia:

> I, for one, was concerned only with school and the social life connected with it. But in Karelia, each school, each factory, every workplace had its political organizer or teacher. They held meetings regularly at which the workers and students were taught the tenets of communism. They would also hold meetings at the various barracks, and although attendance was not required, it was what we called "voluntary compulsion" – it was best to go.[34]

Though the Communist Party viewed the role of political organizations and spaces as key sites for developing socialist consciousness in the masses, these sites served as much more for citizens throughout the Soviet Union. Karelian life writing primarily describes the writers' involvement in the political sphere in terms of the opportunities for socialization that they provided. Take for example a description offered by Terttu Kangas, writing to her sister: "We have a radio right here in our downstairs. There, there is also a Red Corner so we don't have to go far. There we always spend our evenings and have fun."[35] The radio and Red Corner, held as key tools of politicization by the Soviet leadership,[36] were, instead, for Kangas, an object and space of leisure and entertainment. Lewis Siegelbaum, using the example of Soviet workers' clubs, succinctly summarizes the primary value of political spaces, arguing that they "functioned as sites for friendship-making and bonding, courtship, informal exchanges of information, sheer entertainment or fun, and a host of other purposes not officially acknowledged or sanctioned."[37]

Iltamat

Iltamat, or evening entertainment programs, were a staple of Finnish North American hall life. An *iltama* program could consist of a variety of activities, including dances, auctions, musical or theatrical performances, and guest speakers.[38] Personal letters reveal that the tradition of the *iltama* was just as ubiquitous in Karelia. On many evenings of the week, Finns in the region's larger centres, like Petrozavodsk and Kondopoga, could rush to the *Kulttuuritalo* (House of Culture) to take part in whatever event was scheduled.[39] In 1935, construction was completed on the *Kansantaiteentalo*, or the House of (Finnish) National Arts. Klaus Maunu remembered the centre's large auditorium, multiple meeting rooms, and gymnasium.[40] In Mayme Sevander's view, the Kondopoga House of Culture, completed in the same year, "truly was a place connected with culture and entertainment."[41] Writing a retrospective piece on the cultural work of Finnish North Americans in Karelia, "They Built Culture," émigré Impi Vauhkonen noted: "It felt then, like everyone took part in something. The Clubs were in diligent use. The American workers' Uritski Street ... Club was the youth's almost nightly gathering place. There, all kinds of activities were organized, [such as] dance, dramatic, [and] athletic program evenings, for example."[42] Lumber camps, like Vonganperä, also organized evening entertainments, as described by Lisi Hirvonen in early 1933: "from other villages people come to have *iltamat* and perform[.] at Christmas time, two school groups came to perform programs[.] was fun to see and hear."[43] Allan Sihvola remembered the Club building in Vilga, where dances, *iltamat*, and touring theatre productions were hosted.[44] The Kondopoga Paper Mill Club was also a popular leisure space.[45] Shortly after moving to Petrozavodsk, Hirvonen wrote about the *iltamat* they had already participated in, including a dramatic performance and films.[46] When Eino Hirvonen began to work for the Finnish National Theatre, the couple were given lodging in Petrozavodsk's Summer Park by the theatre's outdoor stage. The Summer Park was a main site for cultured socialization, which led Hirvonen to note: "during the summer this place is a bit restless because there are entertainments every evening almost [but] I guess we'll manage."[47]

In addition to organized evening programs, the Karelian life writers show that visiting friends and spending time with neighbours were popular ways to pass the time. The letters, especially, frequently mention the back and forth visiting with acquaintances from Canada and the United States. Lisi Hirvonen wrote to her sister that her day's plans had gone awry because "we were out visiting people so late last night that I was very sleepy this morning."[48] Alice Heino wrote to her sister: "Visitors are coming again. We have them every night."[49] Heino explained that during week nights, when not going to the *kultuuritalo*, "the youth gather at our place and we play [the phonograph]."[50] Reino Hämäläinen explained to Benny: "Out here we go from place to place visiting and talk about all thing[s] and so on. We all get together and start singing some of the popular songs. Meaning once [were] popular."[51]

Music and Dancing

In the 1930s, Karelia could boast a rich music scene. Not only did youth gather to listen to recorded music and join together to sing favourite American songs, Karelia had several active musical groups, performed by and for Finnish North Americans. A symphony orchestra, radio orchestra, dance orchestra, brass band, *kantele* orchestra, children's orchestra, two choirs, and smaller Workers' Club bands are all mentioned in Vuohkonen's short overview of Finnish North American music in 1930s Karelia. Allan Sihvola's memoir portrays the numerous performance opportunities he had as a young, ambitious musician. Reino Hämäläinen wrote to Benny about how much he enjoyed music in Petrozavodsk "because these bozos can play and sure got good places to play."[52]

The "Radio Calendar" published in the Finnish newspaper *Punainen Karjala* shows "music performed by the radio orchestra, directed by K. Rautio" on most days, as a break in educational programming, such as "Karelian History," "Forest Workers' Study," "Building Technique Lecture," and children's and youth's programs.[53] Elis Ranta moved his family from Uhtua to Petrozavodsk in the spring of 1933, having been given the opportunity to work as a full-time musician.[54] He was the horn player for the Petrozavodsk Radio Orchestra. Ranta wrote to his brother about the Radio Orchestra: "This orchestra is very good. I have never played in such a good gang, as this our orchestra. We have 32 players and two directors. One of the directors is Russian, [and] has at some time been an American symphony orchestra's director ... We don't play every night, just about twelve times a month. The musicians perform solos on the other evenings."[55] Reino Hämäläinen offered his opinion on the group, writing to Benny that "The Radio orchestra is another good thing to listen to because they play some American pieces once in a while."[56]

Elis Ranta was also the conductor of the Ski Factory's Brass Band, in which Lauri Hokkanen played. Hokkanen wrote about the band:

> I started out playing the trumpet and later switched to baritone ... There were about twenty-five of us in the band, and we practiced every week. Occasionally we even played in a combined group of bands from all over the territory with about a hundred and fifty musicians ... Elis Ranta was the leader of our ski factory band. We were called upon to play at dances, parades, an occasional concert, and various affairs at the ski factory club. We received no pay for this; it was a civic duty, and one we enjoyed. But we did get paid for playing at funerals ... Often we were asked to play at doings some distance from town.[57]

By playing at different events, Hokkanen was able to experience many sides of Karelian cultural life. His memoir gives the impression that involvement with the Brass Band was a highlight of his time in Karelia.

Listening to Karelia's orchestras brought joy to Finnish North Americans. Mayme Sevander wrote about her mother's relationship with music in Karelia:

> My mother, who loved music, often said that the Karelian Radio Symphony Orchestra in Petrozavodsk was one of the finest orchestras she had ever heard. I think she was proud of the fact that most of the musicians were American Finns ... Mother seldom had time to attend [concerts], but she would put on the radio in the evenings and listen to the concerts while she did the mending. She always said that listening to the cheerful folk music and beautiful classical pieces made it easy to forget for a few minutes that our walls were thin, our food poor and our feet cold.[58]

Sevander's description of her mother finding her moments of leisure at home, while performing domestic tasks, rather than out at public cultural events is fitting with what is known about North American and Soviet women's lower participation in leisure due to greater family care burdens.[59] Though women in 1930s Soviet Union were continuously told that their maternal and home duties should not interfere with their cultural and socialist development, the reality of women's lives and lack of support structures impeded their full engagement. Sevander, herself, still with the freedom of youth, formed happy memories and a love of music by attending many symphony concerts at the Philharmonic building, which was destroyed by the Soviets as the Finnish army approached during the war.[60]

With so many orchestras in the region, Finnish North Americans had ample opportunities to dance. Though the value of dancing – especially Western dances – was contested in the revolutionary period, by the Second Five Year Plan, dancing had come to be seen as "almost a duty" for good Soviet citizens.[61] Dancing was certainly a favourite pastime, as it had been in Canada and the United States.[62] For youth, music and dances could offer opportunities to "raise hell" and have a good time with friends.[63] Alice Heino wrote about how she had learned to dance so well in Karelia that she could teach anyone, adding that many boys had asked her to dance but she had yet to promise anyone a "lesson."[64] Reino Mäkelä, likewise, reported having learned to dance in Karelia.[65] Vieno Zlobina remembered learning the popular French *quadrille* square dance set to Russian music from local Karelian youth.[66] Aate Pitkänen wrote to Taimi that "we have quite a few programs and dances. I don't dance very much, once in a while."[67] The dance floor had less to offer others. Lisi Hirvonen, writing at the age of forty, complained: "we went to the summer park yesterday evening but we got so cold that we had to go home[.] there aren't any amusements for someone this old, though you do hear beautiful music there."[68] Elmer Nousiainen, former saxophonist for a popular Finnish North American dance band in 1930s Petrozavodsk, remembered that "we played Russian, Finnish and American dance music, and, of course, jazz."[69] Dancing was as prevalent in the lumber camps and remote areas, but sometimes required a bit more creativity. Youth from Rutanen camp, like Allan Sihvola, would go to neighbouring Isku lumber camp for dances.[70] "Often though," Sihvola remembered, "in the evening we carried Leipälä's cabinet gramophone into the cafeteria, gathered tables and chairs and the dance started."[71] At Säde, when an impromptu dance was about to start, the children would run from door to door spreading the word.[72]

Theatre

In addition to the music scene, "they put on some good plays here," Aate Pitkänen wrote to his sister and brother-in-law in late 1934.[73] Finnish migrants brought popular amateur and working-class theatre with them to Canada and the United States. In North America, stage productions were a mainstay of Finnish hall activities, beginning with the earliest temperance organizations. Theatrical performances were most often political and served to fundraise and rally support for the workers' cause.[74] In Karelia, Finnish theatre also thrived. Soviet policies of minority accommodation placed great importance on building cultural institutions that "civilized" the population in its official minority language. Therefore, the Karelian Finnish National Theatre was established to offer audiences professional, communistic plays year round, and *iltamat* around the region presented amateur productions by workers, youth, and children.

Finnish North Americans, already used to the stage, made a mark on theatre in Karelia, and a lasting impression on those who watched them perform. Mayme Sevander remembered: "I loved to sit in my wooden seat at the theater and smell the musty curtain and see everyone around me, dressed up and expectant as the lights fell low."[75] Klaus Maunu remembered a delightful performance by a Finnish Canadian, and Sevander reminisced about the roles played by many migrants from the United States and Canada.[76] Eino Hirvonen began work with the National Theatre in September 1933. Through Lisi Hirvonen's letters, we learn about the company's busy touring schedule. For example, in August 1934, Hirvonen wrote to her sister that "Eino has been on tour all over Karelia and now he has been given summer vacation for one and a half months and right after summer vacation they will again leave on tour to Leningrad and Ingria."[77] The troupe brought performances to lumber camps, agricultural collectives, and other remote regions, where audiences could escape their difficult lives for a few moments.

Beyond entertainment, the theatre was to culture and educate audiences on socialist living. Mayme Sevander provides a noteworthy description of the accomplishments of the professional Finnish theatre:

> The Karelian Finnish Theatre may rightfully be called a great enlightener. There was neither a small village nor a logging camp in the Republic where actors and singers wouldn't have delighted eager audiences with their performances. Among the most memorable events in the history of the theatre was the month-long, 1,200-kilometer skiing expedition that eight company members undertook in 1936 ... On their backs, they carried sets and costumes. They staged plays in several god-forsaken places. Probably the greatest impact of this heroic venture was that the company often interested illiterate people in learning to read and write. Often, they were the ones to give the first lessons.[78]

Sevander's depiction of the Theatre Company casts it as "a great enlightener" on a "heroic venture," bringing culture and literacy to the "god-forsaken" and "backwards" Soviet periphery. Though not explicitly communicated, Sevander's description implies that those receiving the "lessons" were not Finnish or North Americans – since their literacy has been a significant point of pride in their collective history – but the "others" of the region, likely Russian, Karelian, Ingrian, and Veps peasants. Sevander's characterizations echo formal communist enlightenment rhetoric and reveal how Finnish North Americans internalized scripts that supported their elite status in Karelia.

Cinema

By the late 1920s, Finnish migrants in Canada and the United States were among the masses that flocked to movie theatres to see the latest Hollywood offerings. Even with families facing economic hardships during the depression, people continued to see movies regularly, with youth reportedly still attending at least once a month.[79] Moviegoing was an important part of Soviet people's lives in the 1930s, as it was in many other places, worldwide. In Karelia, Finnish North Americans continued to have frequent access to movies (*kino*). Movies could be viewed almost daily in the capital in theatres such as the "Triumf," "*Kino-Teatteri Puna-Tähti*" ("Movie Theatre Red Star") or the Karelian National Dramatic Theatre's "Little Hall" ("*Pieni Sali*") cinema.[80] Even in Karelia's remote lumber camps, like Vonganperä, film projectors were brought in

Figure 14 Film screening for lumber workers in 1938 (photo courtesy of the Karelian Research Centre Russian Academy of Sciences).

regularly.[81] Writing in spring of 1933 from the outskirts of Petrozavodsk, Lisi Hirvonen reported that there "films are shown on two or three evenings each week."[82]

Aate Pitkänen complained to his sister and brother-in-law that the films presented in Karelia "aren't so hot," and that he preferred the odd occasions when foreign films were screened.[83] While old foreign films were still screened at the "Triumf" theatre, as remembered by Klaus Maunu, they had, indeed, become rare.[84] Soviet moviegoers had come to love Hollywood comedies and romances, but, in the 1930s, the government almost wholly ended the importation of foreign films, despite their profitability. As an example, no foreign films were brought into the Soviet Union in 1932 and only three films made abroad entered the country in 1936.[85] It was believed by the leadership that, since films were to serve solely as a political tool, only films made in the Soviet Union could project the correct political message.[86] This reasoning provided the justification needed to direct scarce resources to the film industry.[87] The Soviet film industry was never able to meet its ambitious production goals, but while the number of films made decreased, the number of copies per film increased significantly.[88] This assured that Soviet films would be widely viewed. Through movie attendance, Finnish North Americans in Karelia, like audiences throughout the Soviet Union, had an opportunity to directly view the world as their leader wanted it portrayed. Stalin, as characterized by Peter Kenez, was preoccupied with the national film industry and "personally saw and approved every single film exhibited in the Soviet Union."[89] The approach taken by the Soviet leadership was to use films "not to portray reality but to help deny it."[90] Richard Stites characterized Soviet popular culture, including films, as a "web of fantasy and a giant political cover up."[91] If ordinary people, in their daily lives, were not experiencing the "joyous life" Comrade Stalin had exhorted, then Soviet films would allow them to participate in it, even if only for the duration of the screening.

The Soviet film industry, under the strict micromanagement of top party officials, paid special attention to stirring children and youth through film.[92] A letter from Alice Heino shows how effective Soviet film propaganda could be. Heino, writing in her early teen years, conveyed how impressed she had been by the movies she had watched in Karelia and wrote eagerly to her brother about one that had an especially strong impact on her: a film about the school years of a poet who defied the Tsar by aligning with the Bolshevik cause.[93] *Young Pushkin*, the film Heino likely referred to, was a part of the profusion of Pushkin material created as a part of the 1937 Pushkin Centennial.[94] While Soviet films could successfully indoctrinate key political messages, moviegoing was still, for the ordinary person, a leisure activity, and became an increasingly important form of escapism. For youth, who made up a majority of the audience,[95] the cinema provided a space away from the adult gaze. Mayme Sevander remembered frequently attending movies with friends from the age of twelve, without adult supervision.[96] The movie theatre was a primary site for youth sociability and courtship in Karelia, as it had been in North America. In a letter written just days after arriving in Petrozavodsk, Reino Mäkelä explained to a friend, "This towns [*sic*] got movies like America and American shows translated to Russian. As I was writing this Benny is sitting beside me wanted to go already."[97]

Celebrations

For a few days out of the year, the Soviet Union could take a break from its fast-paced industrialization drive to celebrate what it had already accomplished. The main holidays in the Soviet calendar were May Day (1 May), the Anniversary of the Revolution (7 November), and, after 1935, New Year's Day (1 January). Karen Petrone has analyzed celebrations during Stalin's rule showing "how Soviet officials tried to create legitimacy through emotional appeals and mobilize citizens through apolitical gaiety."[98] These days would transform cities and villages across the nation, and "even the smallest bakery in a quiet back street would remove the plaster loaves from behind its windows for the festival and spread out a red cloth on which to place portraits and busts of the leaders, or at the very least would hang colourful posters."[99] Celebrations, as depicted in the Karelian life writing, incorporated, on a grander scale, many of the leisure activities and entertainments Finnish North Americans participated in regularly. Lisi Hirvonen described her participation in the October Revolution celebrations in Petrozavodsk:

> now again our celebration is over[.] even I was allowed to be free from work for four days[.] it was lots of fun[.] we had a fun shock worker party at the ski factory[.] we ate and drank[.] there was entertainment and at the end we danced[.] everything was free for the shock workers[.] and one evening I was at the national enlightenment house[.] 8 o'clock began a theatre piece and 12 began a concert. And at 2 o'clock began a dance[,] lasted to 5 in the morning and the third evening I was at *kinos* meaning moving pictures. And I was in a parade.[100]

Hirvonen's description, written just days before Stalin proclaimed that "Life has become better, life has become more joyous, comrades,"[101] features many of the primary elements of Soviet celebration in the 1930s. The Ski Factory celebration, like those across the Soviet Union, singled out the heroes of production, and offered them food, drink, and entertainment to reinforce social hierarchy and to show those who were not included what to strive for. Hirvonen's participation in the parade would have been obligatory, as all workers were expected to participate, but she, as a shock worker, may have marched closer to the front of the procession, which replicated Soviet hierarchy.[102] Ironically, parading workers for their production accomplishments and taking people away from work – for four days in Hirvonen's case – resulted in decreased production that then would lead to higher output requirements in the following days.[103] Hirvonen projected Soviet "joy" to her sister, concluding "it was lots of fun."

Celebrations were also held in honour of local accomplishments. Terttu Kangas detailed the events at the opening of the Lososinnoye House of Enlightenment in October 1934:

> Here there was a really big celebration, a real two-dayer. It was Lososiina's new enlightenment house's opening, because they built a really grand enlightenment house. Even almost all of us from here in Lohijärvi were

there. Yes, there you got to hear valuable programming[.] From the city had come a 30 person singing choir and 20 person *pänti* [band] so yes it felt festive that fine playing and singing[.] then there was still lots of other valuable programming[.] there was Martti Henrikson [*sic*], too, quivering his mouth[.] the next evening there was a big theatre production and a dance at the end of both nights[.] I think the events will be written about in *Työmies*.[104]

Kangas's description of the celebration follows the Soviet recipe for mass events, featuring political speeches – Hendrickson's quivering mouth – and entertainment. However, if the Soviet system was, as Richard Stites has stated, "a dual system of politics and fun," then Kangas's description suggests that she primarily internalized the fun of the occasion.[105] Perhaps exercising "a mild form of resistance" against the continuous bombardment of political messaging, Kangas, like others in the Soviet Union, took from the celebration what she wanted, and not necessarily what the officials had intended.[106] Stites has identified the ways in which celebration organizers "attempted to saturate their audience" through "days of pre-festival press coverage, speechifying on the main day, and then the post-mortem congratulatory rhetoric when it was over."[107] None of this messaging obviously transferred over into the letter writers' narratives. It seems that if the letter's recipients wanted to know about the political content of the events, they could turn to North American Finnish newspapers, like *Työmies*, for coverage.

Christmas was not celebrated in the USSR for its ties to religion and Santa Claus's questionable *kulak* background, and in 1928 the festive fir tree was also banned for its religious symbolism and the perceived "economic evil" associated with cutting down young trees.[108] In 1934, Lisi Hirvonen noted "it will be Christmas soon as well although it does not feel like Christmas here," ending by wishing her sister a happy New Year, instead.[109] Though New Year's had been quietly acknowledged throughout the early Soviet years, in December 1935, it became an official holiday. Along with public celebrations and the reinvention of the New Year's Tree, 1935 marked a reversal of the ban on private, home-based celebrations.[110] Sylvi Hokkanen wrote about the small New Year's party that she and Lauri hosted in their room in 1937: "We planned a midnight supper with as much on the table as our purse could stand. The big thing was the tree with homemade decorations – that was great fun."[111]

Private parties were also held on other occasions. Mayme Sevander vividly described a 1938 May Day party at the Finnish North American "Valiparakit" barracks in Petrozavodsk. The Mäkelä brothers, Kalervo

(Cowboy), Rudy, and Reino (one of the studied life writers), hosted the festivities. Sevander wrote:

> They talked it up with the neighbors and we were given a free hand up to 12 [a.m.]: use the kitchen, dance in the corridor, smoking on the stairwell only! Have a good but orderly time! One room was the "Jokes only." That's where Reino Mäkelä, Ansa Sword, and Ensio Haapanen reigned. It was non-stop joking: one got through, laughter hadn't yet subsided when the next one took over. A second room was for games. A third – for hors d'oeuvres and beer (naturally some guys had pocket flasks too. You couldn't exactly picture Russia without them!) The fourth was for coffee, tea and goodies made by the girls. And in the corridor – dancing to gramophone music.[112]

Descriptions of private celebrations and public festivals, like those depicted by Hirvonen, Kangas, Hokkanen, and Sevander, bring to life the social world of Finnish North American Karelia. While the Soviet leadership viewed celebrations as a crucial tool for political indoctrination, ordinary people revelled in the escape they provided from the drearier aspects of Soviet life. For youth, celebrations and leisure were closely linked to courtship.

Dating, Marriage, and Divorce

Mayme Sevander's description of the May Day party provides further insight on the drama of youth:

> It happened that somebody would accidentally stumble on a couple kissing and hugging in the kitchen, or on the stairs that led to the attic or in a neglected corner. A girlish tear was shed here and there. You know how it is: A is in love with B, while B is in love with C etc. That was happening all along ... the party began breaking up and the boys went to see off the girls.[113]

For older teenagers and young adults, Karelia offered abundant opportunities to date. Aate Pitkänen clearly made the point when he wrote to friends in Lakeridge, Ontario, that dating was "like a disease" and that bachelors changed dates as often as "gypsies change horses."[114] Aate and other Finnish North American youths in Karelia were participating in a dating culture that they had known in the United States and Canada. In the interwar period, "dating served as general recreation and social self-affirmation, not necessarily courtship of a potential life companion."[115] In April 1933, Pitkänen confided to his sister:

You asked me about Irma. Oh yes she was one of these summery flares. There's been quit[e] a few of these flares, summery, autumn, wintery and springy and over night flares, I haven't had a steady one for a long time, since last year. Boy she was something you don't get everyday. She was an American. So new years came along and I made a resolution and told her where to get off at. I spose summer will bring some flare again.[116]

In another letter Aate Pitkänen wrote home that "mother wanted to know if I have an *akka* [hag/old woman/wife] yet. Yes, I am ashamed to admit that not a serious one yet."[117] Perhaps playing up the "shame" of not being in a committed relationship for his mother's sake, Pitkänen's writing suggests that he had, in fact, been dating, though casually. Describing the romantic pursuits of a young man who lived in the same communal tent as her and Eino, Lisi Hirvonen noted, "yes those young men get around."[118] Reino Mäkelä explained that "I've learn [*sic*] a lot of Russian when you go with Russian girls."[119] Though describing diverse dating and an array of appealing women, Mäkelä boasted to Benny: "We have a lot of blondes here and I got one myself – a '*hellu*' [steady]."[120]

Many young men, like Mäkelä and the man who lived with the Hirvonens, dated local Karelian and Russian women. Mäkelä explained that "these Russian girls then you sure have fun with them. If you want to go some place there [*sic*] the ones to pay your way."[121] Mäkelä's description of Russian "girls" covering the expenses of dates requires further consideration. Beth L. Bailey has successfully demonstrated how, in the United States, the switch from home courting to public dating created an "economy of dating," which through the use of men's money, resulted in unequal power relations.[122] The very fact that Mäkelä felt that women footing the bill for a date merited remark suggests that he had encountered new customs by dating Russian women in Karelia. Mäkelä seems to have viewed these differences positively. Sylvi Hokkanen's memoir, however, demonstrates a familiar economy of dating at play in some cases in Karelia. Hokkanen remembered that "Many American and Canadian men married Karelian girls; the girls obtained better food norms as wives of recruited workers, and the men were proud of their young wives."[123] The prevalence of marrying Karelian and Russian women also related to the Karelian immigration policy, which excluded single women. Terttu Kangas addressed the issue in late 1933, in order to provide clarification for those in Drummond Island. As Kangas understood it, single women were able to immigrate only if accompanying their father, adding "I don't know why [they] can't come here[.] yes, there are men here so that here too you can get married."[124] She presented the issue of marriage from the woman's perspective, not touching on how the large numbers of single Finnish North American men limited opportunities for forming endogamous relationships.[125]

In 1937 Aate Pitkänen started to date Maria "Maikki" Smolenikova, a Russian, and told his sister that people were very happy for them, except for some bachelors who had their eye on the "sweetest and cutest girl on this side of the north pole."[126] In Pitkänen's letter, Maikki's positive qualities were framed through her community involvement. "She's always active & has responsible jobs at sport meets," Aate proudly wrote, "Now during the celebrations she's been performing at the house of culture every night."[127] The two appear to have married quickly but the relationship proved short-lived, ending a year later.[128] Ultimately, Pitkänen met and married Lilia, a Russian woman from Buzuluk. Youth also often married quickly without the approval of their parents. A 1939 letter written by Alice Heino explains to her sister Martha, how their brother Walter had married against their mother's wishes.[129] Likewise, with an underlying tone of disapproval, Terttu Kangas wrote to her sister in 1937: "So room we have again, because we aren't now but a three person family. Martha she went and got married this summer August 3rd day to one Olavi Niemi named man ... This Olavi has come from somewhere in Minnesota with his parents to Lososiina. He has been the whole time a car driver there. He is 24 years old."[130] When couples did marry, parenthood quickly followed. Tauno Salo referred to the speed at which newlyweds had babies as a "socialist competition."[131]

In addition to forming marriages and families, the Karelian life writings also address relationships ending in divorce. In a 1988 interview with Varpu Lindström, Leini Hietala spoke about her parents' 1933 divorce in Karelia. Hietala noted: "Well, it was at that time just some kind of fever that you left your own wife and got married with another."[132] Hietala gave the example of a man who left his wife for another woman, who had also left her husband, only to have the abandoned individuals marry each other.[133] Hietala, herself a child when her mother left her father for another man, judged that in all of the divorces and "trades," "children had to suffer ... children had to see it all."[134] The letters of Lisi Hirvonen show the breakdown of her marriage, though in limited detail. After beginning to work and tour with the Karelian National Dramatic Theatre in the fall of 1933, mentions of Eino Hirvonen gradually disappear.[135] Then, in August 1936, Hirvonen finally wrote that Eino was in Uhtua and "there's no need to write much about it[.] let it be as if it had only been a dream."[136] A year and a half later, Lisi Hirvonen explained that "here in Petroskoi Hirvonen lives with his wife[.] I rarely come across them[.] it does not feel like anything anymore[.] we say *haloo* that's all[.] one gets used to everything."[137]

Both marrying and divorcing were simple matters in the USSR until 1936. "In fact," wrote Enoch Nelson to his sister,

> now it is not even necessary to get the marriage license if you do not want to. If you want to be legal, the young couple go to the nearest elected official (it makes no difference hardly who he is) and state that you wish to live together as man and wife. He writes a certificate and it is ready. If you want a divorce, go to some official and state the case. If a man wants a divorce he can get it without the consent of the woman and if a woman wants it she can get it without the consent of the husband. In the case of children the man must pay the mother for the support of the children.[138]

Common-law relationships and marriage outside the church had been recognized by a 1917 decree in Revolutionary Russia, and echoed the political beliefs and practices of many Finnish leftists in North America.[139] Acquiring a divorce in Canada and the United States, while on the rise, continued to be difficult well into the 1930s and beyond.[140] In the Soviet Union, not only would non-mutual divorces be granted, one could even request a "post card divorce," where the registry office would inform the spouse on your behalf.[141] Personal freedoms were additionally bolstered with legalization of abortion in 1920. However, with a very low birth rate and increasingly pronatalist rhetoric coming from the Soviet centre, a controversial 1936 decree banned abortion, complicated divorce proceedings, and established a strict formula for child support, boosting conservative family values in the name of building socialism.[142]

Alcohol and Masculinity

Family values, gender roles, and socially conservative attitudes surrounded the use of alcohol. Terttu Kangas reported to her sister Toini in April 1934 about attitudes toward drunkenness in Lohijärvi: "Yes, those temperance champions should come here because that liquor you can buy here from every grocery store as much as you want even though very little is still drank because drunkenness here is held as a very shameful thing[.] if you appear in drunken scenes then soon you find your name in the wall paper."[143] Kangas's explanation was well in keeping within official attitudes toward drinking. Just as the Left in Canada and the United States had admonished drunkenness and smoking, the official Soviet policy was to attack the morality and political weakness of workers who were susceptible to drink.[144]

However, public opinions of drunkenness must not have been too severe, since descriptions of excesses are easy to find. "Theres a lot of vodka to drink out here any way [*sic*]," Reino Hämäläinen noted.[145] In the Strengs' story, men spent many hours drinking at the hotel bar, while waiting for their departure from Halifax, and at a Karelian party, the men went to a neighbour's home for a stronger drink to "add to life's joy."[146] Lauri Hokkanen remembered a careless evening when he sampled a Karelian friend's home-made beer or "*braug*."[147] The "powerful stuff" was "made from sugar, grain and raisins and fermented under pressure." The two drank a few glasses before heading off to the Ski Factory Club, but they could not properly drive the *potkukelkka* (Ski Factory–made kick sled) and got banged up along the way.[148] In another example, Reino Mäkelä wrote to Benny about the previous evening's escapades. Mäkela and a friend "go[t] some 'vodka' and got stewed to the gills. I got kick[ed] out of the dance and the girls are sure sore."[149] Allan Sihvola wrote about how the lumber camp bachelors would drive into Petrozavodsk on Sundays for "amusements at the restaurants and to taste on the park lawn the liquor store's offerings."[150] At the lumber camp, however, Sihvola remembered "rarely seeing drunks, but in the barracks attic we boys once found a big suitcase full of empty bottles, which we brought to Petroskoi and gave them to the store to get some pocket money."[151] At the Mäkelä's May Day party, as portrayed by Mayme Sevander, "some guys" brought pocket flasks with spirits, while "the girls" provided the snacks.[152]

These descriptions of alcoholic consumption all portray drinking in terms of male sociability. Women, as depicted by Hokkanen and Mäkelä, were cast in the role of judge, rather than fellow imbiber. After he got drunk, injured, and missed his award presentation at the Ski Factory Club, Lauri Hokkanen looked to his wife's reaction, remembering that "Sylvi wasn't too harsh on me."[153] Likewise, when Mäkelä was so intoxicated that he was expelled from the dance, "the girls sure [were] sore." In Christer Bucht's telling of the Strengs' Karelian story, narrated in Aino's voice, she states: "at our house vodka is not served, at least during my time."[154] Sylvi Hokkanen thought back on a particularly "spic and span" woman from the US who also lived in the Ski Factory complex.[155] In addition to her meticulous cleanliness, Hokkanen remembered the woman for something she had said: "If a man drinks, it is because of the woman's laxity."[156] Hokkanen reflected on the meaning of this saying: "since drinking was common among us at that time, it put the burden of the problem on the women."[157] The gendering of social acts – like alcoholic indulgence – and the gendering of moral regulation – here in the form of women's chastising – are both made visible in the Karelia life writing.

Athletics

Sports were a primary pastime in Karelia in the 1930s. The Finnish North American letters and memoirs detail involvement in numerous physical activities, ranging from casual leisure to serious competition. For the everyday participant, sport provided leisure and socialization. However, by committing to athletic pursuits, Finnish North Americans engaged in the socialist building of individuals and society, espoused by the North American Left and the Soviet centre. For the Soviet leadership and intelligentsia, sport built health, character, and identification with the state.[158] Finnish North American leftist sports associations, likewise, aimed to "raise the physical, intellectual and cultural level of workers by promoting an interest in physical activity, and to further the country's militant labour movement."[159] In the United States and Canada, many Finnish athletic organizations, representing different religious, temperance, or political identifications, vied for participants.[160] Through these clubs, Finnish migrants participated in gymnastics, wrestling, skiing, skating, baseball, and basketball, among other fields.

The Finnish-Canadian Amateur Sports Federation 1986 organizational history makes clear the Karelian migration's impact on Finnish sports in North America, noting the resultant decline in membership and the loss of top athletes.[161] Medal-winning wrestlers, skiers, and track and field athletes were among the emigrants. Vieno Zlobina's father, Elis Ahokas, was one such prized skier who left his local athletics club "Sports Chaps."[162] Further contextualizing the Karelian experience, *Sports Pioneers* illustrates how members of the federation, and thereby of the communist Finnish Organization of Canada, participated in a range of community sports, arts, politics, and entertainment. Such holistic participation was in keeping with the ideals of socialist enlightenment, and was also practised by Finnish migrants in Karelia.

While Finnish North American athletic organizations struggled in the immediate aftermath of the mass migration, Karelia gained many skilled athletes and experienced a boost in regional sporting and competition. The Karelian letters and memoirs paint an image of a community passionate about sports. The Finnish North American–organized baseball league, along with wrestling and soccer, were popular with both participants and observers.[163] Track and field events were common pastimes and Allan Sihvola remembered the long jump pit and high jump apparatus constructed by Finns at the Rutanen lumber camp.[164] Given Karelia's many rivers and lakes, swimming was another favourite summer amusement.[165] In the lumber camps, horseshoes were among favourite games.[166] During the summer, nearby lumber camps would get together for sporting competitions and community fun.[167] Tauno Salo wrote about how pool rooms were very much "in style" in 1935.[168] Youths could spend their time playing billiards for six rubles per hour.[169] Skiing was definitely the top winter sport in Karelia for all ethnicities, as it was elsewhere in the Soviet Union.[170] Reino Hämäläinen reported to Benny that "they do a lot of skiing and boy do they know how to ski out here."[171] During the long winter, in addition to being an avid cross-country and downhill skier, Aate Pitkänen also played on a hockey team and enjoyed keeping track of the local basketball teams.[172] Skating was another favourite pastime, with skating rinks in most towns across Karelia.[173] Reino Mäkelä's letters demonstrate how rinks were an important site for youth sociability. Mäkelä explained how "we go skatting [sic] with girls here like there too," and that "we go skatting [sic] here every night at the stadium where they have a band playing."[174] Vieno Zlobina also fondly remembered the "brightly illuminated" rink with the brass band, and how "boys used to approach girls stretching a hand ... New acquaintances and friends were made."[175] Skates and skis were among the most widely owned goods in 1930s Soviet Union, and quality skis were made in Petrozavodsk by Finnish North Americans employed at the Ski Factory.[176] It is unclear how easily obtainable skates and skis were in actuality, since Aate Pitkänen wrote about spending days mending and maintaining his equipment in November 1933.[177]

Competitive Sport and Embodying the Soviet Dream

For keen athletes hobbies could become a ticket for travel, Soviet praise, and safety from repression. Aate Pitkänen's letters and remarkable life story show a progression from leisure sporting to a full-time occupation. Pitkänen's love of sport had begun in Kivikoski, Ontario, but in Karelia he excelled. In the earliest available letters, from March and April of 1933, he wrote about his participation in biathlon events and ski meets in the Petrozavodsk area.[178] After a break in available letters that spans over two years, Aate wrote to his parents "about what I have been up to, that is, of course, about sport."[179] This March 1937 letter demonstrates Pitkänen transitioning toward full-time athletics. In February 1937, he placed second in the Soviet Union for slalom, but also participated at the national level in ski jumping. "Based on this," Pitkänen explained to his parents, "our trade union [athletic organization] left me in Moscow for a few days to train some more and then sent me to Svedlovski with my original instructor, to a league-wide camp and to an all trade union wide competition," where he placed second again.[180] At this time, he also competed and dominated in various cross-country skiing events. Pitkänen estimated that during the winter of 1937, sports competitions and training had taken him 17,500 kilometres.[181]

Two years later, Aate Pitkänen wrote again to his parents to fill them in on what had happened since the winter of 1937. He had been moved approximately 2,000 kilometers southeast to the city of Buzuluk to train athletes and to compete. "I will write more about sports, as they have become such a part of daily life," Pitkänen stated.[182] He recounted that, in Petrozavodsk, he had worked as a coach and trainer, though still technically working as a linesman. He had broken Karelian cycling records in the fall of 1937, a fact that is also mentioned in the memoir of Klaus Maunu, who had lived close by the Pitkänen family in the rural Thunder Bay area.[183] Pitkänen also reported having broken ski records, competing in downhill, slalom, ski jumping, and even one-footed ski jumping in 1938.[184] These successes secured Pitkänen a place on a national ski team, sending him to Leningrad and Sverdlovski to train and compete.[185] In 1940, Pitkänen developed a close relationship with future Soviet leader Yuri Andropov, who came to Karelia in 1940 to head the Youth League, which may explain Pitkänen's continuing work with the YCL.[186] Andropov was especially interested in bolstering the sports prowess of Karelian and Soviet youth, and supported Pitkänen's continuing athletic development, leading to another record year in 1941.[187] In an article on "Aate Pitkänen's Life and Death," journalist Anatoli Gordijenko interviewed one of Pitkänen's teammates, Tenho Nygard, also a North American Finn. Nygard portrayed his former colleague as a celebrity, stating that "the name of skier Aate Pitkänen was on everyone's lips."[188]

While Aate Pitkänen's transition from a skilled sports hobbyist to a major national competitor may seem fairly straightforward, Soviet policy regarding athletics complicates the story. Pitkänen's letters illustrate, in action, the Soviet centre's dichotomy between shaping world-class athletes and officially denouncing athletic professionalism.[189] No one in the Soviet Union was officially permitted to work as a full-time athlete, and no one was to earn a salary from sport, so loopholes emerged in the system. In Pitkänen's case, training and trial races took him away from work, but "all the travel costs [were] paid for by the trade union and in addition we get an allowance. In the resort where we were training we had free food and we were still getting full salary (same in all the later competitions)."[190] When Pitkänen was made a "voluntary" ski trainer – "during [his] free time" – the position quickly became priority. Pitkänen confessed that "not much came of my other work [as a telephone linesman] as even my days were spent in organizing sports."[191] He found time to work a day here and there, between travel for races and training. Pitkänen's experience resonates with Robert Edelman's explanation of top athletes having to "pretend" to work in another field.[192] Pitkänen wrote to his parents about how he had been rewarded with a gramophone and a radio in two separate races.[193] However, there may well have been other prizes that were left unmentioned. James Riordan has identified the "general process of elite-creation" that rewarded top athletes: "Even more than their counter-parts in industry, the sports stars began to receive large sums of money, priorities in respect to flats and scarce commodities for establishing records and winning championships."[194]

Aate Pitkänen's story is remarkable in exemplifying what could be called the Soviet Dream. As we have seen, Pitkänen's family history prepared him for a life of socialist commitment. In Karelia, Pitkänen began to embody the Soviet ideals. A common workshop poster in the Soviet Union proclaimed: "Every Sportsman should be a Shock Worker; Every Shock Worker, a Sportsman." Aate Pitkänen epitomized the slogan. He was a competitive athlete at the national level, and he was a rewarded shock worker and Stakhanovite in Karelia, going back to 1933. Pitkänen took seriously his commitment to socialist development, both personal and societal. Pitkänen's responses to return migration, as discussed above, suggest that he believed in the value of full engagement with the socialist project. In addition to all the ground he covered as an athlete in 1937, Pitkänen characterized his additional involvements as: "lots of work, and then I had to train the parachutists, and then I still attended Russian language courses in the evenings, and add still to that meetings (as they still put me in the Youth League's committee) and then I still did my training at the Aero Club."[195] Furthermore, Pitkänen reported to his parents that "I have always filled my norm 100%. During the winter I still continued my physical culture work in the evenings and during my days off."[196] Between 1937 and 1939, most Finns in Karelia were leading a life very different from that described in the letters of Aate Pitkänen. Severe Stalinist purges were striking the region. For Pitkänen, however, involvement in political study and activism through the Young Communist League, military preparedness work in the form of Oso (Special Operations) manoeuvre practices,[197] parachuting, Aero Club, Russian-language study to counter any "bourgeois nationalist' tendencies, Stakhanovite-level productivity, and top ski rankings constructed a safety net that elevated his social standing and protected him from the fate of many with whom he had made the journey to Karelia. Individuals like Aate Pitkänen served as personifications of ideal Soviet traits and the "good life' adamantly promoted by the centre.

Conclusion

Many Finnish North Americans wholeheartedly threw themselves into Karelian community building. They believed that they had been brought to Karelia to educate the region in labour productivity and to bring culture to the wilderness. However, in the process, they exacerbated the gulf between them and other residents of the region. Irina Takala explains the non-Finnish perspective:

> The energy of Finns, the fact that they were engaged in theatrical activities, singing, that they created their own orchestra, provoked open misunderstanding of the local population. The people couldn't believe how anybody could be engaged in a voluntary activity in such a difficult time, not having any means of subsistence. The people had suspicions that the Americans, in addition to the preferential rations for foreigners got some additional payment from Finnish authorities, because they couldn't understand how Finns could sing, play, and go in for sports while others were starving.[198]

For the North Americans, however, community involvement did not occur in spite of hardships: it flourished *because of* hardships. Based on the Karelian letters and memoirs, those who chose to stay in Karelia believed that they were building a flourishing economy and cultural life in "sure steps," as Antti Kangas wrote in 1934.[199] In Canada and the United States, Finnish migrants had stuck together and built a rich community life that integrated politics, the arts, athletics, and socialization – it would be no different in Karelia.

Considering life-writing portrayals of community life and leisure within the contexts of transforming Soviet attitudes and policies provides an opportunity to look at the ways Finnish North Americans chose to engage with the state and socialist building, and the ways they used formal venues to suit their personal needs. Youth remoulded their migrant backgrounds, socialist upbringing, and the avenues that the Soviet state opened to them, like movie theatres, official holidays, and political organizations, to befit courtship, sociability, and fun. Sylvi Hokkanen recalled: "being young and imbued with the idea of building a workers' paradise, as it was called, we took all the difficulties in stride ... And we had fun, real fun."[200] For Karelian life writers, the happy days of dances, dating, and sports came to stand as a foil for the community's tragic repression during the Great Terror, and the narration of those times of optimism somehow lessened the pain in the collective memory formed over time.

Chapter Seven

"Karelia Is Soaked in the Blood of Innocent People": Writing about the Great Terror

The fate of the Finnish North Americans' utopia in Soviet Karelia can, in part, be found in the pine forests of the region. At the northernmost tip of Lake Onega, some 160 kilometres north of Petrozavodsk, lies a horrific site of the Stalinist Great Terror. Up to 9,000 people were shot and buried in the forest of the small village Sandarmokh between 1937 and 1938.[1] The July 1997 excavation of the site found remains that showed that the victims "had been stripped to their underwear, lined up next to a trench with hands and feet tied, and shot in the back of the head with a pistol."[2] The victims were "men and women of sixty ethnicities and nine religions," many of whom had been brought there from hundreds of kilometres away.[3] Many were transported from Karelia's infamous Solovki prison, often referred to as Stalin's first concentration camp. At Sandarmokh, one man, Mikhail Matveev, a Leningrad NKVD administrative officer, personally killed 200 to 250 people every day over a five-day period in late October to early November 1937.[4] Matveev's own interrogation record from 1939, when he was arrested and tried for "excess of zeal," ultimately led to the discovery of the site and the names of many of its victims.[5] Yuri Dmitriev from Petrozavodsk was among the small group of independent researchers who found the Sandarmokh graves. Among those executed there, 268 Finnish North Americans have so far been identified.[6] Included in the list, we find individuals directly linked to this study: Oscar Corgan (Mayme Sevander's father), Frank Heino (husband of Justiina and father of Alice), Enoch Nelson, and Karelian Technical Aid director Matti Tenhunen.

Just 20 kilometres from Petrozavodsk lies another site of murder and unburied memories. In 1997 in Krasny Bor, the bodies of 1,193 people were found in mass, open-pit graves, identified by the depressions in the ground, characteristic of such sites. In the pit, excavators, again led by Dmitriev, found bullet holes in the back of skulls, shards of glass, and pieces of tin. The glass pieces were the remnants of vodka bottles, offered to give courage to the executioners; the tin was from meat cans, given as a reward for a job well done.[7] In addition to Krasny Bor, over 2,500 more bodies are said to have been hidden in the Petrozavodsk vicinity.[8] Many US and Canadian Finns are among them.

The people of Karelia, like those throughout the Soviet Union, fell victim to the Stalinist regime's cruel and murderous program of accusation, arrest, exile, and execution, which peaked in 1937–38. An analysis of how the Great Terror has been narrated, interpreted, and remembered by Finnish North American life writers humanizes the impact of this violent repression and deepens understandings of the ways in which the Terror impacted everyday lives, not only at the time, but also for decades later. Finnish North American letters from the mid-1930s to the first years of the 1940s provide an opportunity to read for glimpses of the Terror in action. What is written and, just as importantly, what is not may show the tenuous circumvention of censors and self-imposed silences. The letters reveal emotions and negotiations of self and place wrapped up in the fear and uncertainty of turbulent times, and the settling in of silences that would enshroud the history of Finnish North Americans for decades. Memoirs and retrospective letter collections written after Stalin's death make it possible to assess the multiple layers of silence in Finnish North American narratives, scars of trauma, the writers' search for "truth," and how the sources, taken together, promote the collective memory of Finnish North American life in Karelia and their community's loss.

The Great Terror

Violence and fear had been tools of the Soviet order since the Revolution, from the brutal containment of enemies during the Civil War to the repressions that accompanied Stalin's consolidation of power. However, the scope and magnitude of violence and repression, as primary tactics of control, reached unparalleled heights in 1937–38. During this time, known as the Great Terror, the Soviet government switched its focus from the hunt for "class enemies" to the uncovering of "enemies of the people." As Sheila Fitzpatrick argues, this change in rhetoric marked the transition from targeted repression to random, all-out attacks.[9] Though compiled numbers are incomplete and debated, Robert Conquest has estimated that in 1937–38, eight million people were arrested in the Soviet Union or, in other words, "one can virtually say that every other family in the country on average must have had one of its members in jail."[10] The gulags in those years held about seven million people, with the ultimate survival rate as low as 10 per cent.[11] At least one million people had been executed by late 1938.[12]

Across the Soviet Union, the formula of the Terror was largely the same. First, the night time arrest:

> Two or three NKVD men, sometimes brutal, sometimes formally correct, would knock and enter. A search was made which might be brief but could take hours, especially when books and documents had to be examined. The victim, and his wife if he had one, sat under guard meanwhile, until finally he was taken off. A quick-witted wife might in the long run save his life by getting him some warm clothes. By dawn, he would usually have been through the formalities and be in his cell.[13]

Then, at the prison, the arrested individual would undergo several rounds of interrogation, with the aim of obtaining a confession.[14] Since the arrested were almost all entirely innocent and the NKVD did not reveal what the alleged charges were, the prisoner would be left struggling until they invented their own crime to confess. Once the arrested had confessed and provided further names to the NKVD, they were sentenced to prison, the gulag, or execution, often without trial. Those who were executed were shot with a Soviet TT-33 pistol, which often required several bullets or the ultimate use of blunt force.[15] Those who were spared from personal arrest were little better off. The families of "enemies of the people" were evicted, removed from their jobs, and "shunned as plague-bearers."[16] Everyone feared their uncertain futures, not knowing if their relatives and friends would return, and whether their own turn was soon approaching.

The Terror in Karelia

Though defying any moral, logical explanation, the government's war on its own people found reason, in part, through the "inextricably intertwined" relationship of ideology and security, which sought to eliminate all dissent.[17] Dissent was defined broadly and arbitrarily. However, those with foreign contacts and the intelligentsia of minority nationalities were categorized, with certainty, as dangerous and needing to be suppressed. Proximity to the Finnish border, alleged "bourgeois nationalism," and perceived foreignness proved to be the undoing of Red Finn Karelia, and the justification for the wide-scale repression of Finns in the region.

Life in Karelia changed very quickly for Finnish North Americans. Sergei Kirov's murder on 1 December 1934 has often been pinpointed as the turning point for Finns in Karelia. As First Secretary of the

Leningrad Regional Party Committee, to whom the Karelian party was subordinate, Kirov had advocated on behalf of the Karelian Red Finn leadership. His successor, Andrei Zhdanov, however, legitimized his leadership by turning toward the Soviet centre and renewing attacks on the Finnish, Karelian, and Ingrian families living in the Karelian border districts, forcefully relocating thousands of individuals.[18] At this time, 400–500 regional political and industrial leaders, primarily Red Finns, were purged.[19] To thwart Finnish nationalism and to transfer local power to the Soviet centre, the Finns' much-respected First Secretary of the Karelian Party, Kustaa Rovio, was stripped of his post in August 1935. Four months later, in late November, Edvard Gylling was removed as Chairman of the Council of People's Commissars, and followed Rovio to Moscow. Both men, first reassigned to insignificant Central Committee work, were arrested in 1937 and executed in 1938. Russians from the Leningrad Party replaced Rovio, Gylling, and many other posts taken from Finns. Nick Baron argues: "from this time on, it is difficult to distinguish an independent Karelian position in any sphere of policy."[20]

By the autumn of 1935, Finnish North Americans, largely spared from the purges up to that point, could not deny that the tide had turned in Karelia.[21] Finnish North Americans working and living in the agricultural communes Säde and Hiilisuo were among the first to feel the weight of the repressions in the region, when their migrant leaders were arrested, exiled, and eventually executed for "bourgeois nationalism" and "wrecking."[22] The year 1936 was the calm before the storm, though people were arrested under no known formal policy or explanation. Early 1937 witnessed the continued removal of Finns in leadership positions. The Terror against the whole population was officially launched in Karelia and across the Soviet Union in July 1937, with Yezhov's signing of Operative Order 00447, the repression of "kulaks, criminals, and other anti-Soviet elements," followed in August by Order 00486, "The operation for the repression of wives of traitors of the Motherland" (also extended to children), and Orders 00439, 00485, and 00593, which specifically outlined the repression of national groups in the Soviet Union. While these national orders did not mention Finns by name, they became the primary target for the region's large-scale repression. A further October Order, number 00693, "Operation for the repression of illegal crossers of the border of the USSR," had especially devastating effects on the Finnish *loikkarit* (border hoppers). At the same time as issuing Order 0047, the Soviet government and NKVD empowered *troikas*, local groups of three people – though often operating as a *dvoika*, or twosome – to impose the death penalty.[23] In Karelia, the regional First Secretary, head of the local NKVD, and the Party Prosecutor served as arrestor, prosecutor, judge, and jury.[24]

Under the all-encompassing Order 00447, Karelia's first target, to be fulfilled between 5 August 1937 and 20 November 1937, demanded the purge of 1,000 people, 300 of whom were to be executed.[25] Heeding Yezhov's warning that "better too far than not enough," local police and the new party leadership were, in Baron's words, "inclined to interpret their quotas not as limits but as starting-points."[26] By the November deadline, the *troika* had, in fact, convicted more than double its target and sentenced 1,690 people to death.[27] Approximately 10,000 people were arrested in Karelia between July 1937 and August 1938, of whom up to 83 per cent were condemned to death.[28] These verdicts were called the "five kopek sentence," by Finnish North Americans in Karelia, referring to the cost of a bullet.[29] Although Finns represented no more than 3 per cent of the Karelian population, more than 40 per cent of the region's purge victims were ethnically Finnish.[30] Irina Takala traced the arrests of 418 Finnish Americans and 323 Canadian Finns (741 total), concluding that Finnish North Americans accounted for 15 per cent of the region's total purges.[31] Finnish North Americans in Karelia in 1938 numbered some 4,750, out of the approximate total free population of 447,000, or, in other words, no more than 1 per cent of the region's population. Therefore, Finnish North Americans, like Finns overall, comprised a disproportionately high percentage of those repressed in Karelia. Out of the North American Finns arrested, Takala has found that 84 per cent of the Canadians and 71 per cent of the Americans were executed.[32] The scale of death sentences imposed on Finns in Karelia led Auvo Kostiainen to label the Terror as "genocide."[33]

The number of arrests does not begin to address the true scope of the Great Terror in Karelia. Families and friends, ostracized and scarred, stand obscured behind the numbers that represent each individual taken by the NKVD. Finnish North American memoirs and oral histories abound with stories of the wives and children of arrested men being sent to places like the dreaded "Lime Island" on Lake Onega, where backbreaking forced labour and inadequate provisions claimed the lives, health, and spirit of many.[34] Fear was ever present. During the sweeping arrests, Klaus Maunu's father built a large wooden chest, knowing that if he were arrested, his family would be evicted.[35] In that case, they could quickly pack their essentials into the chest to bring with them. The chest stood as a constant reminder of what might lurk ahead.

In such a closely knit community, it is reasonable to say that the Terror reached into the lives of every Finnish North American in Soviet Karelia. This runs contrary to Sheila Fitzpatrick's argument that "the terror was not a terror for everyone" and that the Great Purges likely had less impact on the daily lives of ordinary people than disciplinary labour practices.[36] Fitzpatrick's argument rests on the fact that, overall, the Soviet Terror targeted officials and the intelligentsia above all others. However, in Karelia, the Finnish North Americans' privileged position, their very obvious "foreignness," their imported North American outspokenness, and the region's precarious border position in the geopolitical tensions between Finland and the Soviet Union made the migrants obvious targets. Anti-Finnish measures severely restricted the freedoms of the region's Finnish border hoppers, Red Finns, and Finnish North Americans alike. The Finnish language was eliminated in schools and administration, Finnish newspapers were discontinued, and cultural activities had to be conducted in Russian. As early as 1935, many once-desired Finnish teachers were dismissed for "nationalism."[37] Sylvi Hokkanen was among those whose teaching careers came to an abrupt end, ousted for being "foreigners" and insufficient in Russian.[38] Finnish children's education suffered greatly. Whole libraries of Finnish-language books were destroyed, although some, like young Klaus Maunu, hid away their cherished volumes.[39] The change in language policy proved very difficult for many migrants, who struggled to maintain jobs and go about their normal lives, as bravely noted in the letters of Justiina Heino and Lisi Hirvonen.[40] "We were not even supposed to speak Finnish in public," Sylvi Hokkanen remembered, and Allan Sihvola noted that "on the streets you would not dare speak Finnish aloud, as the Finnish language was an 'enemy of the state' language and taboo."[41] Mayme Sevander wrote: "People dared speak Finnish only in whispers, in their own rooms, behind closed doors and around only the most trusted of friends. The rest of the time people like my mother, who knew no other language, stayed silent, worried that the wrong words would slip out and then they, too, would be taken away."[42]

Indeed, the fear of saying the wrong thing began to tear apart friendships. In his memoir, Paavo Alatalo relays his interrogation with the NKVD in early 1938.[43] He had been asked about what his family discussed, to which he replied that he was too busy participating in Soviet-sanctioned activities to take note and that no one visited his home. In a January 2002 interview, Alatalo further elaborated that people did not visit with each other "because everyone feared each other. You didn't dare go, really, anywhere."[44] After the arrest of her father and the Säde leadership in August 1935, Vieno Zlobina remembered that "every following day was filled with fear and insecurity. I was afraid to confide in anyone, afraid to be branded the daughter of a peoples' enemy. I lived under oppressive isolation and kept my grief to myself."[45] Mayme Sevander recalled:

"We didn't know who was friend or who was foe ... Finns were no longer sticking together; no one was sticking together. We all looked out for ourselves and our own families; it was suicide to trust further than that."[46] There was reason to be suspicious and fearful. Denunciations were an unsavoury yet ever-present feature of Soviet life, and the case was no different in Karelia.[47] "It would make me happy to say that there were no turncoats among the Finnish community," Sevander proclaimed. "Alas, my correspondents and interviewees hold to another opinion."[48] Regardless, it was impossible to keep everything inside. Though writing about people's hesitance to speak, Sevander also remembered: "The arrests were all we talked about, but in whispers, always in whispers, and then we felt a knot in our stomachs, a fear that someone would hear us, that a hand would fall on our shoulder and voice would say, 'Come with me,' and that would be the end of us. But we couldn't help ourselves; we had to talk; stories went around despite the risk."[49]

Writing at the Time of Terror

In a world of whispers the letter could speak too loudly. It was widely known in the Soviet Union that the post was intercepted and that foreign contacts placed a person in danger.[50] Whether letters were stopped by censors before leaving the country or whether writers chose to cut off their foreign correspondences when the purges escalated,[51] few letters are available from the peak of the Terror. Those who desired to write utilized several correspondence strategies. Before delving into the covert and muted letter-writing practices, we first turn to a remarkable letter that depicts the life of terror with startling clarity.

Aino and Aatu Pitkänen escaped Karelia sometime between March and early June 1938. The couple travelled over 500 kilometres, surviving the month-long trek to the border and the subsequent eight days of quarantine in a Finnish prison, finally landing in their family village of Urimolahti. From there, Aino Pitkänen wrote a chilling letter to her husband's brother's family (Aate Pitkänen's mother and father) in Ontario, which detailed the dire situation so vividly and accurately that it merits quotation at length. Pitkänen wrote:

> Thank you for your letter that I received in March. I was very happy to receive it. Except there isn't really a place where I could read it because nowadays it's a bad person in the Soviet Union who receives letters from outside ... we poor people have not been feeling well for the entire past winter. This is because Russia is undergoing a big cleansing. The whole winter we were afraid whose turn is it to leave tonight. Soldiers came with

their bayonets to get [people][.] after that nothing more was known [of them]. From the whole river they took Finns so thoroughly that only four men were left when we escaped[.] they have [since] taken the rest of them as well ... You cannot believe what life in the Soviet Union was like last winter. People have not done anything bad, only hard work, and this is the way they are treated, some are imprisoned, others sent away ... All last winter we did not dare sleep[.] always had to watch the door because the soldiers always came at night. This imprisonment of people is because of saboteurs [and] innocent people have to suffer, especially Finns. All the Finnish books had to be burned, Finnish newspapers were discontinued. Karelian and Russian languages came into use [and] we forcibly became illiterate. They did organize night circles for Karelian and Russian language ... This was a good thing, in the country, [use] the country's language. All the women whose husbands had been imprisoned were treated badly by the local leadership. Those women who were working less strenuous tasks, for example in the cafeteria, were taken out of work and sent to the forest, even if they had small children[.] In the forest a woman alone can't keep many children alive. It also happened that they were evicted and told to go where they please ... There were eight widows living together in one small room with three children. But because they were wives and children of the imprisoned they are left [like that]. You may think that I am slandering the welfare of the workers in the Soviet Union. I am not, but writing as things are. It is not the wish of the Party or the Government, but when saboteurs have infiltrated such places where they can do damage, then an honest worker becomes their victim. That is what happened to us ... Injustice wins no matter how good the person is. Because today in Russian prisons there sit hundreds of innocents. At least our conscience does not bother us that we would have done anything wrong against the Soviet Union.[52]

The letter further outlined the names of arrested friends whom the Pitkänen family knew from Canada.

Aino Pitkänen displayed a striking understanding of hostility towards foreign contacts, the nature of the arrests, the attack on the Finnish language, the state of Soviet prisons and justice, and the fate of wives of "enemies of the people." Pitkänen's narrative clearly demonstrates that while the men were taken (and the horrors they endured were not witnessed by those who remained), women and their children were disempowered and displaced. The suffering of women and children served as a powerful symbol of inhumanity.[53] It is not known how Antti and Kirsti Pitkänen reacted to such shocking news. Antti had been in Karelia and learned first-hand that Soviet communism was not what he and other Finnish North Americans had imagined. However, Antti Pitkänen left before the purges in Karelia accelerated. They received positive messages about Karelia's development from son Aate, as we have seen. Furthermore, Antti and Kirsti were staunch communists, who upheld the party line. Yet, here was a letter, from Antti's sister-in-law and brother that told of unbelievable horrors. Aino Pitkänen placed the blame on "saboteurs," explicitly stating that the chaos was "not the wish of the Party or the Government." Pitkänen portrayed herself as a loyal communist, and distanced herself from "slandering," which so many who had left Karelia had been accused of. Though out of the Soviet Union, Aino Pitkänen demonstrated remarkable bravery in "writing as things are," choosing to get the news out, despite the risks of Soviet retribution and North American communist – even family – excommunication. Pitkänen's letter stands as a significant, rare, contemporary first-hand account of the Terror in Karelia.

Other Finnish North Americans, still in Karelia, were more restrained. Some chose to simply discontinue writing letters until life seemed more settled. This seems to have been Aate Pitkänen's strategy, whose available letters contain a gap between early 1937 and 1 January 1939. Aino Pitkänen, however, wrote about Aate to his parents: "well then greetings from Aate. He does not dare write to you or to us. He was very emotional when we left. Aate can't be any surer of when the retrievers attack him."[54] Some migrants nevertheless strove to maintain their correspondence, despite difficulties and never knowing for sure whether the letters would arrive at either end. Writers devised strategies and codes to pass their letters through the system. Through close reading and contextualization, it is possible to identify some of the ways in which Finnish North Americans addressed politically sensitive topics. Instead of writing directly, correspondents often slipped mention of forbidden topics amid typical content. For example, after Frank Heino was arrested, Alice simply asked her brother, "Have you gotten a letter from Pop?" and otherwise left him unmentioned in the letter.[55] However, without knowledge of what was happening inside the Soviet Union, many North American recipients did not understand the hints.[56]

Sometimes frustration and distress led writers to throw subtlety out the window. In a letter written close to the same time as Alice's letter mentioned above, Justiina Heino overtly stated: "I got [a letter] from Martta now and she didn't know that father's been arrested even though I wrote her in as political way as I knew how but I still saw from the letter that she hadn't received my letter."[57] Perhaps exemplifying glitches in the Soviet mail interception system, Heino's letter, explicitly addressing arrest, the act of masking writing, and state censorship reached its destination.

Others remained silent about what was happening around them, but have left clues for the knowing reader. No letters written by Lisi Hirvonen in 1937 have been found. There is no way to know whether she wrote during that year, but in February 1938, Hirvonen wrote that she had received her sister's letter "ages ago." According to Hirvonen, it had been left unanswered "because there isn't any news really."[58] Given Aino Pitkänen's description of the same awful winter in Karelia, one can deduce that Hirvonen had chosen silence. David Gerber argues that it is the historian's task to "explain how it is that intentional, strategic silence, where we might be fortunate enough to find traces of it, may have been integrated into the negotiations that comprise epistolarity."[59] Worries about censorship and the consequences of writing outright added another actor into the epistolary negotiation. In addition to protecting her sister from the truth of what was happening in Karelia, by avoiding the topic and adding assurances that she was "OK," Lisi Hirvonen had to construct her letters in a way that protected her from a third party overseeing the correspondence. Perhaps Hirvonen's silence also indicated her personal process of trying to understand what was happening around her. Although they had already separated, Eino Hirvonen was arrested in 1938 and it seems that Lisi had also at least been interrogated by police.[60] Writing on 10 September 1938, she acknowledged her silence, reporting that she had "so much to say but can't, maybe sometime in the future."[61] She would never reveal all she had hoped to share with her sister. Nothing is known about Lisi Hirvonen after a letter from Petrozavodsk dated 19 July 1939.

Ann Goldberg observes that "because authentic feelings and thoughts mostly could not be communicated, that form had become hollowed out and transformed. Letter-writing thus became a kind of mimicry of authenticity and privacy, a performance in which real communication of real thoughts occurred only in oblique, coded, and disguised form."[62] The letters of Terttu Kangas reveal the strategy of moving attention away from one's self in order to avoid difficult topics. Kangas apologized to her sister for not having written between January 1937 and January 1939 by explaining that the "biggest reason of course has been just laziness."[63] Kangas's letters typically offered elaborate, if not mundane, descriptions of her daily life. However, other than a few very brief lines about her family's work, questions to her sister almost entirely made up the January 1939 letter. Kangas told nothing about what had happened in her life over the last two years. She wanted to reconnect with her sister, but could not write about her life honestly and openly. By posing question after question to her sister, she was able to re-establish their correspondence, while safely maintaining the silence surrounding the two missing years. Like Lisi Hirvonen, the fate of Terttu Kangas and her family is so far unknown beyond the 30 January 1939 letter.

The long gaps and stoppages in correspondence, and the uncertainty of whether one's mail would even arrive, profoundly affected the relationship of correspondents and the emotional condition of the Karelian writers. When one's sense of self could be partially wrapped up in regular connections with the life left behind, being without letters caused a disruption of "personal continuity."[64] Failure to hear from loved ones could lead to a severe sense of loneliness and depression. After losing two young sons in Karelia and not knowing what had happened to her husband after his arrest in 1938, Justiina Heino expressed in her letters a desperate plea for ties to her family and old community. Heino wrote that she had been wondering about all kinds of old friends and looking at the few photographs she had, but confessed she knew nothing of their lives, having been without correspondence for so long.[65] Photographs and letters received, looked at over and over again, made poor substitutes for missed people, but provided a tangible link. While asking her sister questions moved attention away from her own life, Terttu Kangas's January 1939 letter can also be viewed as an attempt to re-entrench herself in the social world of the community she had left behind and now longed for. Uncertainty clouding daily life solidified the desire to maintain the security of belonging in the home community and prompted nostalgic memories of friends, family, and the places left behind.

It became increasingly difficult for Finnish North Americans to stay optimistic about past decisions to move to Karelia. In Lisi Hirvonen's final available letter, from July 1939, she reflected on her life's choices:

> Yes, many times I sadly remember you all because I am so alone here but that is my fate. I have thought that I should have stayed there in Canada and not gone anywhere like a hobo[.] I have come to the view that the person is the most happy and contented who is in one place their whole life even though too late I came to understand. Well, what about it[,] you can't get it back anymore.[66]

Hirvonen, like many of the letter writers, had expressed her belief that life in Karelia would only improve, but the passing of time and the hostile environment challenged her hopefulness.[67] With the possibility of leaving the Soviet Union practically eliminated by 1936, many Finnish North Americans, like Hirvonen, were saddened yet resigned to their "fate" of life in Karelia.

Others, still, would not accept their place in Karelia and became increasingly desperate to leave.[68] The letters of Kalle Korhonen to his estranged daughter Aune inflict readers with the uneasy emotions of strained relationships, regrets, and losses. The very intimate details of this letter exchange can only truly be understood by the correspondents, and since Aune's voice is missing, the analysis of this collection proves challenging. However, being mindful of the ways that letter writers shape their narratives to best convey their needs and to suit their audience, it is possible to read the strain caused by political upheaval in Karelia across the strain of the relationship depicted in Korhonen's letters. The span of the correspondence reveals Korhonen's ever-growing desire to leave Karelia and the strategies he employed to discuss his return with his daughter, in light of both the nature of their relationship and the turmoil in Karelia.

Korhonen extended his first letter to Aune in August 1935, noting three years of silence between them.[69] The letter portrays the positive sides of Soviet and Karelian life, leaning heavily on ideological language. By late October 1936, Korhonen admitted that he and his wife had begun to think about returning to North America.[70] He wrote about his preference for the United States rather than Canada, but noted that getting into the United States would be more difficult. Korhonen warned his daughter not to tell anyone about his plans. In the next letter, written 30 January 1937, Korhonen again noted: "I have begun to grow the idea of moving still to the USA. but it is now a bit difficult. Requires organization and can't travel whenever you want."[71] Korhonen's writing may signal the growing tensions in Karelia. In May 1937, Korhonen did not write directly about returning, but expressed his desire to be with his daughter in emotional terms. He wrote: "Only now I too feel, with a serious mind, that I wish to be near you, I wish to see you often – your child, your husband I wish to see often ... but especially you ... Before I didn't feel this matter, did not comprehend with love. Now I feel it."[72] Korhonen's letters in January and May 1937 did not speak directly to the increasing arrests and unease gripping the Finnish community, but his emotion may hint at the fear and uncertainty with which he and others were becoming acquainted.

Korhonen's letter dated 30 November 1937 is rare both because it was written during the peak of the Terror and because it shows signs of strategic writing. This letter is devoid of the emotion seen in the previous one. Given how frankly Korhonen had written about his desire to return to North America less than a year prior and the horrors we know were occurring in Karelia at the time of writing, this letter suggests active self-censorship. Korhonen wrote: "I, because I am ill so much, think sometimes that [I'll] move there again, for health's sake, but from the other side rises counter-points against. I know that my health is [best] in that climate but the socialist system has already strongly taken hold. It says: here is your home! For health reasons only, if at all, otherwise no."[73] Korhonen masked his desire to leave in the safety of a discussion of his health. Korhonen framed this letter narrative as a debate with himself, but one can question who exactly raised the counterpoints. Reading between the lines, the socialist state had, indeed, taken hold and told Finnish North Americans, Korhonen among them, that Karelia and the Soviet Union was their home, which they could not leave.

No letter from the following year has been found, and it is unknown if Korhonen wrote during that time. On 30 November 1938, exactly one year after the last letter and as the Terror subsided, Korhonen again wrote directly about his plan to leave Karelia. He listed his work experience and capabilities, and directed Aune to go to the local immigration authorities.[74] In February 1939, Korhonen wrote again, revealing that he had not heard back from her. This time, he explicitly referred to "my aspiration to return again to the United States," to obtaining travel permits, and asked Aune to seek the advice of both a lawyer and the Finnish Consulate to see whether he could return directly or whether he should go through Finland.[75] Not having heard from his daughter, Korhonen could only "assume that you have tried to accomplish something" regarding his return plans.[76] A letter from George Halonen, from Superior, Wisconsin, to Mrs Aune Batson, dated 5 April 1939, accompanies Korhonen's letter collection. Halonen wrote: "I received a confidential letter from your father stating that he would like to come back to America. He also informed me that he has written you about the same question. Consulting our attorneys here I found that you as his daughter have the only possibility to apply for his re-entrance."[77] Halonen made suggestions about how Aune should best proceed. By 30 October 1939, Korhonen had still not heard from Aune. In his last available letter, he scolds his daughter for not writing and pleads for her help to get back to the United States.[78]

Kalle Korhonen never made it back. Allegedly, he died alone in Petrozavodsk from long-plaguing tuberculosis, just half a year after writing the final available letter.[79] Though denying his existence to her own daughter and husband, Aune saved her father's letters.[80] Aune could not have known what her father was experiencing in Karelia when he wrote her about wanting to return. Employing different strategies and approaches to get his message past the censors to his daughter, Korhonen's letters likely read, to Aune, as too cryptic and confused, and perhaps too self-serving. Kalle Korhonen's letters depict a time when little was heard from Finnish North Americans in Karelia, show the increasingly desperate desire by some to escape, and shed light on some of the ways in which letters were shaped to get the message out, without saying too much.

Life Writing and Returning to the Terror

"Now I will continue these lines in this tranquil quietness with just the clock on my desk ticking away the time of eternity and let my thoughts roam to the far off years of strife and struggle," wrote Jack Forsell to his niece in February 1979.[81] He continued:

> So unreal it seems now that if I wrote to you about those years you wouldn't believe me, for even to me they seem so unbelievable. It's a miracle that I happened to survive those years when thousands and millions succumbed who were in the same conditions as I was. All of this was no earning or heroism of mine, just pure luck and chance [in] which I believe, but not in heros [sic].[82]

In this remarkable statement, Forsell addressed the processes of thinking and writing about his experiences with Stalinist repressions and war, making sense of what had happened, making peace with why he had survived, and the problems of conveying an extremely difficult past, of which little was known or understood, especially by outsiders. For Forsell and other Finnish North American life writers, narrating the Great Terror proved difficult, even long after the death of Stalin. In their memoirs and retrospective letters, they continued to utilize various tactics to convey their experiences in 1930s Soviet Karelia in a way that offered them protection from the past. Their narratives reveal silences, the scars of trauma, the quest for "truth," and a sense of belonging in a collective of grief and memory.

Finnish North Americans had multiple factors to overcome to bring their past to light, and many, instead, kept their stories to themselves. Stalin's regime actively concealed the nature of its reign from the West, and found protection in communist parties outside of the Soviet Union.[83] Migrants who managed to return to North America did not find a receptive audience in the very communities that had stood by them in the fight for workers' rights and had seen them off to Karelia. While the significant and well-documented Finnish migrant involvement in Left politics in Canada and the United States was in decline by the late 1930s, many still strongly believed into the 1950s and well beyond that the Soviet Union was a workers' paradise and that Stalin was the true leader of working people. It was difficult to believe that paradise had become hell on earth and that the Father of the Soviet Union could wilfully harm his own people. Mayme Sevander blamed North American communists for silencing those who had lived through the purges, using "misrepresentations" to protect the movement.[84] Lauri Hokkanen remembered an incident at their welcoming party, when they returned to the United States in 1941:

> But there was one sour note to that afternoon. A fellow from the Soo made a welcoming speech. He said very little about us but got into politics, bragging about the Soviet Union. Among other things, he said that no innocent people had been arrested there. I was about to object but could not get a word in at that point, and so I let it go. I have regretted ever since that I did not speak up, but because I knew how my mother felt, I remained silent.[85]

Even Hokkanen's mother, a committed communist, would not believe what her son and daughter-in-law recounted.[86] Furthermore, in the eyes of the rising Finnish right wing in North America, people "foolish" enough to have turned their backs on capitalism and religion, or even worse, on their Canadian or US citizenship, largely deserved what they had experienced.[87] As the Cold War intensified, those who had been to Karelia were forced to hide their pasts for fear of anti-communist retribution. Many returnees moved away from their old home communities to be freed from the stigma of their Soviet experiences. Finnish migrant communities were not safe places for survivors to speak. Lauri Hokkanen wrote: "I really wouldn't have minded telling them about it, but that subject always stirred up strong feelings."[88]

While Canadian and US Finnish returnees had a difficult time sharing their Karelian experiences in North America, those who remained in Karelia internalized the Soviet culture of silence. During Stalin's reign, the phrase "we do not arrest innocent people" was repeated ad nauseam, though people in the Soviet Union knew otherwise.[89] Khrushchev's "Secret Speech" in 1956 at long last began to tell the story of what had happened in the late 1930s. He exposed the Stalinist regime's crimes, and explained them with the concepts of "cult of personality" and "unjustified repression." Khrushchev's Thaw, placing the blame on Stalin, focused on party members and the political elite, saying little about the crimes against ordinary people. Families began to seek answers from the government, but received falsified death certificates that cited natural causes and, most often, dating the deaths to the time of the war.[90] Though the public work of mourning could cautiously begin, there were still many things that could not be said, by the state or its citizens. Soviet openness proved relatively short-lived, as the Brezhnev "Stagnation," beginning in 1964, has been referred to as the "repression of repressions."[91] Mikhail Gorbachev's *glasnost* of the late 1980s again reintroduced the hope of uncovering and redressing the horrors endured by the population in the first half of the twentieth century. The era saw the successful work of many memorial societies, such as the discovery and memorialization of the Krasny Bor and Sandarmokh sites in Karelia. It seems the current political situation in Russia has again drawn a veil over the past.

The Soviet Union (and now Russian Federation) has concealed and revealed parts of its dark history in waves that have hindered both society's and individuals' ability to make sense of their past.[92] Mayme Sevander wrote about getting a friend to open up about his arrest years later, when he left Karelia for Finland: "of course, I had to give a vow of silence, but I dare break it now as he is gone, almost 50 years have passed since then and the truth is coming out."[93] Following an oral history interview about his life in Karelia, Harold Hietala wrote a series of letters to Varpu Lindström that touched on his feelings about having become a historical subject. In one letter, Hietala apologized for the "tight-worded" replies he had given in the interview.[94] He explained that he did "not yet believe that [in Russia] you can speak about things as they in reality are for many have totally without guilt been made to spend years in prison camps and those who have been there don't have the mind to go there again."[95] His memories of imprisonment stayed with him, as had the Soviet culture of silence. Hietala felt comfortable enough to write about his hesitancy to speak. Instead of viewing the migrants' silence as "submission," it should be viewed as an active process of guarding their life narratives against psychological pain.[96]

"If all my letters to Canada were gathered into one pile it would be quite a package," Jack Forsell wrote, "but in these letters I have never written about our 'political life' here. This part of our life has been a 'closed book' to you people there in Canada. Why? Simply because if I wrote about it you people there wouldn't understand anything about it or even believe it!"[97] The Karelian survivors had difficulty seeing how others could relate to their experiences and were rarely willing to break the silence that could lead to mutual understanding. Like Aino Pitkänen, who twice wrote that the recipients of letters would be unable to understand what had happened,[98] fifty years later Jack Forsell still believed that a definite line existed between those in Karelia and "you people there." Some years later, Forsell warned his niece that "the actual tragedies would be too hard for you to digest."[99] Sylvi Hokkanen reflected: "I found it sad that we could not talk about [the Karelian experience] with others because they wouldn't have or couldn't have understood."[100] Indeed, an experiential gulf existed between those who had lived through the Terror and those on the outside who had not and did not know what had occurred in the Soviet Union.[101]

Very few Finnish North American survivors have been willing to draw attention to the period of the purges in their life writing. The Hokkanens' memoir begins and ends with emotional, indirect references to what they experienced in Karelia and how they were subsequently silenced in North America. However, the body of the memoir says very little about specific encounters with the Terror and state repression.[102] Smith and Watson note that "since a narrative cannot recount all time of experience, its gaps as well as its articulated time produce meaning."[103] In a 1972 letter, Forsell set out to "write at least a few sentences of our life here in the past and present."[104] That life story jumps from the birth of his son in 1931 to the death of his daughter in the fall of 1939, with no discussion of anything between. With so many layers of silence surrounding their pasts, the Karelian life writers undoubtedly questioned how much they could say and how their stories would be received. In addition to considerations of audience and reception, the Finnish North American writers were confronted with the emotional discovery inherent in the life-writing process.[105] Discussing her research, Mayme Sevander noted that "not every Finnish-American responded to my articles and questionnaires. Many of those in the Soviet Union who had gone through the drastic experiences of the thirties were reluctant to let their memories go back to the days when they had lost their loved ones."[106] Though willing to tell her own story of struggle and loss, Sevander acknowledged that "recalling the horrendous past is torture."[107] Perhaps some, as Jay Winter suggests, "remain silent, since ... the pain described is inflicted once again through testimony."[108]

Working through Wounds

Antze and Lambek recognize that unwillingness to discuss or remember traumatic events "are less refusals to continue telling stories than to continue interpreting them."[109] Interpretation proves painfully difficult, as "trauma is a disruptive experience that disarticulates the self and creates holes in existence."[110] The extensive letter collections of Jack Forsell and Reino Mäkelä demonstrate how the Terror of 1937–38 and the war years continued to occupy their thoughts and writing, even after many years, but representing these difficult pasts required protective strategies. Jack Forsell used the narrative device of "disowning" the voice or self that had experienced trauma in order to confront it.[111] Forsell began "disowning" years earlier, during his childhood in rural northwestern Ontario.[112] As remembered in letters to his niece, nature had served as the line between a severe father–son relationship and his dreams of a brighter future. Jack remembered: "The biggest joy and peace I felt [was] when I rambled in the bush listening to the sounds of nature."[113] His letters repeatedly return to the same wording and imagery to emphasize the serenity he found in the forest; time spent there represented Jack's "other life."[114] Like marking a distinction between his "real," troubled life and his "other life" in his youth, Jack turned to other voices (selves) to explain and make sense of what he had experienced during the purges and war. Although Forsell wrote about these experiences in several letters over the twenty-five-year span of his correspondence, he never once described his personal experiences directly. In 1979, he wrote about a chance meeting with a woman he had originally met during the war.[115] Jack and the woman had shared a difficult evacuation experience, but he narrated the circumstances of their initial meeting in the voice of the woman.[116] When Jack wanted to broach the topic of the Terror with his niece in Canada, rather than using his own experiences and knowledge, he sent a newspaper article on the subject.[117] Again, Forsell used someone else's voice to tell his lived experiences.

Reino Mäkelä's letters reveal similar strategies. Over the twenty-one years of correspondence, Mäkelä wrote mostly about family and work, and, as Mayme Sevander remarked, "he had his own troubles, but up to his dying day he preserved a positive outlook on life."[118] Though he may have been generally happy in his life, when Mäkelä's letters are read closely, they reveal that memories of the Terror and war were never far from his mind. However, Mäkelä stopped himself from elaborating on those experiences. The Terror explicitly enters Mäkelä's correspondence on two occasions, when he addressed the arrest and death of his brother. In August 1967, Mäkelä wrote: "Kalervo was never married. He was 19 years old when they took him and he died there in 1946."[119] Mäkelä wrote nothing about who "they" were, why Kalervo was taken, or where "there" was. Eleven years later, in the midst of writing about family (likely responding to questions from his correspondent), Mäkelä wrote:

> Kalervo wasn't married. He was young when he was arrested. We had a bad time in 1938 when a lot of Finns were arrested for nothing. Kalervo was in prison for 8 years and died in prison in 1946.[120] When he died we got papers that he was innocent like a lot of people arrested at that time were and [never] came home again. It was the enemies of this country that got into our higher organization. They were all arrested in 1939. Annikki's father

was arrested too and he died in prison too. Innocent. Get the papers after they died.

Enough of this.[121]

Mäkelä wrote in a very matter-of-fact way, presenting facts as he understood them, and avoiding overtly emotional language. It is worth noting that while he got caught up in memories of the Terror, no "I" appears in the description. He abruptly ends the discussion; the space between the description and "enough of this" stands as a physical, tangible separation between "this" past and the present Mäkelä wanted to write about in his letter. The strategies employed by Forsell and Mäkelä – while likely subconscious – exemplify the distancing, deference, and disowning of the victim-self that is common to narratives of trauma.

Laurence Kirmayer argues that "if a community agrees that traumatic events occurred and weaves this fact into its identity, then collective memory survives and individual memory can find a place (albeit transformed) within that landscape." If, however, the community does not believe in the occurrence of trauma, "the possibility for individual memory is severely strained."[122] Finnish North American survivors of the Terror can be seen as fitting into both categories. Those individuals who wrote during the purges (through heavily censored mail) and immediately following their return to North America, when many Finnish North American leftist communities continued to support the Soviet regime, did not have the opportunity to remember and share their experiences with fear, violence, and loss on the communal or social level. On the other hand, Finnish North Americans experienced the purges collectively and talked, though in hushed voices, about events as they unfolded. Among the Finnish North American survivors, breaking silence has resulted in a collective "founding trauma"[123] and a strong urgency to depict what they believed to be the truth of life under Stalin.

"Truth"

In 1996, at the age of ninety-one, Jack Forsell looked back on sixty-six years of life in Karelia and wrote: "I do hope that all the 'enlightened' people of the world will someday know the truth of life & death in the USSR."[124] While struggling to find a way to tell their stories, Forsell and other Karelian life writers believed that their narratives had to contribute to getting the "truth" into the open. In this way, the Finnish North American memoirs and retrospective letters belong, in part, to the genre of testimonial narrative. In this type of writing, "the emphasis is on the I as an *eye*, a witness, of some injustice that the narrative seeks to put on record, if not redress."[125] However, the life writers were faced with a daunting task. Writers had to work through what happened, applying order to the uncertainty, mourning the failure of the socialist project, and finding a voice for their multifaceted truths.

La Capra goes so far as to suggest that the "literal truth" of victim narratives may be irrelevant to the value they offer.[126] Instead, as David Gerber argues, "narrative truth, which assists in establishing continuity and stability amidst the inconsistencies and the frequent contradictions of life, is more important for individuals than literal truth when it comes to the ongoing work of constructing personal identities."[127] Karen Armstrong's analysis of narratives by women evacuated from their Karelian homes to Finland after the Winter and Continuation Wars likewise found that they "aim at an emotional truth rather than the truly true."[128] The emotional truth allows life writers to get at the essence of their personal experience and brings what is important to them to the surface. For Karelian life writers, the quest for truth gets caught somewhere at the intersections of "emotional truth," "narrative truth," and "literal truth." Having endured immense hardships and witnessed *untold* horrors, those who felt secure enough to voice their stories had begun to insist on telling and being told the "literal truth" of what had happened in decades past. At the same time, though, these survivors came to formulate their own "narrative truths" to explain what happened and why they made it through alive. Catherine Merridale reflects on the uniqueness of Russian elders' memorized "monologues," concluding that

> It makes a difference if you spent the best part of your life without the luxury of comparison or collective context, relating the story only to your closest friends, and sometimes even not to them, without re-focusing the images. It also makes a difference if you never had the chance to acquire the knack, the discipline, of listening.[129]

A part of finding one's "truth" was the process of "making sense."[130] Klaus Maunu's memoir demonstrates attempts to bring order to what he experienced during the Great Terror and war. Maunu's memoir searches for explanations in the past. He remembered the fortune cake a family friend in Pike Lake, Ontario, had made. Each slice contained a small item that was to provide a glimpse into the future. When Maunu's revealed a piece of chain, he recalled, they all joked that perhaps he would end up in jail someday. Some seventy years later, after surviving his time in a Ukrainian labour camp, Maunu wrote: "wasn't that a true prediction."[131] He pinpoints the murder of Kirov as "some kind of turning point in my life."[132] The role of this event in his writing suggests that its impact became apparent after the fact, rather than at the time. He conceded that the talk about the murder quickly died down but believed that it made a "lasting impression" on people.[133] The overall "turning point" of the narrative occurs in Maunu's telling of 1936. The narrative transitions immediately from a description of what he called his "most pleasant times" to "the 'grey' times."[134] His writing marks a clear delineation between carefree, youthful life, and the onset of confusion and fear caused, first, in Maunu's chronology, by the arrest of Finnish writers accused of nationalism. By looking to the past to find foreshadowing of what was to come, Klaus Maunu pieced together an unstable logical chain of events that could offer some coherence in the disrupted timeline of traumatic events.

Committed to the process of recording their life stories, the memoirists studied here each shaped their narrative in a chronological sequence that moved from North America, to the early days of Karelian life, to the Terror, and through wartime. This ordering allowed the writers to present a coherent portrayal of their life. However, in the case of Jack Forsell and Reino Mäkelä, who narrated their life stories through letter correspondence over the span of many decades, the formulation of such order and progression was not possible. It is clear in both letter collections that the act of writing to their old home communities had the effect of transporting their memories to the past. For Forsell and Mäkelä, the past in North America, the present day at the time of writing, and their Karelian past became entangled. The narratives of both men conflate the hardships of the Terror and war years. Perhaps because the form of letter writing hindered the establishment of a narrative chronology and a sense of order for their life stories, and because of the intimate presence of the letter recipient as audience, these two life writers proved least able to approach their experiences with Terror head-on in writing.

Along with making sense of one's life trajectory and how the Terror had come to be, a part of the survivors' work was coming to terms with what had become of the socialist project. Jack Forsell wrote about his disenchantment with the Soviet political system on several occasions and lamented the loss of both the idea of socialism and the lives sacrificed. Forsell claimed: "the very first winter here I realized that this isn't the Socialism which I had *dreamed* about & I doubt if there has ever been any Socialism in the USSR."[135] He blamed all that had happened on Lenin, writing: "Lenin was the greatest despot of the 20th century. It was he that founded the USSR with its terrorist & totalitarian methods of rule. The blood of millions upon millions of people are on the conscience of the party he created."[136] Sylvi Hokkanen recalled a night in July 1938 when the Finnish North American barracks were assaulted with arrests on a vast and brutal scale. Hokkanen remembered hearing her beloved anthem "Internationale" playing from the outdoor speakers, as the NKVD raided. She wrote: "Until then, the 'Internationale' to us had been an expression of hope for a better world in the future, for freedom from fear. But now, hearing its stirring notes and, at the same time, being witness to a mass arrest of friends and fellow workers horrified us."[137]

The failure of the socialist project weighed heavily on Mayme Sevander. Sevander devoted herself to disseminating the history and "truth" of what had happened to Finnish North American immigrants in Karelia, or "My People," as she preferred to call them.[138] Taking responsibility for the fates of Finnish North Americans, Sevander expressed her need to

> apologize for my father and his comrades who, due to their firm convictions, due to their zeal in furthering the Cause, found hundreds of followers among Finnish-Americans willing to be among the foreign pioneers, to help the newborn State which was to become a haven for workers and peasants. Remembering my father's profound honesty and dedication, I'm sure he'd approve of the work I undertook and these logical conclusions. I'm not denouncing these idealists. I'm bowing my head in reverence to those committed Finnish men and women whose moral obligations were so high, that they completely disregarded their own interests.[139]

In addition to making peace with her father's role in the Karelian project and bringing attention to the plight of Finnish North Americans, Sevander emphasized the lessons that the Karelian tragedy offered the present day. She concludes *Red Exodus* by stating:

> I'm convinced that a profound knowledge of the crimes and blunders of the so-called socialist epoch is imperative to avoid repetition of the past ... I wanted to let the world know about a very unusual, outmoded set of believers, to prevent those honest people from falling into oblivion, and to rehabilitate true democratic socialism, which many have lost their faith in, and its supporters.[140]

Contemporary life in the Soviet Union (later Russian Federation) provided both Sevander and Jack Forsell with continuous parallels. In *Of Soviet Bondage*, Mayme Sevander argued: "You may agree with me or you may not. But with criminality running riot in Russia today I find a direct connection between the crimes of the past and those of today."[141] The widespread hunger and economic crisis of the 1990s brought Forsell back to memories of secretly helping families of "enemies of the people" and to the "hungry years" of the war.[142] By drawing connections between events of the past and those of the present day, life writers also connected understandings of their past selves with their present selves.

As the history of Finnish North Americans in Karelia began to be publicized, those who lived through the Terror judged how well their experiences were represented. Jack Forsell criticized Mayme Sevander's *They Took My Father* for covering "all this awful bloodshed in a couple of paragraphs."[143] For Forsell, the "truth [was] much more tradgic [*sic*]."[144] However, he concluded that "all in all I hope many people will read this book. It's better than nothing."[145] Although Forsell was happy that journalists and other researchers were beginning to reveal the story of the Finnish North Americans in Karelia, he was critical of the trends he saw: "now the 'fad' of the times is that writers & journalists write about the crimes of that time & of people who fell victims to this crime, but they are silent about the criminals that convicted & shot these innocent people!"[146] The "truth" for Jack Forsell had to look beyond the role of Stalin.[147] Perhaps his intimate knowledge of the victims and the crimes against them made Forsell want to turn the focus away from his community's suffering to the deeds of those who had betrayed them. Harold Hietala expressed more satisfaction with the work of researchers: "I am thankful that I have been able to live so long that I have seen the day that the truth has after all become apparent."[148] He went on to thank researchers Lindström and Vähämäki for bringing "to the whole world this truth."[149]

Collective Grief

Writers who openly discussed the effects of arrests and dislocation downplayed their own losses and pain to lament the overall consequences of the Terror on Finns. While Justiina Heino was not sure whether her husband was alive or dead, she deflected her own very evident mourning by saying that he was only one of thousands missing.[150] Just as Aino Pitkänen described the Karelia Terror through the community's suffering, rather than her own, Aate Pitkänen's final letter to his parents followed the pattern of transferring personal loss to the community's grief. Pitkänen stated: "I was hoping that when the war is over we would all somehow get together and that we could help you when you need help, but one cannot change fate. And so many boys, and much better ones than me, have died after all."[151] Following this tendency, Jack Forsell was frustrated by Mayme Sevander's memoir, *They Took My Father*, because he felt that the book focused too much on the struggles of one family rather than the community.[152] Likely unbeknown to Forsell, however, Sevander herself struggled with the book. While she had been contracted to publish her family memoir by supporters and friends in the United States, she, instead, pursued a project on the experiences and fates of the broader Finnish North American community in Karelia. Sevander believed the collective story to be more important.[153] While she was obligated to complete her personal memoir, she told the story she wanted to tell – the collective story – in her subsequent works, *Red Exodus*, *Of Soviet Bondage*, and *Vaeltajat*. Kaarlo Tuomi's memoir concludes with a commitment and dedication "to those thousands of our countrymen who lost their lives in such a senseless way. It is in tribute to those thousands who had the foresight to turn back in time. And finally it is in tribute to those few who are still living in the Soviet Union."[154]

In *The Politics of Storytelling*, Michael Jackson argues: "the need for stories is linked to the human need to be a part of some kindred community, [but] this need is most deeply felt when the bonds of such belonging are violently sundered."[155] Finnish North American life writers formed a sense of self that placed them within a new community, based on language, ethnicity, and the shared building of socialism, further solidified by collectively experienced terror. Focusing on collective experience and remembrance, the Karelian memoirs and retrospective letters can be viewed as belonging, in part, to the genre of *testimonio*. Testimonio, as defined by Thomas Couser, is "understood to *issue from* an individual, who testifies to its truthfulness, but also to *speak for* a larger community to which its author belongs."[156] In this way, when Finnish North Americans, like other Soviet life writers, portray, for example, the *troika* arriving in the night, the description extends beyond personal experience to the collective one.[157] The story of Katri Lammi's arrest provides another example of the testimonio function.

Katri Lammi's name was well known among the Finnish population of North America and Karelia. Lammi and her husband, Jukka Ahti, regularly entertained the Karelian community in concert and on Finnish-language radio programming. However, more than her talent, the story of her exile has made a mark on the memories of Finnish North Americans. An examination of five different retellings of Lammi's story provides insights into the making of collective memory. Only one of the versions, written by Impi Vauhkonen, claims to tell the story from first-hand experience. The recollections of Mayme Sevander, Lauri Hokkanen, Vieno Zlobina, and Miriam "Margaret" Rikkinen convey Lammi's arrest through what they had been told, confirming the important role of gossip in forming communal history.[158]

Impi Vauhkonen explains that Lammi had been arrested, released, and re-arrested in Petrozavodsk to be taken to Lime Island. Vauhkonen wrote:

Figure 15 Katri Lammi and Jukka Ahti in New York (photo courtesy of Migration Institute of Finland Archives, Toivo Tamminen collection, USA_3221a).

> Katri was Katri, could not be humbled. I remember her departure. When her things had been lifted on to the back of the [truck] and she was helped into the mix, she wrapped an old quilt around her shoulders, straightened up and sang out with her strong voice: *Laaja on mun kotimaani kallis* [wide is my homeland dear] ... Maybe somebody else who lived at *väliparakeilla* [Finnish North American barracks in Petrozavodsk] then remembers it.[159]

In Vieno Zlobina's telling "a singer named Katri Lammi stood on the back of a truck and started to sing clearly the popular Soviet song 'My land is vast ...' about a vast and beautiful homeland where a man breaths [*sic*] freely and is master of the land. She sang the whole way to the port."[160] Mayme Sevander's version of the story shares much in common with Vauhkonen's and Zlobina's versions:

> A friend wrote me in Latushka, telling me the story of Katri Lammi, a Petrozavodsk opera singer. "The truck came to take her away to Lime Island," my friend wrote. "She stood on the back, holding onto its sides and surrounded by pots and pans and a few broken chairs, singing the national anthem. It made quite a picture, this old green military truck driving off down the road in a cloud of dust, and Katri Lammi standing in the back, singing at the top of her lungs: Boundless is my Motherland beloved. / Thousands are the rivers, lakes and woods. / There's no other land you'd ever covet. / Here you breathe as freely as you should. It gave the song a whole new meaning, let me tell you."[161]

These versions feature Lammi on the back of the truck taking her away, and report her singing the anthemic "Song of the Motherland," first performed in the enormously successful 1936 Soviet film *Circus*, then expanded in 1937. It has gone on to be a beloved Russian patriotic song. *Circus* tells the story of a woman who flees America and becomes enamoured by and devoted to Soviet society. The lyrics include:

> At our table,
> no one is excluded,
> Each is awarded on merit,
> In golden letters we write
> The people's Stalinist law.
> These words of greatness and glory
> Cannot be taken back through the years:
> A person always has the right
> To exercise, rest, and work.[162]

The song exemplifies the reinforcement of the Stalinist myth of plenty and draws on the facade of rights written into the 1936 Stalin Constitution. Sheila Fitzpatrick has drawn on the lyrics "Broad is my native land" to refer to the practice of exiling and relocating undesirable elements from Soviet society, pushing problems to the edges, made possible by the Soviet Union's vast geography.[163] Katri Lammi's song choice, whether actual or a created element in the collective retelling of the story, serves to reinforce the tragedy and irony of the Finnish North American fate in Karelia.

Lauri Hokkanen's version of the story contributes additional elements:

> One of the ladies taken to the island was Katri Lammi, an actress and singer who worked at the Finnish Dramatic Theatre in Petrozavodsk. Katri was married to a well-known singer, Jukka Ahti, who had been arrested some time earlier. They used to sing together a lot, which is what they had done while the police were searching their apartment before they arrested Jukka. Those who saw Katri leave for Lime Island said she put on quite a performance, having the police pack and carry her things onto the scow. Richly dressed in furs and laces from the theatre, she paraded along the dock, singing parts from operas. Once on the island, Katri got the job of driving a horse hauling stone to the dock. People said she was a real sight, dressed in the most ridiculous way – furs, lace, muffs – and acting the part of some character. I wished I had seen it.[164]

Hokkanen's story dresses Lammi in "furs and laces" and follows her "performance" all the way to Lime Island, where she continued to play her role. Conversely, Margaret Rikkinen explained in a 2000 interview that Lammi "knew that they were coming to take her so she stripped everything off and put just a blanket around when they were taking her away."[165] Her interviewer asked why and Rikkinen answered simply: "to damn them."

Though allegedly continuing her performance on Lime Island by taking on a "character," the system of repression may have ultimately broken Lammi. In *Red Exodus*, Sevander explains:

> For many years there was no news of Katri Lammi. When she appeared on the Petrozavodsk scene after a long absence, she had aged beyond recognition; her spirit was broken. She found refuge at the old folks' home on the beautiful island of Valaam where she breathed her last. Upon hearing this sad news, I wondered whether, when they were lowering her into her grave, the beautiful melodies of Lehar, Strauss and Imre Calman she had so exquisitely sung, rung in anyone's ears. She and her husband had sacrificed comfort, popularity and finally life itself for the socialist ideal![166]

Vauhkonen noted that when Lammi returned, "her will seemed to have already gone."[167] Lammi's husband had been killed in 1938.[168] Despite the tragic outcome, Lammi's story symbolizes strength. Rikkinen understood the collective significance of Katri Lammi's story: she challenged her captors "to damn them." Regardless of what Lammi actually did – whether she was naked or dressed in finery and whether she put on a performance or not – her behaviour has come to represent the resistance and perseverance of the Finnish North American community in Karelia. Alessandro Portelli argues that such enduring yet discrepant tales are "generated by memory and imagination in an effort to make sense of crucial events and of history in general."[169]

Katri Lammi's body and physical comportment play vital roles in the telling of the story. In both Vauhkonen and Sevander's stories, Lammi was initially objectified, placed among "pots and pans and a few broken chairs," but from there, she "straightened up and sang out with her strong voice." The images of Lammi standing upright, shoulders back with a quilt worn like a cape, parading around, represent bodily projections of power.[170] Furthermore, the Finnish North American community's strength is embodied as a woman. If the mistreatment and suffering of women and children, as exemplified in Aino Pitkänen's letter, stand for the "unspeakable," then this portrayal of a woman's proud resistance could be proclaimed for all to see. While only one of the narrators claimed to have witnessed the event, all took ownership of the story, drawing on its collective value.

Conclusion

The Great Terror in Karelia solidified the group identity of Finnish North Americans there but also forged their connection to the broader community of Soviet citizens. As seen in both the late 1930s to early 1940s letters and in the retrospective life writing, persecution and survival bound them to a shared history. Letters from the 1930s reveal the strategies of writers who sought to maintain their connections with North American correspondents without compromising their safety. The memoir and retrospective letter narratives reveal the wounds of trauma and the quest for "truth." The dream of Soviet Karelia as a homeland for Finnish workers came to an end with the Great Terror. The tribulations of those who remained in the region after the Terror subsided were far from over. The region was quickly thrown into the panic and preparation of war. Karelia became the front for the Wars with Finland, and in 1941, with the Continuation War, Petrozavodsk and its vicinity were bombed and burned. The war years were a time of further displacement and family separation. Able men and women were called to serve, while mothers, children, the ill, and the elderly were evacuated to the far north and to the Caspian Sea under extremely dangerous conditions.[171] Many perished along the way, and survivors had to overcome extreme hunger and hardships through the war years. Though many returned to Karelia after the war, the vibrant Finnish North American community of the 1930s was never revived. Too many had gone and those who remained carried the great burden of all they had endured. With bodies scattered throughout its forests and "soaked in the blood of innocent people," Karelia holds many stories yet to be told of idealism, hope, and despair.[172]

Conclusion

Jack Forsell reflected on his life in Karelia and wrote: "My coming to this country was like a drowning man grabbing at a straw. I did not wish for anything, just threw my future to destiny. Well, eventually and ultimately this 'straw' was a sturdy log that drifted to the harbour of my existence. What this existence has been is another story. A long, long story of which we didn't talk about with our relatives."[1] The statement poignantly speaks to the broader Finnish North American experience in Karelia. In Canada and the United States, many Finnish migrant-settlers lived a hard life. Language difficulties and their working-class immigrant status had long made the goal of obtaining a fair and fulfilling standard of living nearly impossible, but the Depression stripped people of hope. Finnish migrants on the political Left were finding themselves increasingly under attack by their governments, the growing right-wing Finnish North American community, and the deepening rifts among the Finnish immigrant Left. Young Soviet Russia and the messages of the Karelian Technical Aid's recruiters ignited a new spark of optimism. The possibility of an escape from the capitalist world to pursue meaningful work proved widely appealing. "Destiny" threw many challenges at the migrants in Karelia, such as difficult living conditions, inter-ethnic tensions, and ultimately, the violent repression of Finns and others. With little control over their fates – though with many "tactics"[2] – Finnish North American migrants drifted with the changing tide of Soviet ideology. Those who survived the Great Terror and the war years could begin to see their "straw" as a "sturdy log," though left with the work of making sense of what their "existence ha[d] been."

An attempt to make sense of what their lives have been and have meant is apparent in the retrospective letter collections, including Forsell's, Mäkelä's, and Hietala's, and in the memoirs of Ranta, Sihvola, Alatalo, Maunu, Tuomi, Sevander, Zlobina, and the Hokkanens. Zlobina concluded that "nothing is left" of the Säde Commune and world that the Finnish Canadian "idealists" had come to build: "Only memories are left, some sweet, some heartbreaking."[3] For the Hokkanens, their years in Karelia became something that they "would do well to forget," but, as Sylvi remarked, "of course, we couldn't forget."[4] They could not forget their friends and those who were taken in the purges. For the rest of their lives, the couple was "left with a deep feeling of sorrow and disappointment that the dream we'd had – the dream we'd worked hard to fulfill – had collapsed around us."[5] Lauri Hokkanen remembered the significant changes and modernization he saw upon returning to the United States after seven years in the Soviet Union, which led him to think: "Somehow it felt as if the revolution had happened here in the United States!"[6] The Hokkanens' memoir concludes with a clear statement of their politics. Sylvi wrote: "Although when we left for Karelia, we had no clear concept of what either 'democracy' or 'dictatorship of the proletariat' meant, by degrees we found out. Having become thoroughly disillusioned by the latter, we feel that democracy is the way to go."[7] While they may well have believed in the opportunities and freedoms that democracy afforded, such a statement also successfully distanced the Hokkanens from the uncomfortable communist label that followed them through their lives.

The relationship with Karelia and the Great Socialist Project was more complicated for those who stayed in the region beyond the Stalinist years, building lives and families there. It was not possible to draw clear lines, such as those between Soviet Karelia and capitalist North America. Instead, these life writers had to form understandings of their past and present by weighing their experiences against the long trajectory of Soviet politics and life. As we have seen, Jack Forsell doubted whether socialism had ever existed in the Soviet Union, but he also viewed the collapse of communism with suspicion and saw "no *Reason*" for the shortages and poverty that accompanied the transition.[8] While others did not write as explicitly about how they came to regard communism, it is telling that out of all the retrospective life writers considered in this study, only Jack Forsell and Reino Mäkelä ultimately stayed in Karelia and the former Soviet Union.

Each of the memoirists and retrospective letter writers conveyed their consternation at the injustices they had lived through. No one among the life writers studied here denied the Great Terror and the Stalinist crimes or apologized for the Soviet regime's wrongdoings. A sense of betrayal runs through the collective narratives. Even Mayme Sevander, whose ideological commitment to what she termed "socialist democracy" was made evident throughout her life writing, had to reconcile the betrayal of "My People."

We do not know what happened to many of the 1930s letter writers, including the Kangas family, Lisi Hirvonen, and Justiina and Alice Heino. We cannot know with certainty how they understood the changes and violence that engulfed them. In their last letters, they did not have the freedom to write openly, and it is unlikely that they could have suspected that Stalin and his inner circle had intentionally launched the repression. However, an analysis of the letter collections illuminates a clear change in the letter narratives. The optimism and proud descriptions of the work being accomplished, characteristic of the early letters, were replaced by reflections on the significance of family, laments about distance and migration, and, most often, silences.

Aino Pitkänen's brave description of Karelia in the throes of the Great Terror suggest she was not alone in believing that people who had "not done anything bad" were being victimized.[9] Pitkänen portrayed the repression as the fault of "saboteurs," which, for the researcher, raises questions about how people living through the Terror could understand who was responsible for the attacks. Narratives such as Pitkänen's allow us to consider the internalization of state media and messaging, challenges to one's own commitment to communism, how one conveyed these atrocities to communist sympathizers in North America, and the caution one had to exercise when speaking critically of life in the Soviet Union.

Forsell's observation about his existence and how his life was "a long, long story of which we didn't talk about with our relatives" proves to be especially striking when considered in the context of a larger body of Finnish North Americans' Karelian life writing narratives. Engaging in the life-writing process began to break down the silences and distances that existed between the migrants' experiences and those of their relatives remaining in North America. In the Finnish North American communities, where historic political differences and hard feelings are often still harboured, focusing on the experiences of the US and Canadian Finns who participated in the Karelian project helps to free these ostracized individuals from the community shadows. This research helps to continue opening communication and breaking down myths about who went to Karelia, why, and what happened to them there.

Life-writing narratives teach us that those who participated in the Karelian migration need not be characterized as solely economically or politically motivated. The writers bring to light a community, raised in the revolutionary spirit, who believed in the ideals of the workers' movement, without necessarily engaging in the formal ideological contestations of the communist parties, or even paying membership dues. The economic depression made the inequalities of the capitalist world plainly clear, providing an important additional impetus. The significance of both of these factors is readily apparent in the migrants' own telling of their life stories.

The history of the Karelian migration is very much a part of Finnish North American history. The "Karelian Fever" marked a turning point for the Finnish North American Left, and the character of Finnish communities in Canada and the United States overall. Karelia called away so many of the migrant youth. Their absence created a void in Finnish North American political and community life. When people returned from Karelia with strange tales of poverty and, even worse, repression, the communities in Canada and the United States were fractured. When letter exchanges came to a sudden end and friends and family in Karelia simply seemed to disappear, the losses weighed on Finnish migrant communities in North America. The enthusiastic participation in the Karelian project, manifested through fundraising and migration, can be viewed as the final mass display of Finnish socialist utopianism in North America.

As a migration shaped by a multitude of transnational factors, this history must further be understood as one part of the broader project of Karelian autonomy and within the context of evolving Soviet politics and culture. The study of Finnish North Americans in Karelia joins other community micro-histories to further elucidate daily life under Stalin, showing the ways in which people not only built socialism, but lived it.[10] Together, these studies develop the framework of "Stalinism as an analytical category."[11] By centring life-writing narratives and approaching the migration to Karelia in light of a period of transition in Soviet conceptions of housing, consumer goods, families, gender, and sociability, this work has provided unique vantage points for understanding how such formal ideological shifts manifested themselves in the Karelian hinterland and among this migrant population.

Through Finnish Canadians' and Americans' life writing about Karelia, we gain an understanding of the world they lived in, in a way that does not come to the surface through the study of newspapers, organizational records, or government documents alone. The migrants detail their travel and first impressions, the housing, food, and consumer goods they confronted, as well as their attitudes toward other peoples of the region, their working lives, how they participated in social and cultural life, and their understandings of community. Through these sources, "we see and feel, and occasionally hear, taste, and smell, their experiences."[12] While all of the migrants naturally had their own personal paths and perspectives, the life writing as a whole reveals the significant extent of collectively shared experiences. Both the vivid detailing and quick comments offered by the writers bring to life a Finnish North American's ordinary day in Karelia. These narratives lend themselves to gender analysis. Considering the ways in which home life, working life, and social life are written about by men and women highlights the ideals and practices of masculinities and femininities within this community. In addition to exploring intersections of men's and women's experiences, looking at Karelian life through the eyes of children and youth reminds us of the varying roles and encounters the building of socialism entailed.

Letters written inside Stalin's Soviet Union and sent to North America are a rare source and provide many opportunities. The Karelian letter writers demonstrate how personal correspondence supported the transnational flow of information and material goods, and also created a bridge for migrants to stay connected and engaged with their North American home community, with their forming Karelian community, and with the in-between space where individuals maintain and develop a sense of self in all its complexities. The letters show migrants creating shared frames of reference, which made mutual understanding and connection possible. A close reading of letters also reveals the strategies their writers employed to provide both assurances of health and well-being, as well as the coded and muted writing that signalled distress. The extended letter relays of Lisi Hirvonen, Aate Pitkänen, Terttu Kangas, Justiina and Alice Heino, Kalle Korhonen, Karl Berg, and Enoch Nelson tell us that as much as their letters represented their own lived experience, their thoughts were with their correspondents.

The analytical opportunities offered by the Karelian life writing have not been exhausted. The letters, specifically, can be further examined for what they reveal about the negotiation of relationships. Through the common practice of listing whom they had exchanged letters with and whom they had gotten greetings from, correspondents affirmed their social roles and connections.[13] Scholars have much to gain by paying attention to these seemingly mundane references. Listings and questions were embedded with meaning and purpose and can be seen as attempts to stay actively connected to the fluid social dynamics of the home community. Names and information flowed in both directions across the Atlantic; those in Karelia asked about friends and family, but also reported on all the others from their hometowns living in Karelia. In David Fitzpatrick's words, "The recitation of familiar names, to the impatient historian a mere catalogue, evoked an irrecoverable aura of recognition for the intimate reader."[14] One can imagine the visions of places and people evoked in the minds of letter writers as they reconstructed their social worlds through their lists, providing them with the comfort of social and personal continuity. However, the Karelian letters also reveal that keeping up correspondences and waiting for letters could cause anxiety for the migrants. Further analysis of these intimate negotiations and emotions could lead to a deeper appreciation of the exchange at the core of letters.

In the massive and diverse Soviet Union, ethnicity and background were significant factors for how people were positioned in the social hierarchy and how they encountered the state. Life writing offers opportunities to analyze the migrants' relational identities and how they viewed their own national and ethnic identities, given the complexity of negotiating Finnish and North American backgrounds, with newly adopted Soviet citizenship, and the internationalist world view of their socialism. Further research may also be directed by an examination of the language hybridization and multilingual character of many of the narratives. For example, many letters written in Finnish begin and end with English salutations, include "Finglish" (Finnish-English hybrid) words to describe goods or activities, and utilize Russian terms for work, politics, and organizational life. A linguistic consideration rooted in historical and narrative studies may teach us more about the transnational lives and identities of the migrants.

Personal narratives enrich our understanding of the migrants' lives and minds, but the contribution made by an analysis of these sources extends beyond its importance for understanding a particular community and its individual members. There is an ever-growing interest in examining the ways in which life writing serves our understanding of the past, and the aim of this current study has been to add further perspectives. Through the use of letters and memoirs to build a community social history, while simultaneously exploring what each narrative teaches us about its writer, a broad range of methodological and historical questions have been considered. A transdisciplinary investigation of narrative structures and conventions, modes of self-representation and self-understanding, and the active social and personal constructions of memory add fruitful tools of research, analysis, and thought to historical practice. Bridging the analysis of personal letters and memoirs in one study under the umbrella of life writing addresses the common divide in autobiographical narrative research. Working with the two source types demonstrates that, while letters and memoirs have unique particularities and pose their own challenges, the two share much in common. The framing of time, self, and experience are at the core of both of these sources.

Janet Gurkin Altman contends that "to write a letter is to map one's coordinates – temporal, spatial, emotional, intellectual – in order to tell someone else where one is located at a particular time and how far one has travelled since the last writing."[15] This mapping of the self serves to reinforce the "shared world" of the correspondents, but, arguably, also allows the writers – of either letters or memoirs – to take stock of where they have been, are in the present, and what the future may look like. For the researcher, these coordinates provide access into the writers' everyday lives and their ongoing personal development. Continuing to probe how Finnish North Americans in Karelia constructed and fostered networks of communication, connection, and understanding will enrich our understanding of Finnish migrant life on both continents and also of the migrant experience more broadly.

The retrospective letter collections and memoirs represent and narrate the life writers' personal truths, but also illuminate their uncertainties, avoidances, and traumas. Vieno Zlobina reflected on the impact of 1938 and the day her family and community were arrested and exiled: "That saddest day of my life, those hours of unspeakable horror have remained in my memory in all their gloomy details through all my life. Emotional memories are hard to forget. It is said that time cures the wounds. Indeed, the pain of agonizing memories slackens but never fades away. Instead, it becomes a chronic ailment of your soul."[16] Thoughts and memories of community and lost friends and family are often found at the heart of these sources. Offering testimonial narrative and *testimonio*, as we have seen, life writers wanted to set the record straight. They wanted to reconcile their life with what had happened to the community. Writers could reclaim their agency, assaulted by repression and violence, by participating in life writing. Personal narratives and memory hold ongoing importance for the people of the former USSR and those who have lived through repression, terror, and war. Alexander Etkind argues that the Russian state has not adequately met citizens' needs for making sense of their collective past of violence. He argues: "While the state is led by former KGB officers who avoid giving public apologies, building monuments, or opening archives, the struggling civil society and the intrepid reading public are possessed by the unquiet ghosts of the Soviet era."[17] Personal stories and the examination of life under Stalin contribute to the communal task of unearthing the past. The letters and memoirs of Finnish North Americans in Karelia add new voices from the edge of the Soviet Union to this important work. Given the current political climate of Russia, in which individual narratives that do not fit the national meta-narrative are increasingly suppressed, allowing the past to speak has timely importance.

In recent years in Finland, the general public, along with researchers and the government, have taken renewed interest in understanding the fates of Finns in Stalin's Russia. The history of Finnish North Americans in Soviet Karelia contributes a distinct yet connected piece to the histories of Finnish *loikkarit* (border hoppers), Finns displaced from their border Karelian homes, socialist émigrés, and Ingrians, among other Finnish migrant and displaced communities in the USSR. Together, these histories and intimate narratives allow Finns to delve more deeply into our complicated, transnational entanglements. With new family histories coming out and new archives being created to preserve more life stories,[18] I hope this book will help historically contextualize these complex moments and offer ways of reading and interpreting these challenging and wholly absorbing sources.

While the individual stories of remaining Finnish North Americans in Karelia continue beyond the Terror years, concluding the study before the outbreak of war seems fitting. For the life writers, the war years of evacuation, displacement, army conscription, and labour camps mark the beginning of a new chapter – literally, in many memoirs. When Finnish North Americans returned to Karelia in 1946 and later, it was no longer the Karelia they had come to build. The buildings had been destroyed, as had the community the Red Finn leadership had strived to create. With new marriages and new births, the identities of the migrants and their children continued to evolve. Many further developed a sense of self that included strong identification with the Russian language and with being a Soviet citizen. The intergenerational experiences and identities of Finnish North American-Karelian-Soviets after the war offer many possibilities for future analysis.

Canadian and US Finns did not find their socialist society in Karelia. Those who survived the Great Terror and the war, heard Khrushchev's Secret Speech, and lived through the disintegration of communism were left wondering if there ever had been socialism in the Soviet Union. While the Karelian project ultimately failed and so many lost their lives, the life writers reveal that their hope for the future gave the migration meaning. Forsell claimed he "did not wish for anything" when he left Canada, but the letters and memoirs taken as a whole suggest, instead, that the revolutionary spirit and the spirit of idealism were palpable features of community life. While the outcome proved tragic, we can glean inspiration for today from the history of this migration. It provides a reminder of the power and possibility of cooperative living and collective improvement. The migrants' belief that they could concretely contribute to building the better world they envisioned motivated them to take a risk and unsettle themselves. Surely we today could more often act on behalf of the brighter future we envision – even if it requires a sacrifice of some of our comfort.

Life in Karelia moved forward at a pace that left many struggling to keep up. Caught in the midst of rapid-fire regional economic modernization, the growth of the non-Finnish population, and the termination of Red Finn control, Finnish North American migrants looked to secure their place in the insecure Karelian project. Quickly jolted from the position of privileged "foreign specialists" to the ranks of distrusted "bourgeois nationalists" and alleged spies, the short span of time that has come to mark the height of the Finnish North American community in Soviet Karelia had many highs and lows. The optimism and despair both made their mark on the daily lives of the migrants. As Vieno Zlobina reflected, "life alternated between joy and sorrow ... We endured hardships and had struggles, but we also found pleasure in our lives ... One had to find a sound balance in life."[19] In the 1930s and after Stalin's death, many of these migrants set their experiences to paper, leaving us with a view of their dreams and their everyday, their joys, and their heartaches.

Notes

Introduction

1 Marlene Kadar, "Coming to Terms: Life Writing – from Genre to Critical Practice," in *Essays on Life Writing: From Genre to Critical Practice*, ed. Marlene Kadar (Toronto: University of Toronto Press, 1992), 10. Life-writing studies informing my approach include Sidonie Smith and Julia Watson, *Reading Autobiography: A Guide to Interpreting Life Narratives*, 2nd ed. (Minneapolis: University of Minnesota Press, 2010); Laura Ishiguro, *Nothing to Write Home About: British Family Correspondence and the Settler Colonial Everyday in British Columbia* (Vancouver: University of British Columbia Press, 2019); David A. Gerber, *Authors of Their Lives: The Personal Correspondence of British Immigrants to North America in the Nineteenth Century* (New York: New York University Press, 2006); David Fitzpatrick, *Oceans of Consolation: Personal Accounts of Irish Migration to Australia* (Ithaca, NY: Cornell University Press, 1994); and Ashley Barnwell and Kate Douglas, eds., *Research Methodologies for Auto/biography Studies* (London: Routledge, 2019).

2 I see this work as fitting into scholarly lineages of Soviet Karelian studies, Soviet histories of everyday life, and North American (and particularly Canadian) social histories. Works that have informed my thinking include Reino Kero, *Neuvosto-Karjalaa rakentamassa – Pohjois-Amerikan suomalaiset tekniikan tuojina 1930-luvun Neovosta-Karjalassa* (Helsinki: SHS, 1983); Alexey Golubev and Irina Takala, *The Search for a Socialist El Dorado: Finnish Immigration to Soviet Karelia from the United States and Canada in the 1930s* (Michigan State University Press, 2014); Nick Baron, *Soviet Karelia: Politics, Planning, and Terror in Stalin's Russia, 1920–1939* (New York: Routledge, 2007); Sheila Fitzpatrick, *Everyday Stalinism: Ordinary Life in Extraordinary Times: Soviet Russia in the 1930s* (New York: Oxford University Press, 1999); Stephen Kotkin, *Magnetic Mountain: Stalinism as a Civilization* (Los Angeles: University of California Press, 1995); Varpu Lindström, *Defiant Sisters: A*

Social History of Finnish Immigrant Women in Canada, 3rd ed. (Beaverton, ON: Aspasia Books, 2003); and Marlene Epp, Franca Iacovetta, and Frances Swyripa, eds., *Sisters or Strangers? Immigrant, Ethnic, and Racialized Women in Canadian History* (Toronto: University of Toronto Press, 2004).

3 Evgeny Efremkin argues "migrants' identities became a terrain where national and diasporic imaginaries were constructed." Efremkin, "At the Intersections of Nations, Diasporas, and Modernities: North American Finns in the Soviet Union in the 1930s" (PhD dissertation, York University, 2014), 28.

4 Recent contributions to studies of Finnish communities and identities in Canada and the United States include Michel S. Beaulieu, David K. Ratz, and Ronald N. Harpelle, eds., *Hard Work Conquers All: Building the Finnish Community in Canada* (Vancouver: University of British Columbia Press, 2018), and Auvo Kostiainen, ed., *Finns in the United States: A History of Settlement, Dissent, and Integration* (East Lansing: Michigan University Press, 2014).

5 As the history of migrants from Finland to Karelia, especially "Red Finns" and border hoppers (*loikkarit*), is different from that of the North Americans, and not analyzed here, see Eila Lahti-Argutina, *Olimme joukko vieras vaan. Venäjänsuomalaiset vainonuhrit Neuvostoliitossa 1930-luvun alusta 1950-luvun alkuun* (Turku: Siirtolaisuusinstituutti, 2001); Hannu Rautkallio, *Suuri viha. Stalinin suomalsiet uhrit 1930-luvulla* (Helsinki-Porvoo-Juva: WSOY, 1995); Auvo Kostiainen, *Loikkarit: Suuren lamakauden laiton siirtolaisuus Neuvostoliittoon* (Keuruu, Finland: NP, 1988); and Jukka Rislakki and Eila Lahti-Argutina, *No Home for Us Here: The Mass Annihilation of the Finnish Border-Hoppers in the Urals in 1938*, trans. Richard Impola (St. Cloud, MN: North Star Press of St. Cloud, 2002).

6 Samira Saramo, "Capitalism as Death: Loss of Life and the Finnish Migrant Left in the Early Twentieth Century," *Journal of Social History* (2021). doi: 10.1093/jsh/shab039.

7 Oleksa Drachewych and Ian McKay, eds., *Left Transnationalism: The Communist International and the National, Colonial, and Racial Questions* (Montreal and Kingston: McGill-Queen's University Press, 2020).

8 Aleksi Huhta, "Toward a Red Melting Pot: The Racial Thinking of Finnish-American Radicals, 1900–1938" (PhD diss., University of Turku, 2017), 10.

9 See also Golubev and Takala, *The Search for a Socialist El Dorado*, 120.

10 Aleida Assmann, "Re-Framing Memory: Between Individuals and Collective Forms of Constructing the Past," in *The Performance of the Past: Memory, History, and Identity in Modern Europe*, ed. Karin Tilmans et al. (Amsterdam: Amsterdam University Press, 2010), 37. Paul Connerton has similarly argued: "The narrative of one life is part of an interconnecting set of narratives; it is embedded in the story of those groups from which

individuals derive their identity." Connerton, *How Societies Remember* (New York: Cambridge University Press, 1989), 21.
11 On bridging migration history and (settler) colonialism, see Laura Madokoro, "On future Directions: Temporalities and Permanency in the Study of Migration and Settler Colonialism in Canada," *History Compass* 17 (2019): 1–6, and Lucy Mayblin and Joe Turner, *Migration Studies and Colonialism* (Cambridge: Polity, 2021).
12 Irina Takala, "From the Frying Pan into the Fire: North American Finns in Soviet Karelia," in *Karelian Exodus: Finnish Communities in North America and Soviet Karelia during the Depression Era*, ed. R. Harpelle, V. Lindström, and A. Pogorelskin (Beaverton, ON: Aspasia Books, 2004), 115.
13 Smith and Watson, *Reading Autobiography*, 15–16.
14 Gerber, *Authors of Their Lives*, 54–5.
15 Quoted in Jane Couchman and Ann Crabb, in the Introduction to *Women's Letters Across Europe, 1400–1700* (Aldershot: Ashgate, 2005), 6.

The Life Writers

1 Claudia Mills, "Friendship, Fiction, and Memoirs: Trust and Betrayal in Writing from One's Own Life," in *The Ethics of Life Writing*, ed. Paul John Eakin (Ithaca, NY: Cornell University Press, 2004), 112.
2 Sevander's lists of arrested Finnish North Americans dates Lisi and Eino Hirvonen's move as 3 March 1932. Mayme Sevander, *Vaeltajat* (Turku: Siirtolaisuusinstituutti, 2000), 189.
3 The letters were recovered by family twenty-six years after Anna Mattson's death. Nancy Mattson, granddaughter of Anna Mattson, has since delved into Hirvonen's letters and her family history, which led to *Lines from Karelia*, a collection of translated letters and poems inspired by Hirvonen's story (Durham: Arrowhead Press, 2011), and the poetry collection *Finns and Amazons* (Durham: Arrowhead Press, 2012). Lisi Hirvonen's letters are now available at Clara Thomas Archives and Special Collections, York University, Varpu Lindström fonds, 2009-025/042, Nancy Mattson Collection.
4 Clara Thomas Archives and Special Collections, York University, Varpu Lindström fonds, 2009-025/033, 14, Taimi Davis Collection, Aate Pitkänen.
5 Taimi Davis received Aate's final letters sixty years after he had written them. The story of Aate's long-lost mail was introduced to the public in the documentary film *Letters from Karelia*, directed by Kelly Saxberg (National Film Board of Canada, 2004).
6 Clara Thomas Archives and Special Collections at York University, Varpu Lindström fonds, 2009-025/033, 14–18, and 2009-025/034, 1–7. The Pitkänen family biography has been examined in Varpu Lindström, "The Radicalization of Finnish Farm Women in Northwestern Ontario,

1910–1930" in *I Won't Be a Slave: Selected Articles on Finnish Canadian Women's History* (Beaverton, ON: Aspasia Books, 2010): 59–98, and Anatoli Gordijenko, "Aate Pitkäsen Elämä ja Kuolema," *Carelia* 7 (2006): 116–31.

7 Martha's own recollections tell us that her parents paid for her family's passage. Clara Thomas Archives and Special Collections at York University, Varpu Lindström fonds, 2009-025/034, 8, Heino Family Info, Martha's (partial) autobiographical sketch. Martha is listed among the Heino family in some records and with Arvo Tieva's family in others. Compare "Missing in Karelia" database, where Martta is listed as a Tieva, with Mayme Sevander's compiled data in *Vaeltajat*, 188.

8 See, for example, Clara Thomas Archives and Special Collections, York University, Varpu Lindström fonds, 2009-025/036, 4, Rikhard Laiho: List of Finnish-American emigrants to Soviet Karelia.

9 Based on family information and taped conversations with Martta Tieva. Samira Saramo correspondence with Leonore Heino, August 2013.

10 Clara Thomas Archives and Special Collections, York University, Varpu Lindström fonds, 2009-025/034, 14, Heino collection, Tauno Salo.

11 "List of Finnish-American Emigrants to Soviet Karelia." Because of the common occurrence of both the first name Tauno and the last name Salo, it has been difficult to pinpoint with certainty that Tauno Salo from Balsam, MN, is the same as the letter writer.

12 "Missing in Karelia" database, Kustaa Salo.

13 Clara Thomas Archives and Special Collections, York University, Varpu Lindström fonds, 2009-025/035, 4, Judith Batson Collection.

14 Judith D. Batson, "On Being Half-Finnished," unpublished personal essay, 2007. Clara Thomas Archives and Special Collections, York University, Varpu Lindström fonds, 2009-025/035, 5, Judith Batson Collection.

15 The Nelson, Arvid Papers, Finnish American Collection, Immigration History Research Center, University of Minnesota, Box 5a, Folder 12.

16 Allan Nelson, *The Nelson Brothers: Finnish-American Radicals from the Mendocino Coast* (Ukiah, CA: Mendocino Historical Society/IHRC, 2005).

17 Rehabilitation letter from the Ministry of Security of the Republic of Karelia, reproduced in Nelson, *The Nelson Brothers*, Appendix C, 152.

18 Clara Thomas Archives and Special Collections, York University, Varpu Lindström fonds, 2009-025/042, 11, Marilee Coughlin–Karl Berg correspondence.

19 Clara Thomas Archives and Special Collections, York University, Varpu Lindström fonds, 2009-025/035, 6, Arthur Koski letter collection.

20 Sevander, *Vaeltajat*, 227.

21 Clara Thomas Archives and Special Collections, York University, Varpu Lindström fonds, 2009-025/035, 17, Sinisalo collection.

22 Sevander, *Vaeltajat*, 214.

23 Viola Ranta, untitled memoir, unpublished, 1992, 6 pages. Clara Thomas Archives and Special Collections, York University, Varpu Lindström fonds, 2009-025/035, 17, Sinisalo collection.
24 Sevander, *Vaeltajat*, 214.
25 The Makela, Reino, Papers, Finnish American Collection, Immigration History Research Center, University of Minnesota, Folder 1–2.
26 The letters of the two Reinos are filed together in the archive. It is difficult to confirm with certainty who exactly Reino Hämäläinen was. A cross-examination of the following sources has led to this very basic sketch: Sevander, *Vaeltajat*, 190, "Yrjö Hämäläinen"; Missing in Karelia database, "Hämäläinen," "Finnish-American Emigrants to Soviet Karelia, 1930s" list, "Hämäläinen," "List of US Citizens," recorded on board the SS *Britannia*, which arrived from Southhampton in New York on 5 October 1935. (www.ancestry.ca).
27 Clara Thomas Archives and Special Collections, York University, Varpu Lindström fonds, 2009-025/035, 13, Janet Lehto letter collection.
28 Clara Thomas Archives and Special Collections, York University, Varpu Lindström fonds, 2009-025/037, 6, Leini and Harold Hietala correspondence.
29 Sevander, *Vaeltajat*, 234.
30 Clara Thomas Archives and Special Collections, York University, Varpu Lindström fonds, 2009-025/038, 2009-025/038, 1 (Side B) and 2 (Side A), Leini Hietala interview, and 2009-025/037, 4, Leini Hietala interview transcript.
31 Maunu's memoirs have been accessed through the private collection of the late Mrs. Eini Tuomi in Thunder Bay, ON. Maunu's 2000 oral history interview with Raija Warkentin has also been consulted. Raija Warkentin research materials, "Finnish-Canadian-American-Russians," Lakehead University Archives.
32 "Piikilangan Takana" was published by *Carelia* in three instalments, Numbers 11–12 (2006) and Number 1 (2007).
33 Paavo Alatalo, "Sylvin ja Paavon Tarina," 1. Raija Warkentin research materials, "Finnish-Canadian-American-Russians," Lakehead University Archives.
34 Allan Sihvola, "Elämänkeronta," Raija Warkentin research materials, "Finnish-Canadian-American-Russians," Lakehead University Archives.
35 Allan Sihvola, *Stalinin taivaan alle – lapsena Yhdysvalloista Neuvosto-Karjalaan* (Turku: OK-kirja, 2021).
36 Kaarlo R. Tuomi, "The Karelian 'Fever' of the Early 1930s," *Finnish Americana* 3 (1980): 61–75.
37 Ibid., 61. Tuomi's stepfather was arrested and executed during the Great Terror.

38 Kaarlo R. Tuomi, *Isanmaattoman tarina: Amerikansuomalaisen vakoojan muistelmat* (Helsinki: WSOY, 1984). This work was translated from Finnish into English and republished in the United States in 2012 as *Spy Lost: Caught between the KGB and the FBI* (New York: Enigma Books, 2012). See also John Earl Haynes and Harvey Klehr, *In Denial: Historians, Communism and Espionage* (San Francisco: Encounter Books, 2003).
39 Lawrence and Sylvia Hokkanen with Anita Middleton, *Karelia: A Finnish-American Couple in Stalin's Russia, 1934–1941* (St. Cloud, MN: North Star Press, 1991).
40 Here I have used Vieno Zlobina, *Their Ideals Were Crushed: A Daughter's Story of the Säde Commune in Soviet Karelia* (Turku: Migration Institute of Finland, 2017).
41 Mayme Sevander with Lauri Hertzel, *They Took My Father: Finnish Americans in Stalin's Russia* (Minneapolis: University of Minnesota Press, 2004), 180. The book was originally published in 1992 by Pfeifer-Hamilton.
42 Mayme Sevander, *Red Exodus: Finnish-American Emigration to Russia* (Duluth, MN: OSCAT, 1993); Sevander, *Of Soviet Bondage: Sequel to "Red Exodus"* (Duluth, MN: OSCAT, 1996); Sevander, *Vaeltajat* (Turku: Siirtolaisuusinstituutti, 2000).
43 The majority of letters used in this study were collected through the international Missing in Karelia research project, 2006–2009, headed by Varpu Lindström.
44 Further complemented by additional oral history interviews conducted by Varpu Lindström and Raija Warkentin.

1. The Call of *Karjala*: Contextualizing the Karelian "Fever"

1 Statistics Canada, 1931 Census.
2 Peter Kivisto, *Immigrant Socialists in the United States: The Case of Finns and the Left* (Rutherford, NJ: Fairleigh Dickinson University Press, 1984), 71.
3 Samira Saramo, "Terveisiä: A Century of Finnish Canadian Letters," in *Hard Work Conquers All*, ed. M. Beaulieu, R. Harpelle, and D. Ratz (Vancouver: UBC Press, 2018), 168. Efremkin, "Intersections," 27–8.
4 Varpu Lindström, "The Socialist Party of Canada and the Finnish Connection, 1905–1911," in *Ethnicity, Power and Politics in Canada*, ed. Jorgen Dahlie and Tissa Fernando (Toronto: Methuen, 1981), 119.
5 Kivisto, *Immigrant Socialists*, 79.
6 Lindström, *Defiant Sisters*, 115.
7 William A. Hoglund, "Breaking with Religious Tradition: Finnish Immigrant Workers and the Church, 1890–1915," in *For the Common Good: Finnish Immigrants and the Radical Response to Industrial America*, ed. M. Karni and D. Ollila, Jr. (Superior WI: Työmies Society, 1977), 23.

8 Carl Ross, *The Finn Factor in American Labor, Culture, and Society*, 2nd ed. (New York Mills, MN: Parta Printers, 1982), 26 and 23.
9 Edward Laine, "Finnish Canadian Radicalism and Canadian Politics: The First Forty Years, 1900–1940," in *Ethnicity, Power and Politics in Canada*, ed. Jorgen Dahlie and Tissa Fernando (Toronto: Methuen, 1981), 94.
10 For an overview of this trajectory, as seen from the Thunder Bay area, see Michel Beaulieu, "The Finnish Contribution to Early Canadian Socialist Organizations," in *Hard Work Conquers All: Building the Finnish Community in Canada*, ed. Michel S. Beaulieu et al. (Vancouver: UBC Press, 2017): 29–50.
11 Linda Kealey, *Enlisting Women for the Cause: Women, Labour, and the Left in Canada, 1890–1920* (Toronto: University of Toronto Press, 1998), 115; Lindström, "The Socialist Party," 113.
12 Ross, *The Finn Factor*, 68.
13 Janice Newton, *The Feminist Challenge to the Canadian Left 1900–1918* (Montreal & Kingston: McGill-Queen's University Press, 1995), 142.
14 Saku Pinta, "The Wobblies of the North Woods: Finnish Labor Radicalism and the IWW in Northern Ontario," in *Wobblies of the World: A Global History of the IWW*, ed. Peter Cole, David Struthers, and Kenyon Zimmer (London: Pluto Press, 2017): 140–55; Peter J. Campbell, "The Cult of Spontaneity: Finnish-Canadian Bushworkers and the Industrial Workers of the World in Northern Ontario, 1919–1934," in *Essays in Northwestern Ontario Working Class History: Thunder Bay and Its Environs*, ed. Michel Beaulieu (Thunder Bay, ON: Lakehead University Centre for Northern Studies, 2008).
15 The FSOC was banned through the War Measures Act. After regrouping, the organization largely dropped the use of "Socialist" in its name, becoming the Finnish Organization of Canada (FOC).
16 For an organizational history, see William Eklund, *Builders of Canada: History of the Finnish Organization of Canada, 1911–1971* (Toronto: Finnish Organization of Canada, 1987).
17 See Matti Halminen, *Sointula – Kalevan Kansan ja Kanadan suomalaisten historiaa* (Mikkeli: Kustantaja Mikko Ampuja 1936).
18 Timothy Miller, *The Quest for Utopia in Twentieth Century America*, vol. 1: *1900–1960* (Syracuse, NY: Syracuse University Press, 1998), 94–5.
19 Gary Kaunonen, *Finns in Michigan* (East Lansing, MI: Michigan State University Press, 2009), 74–5.
20 Armas K.E. Holmio, *History of the Finns in Michigan*, trans. Ellen M. Ryynanen (Hancock, MI: Great Lakes Books, 2001), 161.
21 Walfrid Jokinen, "The Finnish Cooperative Movement," *Publications of the Institute of General History, University of Turku* 7 (1975): 11.
22 Kaunonen, *Finns in Michigan*, 81.
23 Translation quoted in Peter Kivisto, "The Decline of the Finnish American Left, 1925–1945," *International Migration Review* 17, no. 1 (Spring 1983): 69.

24 William Rodney, *Soldiers of the International: A History of the Communist Party of Canada, 1919–1929* (Toronto: University of Toronto Press, 1968), 51; Donald Avery, "Ethnic Loyalties and the Proletarian Revolution: A Case Study of Communist Political Activity in Winnipeg, 1923–1936," in *Ethnicity, Power and Politics in Canada*, ed. Jorgen Dahlie and Tissa Fernando (Toronto: Methuen, 1981), 70.
25 Donald Avery, "Ethnic Loyalties and the Proletarian Revolution," 76.
26 Ross, *The Finn Factor*, 182.
27 Rodney, *Soldiers of the International*, 41; Avery, "Ethnic Loyalties and the Proletarian Revolution," 71; Norman Penner, *Canadian Communism: The Stalin Years and Beyond* (Toronto: Methuen, 1988), 272.
28 Rodney, *Soldiers of the International*, 41–2.
29 Ibid., 55 and 68.
30 Donald Avery, *Dangerous Foreigners: European Immigrant Workers and Labour Radicalism in Canada, 1896–1932* (Toronto: McClelland & Stewart, 1979), 120.
31 Ross, *The Finn Factor*, 182.
32 Auvo Kostiainen, "The Finns and the Crisis over 'Bolshevization' in the Workers' Party, 1924–25," in *The Finnish Experience in the Western Great Lakes Region: New Perspectives*, ed. Michael Karni et al. (Turku: Migration Institute, 1975), 172.
33 Avery, "Dangerous Foreigners," 116.
34 Kostiainen, "The Finns and the Crisis over 'Bolshevization,'" 174.
35 Ibid., 192; Kivisto, *Immigrant Socialists*, 172.
36 Being wrongly accused of being a socialist was not the only difficulty conservative Finns faced in securing employment. Many "White" Finns accused the "Reds" of using "workplace terrorism" to be sure that only union members were hired. See for example Raili Garth and Kaarina Brooks, *Trailblazers: The Story of Port Arthur Kansallisseura Loyal Finns in Canada* (Toronto: Jack Lake Productions, 2010), 12.
37 Gary London, "The Finnish-American Anti-Socialist Movement, 1908–1918," in *Finns in North America*, ed. M. Karni, O. Koivukangas, and E. Laine (Turku: Institute of Migration, 1988), 211–26.
38 Varpu Lindström, "The Finnish Canadian Communities during the Decade of Depression," in *Karelian Exodus: Finnish Communities in North America and Soviet Karelia during the Depression Era*, ed. Ronald Harpelle et al. (Beaverton, ON: Aspasia Books, 2004), 23.
39 David Kirby, *A Concise History of Finland* (Cambridge: Cambridge University Press, 2006), 93.
40 Eino Friberg, "Translator's Preface: The Significance of the Kalevala to the Finns," in *The Kalevala: Epic of the Finnish People* (Keuruu: Otava Publishing, 1988), 12.

41 On the public memory and commemoration of the Civil War, see Ulla-Maija Peltonen, *Punakapinan Muistot: Tutkimus työväen muistelukerronnan muotoutumisesta vuoden 1918 jälkeen* (Helsinki: SKS, 1996).
42 Kirby, *Concise History of Finland*, 193; Osmo Jussila, Seppo Hentilä, and Jukka Nevakivi, *From Grand Duchy to a Modern State: A Political History of Finland since 1809* (London: Hurst, 1999), 138–41; Markku Kangaspuro, "The Origins of the Karelian Workers Commune, 1920–1923: Nationalism as the Path to Communism," *The NEP Era: Soviet Russia, 1921–1928* 1 (2007): 2–3.
43 Baron, *Soviet Karelia*, 20.
44 John H. Hodgson, *Communism in Finland: A History and Interpretation* (Princeton, NJ: Princeton University Press, 1967), 65 and 147–8; Alexis Pogorelskin, "Edvard Gylling and the Origins of 'Karelian Fever,'" in *The Dividing Line: Borders and National Peripheries*, ed. Lars-Folke Landgren and Maunu Häyrynen (Helsinki: Renvall Institute Publications, 1997), 265.
45 Baron, *Soviet Karelia*, 21; Kangaspuro, "The Origins of the Karelian Workers' Commune," 5.
46 Kangaspuro, "The Origins of the Karelian Workers' Commune," 6; Baron, *Soviet Karelia*, 21.
47 Jussila et al., *From Grand Duchy to a Modern State*, 138. Finland demanded all of Karelia from Lake Ladoga to Lake Onega in the South straight through to the entirety of the Kola Peninsula in the north.
48 For a concise account of the way the "Karelian Question" went through the Soviet bureaucracy in the spring of 1920, see Kangaspuro, "The Origins of the Karelian Workers' Commune," 6–10.
49 See, for example, Markku Kangaspuro, "Russian Patriots and Red Fennomans," in *Rise and Fall of Soviet Karelia*, ed. Antti Laine and Mikko Ylikangas (Helsinki: Kikimora Publications, 2002), 30.
50 Ibid., 33.
51 Peter Kenez, *A History of the Soviet Union from the Beginning to the End*, 2nd ed. (Cambridge: Cambridge University Press, 2006), 53.
52 Baron, *Soviet Karelia*, 36.
53 Kenez, *A History of the Soviet Union*, 64–5.
54 Kangaspuro, "Russian Patriots and Red Fennomans," 26–7; Kenez, *A History of the Soviet Union*, 57.
55 Hodgson, *Communism in Finland*, 153.
56 Auvo Kostiainen, "Genocide in Soviet Karelia: Stalin's Terror and the Finns of Soviet Karelia," *Scandinavian Journal of History* 21, no. 4 (1996): 334. While Karelia had such strong associations with Finnishness, in fact only approximately 10 per cent of Finns in Soviet Russia resided in Karelia, with the majority instead located in the Leningrad area.
57 Markku Kangaspuro, "The Soviet Depression and Finnish Immigrants in Soviet Karelia" in *Karelian Exodus: Finnish Communities in North America and*

Soviet Karelia during the Depression Era, ed. Ronald Harpelle at al. (Beaverton, ON: Aspasia Books, 2004), 132.
58 Hodgson, Communism in Finland, 153fn25.
59 Ibid., 150fn14; Baron, Soviet Karelia, 80.
60 Baron, Soviet Karelia, 38. Kangaspuro, "The Origins of the Karelian Workers' Commune," 19.
61 Paul M. Austin, "Soviet Finnish: The End of a Dream," East European Quarterly 21, no. 2 (June 1987): 187.
62 Hodgson, Communism in Finland, 155; Austin, "Soviet Finnish," 187; Zlobina, Their Ideals Were Crushed, 91–3.
63 Austin, "Soviet Finnish," 187.
64 As quoted in Hodgson, Communism in Finland, 156.
65 Rautkallio provides an overview of Karelian Finnicization in Suuri Viha, especially 36.
66 Hodgson, Communism in Finland, 156–8; Reino Kero, "The Role of Finnish Settlers from North America in the Nationality Question in Soviet Karelia in the 1930's," Scandinavian Journal of History 6, no. 3 (1981): 230–1.
67 Hodgson, Communism in Finland, 156.
68 Ol'ga Iliukha, "Behind the Facade of the Soviet School: Ways and Means of Bringing Up a 'New Individual' in the Schools of Karelia in the 1930s," in Rise and Fall of Soviet Karelia, ed. Antti Laine and Mikko Ylikangas (Helsinki: Kikimora Publications, 2002), 52; Pogorelskin, "Edvard Gylling," 267; Hodgson, Communism in Finland, 158.
69 Kero, Neuvosto Karjalaa Rakentamassa, 14.
70 Baron, Soviet Karelia, 44; Sari Autio, "Soviet Karelian Forests in the Planned Economy of the Soviet Union, 1928–37," in Rise and Fall of Soviet Karelia, ed. Antti Laine and Mikko Ylikangas (Helsinki: Kikimora, 2002), 75.
71 Baron, Soviet Karelia, 74.
72 White Finns, allied with White Russians, used the 1921 food shortages as an opportunity to again encourage the borderland's peasants to revolt against the Soviets. The Red Army, however, violently quelled the uprising that year and the next when the Finns, again, encouraged the locals to take action against Russia. See Jussila et al., From Grand Duchy to a Modern State, 139–40; Baron, Soviet Karelia, 55; and Kangaspuro, "The Origins of the Karelian Workers' Commune," 15.
73 Golubev and Takala, The Search for a Socialist El Dorado, 21.
74 Baron, Soviet Karelia, 86.
75 Auvo Kostiainen, The Forging of Finnish-American Communism, 1917–1924: A Study in Ethnic Radicalism (Turku: Turun Yliopisto, 1978), 164; Irina Takala, "From the Frying Pan into the Fire: North American Finns in Soviet Karelia," in Karelian Exodus: Finnish Communities in North America and Soviet Karelia during the Depression Era, ed. Ronald Harpelle, Varpu Lindström, and Alexis E. Pogorelskin (Beaverton, ON: Aspasia Books, 2004), 106.

76 Zlobina, *Their Ideals Were Crushed*, 21.
77 As provided in Kostiainen, *The Forging of Finnish-American Communism*, 164. Unfortunately, it is not clear whether this amount includes the fundraising efforts of Canadian Finns.
78 Mikko Ylikangas, "The Seattle Commune: An American-Finnish Agricultural Utopia in the Soviet Union in 1920s," in *Victims and Survivors of Karelia*, ed. Markku Kangaspuro and Samira Saramo, *Journal of Finnish Studies*, Special Edition, 15, nos. 1–2 (November 2011): 54.
79 Kostiainen, *The Forging of Finnish-American Communism*, 165. Vesa-Matti Lahti, *Siperia Kutsuu! Kansainvälisen Kuzbas-siirtokunnan ja sen suomalaisten tarina 1921–1927* (Helsinki: Into, 2017).
80 Kero, *Neuvosto Karjalaa Rakentamassa*, 138.
81 Arvid Nelson letter, 22 January 1921. The Nelson, Arvid Papers, Finnish American Collection, Immigration History Research Center, University of Minnesota, Series 2, Subseries 1, Box 2, Folder 11.
82 Ibid.
83 Nelson, *The Nelson Brothers*, 82.
84 Ibid., 89.
85 Ylikangas, "The Seattle Commune," 57. For a recent significant study of the Kylväjä community, see Harri Vanhala, *Kommuuna Kylväjä – Amerikansuomalainen kolhoosi Donin aroilla* (Turku: Migration Institute of Finland, 2021).
86 Ylikangas, "The Seattle Commune," 67.
87 Nelson, *The Nelson Brothers*, 103.
88 Kero, *Neuvosto-Karjalaa Rakentamassa*, 138.
89 Kenez, *A History of the Soviet Union*, 91.
90 See especially Baron, *Soviet Karelia*, 62.
91 Ibid., 61.
92 Autio, "Soviet Karelian Forests," 77–8.
93 Ibid., 77; Baron, *Soviet Karelia*, 105.
94 Baron, *Soviet Karelia*, 82 and 86.
95 Kero, *Neuvosto-Karjalaa Rakentamassa*, 14–15.
96 Ibid., 16–17. However, Wiita did not approve of the idea of a mass migration. The idea of recruiting Finnish workers from Finland was quickly dismissed, as demonstrated by Kangaspuro, *Neuvosto-Karjalan taistelu itsehallinosta*, 243.
97 Kangaspuro, "Russian Patriots and Red Fennomans," 107.

2. "Our Comrades Are Leaving Again": Moving to Soviet Karelia

1 Poem by "a now-forgotten person of the time," as recited in Sevander, *They Took My Father*, 23.
2 Reino Kero, "Emigration of North Americans to Soviet Karelia in the Early 1930s," in *The Finnish Experience in the Great Lakes Region: New Perspectives*,

ed. Michael G. Karni, Matti E. Kaups, and Douglas J. Ollila, Jr. (Turku: Migration Institute, 1975), 216.
3 Huhta, "Toward a Red Melting Pot," 263.
4 A similar body, the Association for Jewish Colonization in the Soviet Union (ICOR), worked in North America to fundraise and recruit for the Jewish settlement project in Birobidzhan.
5 On Tenhunen's role, see Takala, "From the Frying Pan into the Fire," 107.
6 For example, Kaarlo Tuomi's stepfather, Robert Saastamoinen was the volunteer agent in Rock, Michigan. See Tuomi, "The Karelian 'Fever' of the Early 1930s," 64.
7 Takala, "From the Frying Pan into the Fire," 108, and Alexis E. Pogorelskin, "Communism and the Co-ops: Recruiting and Financing the Finnish-American Migration to Karelia," in *Karelian Exodus: Finnish Communities in North America and Soviet Karelia during the Depression Era*, ed. Ronald Harpelle et al. (Beaverton, ON: Aspasia Books, 2004), 37.
8 Pogorelskin, "Communism and the Co-ops," 37. The research of Anita Middleton and memoir of Sylvi Hokkanen reveal that the opportunity for free schooling was especially alluring for women. See Middleton, "Karelian Fever: Interviews with Survivors," *Melting into Great Waters, Journal of Finnish Studies* 1, no. 3 (1997): 179–180, and Hokkanen, *Karelia*, 30–5.
9 Varpu Lindström and Börje Vähämäki, "Ethnicity Twice Removed: North American Finns in Soviet Karelia," *Finnish Americana* 9 (1992): 14.
10 Sevander, *They Took My Father*, 40.
11 Ibid.
12 *Työmies*, 27 June 1931. Reprinted in Peter Kivisto and Mika Roinila, "Reaction to Departure: The Finnish American Community Responds to 'Karelian Fever'" in *North American Finns in Soviet Karelian in the 1930s*, ed. Irina Takala and Ilya Solomeshch (Petrozavodsk: Petrozavodsk State University, 2008), 30–1.
13 Sevander, *Of Soviet Bondage*, 5.
14 Sevander, *Red Exodus*, 48.
15 Kivisto, *Immigrant Socialists*, 172.
16 Zlobina, *Their Ideals Were Crushed*, 22.
17 Kero, "Emigration of North Americans to Soviet Karelia in the Early 1930s," 219.
18 Irina Takala, "From the Frying Pan into the Fire," 109.
19 Golubev and Takala, *The Search for a Socialist El Dorado*, 31.
20 See, for example, Eric Rauchway, *The Great Depression and the New Deal: A Very Short Introduction* (New York: Oxford University Press, 2008), 40.
21 Michael Gelb, "'Karelian Fever': The Finnish Immigrant Community during Stalin's Purges," *Europe-Asia Studies* 45, no. 6 (1993): 1092.

22 Miriam Rikkinen interview with Raija Warkentin, 8 May 2000. Raija Warkentin research materials, "Finnish-Canadian-American-Russians," Lakehead University.
23 Golubev and Takala, *The Search for a Socialist El Dorado*, 36.
24 From William C. Pratt, "Background on 'Karelian Fever,' as Viewed from Communist Party USA Records," in *North American Finns in Soviet Karelian in the 1930s*, ed. Irina Takala and Ilya Solomeshch (Petrozavodsk: Petrozavodsk State University, 2008), 40–1.
25 Ibid., 50.
26 Quoted in ibid., 42.
27 Ibid., 41.
28 For example, Matti Tenhunen letter to Tim Buck, Superior, Wisconsin, 17 May 1931. LAC MG 10 K 3 K-282 Reel 14 (1931) File 128. See also Golubev and Takala, *The Search for a Socialist El Dorado*, 29.
29 Quoted in Evgeny Efremkin, "'Karelian Project' or 'Karelian Fever'? Orders from Above, Reaction from Below: Conflicting Interests in Kremlin, Karelia, and Canada" in *North American Finns in Soviet Karelian in the 1930s*, ed. Irina Takala and Ilya Solomeshch (Petrozavodsk: Petrozavodsk State University, 2008), 65.
30 Lindström, "The Radicalization of Finnish Farm Women," 86.
31 Gordijenko, "Aate Pitkäsen Elämä ja Kuolema," 125.
32 According to *Letters from Karelia*.
33 Sevander, *Red Exodus*, 8.
34 Ibid., 10.
35 Sevander, *They Took My Father*, 32.
36 Hokkanen, *Karelia*, 9.
37 Ibid.
38 Ibid.
39 Cynthia Comacchio, *The Dominion of Youth: Adolescence and the Making of Modern Canada, 1920 to 1950* (Waterloo, ON: Wilfrid Laurier University Press, 2006), 9.
40 Hokkanen, *Karelia*, 9.
41 Ibid., 6–7.
42 Ibid., 7.
43 Golubev and Takala, *The Search for a Socialist El Dorado*, 46.
44 Ibid., 47–9; Efremkin, "Intersections," 289–91.
45 Efremkin, "Intersections," Appendix 1.1 and 1.2.
46 Ibid., Appendix 2.1 and 2.2.
47 Efremkin, "Karelian Project," 71–2.
48 Terttu Kanagas, letter to father and siblings, Lohijärvi, 27 November 1933.
49 Tuomi, "The Karelian 'Fever' of the Early 1930s," 62.

50 Sevander, *Of Soviet Bondage*, 8.
51 Golubev and Takala, *The Search for a Socialist El Dorado*, 31.
52 Pratt, "Background on 'Karelian Fever,'" 42 and 45–6.
53 Antti Pitkänen letter, 25 December 1933.
54 Comparing Antti Pitkänen's experience to Matti Tenhunen's correspondence in 1931 shows a significant difference in processing times. In June 1931, Tenhunen noted how it could take up to six months from the time that individuals signed up for the Karelian project. Matti Tenhunen letter to KTA, 22 June 1931. LAC MG 10 K 3 K-282 Reel 14 (1931) File 128.
55 Zlobina, *Their Ideals Were Crushed*, 24.
56 Maunu, "Muistoja lapsuus ja poikavuosilta," 2.
57 Ibid., 11.
58 Lindström has examined the gender role disruption caused by the North American labour market and economy. See *Defiant Sisters*, 85–8.
59 Tuomi, "The Karelian 'Fever' of the Early 1930s," 65.
60 Ibid., 66.
61 Ibid.
62 Mayme Sevander reported that each family paid the KTA a $400 fee (*They Took My Father*, 23), which presumably included the sail fare. Reino Kero found that the sail ticket by itself cost over $110 in 1931 (*Neuvosto-Karjalaa Rakentamassa*, 80). The costs of getting to New York or Halifax, temporary accommodation on route in North America, and money spent on needed supplies must be added to these amounts.
63 Sihvola, "Elämänkeronta," 17.
64 Kero, *Neuvosto-Karjalaa Rakentamassa*, 80.
65 For example, Terttu Kangas's letter to her father and siblings, 27 November 1933, makes references to a tenant living in their home and asks whether anyone has inquired about purchasing it.
66 Alatalo, "Sylvin ja Paavon Tarina," 21.
67 Zlobina, *Their Ideals Were Crushed*, 28.
68 Hokkanen, *Karelia*, 10.
69 Ibid., 10–11.
70 Sihvola, "Elämänkeronta," 21.
71 Sevander, *They Took My Father*, 32–3.
72 While all of the reviewed memoir, interview, and letter sources list Halifax as the Canadian port of departure, Kero's *Neuvosto-Karjalaa Rakentamassa* names Montreal as the Canadian launching point.
73 Christer Bucht, *Karjala kutsui* (Helsinki: Kirjayhtymä, 1973), 45.
74 Reino Hämäläinen letter to Benny, New York, 20 February 1932.
75 For example Paavo Alatalo's family drove their Ford to New York, where they sold it for a mere $25. Alatalo, "Sylvin ja Paavon Tarina," 21.
76 Hokkanen, *Karelia*, 11.

77 Sihvola, "Elämänkeronta," 17–18.
78 Reino Mäkelä letter to Benny, 19 October 1931, Petrozavodsk.
79 Ibid.
80 Sevander, *Of Soviet Bondage*, 17–18.
81 Hokkanen, *Karelia*, 12.
82 Ibid., 11–12.
83 Ibid., 12.
84 For example, Mäkelä letter to Benny, Petrozavodsk, 19 October 1931.
85 Enoch Nelson letter to Arvid Nelson, Petrozavodsk, 28 December 1930.
86 Reino Mäkelä letter to Benny, Petrozavodsk, 19 October 1932.
87 Terttu Kangas letter to father and siblings, Lohijärvi, 27 November 1933.
88 Golubev and Takala, *The Search for a Socialist El Dorado*, 53–4.
89 Alatalo, "Sylvin ja Paavon Tarina," 21.
90 Ibid.
91 Ranta, untitled memoir, 2.
92 Sihvola, "Elämänkeronta," 24.
93 Tuomi, "The Karelian 'Fever' of the Early 1930s," 67.
94 Hokkanen, *Karelia*, 15.
95 Sihvola, "Elämänkeronta," 24.
96 Sevander, *They Took My Father*, 44.
97 Sihvola, "Elämänkeronta," 25.
98 Hokkanen, *Karelia*, 16.
99 Recited in Sevander, *They Took My Father*, 23.

3. "Of Course Not Like There": Karelian Living Conditions as Experienced by Finnish North Americans

1 Antti Kangas to "Kunnon toverit," Lososiina, 12 October 1934.
2 Cynthia Hooper, "Terror of Intimacy: Family Politics in the 1930s Soviet Union" in *Everyday Life in Early Soviet Russia: Taking the Revolution Inside*, ed. Christina Kiaer and Eric Naiman (Indianapolis: Indiana University Press, 2006), 64.
3 Svetlana Boym, *Common Places: Mythologies of Everyday Life in Russia* (Cambridge: Harvard University Press, 1994), 124.
4 Fitzpatrick, *Everyday Stalinism*, 46. In Magnitogorsk, the available living space in January 1932 amounted to only 1.8 square metres per resident. While conditions improved in the years ahead, Kotkin found that "at no time in the 1930s did the average amount of living space per person in Magnitogorsk exceed 4.0 square meters." Kotkin, *Magnetic Mountain*, 161.
5 Hooper, "Terror of Intimacy," 64–5.
6 David L. Hoffman, *Stalinist Values: The Cultural Norms of Soviet Modernity, 1917–1941* (Ithaca, NY: Cornell University Press, 2003), 22.

7 For example, Jukka Gronow, *Caviar with Champagne: Common Luxury and the Ideals of the Good Life in Stalin's Russia* (New York: Berg, 2003), 77–8.
8 Hoffman, *Stalinist Values*, 144.
9 In addition to skis and sleds, the Ski Factory produced different types of furniture.
10 Lynne Attwood, *Gender and Housing in Soviet Russia: Private Life in a Public Space* (New York: Manchester University Press, 2010), 116.
11 There were, however, significant discrepancies between urban and rural inhabitants.
12 Takala, "From the Frying Pan into the Fire," 113.
13 Golubev and Takala, *The Search for a Socialist El Dorado*, 58–60.
14 Baron, *Soviet Karelia*, 79–80.
15 Ibid., 116.
16 Kero, *Neuvosto-Karjalaa Rakentamassa*, 105.
17 Elis Ranta letter to "Hyvä Veli," Petrozavodsk, 1 April 1934.
18 Baron, *Soviet Karelia*, 140.
19 Hokkanen, *Karelia*, 55.
20 Ernesti J. (Ernest Laine) Komulainen, *A Grave in Karelia*, trans. Ritva Koivu (Ann Arbor: Braun-Brumfield, 1995), 23.
21 For example, Hokkanen, *Karelia*, 49, and Sevander, *They Took My Father*, 46.
22 Sevander, *They Took My Father*, 51.
23 Reino Mäkelä letter to Benny, Petrozavodsk, undated [circa 1932].
24 Emma Mason, in her study of women in the gulag, has found similarities in the daily experiences of arrested, exiled, and free Soviet society. See Mason, "Women in the Gulag in the 1930s" in *Women in the Stalin Era*, ed. Melanie Ilič (New York: Palgrave, 2001), 144.
25 Sevander, *They Took My Father*, 111.
26 Elis Ranta to "Veli hyvä ja perheesi," Petroskoi, 26 September 1933.
27 Hokkanen, *Karelia*, 49.
28 Terttu Kangas to Toini, 28 October 1934.
29 Hokkanen, *Karelia*, 50.
30 Reino Mäkelä letter to Benny, Petrozavodsk, undated [circa 1932].
31 Sevander, *They Took My Father*, 46.
32 Boym, *Common Places*, 146.
33 Vadim Volkov, "The Concept of Kul'turnost': Notes on the Stalinist Civilizing Process," in *Stalinism: New Directions*, ed. Sheila Fitzpatrick (London: Routledge, 2000), 221.
34 Irina Takala, "North American Finns as Viewed by the Population of Soviet Karelia in the 1930s," in *North American Finns in Soviet Karelia in the 1930s*, ed. Irina Takala and Ilya Solomeshch (Petrozavodsk: Petrozavodsk State University Press, 2008), 206.

35 Ian Mosby, "'Food Will Win the War': The Politics and Culture of Food and Nutrition during the Second World War" (PhD dissertation, York University, 2011), 7.
36 Gronow, *Caviar with Champagne*, 98.
37 Julie Hessler, "Cultured Trade: The Stalinist turn towards Consumerism," in *Stalinism: New Directions*, ed. Sheila Fitzpatrick (London: Routledge, 2000), 184.
38 Gronow, *Caviar with Champagne*, 125.
39 Antti Kangas to "Kunnon toverit," Lososiina, 12 October 1934.
40 The symbols of Soviet Russian abundance and prosperity and the focus of Soviet luxury production. See Gronow's *Caviar with Champagne*.
41 Kero, *Neuvosto-Karjalaa Rakentamassa*, 106.
42 Bucht, *Karjala kutsui*, 76. Aino and Eino Streng's account matches quite closely with the rations for "foreign workers" outlined by Golubev and Takala, *The Search for a Socialist El Dorado*, 64.
43 Ranta, untitled memoir, 2.
44 Kero, *Neuvosto-Karjalaa Rakentamassa*, 104.
45 Gronow, *Caviar with Champagne*, 33.
46 Takala, "North American Finns as Viewed by the Population of Soviet Karelia," 203.
47 Kero, *Neuvosto-Karjalaa Rakentamassa*, 104.
48 Lizzie Collingham, *The Taste of War: World War Two and the Battle for Food* (London: Allen Lane, 2011), 328, speaking generally about Soviet rations.
49 David E. Kyvig, *Daily Life in the United States, 1920–1940* (Chicago: Ivan R. Dee, 2004), 118.
50 Baron, *Soviet Karelia*, 54.
51 Takala, "From the Frying Pan into the Fire," 113.
52 See for example the recollections of interviewees in Laura Campbell, *Respectable Citizens: Gender, Family, and Unemployment in Ontario's Great Depression* (Toronto: University of Toronto Press, 2009), 29 and 31.
53 Sevander, *They Took My Father*, 41. Likewise, Suzanne Rosenberg remembered really missing fruit as a child immigrant in Moscow. Suzanne Rosenberg, *A Soviet Odyssey* (Toronto: Oxford University Press, 1988), 35.
54 Zlobina, *Their Ideals Were Crushed*, 73.
55 Mary Leder, *My Life in Stalinist Russia: An American Woman Looks Back*, ed. Laurie Bernstein (Indianapolis: Indiana University Press, 2001), 229.
56 Karl Berg Letter to Bertha and Reino, 17 October 1932.
57 Terttu Kangas to Father and siblings, Lohijärvi, 27 November 1933.
58 Peter Farb and George Armelagos, *Consuming Passions: The Anthropology of Eating* (Boston: Houghton Mifflin, 1980), 108.
59 Collingham, *The Taste of War*, 325.

60 For example, Suzanne Rosenberg recalled the prevalence of bread made with flour and sawdust in her Soviet experience. Rosenberg, *A Soviet Odyssey*, 86.
61 Marlene Epp, "The Semiotics of Zwieback: Feast and Famine in the Narratives of Mennonite Refugee Women" in *Sisters or Strangers? Immigrant, Ethnic, and Racialized Women in Canadian History*, ed. Marlene Epp et al. (Toronto: University of Toronto Press, 2004), 328.
62 Sevander, *They Took My Father*, 107.
63 Farb and Armelagos, *Consuming Passions*, 98.
64 Saramo, "Terveisiä," 173.
65 Terttu Kangas to Toini, Lohijärvi, March 1935.
66 Epp, "The Semiotics of Zwieback," 329.
67 Aate Pitkänen letters to Taimi Davis, Petrozavodsk, 29 March 1933, to "Lakeridge Residents," 20 June 1933, and to Parents, 9 November 1933.
68 Roland Barthes, "Toward a Psychosociology of Contemporary Food Consumption," in *Food and Culture: A Reader*, ed. Carole Counihan and Penny Van Esterik (New York: Routledge, 1997) [originally published in 1961], 26.
69 Frederic M. Roberts, "The Finnish Coffee Ceremony and Notions of Self," *Arctic Anthropology* 26, no. 1 (1989): 20–33.
70 Hokkanen, *Karelia*, 10.
71 Elis Ranta to "Veli hyvä ja perheesi," Petrozavodsk, 26 September 1933.
72 Hokkanen, *Karelia*, 55.
73 Ibid., 19.
74 Harold Hietala letter to Varpu Lindström, Tshalna, February 1989.
75 Farb and Armelagos, *Consuming Passions*, 175–6.
76 Reino Hämäläinen letter to Benny, Petrozavodsk, 5 April 1932.
77 Hokkanen, *Karelia*, 55–6.
78 Gronow, *Caviar with Champagne*, 124.
79 Aate Pitkänen to Taimi and Jim, Petrozavodsk, 21 November 1934.
80 Ranta, untitled memoir, 2.
81 Hokkanen, *Karelia*, 41.
82 Ibid.
83 Golubev and Takala, *The Search for a Socialist El Dorado*, 62.
84 Ibid.
85 See, for example, Antti Pitkänen letter, Lakeridge, 2 April 1933, and Kirsti Pitkänen letter, Lakeridge, 10 April, circa 1935–6.
86 Maunu, "Muistoja lapsuus ja poikavuosilta," 14–15.
87 Terttu Kangas letter to Toini, Lohijärvi, 9 April 1932.
88 Elis Ranta letter to "Hyvä Veli," Petroskoi, 1 April 1934.
89 Attwood, *Gender and Housing in Soviet Russia*, 64.

90 Zlobina, *Their Ideals Were Crushed*, 79.
91 Ibid.
92 Hokkanen, *Karelia*, 47.
93 Epp, "The Semiotics of Zwieback," 315.
94 Sevander, *They Took My Father*, 50.
95 Cynthia R. Comacchio, *The Infinite Bonds of Family: Domesticity in Canada, 1850–1940* (Toronto: University of Toronto Press, 1999), 126.
96 Ibid.
97 Donna Gabaccia, *We Are What We Eat: Ethnic Food and the Making of Americans* (Cambridge, MA: Harvard University Press, 1998), 138 and 145.
98 Laura Hollingsworth and Vappu Tyyska, "The Hidden Producers: Women's Household Production during the Great Depression," *Critical Sociology* 15, no. 3 (October 1988): 15.
99 For example, Sevander, *They Took My Father*, 60.
100 Throughout the vast Soviet land, hungry people foraged for food to make do. Collingham, *The Taste of War*, 225, and Epp, "The Semiotics of Zwieback," 320.
101 Lisi Hirvonen letter to Anna, Petrozavodsk, 6 August 1934. It is unclear which employers, but seems like the Ski Factory (her employer), and whether the practice was common beyond Petrozavodsk.
102 Terttu Kangas letter to Toini, Lohijärvi, 28 October 1934.
103 Lisi Hirvonen to Anna, Wonganperä, 13 October 1932.
104 Hokkanen, *Karelia*, 57.
105 Ibid.
106 Volkov, "The Concept of Kul'turnost'," 217.
107 Fitzpatrick, *Everyday Stalinism*, 44.
108 Enoch Nelson letter to Brother Arvid, Petrozavodsk, 10 January 1933.
109 Zlobina, *Their Ideals Were Crushed*, 74.
110 Quoted in ibid., 66.
111 Reino Hämäläinen letter to Benny, Petrozavodsk, 5 April 1932.
112 Rosenberg, *A Soviet Odyssey*, 38.
113 Gronow, *Caviar with Champagne*, 91.
114 Bucht, *Karjala kutsui*, 77.
115 Zlobina, *Their Ideals Were Crushed*, 72 and 29.
116 Sevander, *They Took My Father*, 51. Vieno Zlobina also referred to their wringer and laundry system in Canada, though emphasizing that it, too, was hard work. Zlobina, *Their Ideals Were Crushed*, 16.
117 Reino Hämäläinen letter to Benny, Petrozavodsk, 5 April 1932.
118 Sevander, *They Took My Father*, 52.
119 See for example, Komulainen, *A Grave in Karelia*, 16, about the values placed on American, Finnish, and Russian clothes.

120 Aate Pitkänen letter to Parents, Petrozavodsk, 9 November 1933, and Buzuluk, 1 January 1939; Alice Heino letter [to Martha], [Kondopoga], circa 1938 (AH3) and Justiina Heino letter to Waino, Kondopoga, 25 January 1933 (JH2).
121 Enoch Nelson letter to Brother Arvid, Petrozavodsk, 10 January 1933.
122 Ibid.
123 Ibid.
124 Terttu Kangas letter to Toini, Lohijärvi, 6 January 1937.
125 Terttu Kangas letter to Toini, Lohijärvi, March 1935.
126 Terttu Kangas letter to Toini, Lohijärvi, 6 January 1937.
127 Gronow, *Caviar with Champagne*, 68–9.
128 Jack Forsell letter to Janet, Tshalna, 12 December 1991.
129 Kero, *Neuvosto-Karjalaa Rakentamassa*, 105.
130 Takala, "From the Frying Pan into the Fire," 113.
131 Aate Pitkänen letters to "Lakeridge Residents," 20 June 1933; to Parents, 9 November 1933, and to Parents, 1 January 1939.
132 Aate Pitkänen letters to "Lakeridge Residents," Petrozavodsk, 8 April 1933, and to Parents, 20 March 1937; Jack Forsell letter to Janet, Tshalna, 29 November 1983.
133 Jack Forsell letter to Janet, 8 April 1978.
134 For more about the social significance of time and calendars, see Eviatar Zerubavel, *Hidden Rhythms: Schedules and Calendars in Social Life* (Chicago: University of Chicago Press, 1981).
135 Aate Pitkänen letter to Parents, Petrozavodsk, 20 March 1937.
136 For example, Terttu Kangas letter to Toini, Lohijärvi, 9 April 1932 and March 1935.
137 Lisi Hirvonen letter to Anna Mattson, Wonganperä, 5 February 1933.
138 Sevander, *They Took My Father*, 113.
139 Marina Malysheva and Daniel Bertaux, "The Social Experiences of a Countrywoman in Soviet Russia," in *Gender and Memory*, ed. Selma Leydesdorff et al. (Oxford: Oxford University Press, 1996), 41.
140 Sihvola, "Elämänkeronta," 27.
141 Rosenberg, *A Soviet Odyssey*, 35.
142 Justiina Heino letter to Laura, Kondopoga, 14 October 1932 (JH1), and Justiina Heino to Waino, Kondopoga, 25 January 1933 (JH2).
143 Maunu, "Muistoja lapsuus ja poikavuosilta," 13.
144 Takala, "From the Frying Pan into the Fire," 113.
145 For example, Kyvig, *Daily Life in the United States*, 139. For the history of Canada's colonial hierarchy of health care, see for example Maureen Lux, *Separate Beds: A History of Indian Hospitals in Canada, 1920s–1980s* (Toronto: University of Toronto Press, 2016).
146 Sevander, *They Took My Father*, 114.

147 Fitzpatrick, *Everyday Stalinism*, 23.
148 Volkov, "The Concept of Kul'turnost,'" 218.
149 Hoffman, *Stalinist Values*, 25. For more on the *Obshchestvennitsa*, see Mary Buckley, "The Untold Story of the *Obshchestvennitsa* in the 1930s," in *Women in the Stalin Era*, ed. Melanie Ilič (New York: Palgrave, 2001): 151–72.
150 Sevander, *They Took My Father*, 111.
151 Boym, *Common Places*, 140.
152 Sihvola, "Elämänkeronta," 25.
153 Hokkanen, *Karelia*, 51.
154 Ibid.
155 For example, Ulla Vuorela, "Colonial Complicity: The 'Postcolonial' in a Nordic Context," in *Complying with Colonialism: Gender, Race and Ethnicity in the Nordic Region*, ed. Suvi Keskinen et al. (London: Routledge, 2009): 48–75.
156 Komulainen, *A Grave in Karelia*, 22.
157 Ibid., 23.
158 Terttu Kangas letter to Toini, Lohijärvi, 30 January 1939.
159 Takala, "North American Finns as Viewed by the Population of Soviet Karelia," 206.
160 Tuomi, "The Karelian 'Fever' of the Early 1930s," 68.
161 Hokkanen, *Karelia*, 17.
162 Ibid. See also Arvo Tuominen, *The Bells of the Kremlin: An Experience in Communism* (Hanover and London: University Press of New England, 1983), 107.
163 Rosenberg, *A Soviet Odyssey*, 57 and 86.
164 Leder, *My Life in Stalinist Russia*, 219.
165 Takala, "From the Frying Pan into the Fire," 114.
166 Sevander, *They Took My Father*, 49.

4. "The Golden Fund of Karelia": Childhood in Finnish North American Karelia

1 Discussed by Sevander in *Red Exodus*, 212.
2 Efremkin, "Intersections," Appendix 1.1 and 1.2.
3 Sevander, *Red Exodus*, 39.
4 My thinking on the history of children is influenced by Mona Gleeson, "Avoiding the Agency Trap: Caveats for Historians of Children, Youth, and Education," *History of Education* 45, no. 4 (2016): 446–59, and by Catriona Kelly, "Shaping the 'Future Race': Regulating the Daily Life of Children in Early Soviet Russia" in *Everyday Life in Early Soviet Russia: Taking the Revolution Inside*, ed. Christina Kiaer and Eric Naiman (Indianapolis: Indiana University Press, 2006).

5 Rhonda Hinther, "Raised in the Spirit of the Class Struggle: Children, Youth, and the Interwar Ukrainian Left in Canada," *Labour/Le Travail* 60 (Fall 2007): 48.
6 Lindström, "The Radicalization of Finnish Farm Women," 77, for example.
7 Sihvola, "Elämänkeronta," 3.
8 See for example, Taimi Davis, "The Pitkanens of Kapalamaki: A History of the Family and Kivikoski School," unpublished, date unknown. York University Archives, Varpu Lindström fond, 2009-025/034.
9 Lindström, "The Radicalization of Finnish Farm Women," 81.
10 Ibid., 72 and 76.
11 Alice Heino mentions their *Työmies* subscription in her 18 March [early 1937] letter to "Rakas Veljeni."
12 LAC, MG 28 V 47, Vol. 191, File 5. Minutes of the Tarmola Women's Branch, 7 May 1930.
13 Davis, "The Pitkanens of Kapalamaki," 2.
14 Zlobina, *Their Ideals Were Crushed*, 18.
15 Hokkanen, *Karelia*, 83.
16 Kenneth Teitelbaum has identified at least 100 English-language Sunday Schools in the United States in the first two decades of the 1900s, in *Schooling for "Good Rebels": Socialist Education for Children in the United States, 1900–1920* (Philadelphia: Temple University Press, 1993), 1 and 42. A similarly thorough study of non-English-language children's socialist programming has not yet been conducted; the inclusion of such Sunday Schools would certainly raise the number significantly.
17 Donald J. Wilson, "Little Comrades: Socialist Sunday Schools as an Alternative to Public Schools," *Curriculum Inquiry* 21, no. 2 (Summer 1991): 218. Rhonda Hinther has likewise shown the dual political-cultural significance of Ukrainian Canadian socialist children's programming in *Perogies and Politics: Canada's Ukrainian Left, 1891–1991* (Toronto: University of Toronto Press, 2018), 80.
18 Sevander, *They Took My Father*, 15.
19 National Children's Council, "Camps and Summer Work for Workers, Children, Groups," May 1931, 1. Nordström Collection, Lakehead University Archives, MG 2.
20 Hermynia Zur Muhlen, *Fairy Tales for Workers' Children*, trans. Ida Dailes (Chicago: Daily Worker, 1925), http://www.archive.org/details/Fairy TalesForWorkersChildren.
21 Ester Reiter, "Camp Naivelt and the Daughters of the Jewish Left," in *Sisters or Strangers? Immigrant, Ethnic, and Racialized Women in Canadian History*, ed. Marlene Epp et al. (Toronto: University of Toronto Press, 2004), 371.
22 Young Pioneers of Canada, "Games for the Pioneer Leader," July 1931. Nordström Collection, Lakehead University Archives, MG2.
23 Young Pioneers of Canada, 1.

24 Ibid., 2.
25 Ibid., 3 and 6.
26 Ibid., 5.
27 Ibid., 5–6.
28 Ibid., 8.
29 Ibid., 2.
30 Julia L. Mickenberg, "The New Generation and the New Russia: Modern Childhood as Collective Fantasy," *American Quarterly* 62, no. 1 (March 2010): 107.
31 Paul C. Mishler, *Raising Reds: The Young Pioneers, Radical Summer Camps, and Communist Political Culture in the United States* (New York: Columbia University Press, 1999), 3.
32 Lisa Kirschenbaum, *Small Comrades: Revolutionizing Childhood in Soviet Russia* (New York: Routledge, 2001), 20.
33 Kirschenbaum, *Small Comrades*, 133.
34 Ibid., 106.
35 Ibid., 192.
36 Sevander, *They Took My Father*, 32.
37 Erwin Niva interview with Varpu Lindström, August 1988, Karelia.
38 Sihvola, "Elämänkeronta," 21.
39 Ranta, untitled memoir, 1.
40 Ibid., 2.
41 Elis Ranta letters to brother, 26 September 1933 and 1 April 1934.
42 Alice Heino letter to "Rakas Veljeni," Kondopoga, 18 March [early 1937] (AH2).
43 E. Thomas Ewing, *The Teachers of Stalinism: Policy, Practice, and Power in Soviet Schools of the 1930s* (New York: Peter Lang, 2002), 67.
44 Ibid., 68.
45 Ibid., 160. The rate had grown considerably from 18 per cent in 1930, before the decree on mandatory primary education.
46 E. Thomas Ewing, "Ethnicity at School: 'Non-Russian' Education in the Soviet Union during the 1930s," *History of Education* 35, nos. 4–5 (2006), 506–7.
47 Iliukha, "Behind the Facade of the Soviet School," 52.
48 Leini Hietala interview with Varpu Lindström, Petrozavodsk, August 1988.
49 Sihvola, "Elämänkeronta," especially 28–30.
50 Ibid., 30.
51 Zlobina, *Their Ideals Were Crushed*, 81.
52 Ranta, untitled memoir, 3.
53 Sevander, *Red Exodus*, 14.
54 Iliukha, "Behind the Facade of the Soviet School," 60–1.
55 Ibid., 63.
56 Ewing, *The Teachers of Stalinism*, 210.

57 Erwin Niva interview with Varpu Lindström, August 1988, Karelia.
58 Ibid.
59 Sevander, *They Took My Father*, 47.
60 Ewing, "Ethnicity at School," 511.
61 Austin, "Soviet Finnish," 189.
62 Terttu Kanagas letter to sister Toini, Lohijärvi, 28 October 1934.
63 Hokkanen, *Karelia*, 30.
64 Paavo Alatalo interview with Raija Warkentin, January 2002, Jokela, Finland.
65 Ibid.
66 Leini Hietala interview with Varpu Lindström, August 1988, Karelia.
67 Sevander, *They Took My Father*, 47.
68 Ibid.
69 Alatalo, "Sylvin ja Paavon Tarina," 6.
70 Neil Sutherland, *Growing Up: Childhood in English Canada from the Great War to the Age of Television* (Toronto: University of Toronto Press, 1997), 14.
71 Sihvola, "Elämänkeronta," 27–8.
72 Golubev and Takala, *The Search for a Socialist El Dorado*, 120.
73 Leini Hietala interview with Varpu Lindström, August 1988, Karelia.
74 Ibid.
75 Paavo Alatalo interview with Raija Warkentin, January 2002, Jokela, Finland.
76 Hokkanen, *Karelia*, 86.
77 Krupskaia letter to P.P. Postyshev, 1932, reproduced in *Stalinism as a Way of Life: A Narrative in Documents*, ed. Lewis Siegelbaum and Andrei Sokolov (New Haven: Yale University Press, 2000), 360–1.
78 Ranta, untitled memoir, 3.
79 Erwin Niva interview with Varpu Lindström, August 1988, Karelia.
80 Sevander, *They Took My Father*, 107.
81 Ibid., 112.
82 Alice Heino letter [to William Heino], Kondopoga, date unknown [circa 1938] (AH4).
83 Sevander, *Red Exodus*, 18.
84 Zlobina, *Their Ideals Were Crushed*, 76.
85 Alice Heino letter to "Rakas Veljeni," Kondopoga, 18 March [early 1937] (AH 2).
86 *Punainen Karjala*, 23 July 1936, no. 168.
87 Sevander, *They Took My Father*, 107.
88 Justiina Heino letter to Waino Lane, Kondopoga, 25 January [1933] (JH2).
89 See Kelly, "Shaping the 'Future Race,'" especially 261.
90 Alice Heino letter to "Rakas Veljeni," Kondopoga, 18 March [early 1937] (AH2).
91 Alice Heino letter [to Martha], [Kondopoga], circa 1938 (AH 3).
92 Sevander, *They Took My Father*, 61.

93 Komulainen, *A Grave in Karelia*, 16.
94 Helena Miettinen and Kyllikki Joganson, *Petettyjen Toiveiden Maa* (Saarijärvi, Finland: Arator, 2001), 21.
95 Takala, "North American Finns as Viewed by the Population of Soviet Karelia in the 1930s," 206.
96 Miettinen and Joganson, *Petettyjen Toiveiden Maa*, 21.
97 Takala, "North American Finns as Viewed by the Population of Soviet Karelia in the 1930s," 206.
98 Paavo Alatalo interview with Raija Warkentin, January 2002, Jokela, Finland.
99 Hokkanen, *Karelia*, 108.
100 Ibid., 42.
101 Kirschenbaum, *Small Comrades*, 34.
102 For an overview of children's homelessness, see Catriona Kelly, *Children's World: Growing Up in Russia, 1890–1991* (New Haven, CT: Yale University Press, 2007), part 2: *Children on Their Own*.
103 Siegelbaum and Sokolov, *Stalinism as a Way of Life*, 390.
104 As an example, see the report on the inspection of the Children's Commune, Barybino, June 1936, reproduced in Siegelbaum and Sokolov, *Stalinism as a Way of Life*, 394–6.
105 Hokkanen, *Karelia*, 47.
106 Kirschenbaum, *Small Comrades*, 134. See also Monica Rüthers, "Picturing Soviet Childhood: Photo Albums of Pioneer Camps," *Jahrbücher für Geschichte Osteuropas* (2019): 65–95.
107 Leini Hietala interview with Varpu Lindström, Petrozavodsk, August 1988.
108 Jeanette D. Pearl in *New York Call*, 29 October 1911, quoted in Kenneth Teitelbaum, "'Critical Lessons' from Our Past: Curricula of Socialist Sunday Schools in the United States," *Curriculum Inquiry* 20, no. 4 (Winter 1990): 419.

5. "Isn't It a Different Land, This Sickle and Hammer Land?": Working in Soviet Karelia

1 Karl Berg letter to Bertha, 17 October 1932.
2 Sevander, *They Took My Father*, 5 and 12.
3 Maunu and Lili Klaus interview with Raija Warkentin, 7 June 2000.
4 Alatalo, "Sylvin ja Paavon Tarina," 20.
5 Sihvola, "Elämänkeronta," 15.
6 Ibid., 17.
7 Ranta, untitled memoir, 1.
8 Hokkanen, *Karelia*, 7.
9 Lindström, *Defiant Sisters*, especially 84–114.
10 Alatalo, "Sylvin ja Paavon Tarina," 20.

11 Sylvi Hokkanen wrote about having to leave her job as a teacher because "people looked askance at married women who held jobs that could have gone to single people." Hokkanen, *Karelia*, 8.
12 Sari Autio-Sarasmo, "The Economic Modernization of Soviet Karelia during the Process of Soviet Industrialization," in *Victims and Survivors of Karelia*, ed. M. Kangaspuro and S. Saramo, Special Issue of *Journal of Finnish Studies* 15, nos. 1/2 (November 2011): 86.
13 Ibid.
14 Golubev and Takala, *The Search for a Socialist El Dorado*, 49.
15 Using greetings published in Finnish North American newspapers, Reino Kero outlines the numbers of North Americans at specific camps in *Neuvosto Karjalaa Rakentamassa*, 95–8.
16 So named in North America, for their use by Scandinavian immigrants.
17 Autio-Sarasmo, "Economic Modernization," 93.
18 Kero outlines the various techniques and technological contributions of Finnish North Americans in *Neuvosto Karjalaa rakentamassa*, 109–21.
19 Autio-Sarasmo, "Economic Modernization," 94.
20 Golubev and Takala, *The Search for a Socialist El Dorado*, 71. Local Karelian lumberjacks averaged 4.3 cubic feet per day; the overall North American average was 8.5 cubic feet.
21 Golubev and Takala, *The Search for a Socialist El Dorado*, 76.
22 Autio-Sarasmo, "Economic Modernization," 93.
23 Golubev and Takala, *The Search for a Socialist El Dorado*, 75–6.
24 Kero, *Neuvosto Karjalaa Rakentamassa*, 116; Ylikangas, *The Sower Commune*, 79.
25 Kero, *Neuvosto Karjalaa Rakentamassa*, 98.
26 Golubev and Takala, *The Search for a Socialist El Dorado*, 75–6.
27 Karl Berg letter to Bertha, 17 October 1932.
28 Enoch Nelson letter to Brother Arvid, Petrozavodsk, 10 January 1933.
29 Ibid.
30 Aate Pitkänen letter to Parents, 12 November 1933.
31 Karl Berg letter to Bertha and Reino, 17 October 1932.
32 Lisi Hirvonen letter to Anna, Petrozavodsk, 20 April 1933.
33 Enoch Nelson letter to Brother Arvid, Petrozavodsk, 10 January 1933.
34 Kalle Korhonen letter to Aune, Judith, and Trenton, Petrozavodsk, 30 January 1937.
35 Kalle Korhonen letter to Aune, Petrozavodsk, 23 August 1935. Emphasis in original.
36 Terttu Kangas letter to Toini, Lohijärvi, 28 October 1934.
37 Ibid.
38 Enoch Nelson letter to Sister Ida, Kem, 2 May 1930.
39 Fitzpatrick, *Everyday Stalinism*, 75.

40 Enoch Nelson letter to Arvid Nelson, Petrozavodsk, 28 July 1930. Two months earlier, Enoch had reported to his sister Ida that he had left Uhtua and was now working in Kem. See Enoch Nelson letter to Sister Ida, Kem, 2 May 1930.
41 Lisi Hirvonen letter to Anna, Vonganperä, 13 October 1932.
42 Lisi Hirvonen letter to Anna, Vonganperä, 5 February 1933.
43 Ibid.
44 Lisi Hirvonen letter to Anna, Petrozavodsk, 20 April 1933.
45 Ibid.
46 Lisi Hirvonen letter to Anna, Petrozavodsk, December 1933.
47 Lisi Hirvonen letter to Anna, Petrozavodsk, 2 February 1938.
48 Lisi Hirvonen letter to Anna, Petrozavodsk, 10 September 1938.
49 Lisi Hirvonen letter to Anna, USSR Karjala, 17 January 1939.
50 Lisi Hirvonen letter to Anna, Petrozavodsk, 19 July 1939.
51 Lisi Hirvonen letter to Anna Mattson, 17 January 1939 and 19 July 1939.
52 Hokkanen, *Karelia*, 17–22.
53 Ibid., 25.
54 Ibid.
55 Ibid., 27.
56 Ibid.
57 Hokkanen, *Karelia*, 22.
58 See for example, Saramo, "Terveisiä," 168.
59 David Shearer, "Elements Near and Alien: Passportization, Policing, and Identity in the Stalinist State, 1932–1952," in *The Journal of Modern History* 76, no. 4 (December 2004): 838.
60 Golubev and Takala, *The Search for a Socialist El Dorado*, 49.
61 Hokkanen, *Karelia*, 22.
62 Ibid., 24.
63 Shearer, "Elements Near and Alien," 845.
64 Aate Pitkänen letter to Taimi, Petrozavodsk, 21 November 1934.
65 Aate Pitkänen letter to friends, Petrozavodsk, 8 April 1933.
66 Enoch Nelson letter to Sister Ida, Kem, 2 May 1930.
67 Kotkin, *Magnetic Mountain*, 42–9.
68 Kero, *Neuvosto-Karjalaa Rakentamassa*, 109–21.
69 Autio-Sarasmo, "The Economic Modernization of Soviet Karelia," 94.
70 Aate Pitkänen letter, 21 November 1934.
71 Ibid.
72 See for example, V. Suomela, *Kuusi kuukautta Karjalassa: Mitä siirtolainen näki ja koki Neuvosto-Karjalassa* (Sudbury: Vapaa Sana, 1935), 12.
73 Stephen Kotkin, "Coercion and Identity: Workers' Lives in Stalin's Showcase City," in *Making Workers Soviet: Power, Class and Identity*, ed. Lewis Siegelbaum and Ronald Grigor Suny (Ithaca, NY: Cornell University Press, 1994), 282.

74 For a thorough analysis that pairs the economic and labour aspects of Stakhanovism with sociological and cultural considerations, see Siegelbaum, *Stakhanovism and the Politics of Productivity in the USSR, 1935–1941*. For a case study of Stakhanovism at Magnitogorsk, see Kotkin, *Magnetic Mountain*, 207–15.
75 Aate Pitkänen letter to Parents, 12 November 1933.
76 T erttu Kangas letter to Toini, Lohijärvi, 9 April 1934.
77 Lisi Hirvonen letter to Anna, Petrozavodsk, 18 March 1935.
78 Lisi Hirvonen letter to Anna, Petrozavodsk, 12 November 1935.
79 Hokkanen, *Karelia*, 66 and 83.
80 Fitzpatrick, *Everyday Stalinism*, 103.
81 Takala, "North American Finns as Viewed by the Population of Soviet Karelia in the 1930s," 202.
82 Fitzpatrick, *Everyday Stalinism*, 9–10.
83 Mayme Sevander, *They Took My Father*, 55.
84 Ibid., 47.
85 Enoch Nelson letter to Sister Ida, Kem, 2 May 1930.
86 Suomela, *Kuusi kuukautta Karjalassa*, 12.
87 Andrea Graziosi, "Foreign Workers in Soviet Russia, 1920–40: Their Experience and Their Legacy," *International Labor and Working-Class History* 33 (Spring 1988): 43.
88 Hokkanen, *Karelia*, 19.
89 Sevander, *They Took My Father*, 49.
90 Hokkanen, *Karelia*, 74.
91 Takala, "North American Finns as Viewed by Soviet Karelians," 203.
92 Ibid.
90 Autio-Sarasmo, "The Economic Modernization of Soviet Karelia," 95–6; Golubev and Takala, *The Search for a Socialist El Dorado*, 67. Such clashes have been noted elsewhere in the Soviet Union, where foreign expertise was recruited. See for example Deborah Fitzgerald, "Blinded by Technology: American Agriculture in the Soviet Union, 1928–1932" in *Agricultural History* 70, no. 3 (Summer 1996): 476–8.
94 See also Kero, *Neuvosto Karjalaa Rakentamassa*, 122–5, for an example of a conflict in Matrosy.
95 Baron, *Soviet Karelia*, 123.
96 Suomela, *Kuusi kuukautta Karjalassa*, 28 and 29.
97 Baron, *Soviet Karelia*, 128.
98 Karl Berg letter to Bertha, 17 October 1932.
99 Baron, *Soviet Karelia*, 134–5.
100 Enoch Nelson letter to Brother Arvid, Petrozavodsk, 10 January 1933.
101 Justiina Heino letter [to Martha], [Kondopoga], circa late 1936 (JH 3).

102 Paavo Alatalo interview with Raija Warkentin, Jokela, Finland, 15 January 2002.
103 Terttu Kangas letter to Toini, Lohijärvi, 27 November 1933.
104 Terttu Kangas letter to Toini, Lohijärvi, 9 April 1934.
105 Lisi Hirvonen letter to Anna, Vonganperä, 5 February 1933.
106 Hokkanen, *Karelia*, 22, 23, and 72.
107 Ibid., 26; see also 20.
108 Ibid., 26.
109 For example, in Komulainen's description of the barracks dwellers, only men were present. *A Grave in Karelia*, 28–36.
110 Hokkanen, *Karelia*, 27.
111 Tuomi, "The Karelian 'Fever' of the Early 1930s," 69.
112 Ibid.
113 See, for example, Takala, "North American Finns as Viewed by Soviet Karelians," 203–4.
114 Hokkanen, *Karelia*, 21.
115 Kotkin, "Coercion and Identity," 283–4.
116 Hokkanen, *Karelia*, 21.
117 Ibid. Due to widespread labour scarcity, managers may have been willing to work around official policy in order to retain their employees. See Kotkin, "Coercion and Identity," 283.
118 Ian Radforth, "Finnish Radicalism and Labour Activism in the Northern Ontario Woods," in *A Nation of Immigrants: Women, Workers, and Communities in Canadian History, 1840s–1960s*, ed. Franca Iacovetta et al. (Toronto: University of Toronto Press, 1998), 295.
119 Hokkanen, *Karelia*, 83–4.
120 Ibid., 86.
121 Ibid.
122 Justiina Heino letter [to Martha], [Kondopoga], circa late 1936 (JH3).
123 Ibid.
124 Justiina Heino letter, unknown details [1938] (JH4).
125 Alice Heino letter [to William], [Kondopoga], circa 1938 (AH 4).
126 Hokkanen, *Karelia*, 89.
127 Lewis Siegelbaum, "1939: Labor Discipline," *Seventeen Moments in Soviet History* website. http://soviethistory.msu.edu/1939-2/labor-discipline/.
128 Fitzpatrick, *Everyday Stalinism*, 8.
129 Hokkanen, *Karelia*, 89.

6. "All Kinds of Hustle and Bustle:" Community Life and Leisure

1 Aate Pitkänen letter to Parents, Petrozavodsk, 12 November 1933.
2 Reino Hämäläinen letter to Benny, Petrozavodsk, 5 April 1932.

3 Efremkin, "Intersections," Appendix 1.1 and 1.2.
4 To extend David Gerber's useful concept of "personal continuity" in *Authors of Their Lives*, 4.
5 Golubev and Takala, *The Search for a Socialist El Dorado*, 139. This number includes those who returned to North America, to Finland, and other regions of the USSR. It became very difficult to leave the USSR after 1936.
6 See Kero, *Neuvosto-Karjalaa Rakentamassa*, 202–4, and Varpu Lindström's analysis of V. Suomela's scathing exposé, *Kuusi kuukautta Karjalassa*, in "'Heaven or Hell on Earth?': Soviet Karelia's Propaganda War of 1943–35 in the Finnish Canadian Press," in *North American Finns in Soviet Karelia in the 1930s*, ed. Irina Takala and Ilya Solomeshch, 83–103 (Petrozavodsk: Petrozavodsk State University Press, 2008).
7 Aate Pitkänen letter to Taimi Davis, Petrozavodsk, 29 March 1933.
8 Kero, *Neuvosto-Karjalaa Rakentamassa*, 200, and Golubev and Takala, *The Search for a Socialist El Dorado*, 139.
9 Aate Pitkänen letter to "Aatut, Mikkolat, Haarat ja ketä vielä," Petrozavodsk, 8 April 1933.
10 Aate Pitkänen letter to Taimi Davis, Petrozavodsk, November 1933.
11 Ibid.
12 Ibid.
13 Ibid.
14 Antti Pitkänen joked to Taimi that Aho had "gone crazy" trying to get back to "kultala," based on the letters Aho had sent Antti. Antti Pitkänen letter to Taimi Davis, Lakeridge, ON, 2 April 1933.
15 Aate Pitkänen letter to "Aatut, Mikkolat, Haarat ja ketä vielä," Petrozavodsk, 8 April 1933. Emphasis in original.
16 Terttu Kangas letter to Toini, Lohijärvi, March 1935.
17 Antti Kangas letter to "Kunnon Toverit," Lososiina, 12 October 1934.
18 Ibid.
19 Ibid.
20 Aate Pitkänen letter to Taimi Davis, Petrozavodsk, November 1933.
21 Sevander, *Of Soviet Bondage*, 29.
22 Kalle Korhonen to Aune Batson, "Tunkuan Piiri," 23 August 1935.
23 Gordijenko, "Aate Pitkäsen Elämä ja Kuolema," 118.
24 Ibid., 125.
25 Sevander, *They Took My Father*, 180.
26 Hokkanen, *Karelia*, 29.
27 Sevander, *They Took My Father*, 48. Also, Zlobina, *Their Ideals Were Crushed*, 86.
28 Lisi Hirvonen letter to Anna Mattson, Wonganperä, 5 February 1933.
29 Lisi Hirvonen letter to Anna Mattson, Petrozavodsk, 20 April 1933.
30 Ranta, untitled memoir, 2.

31 Alice Heino letter to "Rakas Veljeni," Kondopoga, 18 March [1937] (AH 2).
32 Ibid.
33 Reino Hämäläinen letter to Benny, Petrozavodsk, 5 April 1932.
34 Hokkanen, *Karelia*, 34.
35 Terttu Kangas letter to Toini, Lohijärvi, March 1935.
36 Stephen Kotkin, *Magnetic Mountain*, 180–2.
37 Lewis Siegelbaum, "The Shaping of Soviet Workers' Leisure: Workers' Clubs and Palaces of Culture in the 1930s," *International Labor and Working-Class History* 56 (Fall 1999): 85.
38 Samira Saramo, "'A socialist movement which does not attract the women cannot live': Finnish Socialist Women in Port Arthur, 1903–1933," in *Labouring Finns: Transnational Politics in Finland, Canada, and the United States*, ed. Michel Beaulieu et al. (Turku: Institute of Migration, 2011), 151.
39 See for example, Alice Heino to "Rakas Veljeni," Kondopoga, 18 March [1937] (AH 2).
40 Maunu, "Muistoja lapsuus ja poikavuosilta," 19.
41 Sevander, *Red Exodus*, 71.
42 Impi Vauhkonen, "He Rakensivat Kultuuria," *Carelia* 3 (1993): 78.
43 Lisi Hirvonen letter to Anna Mattson, Wonganperä, 5 February 1933.
44 Sihvola, "Elämänkeronta," 27.
45 Vauhkonen, "He Rakensivat Kultuuria," 79.
46 Lisi Hirvonen letter to Anna Mattson, Petrozavodsk, 20 April 1933.
47 Lisi Hirvonen letter to Anna Mattson, Petrozavodsk, December 1933. See also Vauhkonen, "He Rakensivat Kultuuria," 76.
48 Lisi Hirvonen letter to Anna Mattson, Petrozavodsk, 6 August 1934.
49 Alice Heino letter [to Martta], [Kondopoga], circa 1938 (AH 3).
50 Ibid.
51 Reino Hämäläinen letter to Benny, Petrozavodsk, 5 April 1932.
52 Ibid.
53 For example, *Punainen Karjala*, no. 17, 20 January 1932.
54 Ranta, untitled memoir, 3 and Elis Ranta letter to "Hyvä Veli," Petrozavodsk, 26 September 1933.
55 Elis Ranta letter to "Hyvä Veli," Petrozavodsk, 1 April 1934.
56 Reino Hämäläinen letter to Benny, Petrozavodsk, 5 April 1932.
57 Hokkanen, *Karelia*, 45.
58 Sevander, *They Took My Father*, 56.
59 See for example Sarah Davies, "'A Mother's Causes': Women Workers and Popular Opinion in Stalin's Russia, 1934–1941," in *Women in the Stalin Era*, ed. Melanie Ilič (New York: Palgrave, 2001), 93; Saramo, "A socialist movement which does not attract women cannot live," 153.

60 Sevander, *Red Exodus*, 93–4.
61 Hoffman, *Stalinist Values*, 32–3 and 129; Gronow, *Caviar with Champagne*, 39; Fitzpatrick, *Everyday Stalinism*, 93.
62 Kyvig, *Daily Life in the United States*, 209; Comacchio, "Dancing to Perdition: Adolescence and Leisure in Interwar English Canada," *Journal of Canadian Studies / Revue d'études canadiennes* 32, no. 3 (Fall 1997): 9.
63 Tauno Salo letter to Carl Heino, Petrozavodsk, 23 November 1935.
64 Alice Heino letter [to Martha], [Kondopoga], circa 1938 (AH 3).
65 Reino Mäkelä letter to Benny, Petrozavodsk, 24 January 1932.
66 Zlobina, *Their Ideals Were Crushed*, 71.
67 Aate Pitkänen letter to Taimi and Jim Davis, Petrozavodsk, 21 November 1934.
68 Lisi Hirvonen letter to Anna Mattson, Petrozavodsk, 19 July 1939.
69 Vauhkonen, "He Rakensivat Kultuuria," 79.
70 Sihvola, "Elämänkeronta," 27.
71 Ibid.
72 Zlobina, *Their Ideals Were Crushed*, 71.
73 Aate Pitkänen letter to Jim and Taimi Davis, Petrozavodsk, 21 November 1934.
74 See Timo Riippa, "The Finnish American Radical Theater of the 1930s," *Finnish Americana* 9 (1992): 28–35; James A. Roe, "Virginia, Minnesota's Socialist Opera: Showplace of Iron Range Radicalism," *Finnish Americana* 9 (1992): 36–43.
75 Sevander, *They Took My Father*, 57.
76 Maunu, "Muistoja lapsuus ja poikavuosilta," 18; Sevander, *Red Exodus*, 88–92.
77 Lisi Hirvonen letter Anna Mattson, Petrozavodsk, 6 August 1934.
78 Sevander, *Red Exodus*, 92.
79 Comacchio, "Dancing to Perdition," 12. Rates continued to climb. By 1936, a Halifax survey found that 96 out of 100 respondents went to the cinema more than twice a month. See Comacchio, *The Dominion of Youth*, 167.
80 As advertised in *Punainen Karjala*, January 1932–December 1936.
81 Lisi Hirvonen letter to Anna Mattson, Vonganperä, 5 February 1933.
82 Lisi Hirvonen letter to Anna Mattson, Petrozavodsk, 20 April 1933.
83 Aate Pitkänen letter to Taimi Davis, Petrozavodsk, 21 November 1934.
84 Maunu, "Muistoja lapsuus ja poikavuosilta," 19.
85 Peter Kenez, *Cinema and Soviet Society from the Revolution to the Death of Stalin* (New York: I.B. Tauris, 2001), 120. Lewis Siegelbaum, "The Shaping of Soviet Workers' Leisure," 86.
86 Furthermore, movie theatres could act as a political site by serving as a venue for significant political meetings. See the use of the Karelian Triumf

theatre in Markku Kangaspuro, *Neuvosto-Karjalan taistelu itsehallinosta: Nationalismi ja suomalaiset punaiset Neuvostoliiton vallankäytössä 1920–1939* (Helsinki: SKS, 2000), 244.
87 Kenez, *Cinema and Soviet Society*, 2.
88 Richard Stites, *Soviet Popular Culture: Entertainment and Society since 1900* (Cambridge: Cambridge University Press, 1992), 85.
89 Kenez, *Cinema and Soviet Society*, 131.
90 Ibid., 5.
91 Stites, *Soviet Popular Culture*, 95.
92 Ibid., 146.
93 Alice Heino to "Rakas Veljeni" [Wiljam or Waino], Kondopoga, 18 March [1937].
94 For more about the production and celebration of the Pushkin Centennial, see Karen Petrone, *Life Has Become More Joyous, Comrades: Celebrations in the Time of Stalin* (Bloomington and Indianapolis: Indiana University Press, 2000), 113–48.
95 In Canada, for example, boys and girls under eighteen years of age comprised over 60 per cent of cinema audiences. Comacchio, *Infinite Bonds of Family*, 86.
96 Sevander, *They Took My Father*, 61.
97 Reino Mäkelä letter to Benny, Petrozavodsk, 19 October 1931.
98 Petrone, *Life Has Become More Joyous*, 6.
99 Iurii Gerchuk, "Festival Decoration of the City: The Materialization of the Communist Myth in the 1930s," *Journal of Design History* 13, no. 2 (2000): 124.
100 Lisi Hirvonen letter to Anna Mattson, Petrozavodsk, 12 November 1935.
101 Stalin's speech at the Conference of Stakhanovites, 17 November 1935.
102 Gerchuk, "Festival Decoration of the City," 125; Petrone, *Life Has Become More Joyous*, 23–9.
103 For example, Petrone, *Life Has Become More Joyous*, 31.
104 Terttu Kangas letter to Toini, Lohijärvi, 28 October 1934.
105 Richard Stites, "Festivals of Collusion? Provincial Days in the 1930s," *Kritika* 1, no. 3 (Summer 2000): 476.
106 Ibid., 478.
107 Ibid., 477.
108 Petrone, *Life Has Become More Joyous*, 86.
109 Lisi Hirvonen letter to Anna Mattson, Petrozavodsk, 19 December 1934.
110 Petrone, *Life Has Become More Joyous*, 88.
111 Hokkanen, *Karelia*, 87.
112 Sevander, *Of Soviet Bondage*, 53.
113 Ibid.
114 Aate Pitkänen letter to "Lakeridge Residents," Petrozavodsk, 20 June 1933.

115 Kyvig, *Daily Life in the United States*, 133.
116 Aate Pitkänen letter to Taimi Davis, Petrozavodsk, 3 April 1933.
117 Aate Pitkänen letter to "Lakeridge Residents," 20 June 1933.
118 Lisi Hirvonen letter to Anna Mattson, Petrozavodsk, 20 April 1933.
119 Reino Mäkelä letter to Benny, Petrozavodsk, 24 January 1932.
120 Ibid.
121 Ibid.
122 Beth L. Bailey, *From Front Porch to Back Seat: Courtship in Twentieth-Century America* (Baltimore: Johns Hopkins University Press, 1988), 13–14 and 21–2.
123 Hokkanen, *Karelia*, 53.
124 Terttu Kangas letter to "Rakas Isä ja siskot ja veljet," Lohijärvi, 27 November 1933.
125 Varpu Lindström has shown Finnish Canadian men's historical and statistical preference for marrying Finnish women. See, for example, *Defiant Sisters*, 64.
126 Aate Pitkanen letter to Jim, Taimi, and Joan, Petrozavodsk, 2 May 1937.
127 Ibid.
128 Gordijenko, "Aate Pitkäsen Elämä ja Kuolema," 121.
129 Alice Heino letter to Martha, Kondopoga, 3 September 1939 (AH 5).
130 Terttu Kangas letter to Toini, Lohijärvi, 6 January 1937.
131 Tauno Salo letter to Carl Heino, Petrozavodsk, 23 November 1935.
132 Leini Hietala interview with Varpu Lindström, Petrozavodsk, August 1988.
133 Ibid.
134 Ibid.
135 For example, Lisi Hirvonen letters to Anna Mattson, Petrozavodsk, 6 August 1934 and 19 December 1934 to 30 January 1935 and 18 March 1935.
136 Lisi Hirvonen letter to Anna Mattson, Petrozavodsk, 15 August 1936.
137 Lisi Hirvonen letter to Anna Mattson, Petrozavodsk, 2 February 1938.
138 Enoch Nelson letter to Ida Perkut, Uhtua, 30 December 1926. Nelson, *Nelson Brothers*, 106.
139 Hoffman, *Stalinist Values*, 90; Lindström, *Defiant Sisters*, 72–7.
140 Veronica Strong-Boag, "'Janey Canuck': Women in Canada, 1919–1939," *CHA Historical Booklet*, no. 53 (Ottawa: Canadian Historical Association, 1994), 16; Kyvig, *Daily Life in the United States*, 135.
141 Hoffman, *Stalinist Values*, 97.
142 Ibid., 101.
143 Terttu Kangas letter to Toini, Lohijärvi, 9 April 1934.
144 Hoffman, *Stalinist Values*, 76.
145 Reino Hämäläinen letter to Benny, Petrozavodsk, 5 April 1932.
146 Bucht, *Karjala kutsui*, 55 and 91.

147 Hokkanen, *Karelia*, 66.
148 Ibid.
149 Reino Mäkelä letter to Benny, Petrozavodsk, 24 January 1932.
150 Sihvola, "Elämänkeronta," 26.
151 Ibid.
152 Sevander, *Of Soviet Bondage*, 53.
153 Hokkanen, *Karelia*, 66.
154 Bucht, *Karjala kutsui*, 91.
155 Hokkanen, *Karelia*, 55.
156 Ibid.
157 Ibid.
158 James Riordan, *Sport in Soviet Society: Development of Sport and Physical Education in Russia and the USSR* (Cambridge: Cambridge University Press, 1977), 106.
159 Constitution of the Finnish Canadian Workers Sports Federation, quoted in Jim Tester, ed., *Sports Pioneers: A History of the Finnish-Canadian Amateur Sports Federation, 1906–1986* (Sudbury, ON: Alerts AC Historical Committee, 1986), 7.
160 Bruce Kidd, *The Struggle for Canadian Sport* (Toronto: University of Toronto Press, 1996), 160 and 161; Diane Imrie, David Nicholson, and Laura Nigro, eds., *A Century of Sport in the Finnish Community of Thunder Bay* (Thunder Bay, ON: Northwestern Ontario Sports Hall of Fame and the Thunder Bay Finnish Canadian Historical Society, 2013); C. Nathan Hatton, "Wrestling, Immigration, and Working-Class Culture: The Finns of the Thunder Bay District before 1939" in *Hard Work Conquers All: Building the Finnish Community in Canada*, ed. M. Beaulieu, D. Ratz, and R. Harpelle (Vancouver: University of British Columbia Press, 2018), 104; Kaunonen, *Finns in Michigan*, 89.
161 For example, Tester, *Sports Pioneers*, 31, 37, 41, 59, and 61.
162 Zlobina, *Their Ideals Were Crushed*, 19.
163 Sevander, *Red Exodus*, 168; Maunu, "Muistoja lapsuus ja poikavuosilta," 17; Robert Edelman, *Serious Fun: A History of Spectator Sports in the USSR* (New York: Oxford University Press, 1993), 73; Aate Pitkänen letters to "Lakeridge Residents," 8 April 1933, and to Parents, 20 March 1937 and 12 March 1939.
164 Sihvola, "Elämänkeronta," 26.
165 See, for example, Sihvola, "Elämänkeronta," 26; Maunu, "Muistoja lapsuus ja poikavuosilta," 17; Terttu Kanagas letter to Father and Siblings, Lohijärvi, 27 November 1933.
166 Sihvola, "Elämänkeronta," 27.
167 Ibid.
168 Tauno Salo letter to Carl Heino, Petrozavodsk, 23 November 1935.
169 Ibid.

170 Riordan, *Sport in Soviet Society*, 138.
171 Reino Hämäläinen letter to Benny, Petrozavodsk, 5 April 1932.
172 Aate Pitkänen letter to Taimi Davis, Petrozavodsk, 6 April 1933.
173 For example, Alice Heino letter "Rakas Veljeni" [Wiljam or Waino], Kondopoga, 18 March [1937], and Reino Mäkelä letter to Benny, Petrozavodsk, undated [circa Winter 1932].
174 Reino Mäkelä letters to Benny, Petrozavodsk, 24 January 1932 and undated [circa Winter 1932].
175 Zlobina, *Their Ideals Were Crushed*, 76.
176 Gronow, *Caviar with Champagne*, 60.
177 Aate Pitkänen letter to Parents, Petrozavodsk, 12 November 1933.
178 Aate Pitkänen letters to Taimi Davis, Petrozavodsk, 29 March 1933, 3 April 1933, and 6 April 1933.
179 Aate Pitkänen letter to Parents, Petrozavodsk, 20 March 1937.
180 Ibid.
181 Aate Pitkänen letter, Petrozavodsk, 12 April 1937.
182 Aate Pitkänen letter to Parents, Buzuluk, 1 January 1939.
183 Ibid.; Maunu, "Muistoja lapsuus ja poikavuosilta," 17.
184 Aate Pitkänen letter to Parents, Buzuluk, 1 January 1939.
185 Ibid.
186 Gordijenko, "Aate Pitkäsen Elämä ja Kuolema," 125–6.
187 Ibid., 122.
188 Ibid., 120.
189 For a discussion of this dichotomy, see Riordan, *Sport in Soviet Society*, 125–35.
190 Aate Pitkänen letter to Parents, Petrozavodsk, 20 March 1937.
191 Ibid.
192 Edelman, *Serious Fun*, 68.
193 Aate Pitkänen letter to Parents, Buzuluk, 1 January 1939.
194 Riordan, *Sport in Soviet Society*, 134.
195 Aate Pitkänen letter to Parents, Petrozavodsk, 20 March 1937.
196 Ibid.
197 Aate Pitkänen letter to Taimi Davis, Petrozavodsk, 29 March 1933.
198 Takala, "North American Finns as Viewed by Soviet Karelians," 206–7.
199 Antti Kangas letter to "Kunnon Toverit," Lososiina, 12 October 1934.
200 Hokkanen, *Karelia*, 59.

7. "Karelia Is Soaked in the Blood of Innocent People": Writing about the Great Terror

1 Researchers link differing numbers with the Sandarmokh grave. John Earl Haynes and Harvey Klehr note "more than nine thousand bodies"

in *In Denial*, 117. Alexander Etkind describes the discovery of 9,000 corpses in "Post-Soviet Hauntology: Cultural Memory of the Soviet Terror," *Constellations* 16, no. 1 (2009): 182; Nick Baron refers to 5,000–6,000 deceased in *Soviet Karelia*, 220.
2 Haynes and Klehr, *In Denial*, 117.
3 Etkind, "Post-Soviet Hauntology," 182.
4 Baron, *Soviet Karelia*, 220.
5 Etkind, "Post-Soviet Hauntology," 183; Catherine Merridale, *Night of Stone: Death and Memory in Twentieth-Century Russia* (New York: Penguin Books, 2000), 4.
6 Haynes and Klehr, *In Denial*, 117 and 235.
7 Kaa Eneberg, in conversation with the author, Petrozavodsk, May 2008. Eneberg is a Swedish journalist and researcher whose work has uncovered the history of Swedes and Swedish Finns in Soviet Karelia. See for example Eneberg's, "Recruitment of Swedish Immigrants to Soviet Karelia," in *Karelian Exodus: Finnish Communities in North America and Soviet Karelia during the Depression Era*, ed. Ronald Harpelle et al. (Beaverton, ON: Aspasia Books, 2004), 189–200.
8 Krasny Bor 1937–8, http://heninen.net/punakangas/english.
9 Fitzpatrick, *Everyday Stalinism*, 191–2.
10 Robert Conquest, *The Great Terror: A Reassessment* (Edmonton: University of Alberta Press, 1990), 290.
11 Conquest, *The Great Terror*, 485 and 309. Etkind has characterized Soviet camps as "torture camps, not extermination camps" and that the number of deaths "was the result of negligence rather than purposeful intent." Etkind, *Warped Mourning: Stories of the Undead in the Land of the Unburied* (Stanford, CA: Stanford University Press, 2013), 27.
12 Conquest, *The Great Terror*, 485–6. Conquest notes that these numbers may well be underestimations.
13 Ibid., 261.
14 As the Terror intensified, and the NKVD became increasingly overwhelmed by the number of "enemies" to process, interrogations changed from the lengthy "conveyer" method of wearing the prisoner down to so-called "simplified interrogation procedures," which quickly produced confessions through severe beatings and torture. Conquest, *The Great Terror*, 279.
15 Conquest, *The Great Terror*, 287; Merridale, *Night of Stone*, 200.
16 Fitzpatrick, *Everyday Stalinism*, 213; Conquest, *The Great Terror*, 264.
17 Hoffman, *Stalinist Values*, 176.
18 Baron, *Soviet Karelia*, 168.
19 Ibid.
20 Baron, *Soviet Karelia*, 171.
21 Golubev and Takala, *The Search for a Socialist El Dorado*, 126.

22 Ibid.; Ylikangas, "The Sower Commune," 80.
23 Conquest, *The Great Terror*, 286.
24 As the Purge was quick to turn on its own, over the course of the Karelian Terror campaign, the region went through four First Secretaries, after Rovio, and two heads of the NKVD. See, for example, Irina Takala, "The Great Purge," in *Victims and Survivors of Karelia*, ed. Markku Kangaspuro and Samira Saramo, *Journal of Finnish Studies*, Special Issue, 15, nos. 1–2 (November 2011): 149.
25 Takala, "The Great Purge," 148.
26 Baron, *Soviet Karelia*, 211.
27 Takala, "The Great Purge," 151.
28 The Karelian numbers, as everywhere in the Soviet Union, are incomplete and debated. However, Baron and Takala's numbers prove quite reliable and come relatively close to each other. Baron reports that 9,250 individuals were arrested during the July 1937–August 1938 time period (*Soviet Karelia*, 211), while Takala posits that by 1 January 1938, 5,340 people had been arrested, with 5,164 further arrests taking place between January and August 1938, totalling 10,504 ("The Great Purge," 155).
29 Hokkanen, *Karelia*, 96.
30 Takala, "The Great Purge," 147–8. Twenty-seven per cent of the purge victims were ethnic Karelians and 25 per cent were Russian. Baron contends that Finns represented 2.5 per cent of the population and represented one-third of the purge victims. See *Soviet Karelia*, 211.
31 Takala, "The Great Purge," 159.
32 Ibid., 156.
33 See Kostiainen, "Genocide in Soviet Karelia."
34 See, for example, Maunu, "Muistoja lapsuus ja poikavuosilta," 21; Alatalo, "Sylvin ja Paavon Tarina," 26; Hokkanen, *Karelia*, 95; Sevander, *Red Exodus*, 110.
35 Maunu, "Muistoja lapsuus ja poikavuosilta," 21.
36 Fitzpatrick, *Everyday Stalinism*, 202. Merridale puts forward a similar argument. Merridale, *Night of Stone*, 198.
37 Alatalo, "Sylvin ja Paavon Tarina," 25.
38 Hokkanen, *Karelia*, 85–6.
39 Maunu, "Muistoja lapsuus ja poikavuosilta," 22.
40 Justiina Heino partial letter to unknown recipient [one of her sons], unknown date, circa 1938 (JH4); Lisi Hirvonen letter to Anna Mattson, "U.S.S.R. Karjala," 17 January 1939.
41 Hokkanen, *Karelia*, 85; Sihvola, "Elämänkeronta," 41.
42 Sevander, *They Took My Father*, 100–1.
43 Alatalo, "Sylvin ja Paavon Tarina," 27.

44 Paavo Alatalo interview with Raija Warkentin, Jokela, Finland, 15 January 2002.
45 Zlobina, *Their Ideals Were Crushed*, 96.
46 Sevander, *They Took My Father*, 99.
47 Siegelbaum and Sokolov, *Stalinism as a Way of Life*, 181–2; Fitzpatrick, *Everyday Stalinism*, 116; Kotkin, *Magnetic Mountain*, 174.
48 Sevander, *Red Exodus*, 124.
49 Sevander, *They Took My Father*, 101. Allan Sihvola also noted that news of the arrests immediately circulated through the community, "Elämänkeronta," 42.
50 Glenna Roberts and Serge Cipko, *One-Way Ticket: The Soviet Return-to-the-Homeland Campaign, 1955–1960* (Manotick, ON: Penumbra Press, 2008), 40–1; Conquest, *The Great Terror*, 271.
51 See Sevander, *Red Exodus*, 124 and 126.
52 Aino Pitkänen letter to Antti and Kirsti Pitkänen, Urimolahti, Finland, 25 July 1938.
53 Such symbolism has been utilized in other moments of crisis, such as in the Irish Famine. See Margaret Kelleher, "Woman as Famine Victim: The Figure of Woman in Irish Famine Narratives," in *Gender and Catastrophe*, ed. Ronit Lentin (London: Zed Books, 1997), 249.
54 Aino Pitkänen letter to Antti and Kirsti Pitkänen, Urimolahti, Finland, 25 July 1938.
55 Alice Heino letter to Wiljam, Kondopoga, unknown date, circa 1938 (AH4). Goldberg similarly found that one of her studied correspondents signalled the arrest of her husband by simply not mentioning him until he was released from prison. See "Reading and Writing across the Borders of Dictatorship," in *Letters across Borders: The Epistolary Practices of International Migrants*, ed. Bruce S. Elliott et al. (Ottawa: Palgrave MacMillan, 2006), 163.
56 Leder, *My Life in Stalinist Russia*, 297.
57 Justiina Heino partial letter to unknown recipient [one of her sons], date unknown, circa early 1938 (JH4).
58 Lisi Hirvonen letter to Anna Mattson, Petrozavodsk, 2 February 1938.
59 David A. Gerber, "Epistolary Masquerades: Acts of Deceiving and Withholding in Immigrant Letters," in *Letters across Borders: The Epistolary Practices of International Migrants*, ed. Bruce S. Elliott et al. (Ottawa: Palgrave MacMillan, 2006), 151.
60 Sevander, *Vaeltajat*, 189; Anatoli Shishkin correspondence with Nancy Mattson, 6 December 2009. Eino Hirvonen spent ten years in prison.
61 Lisi Hirvonen letter to Anna Mattson, Petrozavodsk, 10 September 1938.
62 Goldberg, "Reading and Writing across the Borders of Dictatorship," 167.
63 Terttu Kangas letter to Toini, Lohijärvi, 30 January 1939.
64 Gerber, *Authors of Their Lives*, 4.

65 Justiina Heino letter to Wiljam, Salmi, 16 June 1941.
66 Lisi Hirvonen letter to Anna Mattson, Petrozavodsk, 19 July 1939.
67 Lisi Hirvonen letter to Anna Mattson, Wonganperä, 5 February 1933.
68 For example, the Heino letter collection is accompanied by a 1 August 1938 letter from Minnesota Congressman Harold Knutson to Bill Heino that reveals that the Heino family, in both the United States and in Karelia, were working to get Justiina, Alice, and Walter out of the Soviet Union.
69 Kalle Korhonen letter to Aune Batson, Tunkua District, Soviet Karelia, 23 August 1935.
70 Kalle Korhonen letter to Aune Batson, Petrozavodsk, 25 October 1936.
71 Kalle Korhonen letter to Aune Batson, Petrozavodsk, 30 January 1937.
72 Kalle Korhonen letter to Aune Batson, Petrozavodsk, 5 May 1937.
73 Kalle Korhonen letter to Aune Batson, Petrozavodsk, 30 November 1937.
74 Kalle Korhonen letter to Aune Batson, Petrozavodsk, 30 November 1938.
75 Kalle Korhonen letter to Aune Batson, Petrozavodsk, 22 February 1939.
76 Ibid.
77 George Halonen letter to Mrs. T. W. Batson, Superior, Wis., 5 April 1939.
78 Kalle Korhonen letter to Aune Batson, Petrozavodsk, 30 October 1939.
79 Batson, "On Being Half-Finnished."
80 Ibid.
81 Jack Forsell letter to Janet Lehto, "Karelia," 6 February 1979.
82 Ibid.
83 Conquest, *The Great Terror*, 308 and 467.
84 Sevander, *Red Exodus*, 8; Elis Sulkanen also wrote about how returnees were kept silent through "threats." Sulkanen, *Amerikan suomalaisen työväenliikkeen historia* (Fitchburg: Raivaaja Publishing, 1951), 278.
85 Hokkanen, *Karelia*, 125.
86 Ibid., 1–3.
87 Lindström and Vähämäki, "Ethnicity Twice Removed," 15.
88 Hokkanen, *Karelia*, 126.
89 For example, Sevander, *They Took My Father*, 102, and Hokkanen, *Karelia*, 92.
90 The Corgan family received a death certificate that claimed Oscar Corgan had died of cancer in 1940, rather than execution in 1938. Sevander, *They Took My Father*, 175. Lahti-Argutina has explained the falsification of dates: "The thinking was that it was easier for people to accept the death of a loved one if they thought the person died in the war." In Eila Lahti-Argutina, "The Fate of Finnish Canadians in Soviet Karelia" in *Karelian Exodus: Finnish Communities in North America and Soviet Karelia during the Depression Era*, ed. Ronald Harpelle et al., 118–31 (Beaverton, ON: Aspasia Books, 2004), 123.
91 Etkind, *Warped Mourning*, 38.
92 See Etkind's "Post-Soviet Hauntology" and *Warped Mourning*.
93 Sevander, *Of Soviet Bondage*, 48.

94 Harold Hietala letter to Varpu Lindström, Tshalna, 1 February 1989.
95 Ibid.
96 For a discussion about silence as active, see Eviatar Zerubavel, "The Social Sound of Silence: Toward a Sociology of Denial," in *Shadows of War: A Social History of Silence in the Twentieth Century*, ed. Efrat Ben-Ze'ev, Ruth Ginio, and Jay Winter (Cambridge: Cambridge University Press, 2010), 33.
97 Jack Forsell letter to Janet Lehto, Tsalna, 4 December 1988.
98 Aino Pitkänen letter to Kirsti Pitkänen, Urimolahti, Finland, 25 July 1938.
99 Jack Forsell letter to Janet Lehto, Tsalna, 14 January 1993.
100 Hokkanen, *Karelia*, 128.
101 Conquest argues that "an almost instinctive feeling that this did not accord with common sense, with normal experience" struck outsiders, even "people of good will," when they were faced with facts about the Terror and the Soviet labour camp system. *The Great Terror*, 309.
102 The main discussion of the Purges is found in the chapter, "How Can They All Be Guilty?" Hokkanen, *Karelia*, 89–96.
103 Smith and Watson, *Reading Autobiography*, 93.
104 Jack Forsell letter to Janet Lehto, Tsalna, 20 February 1972.
105 Amy-Katerini Prodromou, *Navigating Loss in Women's Contemporary Memoir* (London: Palgrave, 2015).
106 Sevander, *Red Exodus*, 4. See also Miettinen, 315.
107 Sevander, *Red Exodus*, 110.
108 Jay Winter, "Thinking about Silence," in *Shadows of War: A Social History of Silence in the Twentieth Century*, ed. Efrat Ben-Ze'ev, Ruth Ginio, and Jay Winter (Cambridge: Cambridge University Press, 2010), 14.
109 Paul Antze and Michael Lambek, "Introduction," in *Tense Past: Cultural Essays in Trauma and Memory* (New York: Routledge, 1996), xix.
110 Dominick La Capra, *Writing History, Writing Trauma* (Baltimore: Johns Hopkins University Press, 2001), 41.
111 Laurence J. Kirmayer, "Landscapes of Memory: Trauma, Narrative, and Dissociation," in *Tense Past: Cultural Essays in Trauma and Memory*, ed. Paul Antze and Michael Lambek (New York: Routledge, 1996), 189.
112 See Samira Saramo, "The Letters, Memories, and 'Truths' of Finnish North Americans in Soviet Karelia," *Histoire sociale/Social History* 46, no. 92 (November 2013): 487–8.
113 Jack Forsell letter to Janet Lehto, "Karelia," 28 December 1993.
114 See for example, Jack Forsell letters to Janet Lehto, 28 December 1993, [6?] January 1995, and 10 December 1995.
115 Jack Forsell letter to Janet Lehto, "Karelia," 6 February 1979.
116 Marlene Epp has found a similar tendency among Mennonite women's narratives about rape during the Second World War. See, Epp, "The Memory of Violence: Soviet and Eastern European Mennonite Refugees

and Rape in the Second World War," *Journal of Women's History* 9, no. 1 (Spring 1997): 65.
117 Jack Forsell letter to Janet Lehto, Tsalna, 4 December 1988.
118 Sevander, *Red Exodus*, 70.
119 Reino Mäkelä letter to Eva, Säpsä, 20 August 1967.
120 Sevander lists Kalervo Mäkelä's death as 1938. *Vaeltajat*, 206.
121 Reino Mäkelä letter to Eva, Säpsä, 16 October 1978.
122 Kirmayer, "Landscapes of Memory," 189.
123 La Capra, *Writing History, Writing Trauma*, 161–2.
124 Jack Forsell letter to Janet Lehto, "Karelia," 23 December 1996.
125 G. Thomas Couser, *Memoir: An Introduction* (New York: Oxford University Press, 2012), 41.
126 La Capra, *Writing History, Writing Trauma*, 88–9.
127 Gerber, "Epistolary Masquerades," 147.
128 Karen Armstrong, *Remembering Karelia: A Family's Story of Displacement during and after the Finnish Wars* (New York: Berghahn Books, 2004), 112.
129 Merridale, *Night of Stone*, 190.
130 Dominick La Capra has fruitfully explored this concept, along with "working through" and "acting out," in *Writing History, Writing Trauma*.
131 Maunu, "Muistoja lapsuus ja poikavuosilta," 7.
132 Ibid., 16.
133 Ibid.
134 Maunu, "Muistoja lapsuus ja poikavuosilta," 19.
135 Jack Forsell letter to Janet Lehto, "Karelia," 12 December 1991. Emphasis in original.
136 Jack Forsell letter to Janet Lehto, "Karelia," 4 December 1990.
137 Hokkanen, *Karelia*, 94.
138 Sevander uses this term throughout *Red Exodus* and *Of Soviet Bondage*.
139 Sevander, *Red Exodus*, 188–9.
140 Ibid., 190.
141 Sevander, *Of Soviet Bondage*, 61.
142 Jack Forsell letters to Janet Lehto, Tsalna, 4 December 1990 and 14 January 1993.
143 Jack Forsell letter to Janet Lehto, Tsalna, 14 January 1993.
144 Ibid.
145 Ibid.
146 Jack Forsell letter to Janet Lehto, Tsalna, [day unknown] October 1994.
147 Ibid.
148 Harold Hietala letter to Varpu Lindström, Tsalna, 26 August 1989.
149 Ibid.
150 Justiina Heino letter to Wiljam, Salmi, 16 June 1941.
151 Aate Pitkänen letter to parents, Äänislinna, 12 June 1942.

152 Jack Forsell letter to Janet Lehto, "Karelia," [day unknown] October 1992.
153 Author's personal email correspondence with Laurie Hertzel, co-writer of *They Took My Father*, November-December 2013.
154 Tuomi, "The Karelian 'Fever' of the Early 1930s," 75.
155 Michael Jackson, *The Politics of Storytelling: Violence, Transgression, and Intersubjectivity* (Copenhagen: Museum Tusculanum Press, 2002), 33–4.
156 Couser, *Memoir*, 86. Emphasis in original.
157 For example, Ranta, untitled memoir, 3; Hokkanen, *Karelia*, 94. Fitzpatrick notes the prevalence of such descriptions in Soviet memoirs. *Everyday Stalinism*, 209.
158 Connerton, *How Societies Remember*, 17.
159 Vauhkonen, "He Rakensivat Kultuuria," 77.
160 Zlobina, *Their Ideals Were Crushed*, 100.
161 Sevander, *They Took My Father*, 118.
162 Translated lyrics from "Wide Is My Motherland," http://en.wikipedia.org/wiki/Wide_Is_My_Motherland (accessed 12 December 2013). The quoted verse was removed from the song at some point during de-Stalinization campaigns. Thanks to Alexey Golubev for originally helping me find this song.
163 Fitzpatrick, *Everyday Stalinism*, 217.
164 Hokkanen, *Karelia*, 95.
165 Margaret Rikkinen interview with Raija Warkentin, 8 May 2000.
166 Sevander, *Red Exodus*, 111.
167 Vauhkonen, "He Rakensivat Kultuuria," 77.
168 Sevander, *Vaeltajat*, 182.
169 Alessandro Portelli, *The Death of Luigi Trastulli and Other Stories: Form and Meaning in Oral History* (New York: State University of New York Press, 1991), 26.
170 Connerton, *How Societies Remember*, 73–4.
171 Ranta, untitled memoir, 5.
172 Sevander, *Of Soviet Bondage*, 82.

Conclusion

1 Jack Forsell letter to Janet Lehto, Tsalna, 2 December 1984.
2 Kotkin successfully demonstrated the "little tactics of the habitat" that people employed to live within the Soviet system in *Magnetic Mountain*. Timothy Johnston has categorized further strategies to complement Kotkin's approach in *Being Soviet: Identity, Rumour, and Everyday Life under Stalin 1939–1953* (Oxford: Oxford University Press, 2011), xxxi–xxxii.
3 Zlobina, *Their Ideals Were Crushed*, 112.
4 Hokkanen, *Karelia*, 126.

5 Ibid., 130.
6 Ibid., 125.
7 Ibid., 130.
8 Jack Forsell letter to Janet, Tshalna, 4 December 1990.
9 Aino Pitkänen letter to Kirsti and Antti Pitkänen, Urimolahti, Finland, 25 July 1938.
10 Kotkin, *Magnetic Mountain*, 154.
11 Siegelbaum and Sokolov, *Stalinism as a Way of Life*, 3.
12 Jennifer Eastman Attebery, *Up in the Rocky Mountains: Writing the Swedish Immigrant Experience* (Minneapolis: University of Minnesota Press, 2007), 166.
13 See, for example, Alice Heino letter to "Rakas Veljeni," Kondopoga, 18 March 1938, and Lisi Hirvonen letters to Anna Mattson, Petrozavodsk, 6 August 1934 and 30 January 1935.
14 Fitzpatrick, *Oceans of Consolation*, 550.
15 Janet Gurkin Altman, *Epistolarity: Approaches to a Form* (Columbus: Ohio State University Press, 1982), 119.
16 Zlobina, *Their Ideals Were Crushed*, 101.
17 Etkind, "Post-Soviet Hauntology," 182.
18 For example, The Finnish Literature Society has created a new archive for memory-based sources about "Stalin's Victims." New publications include Päivi Sihvola, *Kirjeitä Karjalasta – Amerikansuomalaisen Saaren perheen kolme poikaa Neuvosto-Karjalan ihannevaltiota rakentamassa 1930-luvulla* (Turku: Migration Institute of Finland, 2020); Aimo Ruusunen, *Punakankaan Suomalaiset: Teoloitus – ja hautapaikka Krasnyi bor 1937–1938* (Lappeenranta: Warelia, 2020).
19 Zlobina, *Their Ideals Were Crushed*, 108.

Bibliography

Letters

Clara Thomas Archives and Special Collections, York University, Varpu Lindström fonds:
2009-025/034, 6, Taimi Davis Personal Letters: AATE PITKÄNEN
2009-025/034, 6, Taimi Davis Personal Letters: AINO PITKÄNEN
2009-025/034, 6, Taimi Davis Personal Letters: ANTTI PITKÄNEN
2009-025/034, 9, Heino Letter Collection: JUSTIINA HEINO
2009-025/034, 9, Heino Letter Collection: ALICE HEINO
2009-025/034, 9, Heino Letter Collection: Miscellaneous
2009-025/034, 14: TAUNO SALO
2009-025/042, 12, Nancy Mattson Collection: LISI HIRVONEN
2009-025/035, 4, Judith Batson Collection: KALLE KORHONEN
2009-025/035, 4, Judith Batson Collection: Miscellaneous
2009-025/035, 6, Arthur Koski letter collection: TERTTU KANGAS
2009-025/035, 6, Arthur Koski letter collection: Antti Kangas
2009-025/035, 13, Janet Lehto Letter Collection: JACK FORSELL
2009-025/035, 13, Janet Lehto Letter Collection: Elvie Forsell
2009-025/035, 17, Sinisalo collection: ELIS RANTA
2009-025/037, 6, Leini and Harold Hietala correspondence: HAROLD HIETALA
2009-025/042, 11, Marilee Coughlin Collection: KARL BERG

Immigration History Research Center and Archives, University of Minnesota:
The Nelson, Arvid Papers, Finnish American Collection, Series 2, Box 2, Folder 11: ARVID NELSON
The Nelson, Arvid Papers, Finnish American Collection, Series 2, Box 5a, Folder 12: ARVID NELSON
The Nelson, Arvid Papers, Finnish American Collection, Series 2, Box 5a, Folder 12: ENOCH NELSON

The Makela, Reino, Papers, Finnish American Collection, Folder 1–2: REINO MÄKELÄ
The Makela, Reino, Papers, Finnish American Collection, Folder 2: ANNIKKI MÄKELÄ
The Makela, Reino, Papers, Finnish American Collection, Folder 3: REINO MÄKELÄ
The Makela, Reino, Papers, Finnish American Collection, Folder 3: REINO HÄMÄLÄINEN
Library and Archives of Canada, Comintern Papers, MG 10 K 3 K-282 Reel 14 (1931) File 128: MATTI TENHUNEN

Memoirs

Published

Bucht, Christer. *Karjala kutsui*. Helsinki: Kirjayhtymä, 1973.
Hokkanen, Lawrence and Sylvia Hokkanen, with Anita Middleton. *Karelia: A Finnish-American Couple in Stalin's Russia, 1934–1941*. St. Cloud, Minnesota: North Star Press, 1991.
Leder, Mary M. *My Life in Stalinist Russia: An American Woman Looks Back*. Edited by Laurie Bernstein. Indianapolis: Indiana University Press, 2001.
Maunu, Klaus. "Piikilangan Takana," Three Installments. *Carelia* 11 and 12 (2006) and 1 (2007).
Miettinen, Helena, and Kyllikki Joganson. *Petettyjen Toiveiden Maa*. Saarijärvi, Finland: Arator, 2001.
Rosenberg, Suzanne. *A Soviet Odyssey*. Toronto: Oxford University Press, 1988.
Sevander, Mayme. "A Magic Circle." *Finnish Americana*, 9 (1992): 21–26.
– *Of Soviet Bondage: Sequel to "Red Exodus."* Duluth, MN: OSCAT, 1996.
– *Red Exodus: Finnish-American Emigration to Russia*. Duluth, MN: OSCAT, 1993.
– *Vaeltajat*. Turku: Siirtolaisuusinstituutti, 2000.
Sevander, Mayme, with Lauri Hertzel. *They Took My Father: Finnish Americans in Stalin's Russia*. Minneapolis: University of Minnesota Press, 2004, originally published in 1992.
Sihvola, Allan. *Stalinin taivaan alle – lapsena Yhdysvalloista Neuvosto-Karjalaan*. Turku: OK-kirja, 2021.
Tuomi, Kaarlo R. *Isanmaattoman tarina: Amerikansuomalaisen vakoojan muistelmat*. Helsinki: WSOY, 1984. Translated as *Spy Lost: Caught between the KGB and the FBI*. Introduction by John Earl Haynes. New York: Enigma Books, 2012.
– "The Karelian 'Fever' of the Early 1930s." *Finnish Americana* 3 (1980): 61–75.
Zlobina, Vieno. *Their Ideals Were Crushed: A Daughter's Story of the Säde Commune in Soviet Karelia*. Turku: Migration Institute of Finland, 2017.

Unpublished

Alatalo, Paavo. "Sylvin ja Paavon Tarina." Unpublished memoir, 2002. Raija Warkentin Collection, "Finnish-Canadian-America Russians Project," Lakehead University Archives.

Maunu, Klaus. "Evakossa." Unpublished memoir, circa 1990. Private Collection of family of Mrs. Eini Tuomi, Thunder Bay, ON.

– "Muistoja lapsuus ja poikavuosilta." Unpublished memoir, circa 1990. Private Collection of family of Mrs. Eini Tuomi, Thunder Bay, ON. Also available through Raija Warkentin Collection, "Finnish-Canadian-America Russians Project," Lakehead University Archives.

Ranta, Viola. Untitled, unpublished memoir, 1992. Clara Thomas Archives and Special Collection, York University, Varpu Lindström fonds: 2009-025/035, 17, Sinisalo donation.

Sihvola, Allan. "Elämänkeronta." Unpublished Memoir, 1996. Raija Warkentin Collection, "Finnish-Canadian-America Russians Project," Lakehead University Archives.

Interviews

Clara Thomas Archives and Special Collection, York University, Varpu Lindström fonds, interviews by Varpu Lindström:
2009-025/038, 1 (Side B) and 2 (Side A), LEINI HIETALA interview, August 1988.
2009-025/037, 4, LEINI HIETALA interview transcript.
2009-025/038, 2 (Side B) and 3 (Side A), ERWIN NIVA interview, August 1988.
2009-025/037, 5, ERWIN NIVA interview transcript.

Raija Warkentin Collection, "Finnish-Canadian-America Russians Project," Lakehead University Archives, interviews by Raija Warkentin:
ALATALO, PAAVO. 15 January 2002.
MAUNU, KLAUS AND LILI. 7 June 2000.
RIKKINEN, MIRIAM "MARGARET." 8 May 2000.

Miscellaneous Published Primary Sources

"Karelia for Travellers" (tourist map). APIS, 1999.

Komulainen, Ernesti J. (Ernest Laine). *A Grave in Karelia*. Translated by Ritva Koivu. Ann Arbor: Braun-Brumfield, 1995.

Muhlen, Hermynia Zur. *Fairy Tales for Workers' Children*. Translated by Ida Dailes. Chicago: Daily Worker Publishing, 1925. Available online: http://www.archive.org/details/FairyTalesForWorkersChildren.

National Children's Council. "Camps and Summer Work for Workers,
Children, Groups," May 1931. Lakehead University Archives, Nordström
Collection, MG 2.

Suomela, V. *Kuusi kuukautta Karjalassa: Mitä siirtolainen näki ja koki Neuvosto-Karjalassa.* Sudbury, ON: Vapaa Sana, 1935.

Vauhkonen, Impi. "He rakensivat kulttuuria." *Carelia* 3 (1993): 73–9.

Young Pioneers of Canada. "Games for the Pioneer Leader," July 1931. Lakehead University Archives, Nordström Collection, MG2.

Miscellaneous Unpublished Primary Sources

Batson, Judith D. "On Being Half-Finnished," unpublished personal essay, 2007. Clara Thomas Archives and Special Collection, York University, Varpu Lindström fonds, 2009-025/035, 5, Judith Batson Collection.

Davis, Taimi. "The Pitkanens of Kapalamaki: A History of the Family and Kivikoski School," unpublished, date unknown. York University Archives, Varpu Lindström fond, 2009-025/034.

"List of Finnish-American Emigrants to Soviet Karelia." Clara Thomas Archives and Special Collection, York University, Varpu Lindström fonds, 2009-025/036, 4, Rikhard Laiho.

Minutes of the Tarmola Women's Branch, 7 May 1930. Library and Archives of Canada, Finnish Organization of Canada fonds, MG 28 V 47, Vol. 191, File 5.

Missing in Karelia Database. National Archives of Finland.

Tieva, Martha. Unpublished, partial autobiographical description, unknown date. Clara Thomas Archives and Special Collection, York University, Varpu Lindström fonds, 2009-025/034, Heino Family Info.

Newspapers

Punainen Karjala
Työmies
Vapaus

Music

Dunaevsky, Isaac, composer, and Vasily Lebedev-Kumach, lyricist. "Wide Is My Motherland" (*Pesnya o rodinye*). 1936.

Books and Articles

Altman, Janet Gurkin. *Epistolarity: Approaches to a Form.* Columbus: Ohio State University Press, 1982.

Antze, Paul, and Michael Lambek, eds. *Tense Past: Cultural Essays in Trauma and Memory.* New York: Routledge, 1996.

Armstrong, Karen. *Remembering Karelia: A Family's Story of Displacement during and after the Finnish Wars.* New York: Berghahn Books, 2004.

Assmann, Aleida. "Re-Framing Memory: Between Individuals and Collective Forms of Constructing the Past." In *The Performance of the Past: Memory, History, and Identity in Modern Europe,* ed. Karin Tilmans, Frank van Vree, and Jay Winter, 35–50. Amsterdam: Amsterdam University Press, 2010.

Attebery, Jennifer Eastman. *Up in the Rocky Mountains: Writing the Swedish Immigrant Experience.* Minneapolis: University of Minnesota Press, 2007.

Attwood, Lynne. *Gender and Housing in Soviet Russia: Private Life in a Public Space.* New York: Manchester University Press, 2010.

Austin, Paul M. "Soviet Finnish: The End of a Dream." *East European Quarterly* 21, no. 2 (June 1987): 183–205.

Autio, Paula. "Haaveet jäivät haaveiksi." *Carelia* 3 (1993): 37–43.

Avery, Donald. *Dangerous Foreigners: European Immigrant Workers and Labour Radicalism in Canada, 1896–1932.* Toronto: McClelland & Stewart, 1979.

Bailey, Beth L. *From Front Porch to Back Seat: Courtship in Twentieth-Century America.* Baltimore: John Hopkins University Press, 1988.

Barnwell, Ashley, and Kate Douglas, eds. *Research Methodologies for Auto/biography Studies.* London: Routledge, 2019.

Baron, Nick. *Soviet Karelia: Politics, Planning, and Terror in Stalin's Russia, 1920–1939.* New York: Routledge, 2007.

Barthes, Roland. "Toward a Psychosociology of Contemporary Food Consumption." Reprinted in *Food and Culture: A Reader,* edited by Carole Counihan and Penny Van Esterik, 20–7. New York: Routledge, 1997.

Beaulieu, Michel S., David K. Ratz, and Ronald N. Harpelle, eds. *Hard Work Conquers All: Building the Finnish Community in Canada.* Vancouver: University of British Columbia Press, 2018.

Boym, Svetlana. *Common Places: Mythologies of Everyday Life in Russia.* Cambridge, MA: Harvard University Press, 1994.

Campbell, J. Peter. "The Cult of Spontaneity: Finnish-Canadian Bushworkers and the Industrial Workers of the World in Northern Ontario, 1919–1934." In *Essays in Northwestern Ontario Working Class History: Thunder Bay and Its Environs,* ed. Michel Beaulieu, 91–124. Thunder Bay, ON: Lakehead University Centre for Northern Studies, 2008.

Campbell, Laura. *Respectable Citizens: Gender, Family, and Unemployment in Ontario's Great Depression.* Toronto: University of Toronto Press, 2009.

Collingham, Lizzie. *The Taste of War: World War Two and the Battle for Food.* London: Allen Lane, 2011.

Comacchio, Cynthia R. "Dancing to Perdition: Adolescence and Leisure in Interwar English Canada." *Journal of Canadian Studies / Revue d'études canadiennes* 32, no. 3 (Fall 1997): 5–35.

- *The Dominion of Youth: Adolescence and the Making of Modern Canada, 1920 to 1950*. Waterloo, ON: Wilfrid Laurier University Press, 2006.
- *The Infinite Bonds of Family: Domesticity in Canada, 1850–1940*. Toronto: University of Toronto Press, 1999.

Connerton, Paul. *How Societies Remember*. New York: Cambridge University Press, 1989.

Conquest, Robert. *The Great Terror: A Reassessment*. Edmonton: University of Alberta Press, 1990.

Couchman, Jane, and Ann Crabb, eds. *Women's Letters across Europe, 1400–1700*. Aldershot: Ashgate, 2005.

Couser, G. Thomas. *Memoir: An Introduction*. New York: Oxford University Press, 2012.

Dahlie, Jorgen, and Tissa Fernando, eds. *Ethnicity, Power and Politics in Canada*. Toronto: Methuen, 1981.

Drachewych, Oleksa, and Ian McKay, eds. *Left Transnationalism: The Communist International and the National, Colonial, and Racial Questions*. Montreal and Kingston: McGill-Queen's University Press, 2020.

Edelman, Robert. *Serious Fun: A History of Spectator Sports in the USSR*. New York: Oxford University Press, 1993.

Efremkin, Evgeny. "At the Intersections of Nations, Diasporas, and Modernities: North American Finns in the Soviet Union in the 1930s." PhD Dissertation, York University, 2014.

Eklund, William. *Builders of Canada: History of the Finnish Organization of Canada, 1911–1971*. Toronto: Finnish Organization of Canada, 1987.

Epp, Marlene. "The Memory of Violence: Soviet and Eastern European Mennonite Refugees and Rape in the Second World War." *Journal of Women's History* 9, no. 1 (Spring 1997): 58–87.

Epp, Marlene, Franca Iacovetta, and Frances Swyripa, eds. *Sisters of Strangers? Immigrant, Ethnic, and Racialized Women in Canadian History*. Toronto: University of Toronto Press, 2004.

Etkind, Alexander. "Post-Soviet Hauntology: Cultural Memory of the Soviet Terror." *Constellations* 16, no. 1 (2009): 182–200.

- *Warped Mourning: Stories of the Undead in the Land of the Unburied*. Stanford, CA: Stanford University Press, 2013.

Ewing, E. Thomas. "Ethnicity at School: 'Non-Russian' Education in the Soviet Union during the 1930s." *History of Education* 35, nos. 4–5 (2006): 499–519.

- *The Teachers of Stalinism: Policy, Practice, and Power in Soviet Schools of the 1930s*. New York: Peter Lang, 2002.

Farb, Peter, and George Armelagos. *Consuming Passions: The Anthropology of Eating*. Boston: Houghton Mifflin, 1980.

Fitzgerald, Deborah. "Blinded by Technology: American Agriculture in the Soviet Union, 1928–1932." *Agricultural History* 70, no. 3 (Summer 1996): 459–86.

Fitzpatrick, David. *Oceans of Consolation: Personal Accounts of Irish Migration to Australia.* Ithaca, NY: Cornell University Press, 1994.
Fitzpatrick, Sheila. *Everyday Stalinism: Ordinary Life in Extraordinary Times: Soviet Russia in the 1930s.* New York: Oxford University Press, 1999.
– ed. *Stalinism: New Directions.* London: Routledge, 2000.
Friberg, Eino, trans. *The Kalevala: Epic of the Finnish People*, 5th ed. Keuruu, Finland: Otava Publishing, 2004.
Gabaccia, Donna. *We Are What We Eat: Ethnic Food and the Making of Americans.* Cambridge, MA: Harvard University Press, 1998.
Garth, Raili, and Kaarina Brooks. *Trailblazers: The Story of Port Arthur Kansallisseura Loyal Finns in Canada.* Toronto: Jack Lake Productions, 2010.
Gelb, Michael. "'Karelian Fever': The Finnish Immigrant Community during Stalin's Purges." *Europe-Asia Studies* 45 no. 6 (1993): 1091–1116.
Gerber, David A. *Authors of Their Lives: The Personal Correspondence of British Immigrants to North America in the Nineteenth Century.* New York: New York University Press, 2006.
– "Epistolary Masquerades: Acts of Deceiving and Withholding in Immigrant Letters." In *Letters across Borders: The Epistolary Practices of International Migrants*, ed. Bruce S. Elliott, David A. Gerber, and Suzanne M. Sinke, 141–57. Ottawa: Palgrave MacMillan, 2006.
Gerchuk, Iurii. "Festival Decoration of the City: The Materialization of the Communist Myth in the 1930s." *Journal of Design History* 13, no. 2 (2000): 123–36.
Gleeson, Mona. "Avoiding the Agency Trap: Caveats for Historians of Children, Youth, and Education." *History of Education* 45, no. 4 (2016): 446–59.
Goldberg, Ann. "Reading and Writing across the Borders of Dictatorship: Self-Censorship and Emigrant Experience in Nazi and Stalinist Europe." In *Letters across Borders: The Epistolary Practices of International Migrants*, ed. Bruce S. Elliott, David A. Gerber, and Suzanne M. Sinke, 158–72. Ottawa: Palgrave MacMillan, 2006.
Golubev, Alexey, and Irina Takala. *The Search for a Socialist El Dorado: Finnish Immigration to Soviet Karelia from the United States and Canada in the 1930s.* East Lansing: Michigan State University Press, 2014.
Gordijenko, Anatoli. "Aate Pitkäsen Elämä ja Kuolema." *Carelia* 7 (2006): 116–31.
Graziosi, Andrea. "Foreign Workers in Soviet Russia, 1920–40: Their Experience and Their Legacy." *International Labor and Working-Class History* 33 (Spring 1988): 38–59.
Gronow, Jukka. *Caviar with Champagne: Common Luxury and the Ideals of the Good Life in Stalin's Russia.* New York: Berg, 2003.
Halminen, Matti. *Sointula – Kalevan Kansan ja Kanadan suomalaisten historiaa.* Mikkeli: Kustantaja Mikko Ampuja, 1936.

Harpelle, Ronald N., Varpu Lindström, and Alexis E. Pogorelskin, eds. *Karelian Exodus: Finnish Communities in North America and Soviet Karelia during the Depression Era*. Beaverton, ON: Aspasia Books, 2004.
Haynes, John Earl, and Harvey Klehr. *In Denial: Historians, Communism and Espionage*. San Francisco: Encounter Books, 2003.
Hinther, Rhonda L. "Raised in the Spirit of the Class Struggle: Children, Youth, and the Interwar Ukrainian Left in Canada." *Labour/Le Travail* 60 (Fall 2007): 43–76.
– *Perogies and Politics: Canada's Ukrainian Left, 1891–1991*. Toronto: University of Toronto Press, 2018.
Hodgson, John H. *Communism in Finland: A History and Interpretation*. Princeton, NJ: Princeton University Press, 1967.
Hoffman, David L. *Stalinist Values: The Cultural Norms of Soviet Modernity, 1917–1941*. Ithaca, NY: Cornell University Press, 2003.
Hollingsworth, Laura, and Vappu Tyyska. "The Hidden Producers: Women's Household Production during the Great Depression." *Critical Sociology* 15, no. 3 (October 1988): 3–27.
Holmio, Armas K.E. *History of the Finns in Michigan*. Trans. Ellen M. Ryynanen. Hancock, MI: Great Lakes Books, 2001.
Hooper, Cynthia. "Terror of Intimacy: Family Politics in the 1930s Soviet Union." In *Everyday Life in Early Soviet Russia: Taking the Revolution Inside*, ed. Christina Kiaer and Eric Naiman, 61–91. Indianapolis: Indiana University Press, 2006.
Huhta, Aleksi. "Toward a Red Melting Pot: The Racial Thinking of Finnish-American Radicals, 1900–1938." PhD dissertation, University of Turku, 2017.
Ilič, Melanie, ed. *Women in the Stalin Era*. New York: Palgrave, 2001.
Imrie, Diane, David Nicholson, and Laura Nigro, eds. *A Century of Sport in the Finnish Community of Thunder Bay*. Thunder Bay, ON: Northwestern Ontario Sports Hall of Fame and the Thunder Bay Finnish Canadian Historical Society, 2013.
Ishiguro, Laura. *Nothing to Write Home About: British Family Correspondence and the Settler Colonial Everyday in British Columbia*. Vancouver: University of British Columbia Press, 2019.
Jackson, Michael. *The Politics of Storytelling: Violence, Transgression, and Intersubjectivity*. Copenhagen: Museum Tusculanum Press, 2002.
Johnston, Timothy. *Being Soviet: Identity, Rumour, and Everyday Life under Stalin 1939–1953*. Oxford: Oxford University Press, 2011.
Jokinen, Walfrid. "The Finnish Cooperative Movement." *Publications of the Institute of General History, University of Turku*, no. 7 (1975): 10–24.
Jussila, Osmo, Seppo Hentilä, and Jukka Nevakivi. *From Grand Duchy to a Modern State: A Political History of Finland since 1809*. London: Hurst, 1999.

Kadar, Marlene. "Coming to Terms: Life Writing – from Genre to Critical Practice." In *Essays on Life Writing: From Genre to Critical Practice*, ed. Marlene Kadar, 3–16. Toronto: University of Toronto Press, 1992.

Kangaspuro, Markku. *Neuvosto-Karajan taistelu itsehallinnosta: Nationalismi ja suomalaiset punaiset Neuvostoliiton vallankäytössä 1920–1939.* Helsinki: SKS, 2000.

– "The Origins of the Karelian Workers Commune, 1920–1923: Nationalism as the Path to Communism." *The NEP Era: Soviet Russia, 1921–1928*, 1 (2007): 1–20.

Kangaspuro, Markku, and Samira Saramo, eds. *Victims and Survivors of Karelia.* Special Issue of *Journal of Finnish Studies* 15, nos. 1–2 (November 2011).

Karni, Michael G., and Douglas J. Ollila, Jr, eds. *For the Common Good: Finnish Immigrants and the Radical Response to Industrial America.* Superior, WI: Työmies Society, 1977.

Kaunonen, Gary. *Finns in Michigan.* East Lansing: Michigan State University Press, 2009.

Kealey, Linda. *Enlisting Women for the Cause: Women, Labour, and the Left in Canada, 1890–1920.* Toronto: University of Toronto Press, 1998.

Kelleher, Margaret. "Woman as Famine Victim: The Figure of Woman in Irish Famine Narratives." In *Gender and Catastrophe*, ed. Ronit Lentin. London: Zed Books, 1997, 241–54.

Kelly, Catriona. *Children's World: Growing Up in Russia, 1890–1991.* New Haven, CT: Yale University Press, 2007.

– "Shaping the 'Future Race': Regulating the Daily Life of Children in Early Soviet Russia." In *Everyday Life in Early Soviet Russia: Taking the Revolution Inside*, ed. Christina Kiaer and Eric Naiman, 256–81. Indianapolis: Indiana University Press, 2006.

Kenez, Peter. *Cinema and Soviet Society from the Revolution to the Death of Stalin.* New York: I.B. Tauris, 2001.

– *A History of the Soviet Union from the Beginning to the End*, 2nd ed. Cambridge: Cambridge University Press, 2006.

Kero, Reino. "Emigration of North Americans to Soviet Karelia in the Early 1930s." In *The Finnish Experience in the Great Lakes Region: New Perspectives, Migration Studies*, C 3, ed. Michael G. Karni, Matti E. Kaups, and Douglas J. Ollila, Jr., 212–21. Turku: Institute for Migration, 1975.

– *Neuvosto Karjalaa Rakentamassa: Pohjois-Amerikan suomalaiset tekniikan tuojina 1930-luvun Neuvosta-Karjalassa.* Helsinki: SHS, 1983.

– "The Role of Finnish Settlers from North America in the Nationality Question in Soviet Karelia in the 1930's." *Scandinavian Journal of History* 6, no. 3 (1981): 229–41.

Kidd, Bruce. *The Struggle for Canadian Sport.* Toronto: University of Toronto Press, 1996.

Kirby, David. *A Concise History of Finland*. Cambridge: Cambridge University Press, 2006.

Kirmayer, Laurence J. "Landscapes of Memory: Trauma, Narrative, and Dissociation." In *Tense Past: Cultural Essays in Trauma and Memory*, ed. Paul Antze and Michael Lambek, 173–98. New York: Routledge, 1996.

Kirschenbaum, Lisa A. *Small Comrades: Revolutionizing Childhood in Soviet Russia*. New York: Routledge Falmer, 2001.

Kivisto, Peter. "The Decline of the Finnish American Left, 1925–1945." *International Migration Review* 17, no. 1 (Spring 1983): 65–94.

– *Immigrant Socialists in the United States: The Case of Finns and the Left*. Rutherford, NJ: Fairleigh Dickinson University Press, 1984.

Kostiainen, Auvo. "The Finns and the Crisis over "Bolshevization' in the Worker's Party, 1924–25." In *The Finnish Experience in the Western Great Lakes Region: New Perspectives*, ed. Michael Karni, Matti E. Kaups, and Douglas J. Ollila Jr, 171–85. Turku: Migration Institute, 1975.

– ed. *Finns in the United States: A History of Settlement, Dissent, and Integration*. East Lansing: Michigan University Press, 2014.

– *The Forging of Finnish-American Communism, 1917–1924: A Study in Ethnic Radicalism*. Turku: Turun Yliopisto, 1978.

– "Genocide in Soviet Karelia: Stalin's Terror and the Finns of Soviet Karelia." *Scandinavian Journal of History* 21, no. 4 (1996): 332–41.

– *Loikkarit: Suuren lamakauden laiton siirtolaisuus Neuvostoliittoon*. Keuruu, Finland: NP, 1988.

Kotkin, Stephen. "Coercion and Identity: Workers' Lives in Stalin's Showcase City." In *Making Workers Soviet: Power, Class, and Identity*, ed. Lewis H. Siegelbaum and Ronald Grigor Suny, 274–310. Ithaca, NY: Cornell University Press, 1994.

– *Magnetic Mountain: Stalinism as a Civilization*. Los Angeles: University of California Press, 1995.

Kyvig, David E. *Daily Life in the United States, 1920–1940*. Chicago: Ivan R. Dee, 2004.

La Capra, Dominick. *Writing History, Writing Trauma*. Baltimore: John Hopkins University Press, 2001.

Lahti, Vesa-Matti. *Siperia Kutsuu! Kansainvälisen Kuzbas-siirtokunnan ja sen suomalaisten tarina 1921–1927*. Helsinki: Into, 2017.

Lahti-Argutina, Eila. *Olimme joukko vieras vaan. Venäjänsuomalaiset vainonuhrit Neuvostoliitossa 1930-luvun alusta 1950-luvun alkuun*. Turku: Siirtolaisuusinstituutti, 2001.

Laine, Antti, and Mikko Ylikangas, eds. *Rise and Fall of Soviet Karelia*. Helsinki: Kikimora, 2002.

Larson, Thomas. *The Memoir and the Memoirist: Reading and Writing Personal Narrative*. Athens: Swallow Press/Ohio University Press, 2007.

Lindström, Varpu. *Defiant Sisters: A Social History of Finnish Immigrant Women in Canada*, 3rd ed. Beaverton, ON: Aspasia Books, 2003.
– *I Won't Be a Slave: Selected Articles on Finnish Canadian Women's History.* Beaverton, ON: Aspasia Books, 2010.
Lindström, Varpu, and Börje Vähamäki. "Ethnicity Twice Removed: North American Finns in Soviet Karelia." *Finnish Americana* 9 (1992): 14–20.
London, Gary. "The Finnish-American Anti-Socialist Movement, 1908–1918." In *Finns in North America: Proceedings of Finn Forum III*, ed. Michael Karni, Olavi Koivukangas, and Edward W. Laine, 211–26. Turku: Migration Institute, 1988.
Lux, Maureen K. *Separate Beds: A History of Indian Hospitals in Canada, 1920s–1980s.* Toronto: University of Toronto Press, 2016.
Madokoro, Laura. "On Future Directions: Temporalities and Permanency in the Study of Migration and Settler Colonialism in Canada." *History Compass* 17 (2019): 1–6.
Malysheva, Marina, and Daniel Bertaux. "The Social Experiences of a Countrywoman in Soviet Russia." In *Gender and Memory*, edited by Selma Leydesdorff, Luisa Passerini, and Paul Thompson, 31–43. Oxford: Oxford University Press, 1996.
Mattson, Nancy. *Finns and Amazons.* Durham, UK: Arrowhead Press, 2012.
– *Lines From Karelia.* Durham: Arrowhead Press, 2011.
Mayblin, Lucy, and Joe Turner. *Migration Studies and Colonialism.* Cambridge: Polity, 2021.
Merridale, Catherine. *Night of Stone: Death and Memory in Twentieth-Century Russia.* New York: Penguin Books, 2000.
Metsaranta, Marc, ed. *Project Bay Street: Activities of Finnish-Canadians in Thunder Bay before 1915.* Thunder Bay: Thunder Bay Finnish-Canadian Historical Society, 1989.
Mickenberg, Julia L. "The New Generation and the New Russia: Modern Childhood as Collective Fantasy." *American Quarterly* 62, no. 1 (March 2010): 103–34.
Middleton, Anita. "Karelian Fever: Interviews with Survivors." *Melting into Great Waters, Journal of Finnish Studies* 1, no. 3 (1997): 179–82.
Miller, Timothy. *The Quest for Utopia in Twentieth Century America*, vol. 1: *1900–1960.* Syracuse: Syracuse University Press, 1998.
Mills, Claudia. "Friendship, Fiction, and Memoirs: Trust and Betrayal in Writing from One's Own Life." In *The Ethics of Life Writing*, ed. Paul John Eakin, 101–20. Ithaca, NY: Cornell University Press, 2004.
Mishler, Paul C. *Raising Reds: The Young Pioneers, Radical Summer Camps, and Communist Political Culture in the United States.* New York: Columbia University Press, 1999.

Mosby, Ian. "'Food Will Win the War': The Politics and Culture of Food and Nutrition during the Second World War." PhD dissertation, York University, 2011.

Nelson, Allan. *The Nelson Brothers: Finnish-American Radicals from the Mendocino Coast.* Ukiah, CA: Mendocino County Historical Society/Immigration History Research Center, 2005.

Newton, Janice. *The Feminist Challenge to the Canadian Left 1900–1918.* Montreal and Kingston: McGill-Queen's University Press, 1995.

Ollila, Douglas Jr. "The Emergence of Radical Industrial Unionism in the Finnish Socialist Movement." *Publications of the Institute of General History, University of Turku* 7 (1975): 25–54.

Peltonen, Ulla-Maija. *Punakapinan Muistot: Tutkimus työväen muistelukerronnan muotoutumisesta vuoden 1918 jälkeen.* Helsinki: SKS, 1996.

Penner, Norman. *Canadian Communism: The Stalin Years and Beyond.* Toronto: Methuen, 1988.

Petrone, Karen. *Life Has Become More Joyous, Comrades: Celebrations in the Time of Stalin.* Bloomington and Indianapolis: Indiana University Press, 2000.

Pinta, Saku. "The Wobblies of the North Woods: Finnish Labor Radicalism and the IWW in Northern Ontario." In *Wobblies of the World: A Global History of the IWW*, ed. Peter Cole, David Struthers, and Kenyon Zimmer, 140–55. London: Pluto Press, 2017.

Pogorelskin, Alexis E. "Edvard Gylling and the Origins of Karelian Fever." In *The Dividing Line: Borders and Peripheries*, ed. Lars-Folke Landgren and Maunu Häyryen, 261–71. Helsinki: Renvall Institute Publications, 1997.

Portelli, Alessandro. *The Death of Luigi Trastulli and Other Stories: Form and Meaning in Oral History.* New York: State University of New York Press, 1991.

Prodromou, Amy-Katerini. *Navigating Loss in Women's Contemporary Memoir.* London: Palgrave, 2015.

Radforth, Ian. "Finnish Radicalism and Labour Activism in the Northern Ontario Woods." In *A Nation of Immigrants: Women, Workers, and Communities in Canadian History, 1840s–1960s*, ed. Franca Iacovetta, Paula Draper, and Robert Ventresca, 293–316. Toronto: University of Toronto Press, 1998.

Rauchway, Eric. *The Great Depression and the New Deal: A Very Short Introduction.* New York: Oxford University Press, 2008.

Rautkallio, Hannu. *Suuri viha. Stalinin suomalsiet uhrit 1930-luvulla.* Helsinki-Porvoo-Juva: WSOY, 1995.

Riippa, Timo. "The Finnish American Radical Theater of the 1930s," *Finnish Americana* 9 (1992): 28–35.

Riordan, James. *Sport in Soviet Society: Development of Sport and Physical Education in Russia and the USSR.* Cambridge: Cambridge University Press, 1977.

Rislakki, Jukka, and Eila Lahti-Argutina. *No Home for Us Here: The Mass Annihilation of the Finnish Border-Hoppers in the Urals in 1938.* Trans. Richard Impola. St. Cloud, MN: North Star Press of St. Cloud, 2002.
Roberts, Fredric M. "The Finnish Coffee Ceremony and Notions of Self." *Arctic Anthropology* 26, no. 1 (1989): 20–33.
Roberts, Glenna, and Serge Cipko. *One-Way Ticket: The Soviet Return-to-the-Homeland Campaign, 1955–1960.* Manotick, ON: Penumbra Press, 2008.
Rodney, William. *Soldiers of the International: A History of the Communist Party of Canada, 1919–1929.* Toronto: University of Toronto Press, 1968.
Roe, James A. "Virginia, Minnesota's Socialist Opera: Showplace of Iron Range Radicalism." *Finnish Americana*, 9 (1992): 36–43.
Ross, Carl. *The Finn Factor in American Labor, Culture and Society,* 2nd ed. New York Mills: Parta Printers, 1978.
Rüthers, Monica. "Picturing Soviet Childhood: Photo Albums of Pioneer Camps." *Jahrbücher für Geschichte Osteuropas* (2019): 65–95.
Ruusunen, Aimo. *Punakankaan Suomalaiset: Teoloitus – ja hautapaikka Krasnyi bor 1937–1938.* Lappeenranta: Warelia, 2020.
Saramo, Samira. "Capitalism as Death: Loss of Life and the Finnish Migrant Left in the Early Twentieth Century." *Journal of Social History* (2021). doi:10.1093/jsh/shab039.
– "The Letters, Memories, and 'Truths' of Finnish North Americans in Soviet Karelia." *Histoire sociale/Social History* 46, no. 92 (November 2013): 471–95.
– "'A socialist movement which does not attract the women cannot live': Finnish Socialist Women in Port Arthur, 1903–1933." In *Labouring Finns: Transnational Politics in Finland, Canada, and the United States,* ed. Michel Beaulieu, Ronald Harpelle, and Jaimi Penney, 145–66. Turku: Institute of Migration, 2011.
Shearer, David. "Elements Near and Alien: Passportization, Policing, and Identity in the Stalinist State, 1932–1952." *Journal of Modern History* 76, no. 4 (December 2004): 838–81.
Siegelbaum, Lewis H. "The Shaping of Soviet Workers' Leisure: Workers' Clubs and Palaces of Culture in the 1930s." *International Labor and Working-Class History* 56 (Fall 1999): 78–92.
– *Stakhanovism and the Politics of Productivity in the USSR, 1935–1941.* Cambridge: Cambridge University Press, 1988.
Siegelbaum, Lewis, and Andrei Sokolov, eds. *Stalinism as a Way of Life: A Narrative in Documents.* New Haven, CT: Yale University Press, 2000.
Sihvola, Päivi. *Kirjeitä Karjalasta - Amerikansuomalaisen Saaren perheen kolme poikaa Neuvosto-Karjalan ihannevaltiota rakentamassa 1930-luvulla.* Turku: Migration Institute of Finland, 2020.

Smith, Sidonie, and Julia Watson. *Reading Autobiography: A Guide to Interpreting Life Narratives*, 2nd ed. Minneapolis: University of Minnesota Press, 2010.

Stites, Richard. "Festivals of Collusion? Provincial Days in the 1930s." *Kritika* 1, no. 3 (Summer 2000): 475–9.

– *Soviet Popular Culture: Entertainment and Society since 1900*. Cambridge: Cambridge University Press, 1992.

Strong-Boag, Veronica. "'Janey Canuck': Women in Canada, 1919–1939." *CHA Historical Booklet*, No. 53. Ottawa: Canadian Historical Association, 1994.

Sulkanen, Elis. *Amerikan suomalaisen työväenliikkeen historia*. Fitchburg: Raivaaja Publishing, 1951.

Sutherland, Neil. *Growing Up: Childhood in English Canada from the Great War to the Age of Television*. Toronto: University of Toronto Press, 1997.

Takala, Irina, and Ilya Solomeshch, eds. *North American Finns in Soviet Karelia in the 1930s*. Petrozavodsk: Petrozavodsk State University Press, 2008.

Teitelbaum, Kenneth. "'Critical Lessons' from Our Past: Curricula of Socialist Sunday Schools in the United States." *Curriculum Inquiry* 20, no. 4 (Winter 1990): 407–36.

– *Schooling for "Good Rebels": Socialist Education for Children in the United States, 1900–1920*. Philadelphia: Temple University Press, 1993.

Tester, Jim, ed. *Sports Pioneers: A History of the Finnish-Canadian Amateur Sports Federation, 1906–1986*. Sudbury, ON: Alerts AC Historical Committee, 1986.

Tuominen, Arvo. *The Bells of the Kremlin: An Experience in Communism*. Hanover and London: University Press of New England, 1983.

Vanhala, Harri. *Kommuuna Kylväjä – Amerikansuomalainen kolhoosi Donin aroilla*. Turku: Migration Institute of Finland, 2021.

Vuorela, Ulla. "Colonial Complicity: The 'Postcolonial' in a Nordic Context." In *Complying with Colonialism: Gender, Race and Ethnicity in the Nordic Region*, ed. Suvi Keskinen, Salla Tuori, Sara Irni, and Diana Mulinari, 48–75. London: Routledge, 2009.

Wilson, Donald J. "Little Comrades: Socialist Sunday Schools as an Alternative to Public Schools." *Curriculum Inquiry* 21, no. 2 (Summer 1991): 217–22.

Winter, Jay. "Thinking about Silence." In *Shadows of War: A Social History of Silence in the Twentieth Century*, ed Efrat Ben-Ze'ev, Ruth Ginio, and Jay Winter, 3–31. Cambridge: Cambridge University Press, 2010.

Zerubavel, Eviatar. *Hidden Rhythms: Schedules and Calendars in Social Life*. Chicago: University of Chicago Press, 1981.

– "The Social Sound of Silence: Toward a Sociology of Denial." In *Shadows of War: A Social History of Silence in the Twentieth Century*, ed. Efrat Ben-Ze'ev, Ruth Ginio, and Jay Winter, 32–44. Cambridge: Cambridge University Press, 2010.

Film

"Letters from Karelia." Directed by Kelly Saxberg. National Film Board of Canada, 2004.

Websites

"Krasny Bor 1937–1938," http://heninen.net/punakangas/english.htm.
"1939: Labor Discipline." *Seventeen Moments in Soviet History*, http://soviethistory.msu.edu/1939-2/labor-discipline/.

Index

Page numbers in **bold** indicate illustrations

Aero Club, 147
Ahokas, Elis, 18, 144
Ahokas, Emma, 18
Ahti, Jukka, 172, **173**, 175–6
Alatalo, Paavo, 17, 53, 55–6, 64, 92, 94–5, 99, 102–3, 117, 154, 178, 200n75
Alatalo, Sylvi, 17
All-Russian Central Executive Committee, 31, 195n48
Altman, Janet Gurkin: *Epistolarity*, 183
Alton, Liz. *See* Pitkänen, Taimi (later Davis) (aka Liz Alton)
Amerikan suomalaisen työväenliikkeen historia (Sulkanen), 226n84
Andropov, Yuri, 146
Anglo American Youth Club, 126
Antze, Paul (with Lambek), 165
Armelagos, George (with Farb): *Consuming Passions*, 68–9
Armstrong, Karen: *Remembering Karelia*, 168
Aronen, Kalle, 42
Assmann, Aleida, 5–6
Association for Jewish Colonization in the Soviet Union (ICOR), 198n4
Attwood, Lynne: *Gender and Housing in Soviet Russia*, 61, 73

Authors of Their Lives (Gerber), 8, 216n4
Autio-Sarasmo, Sari, 104

Bailey, Beth L.: *From Front Porch to Back Seat*, 140
Baron, Nick: *Soviet Karelia*, 37, 62, 116, 152–3, 196n72, 222–3n1, 224nn28, 30
Barthes, Roland, 69–70
Batson, Aune (née Korhonen), 13, 160–1
Beaulieu, Michel S., 193n10
Beaulieu, Michel S., ed. (with Ratz and Harpelle): *Hard Work Conquers All*, 188n4
Being Soviet (Johnston), 229n2
Benny (surname unknown) (friend of Reino Hämäläinen and Reino Mäkelä), 54, 130–1, 136, 140, 143, 145
Berg, Karl, 14, 68, 102, 105–6, 116, 182
Bertaux, Daniel, 79
Birobidzhan, 198n4
Bolsheviks and bolshevism, 27, 29–30, 32, 37, 60, 90, 94, 136
Boym, Svetlana: *Common Places*, 81
Brezhnev, Leonid, 164
Brooks, Kaarina (with Garth): *Trailblazers*, 194n36
Bucht, Christer: *Karjala kutsui*, 143

Buck, Tim, 46, 199n28
Buckley, Mary, 207n149
Builders of Canada (Eklund), 193n16

Campbell, Laura: *Respectable Citizens*, 203n52
capitalism, 24, 42, 87–8, 101, 105–6, 163, 178–80
Caviar with Champagne (Gronow), 66, 77
Central Organization of Loyal Finns in Canada, 28
children and youth in Karelia: anxiety of school demotions in, 95; apprenticeship system for, 118–19; babies, birth rate, and abortion, 141–2, 165; boarding schools (Internaat) for, 92; "Children's Homes" (communes) for, 100, 211n104; children's labour, 96; child support after divorce, 142; coming of age of, 118–19, 123; competing pulls of assimilation and tradition on, 94; courtship of, 136, 139; daycare for, **79**; death of, 79, 97, 100, 159, 165; death or arrest of parents of, 96; education of, 87–93 (*see also* education in Karelia); encouragement of critical thinking in, 88, 97; experiences and feelings in letters, memoirs, and interviews, 84; fear and bullying in, 93, 99, 154; feelings about migration in, 56, 91; gender ideals of, 118; history of, 207n4; homelessness of, 100, 211n102; at home with mothers, 81; idealism of, 48; indoctrination into revolutionary values of, 86; influence of film propaganda on, 136; inter-ethnic relations of, 98–100; Karelian and Russian, 99–100; "Karelia's Golden Fund," 84, 101; language, education, and employment barriers of, 85, 94–7; large families, 73; lasting impressions on, 87; leisure of (*see* leisure in Karelia); lens to understand cultural-political activism, 85; military practice of, 128; mistreatment and suffering of, 176; multinational identity of, 85; organizations for, 123, 126; overview of, 9, 12–13, 15–17; of prisoners, 156, 225n53; protection of, 85; public acknowledgment of, 97; radio programs for, 131; relative freedom of, 98; role in building socialism of, 182; value placed on, 85; workers' clubs for, 130; workplace youth leagues for, 128; youth clubs for, 126, 128; youth culture, 123–4

Children's World (Kelly), 211n102
cinema and films in Karelia, 98, 130, 134, **135**, 174, 218–19n86; influence of film propaganda on children and youth, 136; Stalin's preoccupation with national film industry, 136
Cinema and Soviet Society (Kenez), 136
Circus (film), 174
clothing in Karelia: bobby pins, 77; boiling for hygiene, 82; boots, 76–7; brought from North America, 53; buttons, 77; coats, 76; denim jackets and jeans, 75; dresses, 77; Finnish made, 99; glasses, 76; jackets, 99; kimonos, 77; knitted garments, 117; laundering, 76, 205n116; military, ascetic fashion, 75; from North America, Finland, and Russia, 76–7, 205n119; patching, 117; of prisoners, 116; shoes, 75, 77; shortage of, 75, 112; slacks, 75;

Index 249

"smart," 75; socks, 76; sweaters, 75; underwear, 76; watches, 76; woollen garments, 76; work clothes, 76
Cobalt, Ontario, 18, 35–6, 45, 87
Collingham, Lizzie: *The Taste of War*, 203n48
colonialism (settler), 6, 81, 189n11, 207n155
Comacchio, Cynthia: *The Dominion of Youth*, 218n79; *Infinite Bonds of Family*, 219n95
Common Places (Boym), 81
Communist International (Comintern), 5, 24–5, 27, 35, 38, 46
communist parties, 5, 25, 162–3; Bolshevization of, 37; "ethnic" language rights in, 88
Communist Party of Canada (CPC), 24, 26, 47, 126; opposition to Karelian project of, 46
Communist Party of Karelia, 32, 110
Communist Party of the Soviet Union (CPSU), 3, 13–14, 18, 27, 38, 47, 123, 126; youth organizations of, 84
Communist Party USA (CPUSA), 38, 126–7; opposition to Karelian project of, 46
Communist Women's Bureau, 87
Communist Young Pioneers, 9, 84–5, 86, 87–9, 91, 97–9, 128
Connerton, Paul: *How Societies Remember*, 189–90n10
Conquest, Robert: *The Great Terror*, 150, 223nn12, 14, 227n101
consumer goods in Karelia: alarm clocks, 77; aspirin, 77; availability of, 59, 77–8; buttons, 77; calendars, 78, 206n134; darning needles, 77; gramophones, 147; iodine, 77; nail scissors, 77; from North America, Finland, and Russia, 76–7, 205n119; radios, 147; razors, 77; skates and skis, 145
Consuming Passions (Farb and Armelagos), 68–9
Co-operative Exchange Board, 42
cooperativism and cooperatives, 25, 35–7, 47, 51, 102
Corgan, Aino, 47, 64
Corgan, Leo, 65
Corgan, Katri, 18, 64–5
Corgan, Oscar, 18–19, 25, 42–4, 47, 53, 64, 102, 127, 149, 226n90
Corgan, Paul, 47, 64, 69, 95–6, 99
Couser, Thomas: *Memoir*, 172

Daily Life in the United States (Kyvig), 206n145, 220n115
Daily Worker, The (newspaper), 26
dating, marriage, separation, and divorce in Karelia, 108, 139–42
Davies, Sarah, 217n59
Davis, Taimi (née Pitkänen). *See* Pitkänen, Taimi (later Davis) (aka Liz Alton)
Death of Luigi Trastulli ..., The (Portelli), 176
Defiant Sisters (Lindström), 200n58, 220n125
Dmitriev, Yuri, 149
Dominion of Youth, The (Comacchio), 218n79
Drummond Island, Michigan, 14, 24–5, 59, 66, 126, 140

Edelman, Robert: *Serious Fun*, 147
education in Karelia: in boarding schools, 92; on communism, 129; contrast between North America and Karelia, 90; educational games, 88–90; in farming, 105; in

250   Index

Finnish language, 87, 94, 120, 154, 208n17; during the Great Terror, 154; parachutist training, 147; political study, 126; presence of fear in, 93; to question capitalism, 88; radio programs, 131; rigid textbook learning in, 93; in Russian language, 95, 120, 154; Russian-language courses, 147; school demotions, 95; school materials, 92; on socialism, 126, 134; study groups, 128; teacher training, 92, 94–6, 110, 120, 209n45; through theatre productions, 134; volunteer inspector of schools, 128
Efremkin, Evgeny, 49, 84, 188n3
Eklund, William: *Builders of Canada*, 193n16
Eneberg, Kaa, 223n7
Epistolarity (Altman), 183
Epp, Marlene, 69, 73, 227–8n116
Etkind, Alexander, 184; *Warped Mourning*, 223n11
everyday life in Karelia: alcohol and masculinity, 142–3; cars, **63**; children and youth, 84–101 (*see also* children and youth in Karelia); clothing (*see* clothing in Karelia); communality, 63; consumer goods (*see* consumer goods in Karelia); culture, community, and leisure, 9, 15–17, 22, 123–48 (*see also* leisure in Karelia); depressing mood, 56; education, 87–93 (*see also* education in Karelia); food, 66–75 (*see also* food in Karelia); gendered division in home and employment, 64, 96, 116–20, 142, 182; health and hygiene, 78–82 (*see also* health and hygiene in Karelia); history of, 4; homesickness, 124–5; "little tactics of the habitat," 178,

229n2; makeshift nature of, 111; negative reports of, 124; "not like there" (North America), 83; rain and snow, 56; state-run cafeterias or canteens, 70–1; tools, 53, 104, 212n16; volunteer community labour, 128; work, 102–22 (*see also* work in Karelia). *See also* dating, marriage, separation, and divorce in Karelia; housing, furnishings, and living conditions in Karelia
Everyday Stalinism (S. Fitzpatrick), 75, 107, 114, 121, 150, 153–4, 175
Ewing, E. Thomas: *The Teachers of Stalinism*, 92, 209n45

Fairy Tales for Workers Children, 88, **89**
Farb, Peter (with Armelagos): *Consuming Passions*, 68–9
FBI (Federal Bureau of Investigation, USA), 17
Finglish, 5, 8, 69, 72, 75, 94, 183
Finland and Finns: archive about "Stalin's Victims," 185, 230n18; changing position, repression, and executions in Karelia, 120, 151–5, 224n30; colonial ideas about racial and cultural hierarchy, 81, 207n155; cultural and linguistic renaissance, 29; culture and independence, 8; *Fennophilia*, 29; Finnish Civil War (1918), 28–30, 89, 195n41; interest in annexing Karelia, 30, 195n47; migrants to Karelia (border hoppers, *loikkarit*), 5, 33, 98–9, 152, 185, 188n5; migration to North America, 29; nationalist spirit, 29; prisons and prisoner-of-war camps, 12, 155; relations with Soviet Union, 4, 29, 197n96
Finn Factor in American Labor ..., The (Ross), 22

Finnish Americana, 17
Finnish American Socialist Federation (FASF), 24, 26
Finnish-Canadian Amateur Sports Federation, 144
Finnish Labour Temple (Port Arthur, Ontario), **23**, 88
Finnish Literature Society, 230n18
Finnish National Federation (Kansallis-Liitto), 28
Finnish National League, 24
Finnish North Americans (in Karelia): abhorrence for Soviet life of, 15, 56; adoption of Soviet citizenship by, 5; arrests, treatment, and executions of during the Great Terror, 5, 7, 10–12, 14–15, 17–19, 120–1, 149–55, 164, 166, 168–70, 172–3, 175, 180, 184, 189n2, 191n37, 225n49, 226n90 (*see also* Great Terror); assessment of positives and negatives by, 59; changes in jobs and residences of, 107–10; changing position, repression, and executions of, 120, 151–5, 178, 180, 186, 229n2; children and youth of, 84–101 (*see also* children and youth in Karelia); collective farming by, 36; commitment to Five Year Plan of, 107; commune movement of, 18, 36; Communist Party members among, 46–7; communist supporters among, 11, 14, 18, 47, 124, 157, 179–80; communities and identities of, 4–5, 188n4; concept of masculinity in, 120; confiscation of belongings of, 56; consumer goods of (*see* consumer goods in Karelia); culture, community, and leisure of, 9, 15–17, 22, 123–48 (*see also* leisure in Karelia); death of children of, 79, 97, 100, 159; demographic analyses of, 49, 84, 123; differences from local population of, 7, 9, 65, 67, 75, 81, 83, 114, 118, 134, 148; distinctions from Finland Finns of, 5, 98; early arrivals in Karelia of, 34–5, 55; education of (*see* education in Karelia); employment of (*see* work in Karelia); engagement with socialism and utopianism of, 3, 5, 8, 14, 25, 37, 40, 73, 126–9, 147, 169; escapes and moves to Finland by, 14–17, 155, 164; food of (*see* food in Karelia); gender roles in, 64, 96, 116–20, 142, 182; health of (*see* health and hygiene in Karelia); "hero" narrative in collective memory and historiography of, 9; hostility to their Finnishness of, 120; hybridized language (Finglish) (*see* Finglish); idealized labourers (*see* Shock Workers and Stakhanovites); identities of, 4–5, 188n3; inter-ethnic relations of, 4, 37–8, 43, 115–16, 134; letters and memoirs of, 7, 11–19, 41, 53, 155–77 (*see also* life writers; life writing); migrant organizers and leaders among, 18; nostalgia for home among, 70, 159; not understood by people in North America, 164, 227n101; percentages from Canada and United States of, 49; personal connections used to influence the system by, 110; "political life" of, 164; preferential treatment and elite status of, 5, 9, 60, 62, 66, 77–8, 83, 99, 110, 114, 134, 154; property and assets in the home place of, 7, 52, 200n65; published histories of, 19, 170–1; resistance and perseverance of, 176; return in 1946 after the war by, 185;

return migration to North America by, 12, 16, 18, 43–5, 47, 124–6, 147, 159–62, 216n5, 226nn68, 84; role as "civilizers and modernizers" of, 5–6, 8, 81, 115, 148; role in the Continuation War of, 12, 168, 176; scholarly research and analysis of, 19, 192nn43, 44; survivors of the Great Terror among, 176–9, 185; suspicions against and disapproval of local population of, 73, 114, 148; techniques and technological contributions of, 104, 112–13, 212n18; thoughts about privileged status of, 114; tools from home renamed and rebranded by, 104, 212n16; value of money to, 106; women (*see* women in Karelia); work of (*see* work in Karelia). *See also* Karelia (*Karjala*)

Finnish North Americans (in North America): attitudes toward sports of, 144; attraction to Karelia by free health care of, 80; church affiliations of, 21–2; cinema attendance by, 134, 218nn79, 219n95; conservatives and "Church Finns," 28, 163, 178; cultural halls (*haali*) and entertainment evenings (*iltamat*) of, 22, 53, 88, 129; dating culture of, 139; decision to migrate of, 12, 38–9, 41, 50–2, 159, 197n96; effect of emigration on sports of, 144; effect of Russian Revolution on, 25, 107; employment and economic status of, 45, 102–3, 107; employment and "workplace terrorism" of, 21, 194n36; engagement with communism of, 25–7, 49, 157, 163, 179–80; engagement with socialism and utopianism of, 20–5, 28, 35, 37, 40, 45, 49, 119, 147, 169, 181, 193n10; family operations and negotiations of, 51–2; farewell parties for, 53; Finnish-language leftist (communist) press of, 37, 41–3, 47, 52, 87, 124, 212n15; fundraising for Soviet Russia and Karelia by, 35, 197n77; gender roles of, 52, 200n58; home communities of, 14, 16, 21–2, 36, 45, 59, 66, 72, **86**, 87–8, 91, 102–3, 126, 139–40, 145, 159, 161, 163, 198n6; living and working conditions of, 61, 110, 124, 202n11; idealism of, 45, 179; immersion in English language of, 88, 178; "Karelian Fever" of, 41, 44, 51, 85, 90, 125, 181; labour practices and policies of, 119; marriage and divorce of, 142; marriage preferences of, 220n125; migrant communist press, 3; notions of "women's work" of, 118; political and economic motivations for migrating to Karelia of, 44–9, 178; reaction to the Great Terror and Purge in Karelia of, 156, 165, 227n101; recruitment for the Karelian project of, 42–4, 198n8; "Reds" and "Whites," 28, 43, 87, 194n36; requirements, applications, and preparations for migration of, 50–3, 200n62; Socialist Sunday Schools of, 87–8; temperance societies of, 22; theatre productions of, 133

Finnish Socialist Federation, 35

Finnish (Socialist) Organization of Canada (FSOC/FOC), 24, 26, 88, 124, 144, 193nn15, 16

Finnish Workers' Society, 86

Finns and Amazons (Mattson), 189n3

Finns in the United States (Kostiainen, ed.), 188n4
Fitzgerald, Deborah, 214n93
Fitzpatrick, David: *Oceans of Consolation*, 182
Fitzpatrick, Sheila: *Everyday Stalinism*, 75, 107, 114, 121, 150, 153–4, 175
food in Karelia: absence of fresh fruit and vegetables, 67–8; beer and alcohol, 139, 142–3; berries (blueberries, lingonberries, cranberries), 74–5, 79, 108, 116; bread, 66, 68–9, 71, 204n60; butter, 67, 71, 73; cabbage, 67, 81; caramels, 67; care packages from North America, 69; cheap, 117; chicken, 100; coffee, 69–70, 73, 139; cookies, candies, chewing gum, 69; eggs, 68; fish (pickled herring), 67–8, 71, 108; flour, cornmeal, and hulled grain, 67–8, 73; "foreigner's rations," 66–7, 148; fruit (citrus, oranges, bananas), 67–8, 203n53; hors d'oeuvres, 139; jam, 69; for local people, 140; macaroni, 67; meat, 67–8, 71, 150; milk, cream, and cheese, 67–8, 73; mushrooms, 116; myth of plenty, 175; oats, 67; pirogi, 73; porridge (*velli*), 71; potatoes, 67, 71, 74, 81, 108; preparation of, 71–2; rationing of, 66–7, 113, 203n48; shortages and inadequate diet, 62, 67, 78, 99–100, 121, 124, 132; snacks at parties, 143; soup, 71, 74; in state-run cafeterias or canteens, 70–2; sugar, 67, 69, 71, 73; at summer camps, 97; sweets and baking, 69, 71, 73, 139; symbolic status of, 69, 71; tea (*chai*), 67, 69, 71, 139; tobacco, 73; vegetables, 67, 71; vodka, 67; vouchers for dining hall meals, 70; women's role in providing, 73–4
Forging of Finnish-American Communism, The (Kostiainen), 197n77
Forsell, Elvie, 16
Forsell, Jack, 16, 77, 162, 164–7, 169–71, 178–9, 185
From Front Porch to Back Seat (Bailey), 140
From Grand Duchy to a Modern State (Jusilla, Hentilä, and Nevakivi), 196n72

"Games for the Pioneer Leader," 88–9
Garth, Raili (with Brooks): *Trailblazers*, 194n36
Gelb, Michael, 45
Gender and Housing in Soviet Russia (Attwood), 61, 73
Gerber, David, 158, 168; *Authors of Their Lives*, 8, 216n4
Gleeson, Mona, 207n4
Goldberg, Ann, 158, 225n55
Golubev, Alexey, 229n162
Golubev, Alexey (with Takala): *The Search for a Socialist El Dorado*, 45, 49–50, 62, 71, 104, 110, 124, 203n42
Gorbachev, Mikhail, 164
Gordijenko, Anatoli, 127, 146
Grave in Karelia, A (Komulainen), 62, 81, 98–9, 205n119, 215n109
Great Depression, 40–2, 48–9, 67, 178, 180, 203n52
Great Depression and the New Deal, The (Rauchway), 198n20
Great Terror, 4–5, 7, 10–12, 14–15, 17–18, 149–77, 179, 191n37, 227nn101, 102; arrests, imprisonments, and executions during, 149–51, 166, 168–70, 172–3, 175, 184, 223nn11, 12, 14,

225n49, 226n90; concealed from the West, 162, 180; labelled as "genocide," 153; language policy during, 154; Operative Orders, 152–3; survivors of, 176–8; troika, 152–3, 172; TT-33 pistols in, 151
Great Terror, The (Conquest), 150, 223nn12, 14, 227n101
MS Gripsholm (ship), 15, **54**
Gronow, Jukka: Caviar with Champagne, 66, 77
Growing Up (Sutherland), 95
Gylling, Edvard, 30, **31**, 32–5, 38, 40, 152

Haapanen, Ensio, 139
Halonen, George, 13, 161
Hämäläinen, Reino, 16, 54, 70, 76, 123, 128, 130–1, 139, 143, 145, 191n26
Hard Work Conquers All (Beaulieu, Ratz, and Harpelle, eds.), 188n4
Harpelle, Ronald N., ed. (with Beaulieu and Ratz): Hard Work Conquers All, 188n4
Haynes, John Earl (with Klehr): In Denial, 222–3n1
health and hygiene in Karelia: arthritis, 79; barracks living, 80–1; bed linens, 80; birthing hospitals, 79; blisters, 108; boiling clothing, 82; depression and loneliness, 116, 159; doctors, 80, 106; emotional condition, 159; environmental factors, 79; free health care, 80, 106; gastric illnesses, 79; hair cutting, 82; homesickness, 124–5; infectious diseases (typhoid, smallpox, tuberculosis), 80, 82, 161; insect infestations (lice, cockroaches, bedbugs), 80–2; of Karelian and Russian children, 99; lack of running water, 80; in lumber camps, 80; medical care and hospitals, 79, 106; muddy floors, 81; natural remedies, 79; nurses, 80, 106; outhouses, 81; paid sick leave, 106; physical culture, 147; pneumonia, 79, 97; of prisoners, 116; role of sports in, 144; Russian standards of, 81; sanatoriums, 106; saunas, 98; showers and bathhouses, 80; sick leave for workers, 106; skin conditions, 79; "spic and span" cleanliness, 143; urinating near living space, 81; use of Borax, kerosene, and pyrethrum, 82; water sources, 79; weight loss and malnourishment, 78, 99–100
Heino, Alice, 12–13, 92, 96–8, 121, 128, 130, 132, 136, 141, 149, 157, 180, 182, 208n11, 226n68
Heino, Arte, 79, 97–8
Heino, Bill, 226n68
Heino, Frank, 96, 105, 121, 149, 157
Heino, Justiina, 12–13, 97–8, 117, 120–1, 149, 154, 157, 159, 171, 180, 182, 226n68
Heino, Martha. See Tieva, Martha (née Heino)
Heino, Urho, 79
Heino, Viljam, 96
Heino, Waino (Väinö), 98
Heino, Walter, 141, 226n68
Heino family, 12–13, 120–1, 226n68
Hendrickson, Martti, 25, 138
Hentilä, Seppo (with Jusilla and Nevakivi): From Grand Duchy to a Modern State, 196n72
Hertzel, Laurie (with Sevander): They Took My Father, 19, 43, 63–5, 67, 69, 74, 91, 94–8, 115, 132–3, 136, 154, 171–2, 174, 197n1, 200n62

Hesler, Julie, 66
Hidden Rhythms (Zerubavel), 206n134
Hietala, Harold, 16, 70, 164, 171, 178
Hietala, Leini (née Leipälä), 16, 92, 95, 101, 141
Hiilisuo, Karelia, **79**, 105, 152
Hinther, Rhonda, 85, 208n5; *Perogies and Politics*, 208n17
Hirvonen, Eino, 11, 108, 128, 130, 133, 140–1, 158, 189n2, 225n60
Hirvonen, Elizabeth (Lisi), 11, 78, 105–6, 108, 114, 118, 128, 130, 132–3, 135, 137–8, 140–1, 154, 158–9, 180, 182, 189nn2, 3
Hirvonen family, 104
Hoffman, David: *Stalinist Values*, 61, 80, 201n6
Hokkanen, Lauri (with S. Hokkanen and Middleton): *Karelia: A Finnish-American Couple in Stalin's Russia*, 17–18, 48–9, 53–5, 57–8, 62, 64, 69–71, 73, 81–2, 87, 94–6, 99–100, 103, 105, 108–10, 114, 118–21, 127, 129, 131, 138, 140, 143, 148, 154, 163–5, 169–70, 172, 175, 178–9, 198n8, 212n11, 227n102
Hokkanen, Sylvi (née Kuusisto) (with L. Hokkanen and Middleton): *Karelia: A Finnish-American Couple in Stalin's Russia*, 17–18, 48–9, 53–5, 57–8, 62, 64, 69–71, 73, 81–2, 87, 94–6, 99–100, 103, 105, 108–10, 114, 118–21, 127, 129, 131, 138, 140, 143, 148, 154, 163–5, 169–70, 172, 175, 178–9, 198n8, 212n11, 227n102
Hokkanen family, 104
House of (Finnish) National Arts (*Kansantaiteentalo*), 129
housing, furnishings, and living conditions in Karelia: barracks, 63–4, **65**, 80–1, 169–70, 174, 215n109; coffee service, 53; communal kitchens, 72; cooking, 62; curtains, screens, and partitions, 64–5; danger of indoor fires, 63; decorating family rooms, 64; dishes and kitchen utensils, 65; hauling water, 63; hideaway bed, 53; Hudson's Bay blanket, 53; inadequate housing, 62, 124; insect and rodent infestations, 56, 62, 71, 81–2; lack of furniture, 62; lack of heating and lighting, 62–3; lampshades, tablecloths, and flowers, 65; laundry, 76, 205n116; outdoor privies, 63; pictures and photographs, 64; stacking beds, 64
How Societies Remember (Connerton), 189–90n10

Iliukha, Ol'ga, 92–3
Imatra Workers' League (*Työväenliitto Imatra*), 23
In Denial (Haynes and Klehr), 222–3n1
Industrialisti (newspaper), 124
Industrial Workers of the World (IWW or Wobblies), 24
Infinite Bonds of Family (Comacchio), 219n95
Insnab (store), 77–8
Internaat (boarding school), 92
Internationale lumber camp, 104, 113
Internationale (song), 87, 170
International Red Aid (*Mobriin Oso*), 128
Ishpeming, Michigan, 15, **86**
Isku lumber camp, 133

Jackson, Michael: *The Politics of Storytelling*, 172
Joganson, Kyllikki (with Miettinen): *Petettyjen Toiveiden Maa*, 99
Johnston, Timothy: *Being Soviet*, 229n2

256　Index

Jusilla, Osmo (with Hentilä and Nevakivi): *From Grand Duchy to a Modern State*, 196n72

Kadar, Marlene, 4
Kalervo ("Cowboy") (surname unknown), 138
Kalevala (Lönnrot, ed.), 29, 43
Kalevan Kansa Colonization Company, 24
Kandalaksha (Kantalahti), Karelia, 103
Kangas, Antti, 14, 59, 66, 104, 106, 114, 125–6, 148
Kangas, Martha, 14, 141
Kangas, Olavi, 14, 94
Kangas, Terttu (née Järvinen), 14–15, 50, 56, 64, 68–9, 72, 77–8, 81, 94, 106, 117, 125–6, 129, 137, 140–2, 158–9, 182, 200n65
Kangas, Toini, 14, 69, 77–8
Kangas, Urho, 14–15
Kangas family, 25, 180
Kangaspuro, Markku, 32, 196n72; *Neuvosto-Karjalan taistelu itsehallinosta*, 197n96, 218–19n86
Kannussuo lumber camp, 108–9
Kansallis-Liitto. *See* Finnish National Federation (Kansallis-Liitto)
Karelia: A Finnish-American Couple in Stalin's Russia (L. and S. Hokkanen with Middleton), 17–18, 48–9, 53–5, 57–8, 62, 64, 69–71, 73, 81–2, 87, 94–6, 99–100, 103, 105, 108–10, 114, 118–21, 127, 129, 131, 138, 140, 143, 148, 154, 163–5, 169–70, 172, 175, 178–9, 198n8, 212n11, 227n102
Karelia *(Karjala)*: capital of (*see* Petrozavodsk [Petroskoi], Karelia); changing position, repression, and executions of North Americans and Finns in, 120, 151–5, 175, 178, 180, 229n2; children and youth in, 84–101 (*see also* children and youth in Karelia); civilizers and modernizers of, 5–6, 8, 81, 115, 148; collective farming in, 36, 134; communes in, 18, 36, 45, 53, 75–6, **79**, 103, 105, 152; Communist Party in, 32; consumer goods in (*see* consumer goods in Karelia); Continuation War in, 12, 168, 176; Council of the People's Commissars in, 32; culture, community, and leisure in, 9, 15–17, 22, 123–48 (*see also* leisure in Karelia); differences in ethnic populations of, 65, 67, 75, 81, 83, 114; disputes over, 8, 30; everyday life in (*see* everyday life in Karelia); experimental and educational farm in, 105; Finnicization of, 33, 196n65; Finnish and Russian place names in, 6; "Finnish-Karelian" language in, 33–4; first impressions of, 55–8; food in (*see* food in Karelia); foreign worker barracks in, 63, **65**, 80, 169–70, 174, 215n109; furniture factory in, 105; General Plan (1926) for, 37–8; health and hygiene in, 78–82 (*see also* health and hygiene in Karelia); hydro-electric plant in, 104; impact of Stalinism on, 39, 147; impact of the Great Terror on, 5, 7, 10–12, 14–15, 17–18, 147, 151–5, 165, 191n37, 224nn24, 28, 30, 227n102 (*see also* Great Terror); industry and employment in, 9, 14, 34 (*see also* work in Karelia); insecure economic future of, 37–8; inter-ethnic relations in, 4, 37–8, 43, 115–16; Karelian Autonomous

Soviet Socialist Republic (KASSR), 3, 33; "Karelianization" of, 33; the "Karelian Question," 8, 39, 195n48; languages and dialects in, 33, 94, 196n65; life writers in (*see* life writers); lumber industry and camps in, 3–4, 11, 14, 34–5, 38, 57–8, 61–2, 72, 80–1, 96, 100, 104–5, 112–13, 118, **119**, 130, 133–4, **135**, 143, 212n15; map of (1930s), x; population statistics of, 33–4, 195n56; post-war in, 185; prisoner labourers in, 34, 116, 153, 175; Red Finns in top leadership posts in, 32; roads in, **112**; Russification of, 120–1; Second Five Year Plan for, 62, 107; (settler) colonial projects in, 6, 14; ski factory (*see* Karelia Ski Factory); Soviet Karelian studies, 44, 187–8n2; sports and athletics in (*see* sports and athletics in Karelia); Swedes and Swedish Finns in, 223n7; towns in, 57–8, 62; travel to and within (*see* travel to and within Karelia); war and starvation in, 34, 196n72; war evacuation of (1941), 16, 176–7; Wars with Finland, 4, 132, 176; women in (*see* women in Karelia); working in, 102–22 (*see also* work in Karelia)

"Karelian Fever," 41, 44, 51, 85, 90, 125, 181

Karelian Finnish National Theatre, 108, 130, 133–4, 175

Karelian Finnish National Theatre "Little Hall" ("*Pieni Sali*") (cinema), 134

Karelian Fish Trust, 35–6

Karelian Pedagogical Institute, 94, 110, 120

Karelian Radio Symphony Orchestra, 131, 132

Karelian Resettlement Agency, 42, 49, 55, 107

Karelian Technical Aid Committee (KTA), 3, 18, 27, 37, 40–3, 46–7, 49–51, 90–1, 149, 178, 200n62. *See also* "Society for the Technical Aid of Soviet Karelia"

Karelian Workers' Commune, 30–2, 195n48

Karelian Workers' Cooperative, 35

Karelia Ski Factory, 15, 61–2, 71, 100, 105, 108, **109**, 110, 114, 137, 143, 145

Karelles Timber Trust, 38

Karjala kutsui (Bucht), 143

Kelleher, Margaret, 225n53

Kelly, Catriona, 207n4; *Children's World*, 211n102

Kem, Karelia, 56, 58, 62, 104, 112, 115, 213n40

Kenez, Peter: *Cinema and Soviet Society*, 136

Kero, Reino, 45; *Neuvosto-Karjalaa Rakentamassa*, 77, 113, 200n62, 212nn15, 18, 214n94, 216n6

KGB. *See under* Soviet Union (USSR)

Khrushchev, Nikita, 163, 185

Kirjeitä Karjalasta (P. Sihvola), 230n18

Kirmayer, Laurence, 167

Kirov, Sergei, 151–2, 168

Kirschenbaum, Lisa: *Small Comrades*, 90, 100

Kivi, Aleksis, 29

Kivikoski, Ontario, 47, 51, 72, 87, 145

Kivisto, Peter, 21

Klehr, Harvey (with Haynes): *In Denial*, 222–3n1

Knutson, Harold, 226n68

Kommuuna Kylväjä (Vanhala), 197n85

Komsomol (communist youth organization), 84

Komulainen, Ernesti J. (Ernest Laine): *A Grave in Karelia*, 62, 81, 98–9, 205n119, 215n109
Kondopoga House of Culture, 129
Kondopoga (Kontupohja), Karelia, 12–13, **65**, 98, 104, 120, 129
Kondopoga Paper Mill Club, 130
Kondopoga Pulp and Paper Factory, 13, 38, 104, 105
Korhonen, Kalle Heikki ("Korholen"), 13, 106, 126, 159–61, 182
Korpi, Tilda, 64
Kostiainen, Auvo, 153; *The Forging of Finnish-American Communism*, 197n77
Kostiainen, Auvo, ed.: *Finns in the United States*, 188n4
Kotkin, Stephen: *Magnetic Mountain*, 201n4, 229n2
Krasny Bor, Karelia, 149–50, 164
Krupskaya, Nadezhda, 96
Kurikka, Matti, 24
Kuusi kuukautta Karjalassa (Suomela), 115–16, 216n6
Kwakwaka'wakw territory, British Columbia, 24
Kylväjä (collective farm), 36–7
Kyvig, David E.: *Daily Life in the United States*, 206n145, 220n115

La Capra, Dominick: *Writing History, Writing Trauma*, 168, 228n130
Lahti-Argutina, Eila, 226n90
Laine, Edward, 22
Laine, Ernest. *See* Komulainen, Ernesti J. (Ernest Laine)
Lake Ladoga, Karelia, 103, 195n47
Lake Segozero (Seesjärvi), 72
Lambek, Michael (with Antze), 165
Lammi, Katri, 172, **173**, 174–6
Latva, John (Jussi), 42, 51

Leder, Mary: *My Life in Stalinist Russia*, 68, 82
leisure in Karelia: art, 97; auctions, 129; billiards and pool, 145; celebrations, 123, 136–9; chess and checkers, 97; cinema and films (*see* cinema and films in Karelia); concerts, 114, 132, 137, 172; Cultural Houses (*Kulttuuritalo*) and Houses of Enlightenment of, 22, 98, 129, 137, 141; cycling, 146; guest speakers, 129; handicraft, 97; *iltamat* (evening entertainment programs), 123, 130, 133; military practice, 128; music and dancing, 97–8, 114, 128–33, 139, 148; orchestras, bands, and choirs, 131–2, 145, 148; phonograph, 98, 130, 133, 139; poetry reading, 97; political volunteerism, 126–9, 128; private parties, 138–9, 143; radio, 128–9, 132, 172; Red Corners, 60, 128–9; sports and athletics (*see* sports and athletics in Karelia); summer camps, 97; theatre, 97, 108, 114, 129–30, 133–4, 148, 175; travel, 114, 145–6; visits with friends and neighbours, 98, 130, 154; volunteerism, 128; youth organizations, 84, 123, 126 (*see also* Communist Young Pioneers; Young Communist League [YCL])
Lenin, Vladimir, 29, 31, 91, 96, 169
Letters from Karelia (film), 189n5
Life Has Become More Joyous, Comrades (Petrone), 136, 219n94
life writers. *See* Alatalo, Paavo; Berg, Karl; Forsell, Elvie; Forsell, Jack; Hämäläinen, Reino; Heino, Alice; Heino, Justiina; Hietala, Harold; Hietala, Leini; Hirvonen, Elizabeth (Lisi) Mäntysaari Hilberg;

Hokkanen, Lauri; Hokkanen, Sylvi (née Kuusisto); Kangas, Antti; Kangas, Terttu; Korhonen, Kalle Heikki; Mäkelä, Reino; Maunu, Klaus; Nelson, Enoch; Pitkänen, Aate Veli; Pitkänen, Aino; Pitkänen, Antti; Ranta, Elis; Ranta, Viola; Salo, Tauno; Sevander, Mayme; Sihvola, Allan; Tuomi, Kaarlo; Zlobina, Vieno
life writing: about times of optimism to lessen the pain of times of repression, 148; analytical opportunities in, 8, 10, 12, 56, 148, 150, 178–86; bridge between Finnish North American workers' movement and the communist state, 121–2; collective grief in, 171–6; collectively shared experiences in, 181; community social history in, 183; conflation of time in, 169; to create a collective "founding trauma," 167; crossing disciplinary boundaries, 10; definition of, 4; descriptions of socialization in the political sphere in, 129; "disowning" the voice or self in, 158, 160, 165–7, 227–8n116; distance and migration in, 180; emotional discovery inherent in, 165; emphasis on positive aspects of communist state in, 105–6, 160; ethnic and linguistic analysis of, 183; forbidden topics in, 157, 225n55; gender analysis of, 182; during the Great Terror, 155–77; guarding against psychological pain, 164–5; impact of repression, fear, and war on, 107, 120, 150, 154; influences on, 57; insights into practice and policy in action in, 121–2; Karelian, 6–7, 41, 56, 168, 178–86 (*see also* life writers); letters and memoirs compared, 7, 11–19, 41, 53, 56, 60, 64, 81, 150; "life story of her body" in, 79; mapping of the self in, 183–4; mimicry of authenticity in, 158; negotiation of relationships in, 182; oral history interviews as, 16, 153, 164; as outlet for grief, 17, 162; personal and collective memories conveyed in, 7, 150; purposeful narrative shaping in, 9, 160, 182; relational identities in, 183; role of gossip in retelling of life stories in, 172, 175; scars of trauma in, 162; sense of betrayal in, 179; significance of family in, 180; strategic silences in, 157–8, 162, 164, 180, 227n96; studies of, 56, 187n1; *testimonio*, 172, 184; thoughts with correspondents in, 182; truth telling (emotional, narrative, and literal) in, 7, 150, 156–7, 162, 167–71, 184, 228n130; turning points in, 169; what is *not* said in, 15, 150, 182

Lime Island, 153, 172, 174–5
Lincoln Loyalty League, 28
Lindström, Varpu, 16, 21, 28, 43, 94, 141, 164, 171, 189–90n6, 192nn43, 44, 216n6; *Defiant Sisters*, 200n58, 220n125
Lines from Karelia (Mattson), 189n3
Lohijärvi, Karelia, 14, 68, 72, 104, 114, 137, 142
Lönnrot, Elias, ed.: *Kalevala*, 29, 43
Lososinnoye House of Enlightenment, 137
Lososinnoye (Lososiina), Karelia, 104
Lux, Maureen: *Separate Beds*, 206n145

Machine Fund, 42, 45, 104
Madokoro, Laura, 189n11
Magnetic Mountain (Kotkin), 201n4, 229n2

260 Index

Magnitogorsk, Russia, 201n4, 214n74
Mäkelä, A.B., 24, 138
Mäkelä, Kalervo, 166
Mäkelä, Reino, 15–16, 54–6, 63, 132, 136, 138–40, 143, 165–7, 169, 178–9, 191n26
Mäki, Selma, 125
Malcolm Island, British Columbia, 24
Malysheva, Marina, 79
Marxism, 23–4
Mason, Emma, 202n24
Matrosy (Matroosa), Karelia, 77, 104, **119**, 214n94
Mattson, Anna (née Hirvonen), 11, 108, 189n3; *Lines from Karelia*, 189n3
Mattson, Nancy: *Finns and Amazons*, 189n3
Matveev, Mikhail, 149
Maunu, Klaus, 16–17, 52, 64, 79, 102, 129, 133, 135, 146, 153, 168–9, 178, 191n31
Maunu family, 72
Mayblin, Lucy (with Turner): *Migration Studies and Colonialism*, 189n11
Memoir (Couser), 172
Merridale, Catherine: *Night of Stone*, 168
Mickenberg, Julia, 90
Middleton, Anita (née Hokkanen) (with L. and S. Hokkanen): *Karelia: A Finnish-American Couple in Stalin's Russia*, 17–18, 48–9, 53–5, 57–8, 62, 64, 69–71, 73, 81–2, 87, 94–6, 99–100, 103, 105, 108–10, 114, 118–21, 127, 129, 131, 138, 140, 143, 148, 154, 163–5, 169–70, 172, 175, 178–9, 198n8, 212n11, 227n102
Miettinen, Helena (with Joganson): *Petettyjen Toiveiden Maa*, 99

migration history, 189n11
Migration Studies and Colonialism (Mayblin and Turner), 189n11
Mills, Claudia, 11
Mishler, Paul: *Raising Reds*, 90
"Missing in Karelia" (research project), 190n7, 192n43
Molotov, Vyacheslav, 38
"Movie Theatre Red Star" ("*Kino-Teatteri Puna-Tähti*") (cinema), 134
Murmansk Railway, 30, 32, 34, 103, 116
My Life in Stalinist Russia (Leder), 68, 82

National Culture Centre, **127**
Nelson, Allan: *The Nelson Brothers*, 13
Nelson, Arvid, 13, 35, 105, 213n40
Nelson, Enoch, 13–14, 35, 55, 75–7, 105–7, 112, 115, 117, 142, 149, 182, 213n40
Nelson, Ida, 14, 112, 213n40
Nelson Brothers, The (Nelson), 13
Neuvosto-Karjalaa Rakentamassa (Kero), 77, 113, 200n62, 212nn15, 18, 214n94, 216n6
Neuvosto-Karjalan taistelu itsehallinosta (Kangaspuro), 197n96, 218–19n86
Nevakivi, Jukka (with Jussila and Hentilä): *From Grand Duchy to a Modern State*, 196n72
Niemi, Olavi, 141
Night of Stone (Merridale), 168
Niva, Erwin, 91, 94, 96
NKVD. *See under* Soviet Union (USSR)
Nousiainen, Elmer, 133
Nygard, Tenho, 146

Oceans of Consolation (D. Fitzpatrick), 182
Of Soviet Bondage (Sevander), 19, 44, 126, 138–9, 143, 164, 170, 172, 228n138
Olonets region, Karelia, 18

Index 261

One Big Union, 24
Onega Metallurgic Factory, 105
Oso (Special Operations), 147

"Palace of Pioneers," 97
Pearl, Jeanette D., 101
Perogies and Politics (Hinther), 208n17
Petettyjen Toiveiden Maa (Miettinen and Joganson), 99
Petrone, Karen: *Life Has Become More Joyous, Comrades*, 136, 219n94
Petrozavodsk (Petroskoi), Karelia, 11, 14, 55, **57**, 62, **63**, 64, 72, 75, 77, 79, 92, 97, 104–5, 108, 110, 115, 123, **127**, 132, 138
Petsamo, 29
Philharmonic building, Petrozavodsk, 132
Pioneers. *See* Communist Young Pioneers
Pitkänen, Aate Veli, 11–12, 47, 70–2, 86, 106, 111–14, 123–8, 132–3, 135, 139–41, 145–7, 155, 157, 171, 182, 189n5
Pitkänen, Aatu, 155
Pitkänen, Aino, 12, 155–8, 164, 180
Pitkänen, Antti, 12, 47, 51, 72, 86, 126, 156–7, 200n54, 216n14
Pitkänen, Kirsti, 72, 86, 156–7
Pitkänen, Lilia, 141
Pitkänen, Taimi (later Davis) (aka Liz Alton), 12, 47, 51, 86–7, 124, 126, 132, 189n5, 208n8, 216n14
Pitkänen, Taru, 86
Pitkänen family, 189–90n6
Politics of Storytelling, The (Jackson), 172
Port Arthur, Ontario, 16, 22, **23**, 88
Portelli, Alessandro: *The Death of Luigi Trastulli ...*, 176
Pratt, William, 46, 51
Pravda (newspaper), 32
Punainen Karjala (newspaper), 97, 131, 218n80

Punakankaan Suomalaiset (Ruusunen), 230n18
Pushkin Centennial, 136, 219n94

Radforth, Ian, 120
radio in Karelia, 128–9, 147, 172; programs for children, 131; radio orchestra, 132
Raising Reds (Mishler), 90
Ranta, Alli, 15, 72
Ranta, Elis, 15, 64, 69–70, 72, 103, 105, 131
Ranta, Viola, 15, 55–6, 67, 71, 91, 93, 96, 128, 178
Ranta family, 62
Ratz, David K., ed. (with Beaulieu and Harpelle): *Hard Work Conquers All*, 188n4
Rauchway, Eric: *The Great Depression and the New Deal*, 198n20
Rautio, K., 131
Rautkallio, Hannu: *Suuri Viha*, 196n65
Reading Autobiography (Smith and Watson), 7, 165
Red Cross, 128
Red Exodus (Sevander), 19, 45, 84, 93, 96–7, 129, 132, 134, 155, 163, 166, 170, 172, 175–6, 207n1, 228n138
"Red Scare," 28, 40, 43
Reiter, Ester, 88
Remembering Karelia (Armstrong), 168
Repola, Karelia, 30
Respectable Citizens (Campbell), 203n52
"revolutionary spirit," 9, 27, 48–9, 84, 123, 180, 185
Rikkinen, Miriam "Margaret," 45, 172, 175–6
Riordan, James: *Sport in Soviet Society*, 147, 221n158, 222n189
Rosenberg, Suzanne: *A Soviet Odyssey*, 79, 82, 203n53, 204n60

Ross, Carl: *The Finn Factor in American Labor ...*, 22
Rovio, Kustaa, 32–3, 110, 152, 224n24
Runeberg, Johan Ludvig, 29
Russian Federation, 164, 170, 184
Russian Revolution, 25, 49
Rutanen lumber camp, Karelia, 58, 81, 133, 144
Ruusunen, Aimo: *Punakankaan Suomalaiset*, 230n18

Saastamoinen, Robert, 198n6
Säde (Ray) Commune, Karelia, 18, 36–7, 45, 53, 73, 75, 103, 105, 133, 152, 154, 178
Sakura Järvi lumber camp, 109, 120
Salo, Tauno, 13, 145, 190n11
Sandarmokh, Karelia, 149, 164, 222–3n1
Saxberg, Kelly, 189n5
Search for a Socialist El Dorado, The (Golubev and Takala), 45, 49–50, 62, 71, 104, 110, 124, 203n42
Second World War, 7, 17–18
Separate Beds (Lux), 206n145
Serious Fun (Edelman), 147
Sevander, Mayme (née Corgan), 18–19, 25, 47, 50, 53, 55, 78, 92, 127, 149, 178–9; *Red Exodus*, 19, 45, 84, 93, 96–7, 129, 132, 134, 155, 163, 165–6, 170, 172, 175–6, 207n1, 228n138; *Of Soviet Bondage*, 19, 44, 126, 138–9, 143, 164, 170, 172, 228n138; *Vaeltajat*, 19, 172, 189n2, 190n7
Sevander, Mayme (née Corgan) (with Hertzel): *They Took My Father*, 19, 43, 63–5, 67, 69, 74, 80, 83, 91, 94–8, 115, 132–3, 136, 154, 171–2, 174, 197n1, 200n62

Shock Workers and Stakhanovites, 9, 65, 73, 113–14, 147, 214n74; "iskuri" prize for, 113–14
Siegelbaum, Lewis, 129; *Stakhanovism and the Politics of Productivity ...*, 214n74
Siegelbaum, Lewis (ed. with Sokolov): *Stalinism as a Way of Life*, 211n104
Sihvola, Allan, 17, 52–4, 57, 64, 79, 81, 86, 91–2, 95, 103, 130, 133, 143, 154, 178, 225n49
Sihvola, Päivi: *Kirjeitä Karjalasta*, 230n18
Siikanen, Kalle (Säde chairman), 76
Sirola, Yrjö, 84
Ski Factory. *See* Karelia Ski Factory
Ski Factory Brass Band, 131
Ski Factory Orchestra, 15, 110
Small Comrades (Kirschenbaum), 90, 100
Smith, Sidonie (with Watson): *Reading Autobiography*, 7, 165
Smolenikova, Maria "Maikki," 141
Snellman, J.V., 29
Social Democratic Party of Canada (SDPC), 24
socialism and socialist movements: Finnish, 21; Great Socialist Project, 179; international, 20, 22, 37; Karelian, 18, 35, 50, 97, 126–9; North American, 5, 14, 23–4, 28, 101, 169
Socialist Party of America (SPA), 23–4
Socialist Party of Canada (SPC), 23
"Society for the Technical Aid of Soviet Karelia," 35
"Society for the Technical Aid of Soviet Russia," 34
Sointula (Place of Harmony), 24–5
Sokolov, Andrei (ed. with Siegelbaum): *Stalinism as a Way of Life*, 211n104

Solomennoye (Soloman), Karelia, 77
Solovki prison, 149
"Song of the Motherland," 174–5, 229n162
Sorokina, Lilja, 97
Soviet Karelia. *See* Karelia (*Karjala*)
Soviet Karelia (Baron), 37, 62, 116, 152–3, 196n72, 222–3n1, 224nn28, 30
"Soviet Karelian Aid Committee." *See* "Society for the Technical Aid of Soviet Karelia"
Soviet Odyssey, A (Rosenberg), 79, 82, 203n53, 204n60
Soviet Popular Culture (Stites), 136
"Soviet Republic of Scandinavia," 30
Soviet Union (USSR): abortion policy in, 142; athletics policy and contradictions in, 12, 145–7, 222n189; attitudes toward crime, 116; attitudes toward drunkenness, 142; attitudes toward sports, 144, 221n158; banning of Christmas celebrations, 138; Brezhnev "Stagnation," 164; censorship in, 78, 150, 155, 157, 158, 161, 167; change in rhetoric regarding "enemies," 150; children's affection for, 90; citizens' collective past of violence in, 184; classified matters in, 80; collective farms in, 36, 96; communes in, 52, 211n104; competitive sport in, 145–7; control of travel, 161; control over film industry, 135–6, 218–19n86; corruption, labour inefficiencies, and food shortages in, 57, 62, 67; cultural revolution in, 123; culture of silence in, 163–4; de-Stalinization campaigns in, 229n162; direction of resettlement of Karelia by, 42, 49; displaced and starving peasants in, 56; education and childhood in, 92–5, 209n45; everyday life in, 60–4, 201n4; exile and relocation of undesirable elements in, 175, 184; falsified death certificates in, 163, 226n90; First Five Year Plan of, 3, 37–8, 60, 75, 113; food rationing in, 66–7, 113, 203n48; gendered division of labour in, 117; Gorbachev's *glasnost*, 164; gulags (labour camps) and prisons in, 15–17, 149–51, 164, 168, 175, 202n24, 223n11, 227n101; histories of everyday life in, 187–8n2; housing in, 60–4, 80; identity based on Russianness in, 39; industrialization of, 59, 80; KGB, 17, 184; Krushchev's "Secret Speech" and Thaw, 163, 185; labour laws in, 121; labour shortage in, 38, 111; luxury production in the 1930s by, 77; mail interception system in, 157; marriage and divorce in, 142, 220n139; military preparedness practices in, 147; nationalities policy of, 94; New Economic Policy (NEP) of, 34, 37; New Soviet Citizen in, 97; NKVD, 151–4, 170, 223n14, 224n24; official holidays in, 136, 138; patriotic songs about, 174–5, 229n162; personal hygiene in, 80; post-Stalinist years in, 179; relations with Finland of, 4; resolutions on immigration of, 38; scarcity of household items in, 77; scarcity of manufactured cloth in, 76; 1930s "cultured life" in, 4, 65, 80; Second Five Year Plan of, 62, 107, 119, 132; Siege of Leningrad, 12; social engineering of children in, 90; social inequities in, 66;

socialism in, 169, 185; the Soviet Dream, 147; Stalin Constitution (1936), 175; Stalinist Great Terror, 149–77 (*see also* Great Terror); state-wide passportization in, 110–11; strategy of *korenizatsiia* (minority accommodation) in, 32–4, 133; "terrorist & totalitarian methods of rule" in, 169; United States interest in, 90. *See also* Karelia (*Karjala*)

Sport in Soviet Society (Riordan), 147, 221nn158, 189

sports and athletics in Karelia: baseball, 144; basketball, 145; competitive sport, 145–7; hockey, 145; horseshoes, 144; skating, 90, 145; skiing, 98–9, 144–6; sledding, 98; soccer, 144; Soviet athletics policy and contradictions, 12, 145–7, 222n189; Soviet attitudes toward sport; swimming, 144; track and field, 114, 145–6; wrestling, 144

Sports Pioneers (Tester, ed.), 144

Spy Lost (*Isanmaattoman tarina*) (Tuomi), 17, 192n38

Stakhanov, Alexei, 113

Stakhanovism and the Politics of Productivity ..., 214n74

Stakhanovite Movement. *See* Shock Workers and Stakhanovites

Stalin, Joseph, 32, 37–9, 137, 162–3, 171, 180, 186; first concentration camp, 149; preoccupation with national film industry, 136

Stalinism, 4, 179, 184; "an analytical category," 181; the culture of, 39; daily life under, 181; Great Terror, 149–77 (*see also* Great Terror); myth of plenty, 175; revolution in education, 90, 92; support from communist parties outside USSR, 162–3

Stalinism as a Way of Life (Siegelbaum and Sokolov, eds.), 211n104

Stalinist Values (Hoffman), 61, 80, 201n6

Steen, Sara Jayne, 10

Stites, Richard, 138; *Soviet Popular Culture*, 136

Streng, Aino, 54, 66, 143, 203n42

Streng, Eino, 54, 66, 143, 203n42

Sulkanen, Elis, 25; *Amerikan suomalaisen työväenliikkeen historia*, 226n84

Summer Park, Petrozavodsk, 130, 132

Suomela, V.: *Kuusi kuukautta Karjalassa*, 115–16, 216n6

Sutherland, Neil: *Growing Up*, 95

Suuri Viha (Rautkallio), 196n65

Swedish-American Steamship Company, 43

Takala, Irina, 61, 65, 77, 80–1, 83, 99, 114, 148, 198n5, 224nn24, 28

Takala, Irina (with Golubev): *The Search for a Socialist El Dorado*, 45, 49–50, 62, 71, 104, 110, 124, 203n42

Tarmola, Ontario, 87

Taste of War, The (Collingham), 203n48

Teachers of Stalinism, The (Ewing), 92, 209n45

Tenhunen, Matti, 38, 42, 44, 46, 149, 198n5, 199n28, 200n54

Tester, Jim, ed.: *Sports Pioneers*, 144

Their Ideals Were Crushed (Zlobina), 68, 92, 144–5, 172, 174, 178–9, 184, 186, 192n40, 205n116

They Took My Father (Sevander and Hertzel), 19, 43, 63–5, 67, 69, 74, 80, 83, 91, 94–8, 115, 132–3, 136, 154, 171–2, 174, 197n1, 200n62

Tieva, Arvo Nestor, 12, 190n7

Tieva, Martha (née Heino), 12, 141, 157, 190n7
Torgsin (store), 77
Toveritar (newspaper), 87
Trailblazers (Garth and Brooks), 194n36
travel to and within Karelia: journey and shipboard life, 53–5, 200n75; distances travelled, 35, 47, 55, 145–6
"Triumf" (cinema), 134–5, 218–19n86
Tumba lumber camp, 72
Tuomi, Eini, 50, 191n31
Tuomi, Kaarlo, 17, 52, 56–7, 82, 118–19, 178, 191n37, 198n6; *Spy Lost (Isanmaattoman tarina)*, 17, 192n38
Turner, Joe (with Mayblin): *Migration Studies and Colonialism*, 189n11
Työmies (newspaper), 18, 26, 35, 41, 47, 87, 124, 138, 208n11

Uhtua, Karelia, 15, 56, 58, 104, 109, 112, 131, 141, 213n40
unionism, 24, 28, 119
Union of Soviet Socialist Republics. *See* Soviet Union (USSR)
United Front Communism, 26
utopianism, 4, 8, 20, 24–5, 37, 39–40, 181

Vaeltajat (Sevander), 19, 172, 189n2, 190n7
Vähämäki, Börje, 43, 171
"Valiparakit" barracks, Petrozavodsk, 138, 174
Vanhala, Harri: *Kommuuna Kylväjä*, 197n85
Vapaa Sana (newspaper), 124
Vapaus (newspaper), 26, 41, 87, 124
Vauhkonen, Impi, 130–1, 172, 174, 176

Vilga, Karelia, 104, 130
Vonganperä lumber camp, Karelia, 11, 70, 104, 108–9, 128, 130, 134
Vuorela, Ulla, 207n155

Walz, Maggie, 24–5
Warkentin, Raija, 191n31, 192n44
War Measures Act (Canada), 193n15
Warped Mourning (Etkind), 223n11
Warren, Ohio, 54, 86, 91, 103
Watson, Julia (with Smith): *Reading Autobiography*, 7, 165
White Sea-Baltic Canal, 103, 116
"Wide Is My Motherland" (song). *See* "Song of the Motherland"
Wiita, John, 38, 197n96
Wilson, Donald J., 87
Winter, Jay, 165
women in Karelia: appeal of free schooling to, 198n8; attitudes to alcohol and drunkenness of, 143; Communist Women's Bureau, 87; courting, marriage, and divorce of, 139–42; creation of domestic comfort by, 64; different ethnic cultural values of, 81; disinterest in communal cooking, 73; "economy of dating" in, 140; embodiment of community's strength, 176; employment of, 103, 116–20; evacuees, 168; farming in Karelia by, 189–90n6; fundraising by, 128; in gulags (labour camps), 202n24; hairstyles of, 77; housewife activists (*obshchestvennitsa*), 80, 207n149; laundry work by, 76, 205n116; local Karelian, 118; lumbering work by, 118, **119**; married and working, 212n11; migration of single women to Karelia, 50; mistreatment and suffering of, 176; more details than men

266 Index

in letters and memoirs by, 64; newspapers for, 87; perfumes and makeup for, 75; role in domestic and family labour, 60–1, 70, 72, 117, 132, 217n59; role in providing family food, 73–4; separation from spouse of, 108; single mothers, 99; ski factory workers, **109**; status and rights of single, 140; wives of prisoners, 156, 158, 225nn53, 55

Worker, The (newspaper), 26
Worker's Cooperative Bonds, 37
Workers' Parties, 25
Workers' Party of Canada, 26
Workers' Party of the United States, 26
work in Karelia: adaptation to Karelian conditions, 111; agriculture, 35, 103, 105; auto mechanics, 110; availability of, 106; berry picking, 108; brick making, 109; cafeteria, 121; Canadian expertise in lumber industry, 104, 113; canal construction, 116; car driver, 141; by children, 96; cleaning fish, 108; coach and trainer, 146; construction, 103, 105, 108–9; cooking, 103, 109; daycare, 117–18, 121; difficult conditions, 124; electricity and telephone construction, 105; factory production, 102, 105, 108; farming, 102; fatalities, 103; fisheries, 35, 105; "foreign experts," 114–15, 214n93; foremen and managers, 114–15; forest, 121; freight handling, 102; gathering moss, 108–9; gendered division of, 116–20; handmade tools, 119; haying, 109; idealized labourers (*see* Shock Workers and Stakhonvites); job changes, 107–9, 213n40; job satisfaction, 109; knitting, 117–18; labour cooperatives, 35; labour force statistics, 104–5, 212nn15, 20; labour laws, 115, 121; labour projects, 103; labour shortages, 38, 111, 215n117; language restrictions on, 120, 154; laundering, 103, 108; by local Karelian women, 118; loss of, 120–1; lumbering and logging, 35, 102–5, 108, 116, 118, **119**, 212n15; manufacturing and processing, 105; mechanical and metal work, 110; mining, 102; mixing clay, 109; monetary bonuses, 114; musicians, 110, 131, 172; paid vacation, 106; preparedness for, 109; prisoner labourers, 34, 116, 153, 175; production quotas, 113, 119; railroad construction, 102, 116; road and other infrastructure construction, 105, **112**; rowing boats, 118; sawing firewood, 117–18; sawmills, 110; shingle making, 109; strikes, 103; summer vacations, 133; teachers, 109, 115, 120, 154, 212n11; telephone cable linesman, 111, 113, 146; theatre, 108, 134, 175; tractor operators, 115; trade unions, 145–6; transfer of skills, 112; unemployment, 103, 108; volunteer community labour, 128; wages, 103, 106, 115, 119–21, 146, 215n117; "women's work," 117–18, **119** (*see also under* women in Karelia); worker equality and inequality, 106–7, 116; workers' benefits: health care and sick leave, 106; workers' rights, 107, 115; work ethics, 114–15; work gangs, 119; workplace interactions and clashes, 114, 116, 214nn93, 94;

workplace youth leagues, 128; work settlements, 103
Writing History, Writing Trauma (La Capra), 168

Yezhov, Nikolay, 152–3
Young Communist League (YCL), 47, 126–8, 146–7
Young Pushkin (film), 136

Zerubavel, Eviatar, 227n96; *Hidden Rhythms*, 206n134
Zhdanov, Andrei, 151
Zlobina, Vieno (née Ahokas), 18, 36, 45, 52–3, 75–6, 87, 132, 154; *Their Ideals Were Crushed*, 68, 92, 144–5, 172, 174, 178–9, 184, 186, 192n40, 205n116
Zolotareva, Marina, 79

www.ingramcontent.com/pod-product-compliance
Lightning Source LLC
Chambersburg PA
CBHW030310080526
44584CB00012B/513